The Archaeology of Meaningful Places

Foundations of Archaeological Inquiry

James M. Skibo, series editor

Living with Pottery: Ethnoarchaeology Among the Gamo of Southwest Ethiopia
John W. Arthur

Complex Systems and Archaeology: Empirical and Theoretical Applications
R. Alexander Bentley and Herbert D. G. Maschner, editors

Invisible Citizens: Captives and Their Consequences
Catherine M. Cameron, editor

Material Meanings: Critical Approaches to the Interpretation of Material Culture
Elizabeth S. Chilton, editor

Pottery Ethnoarchaeology in the Central Maya Highlands
Michael Deal

Archaeological Perspectives on Political Economies
Gary M. Feinman and Linda M. Nicholas, editors

Archaeology Beyond Dialogue
Ian Hodder

The Archaeology of Settlement Abandonment in Middle America
Takeshi Inomata and Ronald W. Webb, editors

Evolutionary Archaeology: Theory and Application
Michael J. O'Brien, editor

Style, Function, Transmission: Evolutionary Archaeological Perspectives
Michael J. O'Brien and R. Lee Lyman, editors

Race and the Archaeology of Identity
Charles E. Orser Jr., editor

Ancient Human Migrations: A Multidisciplinary Approach
Peter N. Peregrine, Ilia Peiros, and Marcus Feldman

Unit Issues in Archaeology: Measuring Time, Space, and Material
Ann F. Ramenofsky and Anastasia Steffen, editors

Behavioral Archaeology: First Principles
Michael Brian Schiffer

Social Theory in Archaeology
Michael Brian Schiffer, editor

Craft Production in Complex Societies
Izumi Shimada, editor

Pottery and People: A Dynamic Interaction
James M. Skibo and Gary M. Feinman, editors

Expanding Archaeology
James M. Skibo, William H. Walker, and Axel E. Nielsen, editors

Archaeological Concepts for the Study of the Cultural Past
Alan P. Sullivan III

Essential Tensions in Archaeological Method and Theory
Todd L. VanPool and Christine S. VanPool, editors

THE ARCHAEOLOGY OF MEANINGFUL PLACES

Edited by
Brenda J. Bowser
and **María Nieves Zedeño**

THE UNIVERSITY OF UTAH PRESS
Salt Lake City

Foundations of Archaeological Inquiry
James M. Skibo, series editor

Copyright © 2009 by The University of Utah Press. All rights reserved.

 The Defiance House Man colophon is a registered trademark of the University of Utah Press. It is based on a four-foot-tall, Ancient Puebloan pictograph (late PIII) near Glen Canyon, Utah.

13 12 11 10 09   1 2 3 4 5

Library of Congress Cataloging-in-Publication Data

The archaeology of meaningful places / edited by Brenda J. Bowser and María Nieves Zedeño.
     p. cm.
  Includes bibliographical references and index.
  ISBN 978-0-87480-882-7 (alk. paper)
  1. Indians of Central America—Antiquities.   2. Indians of Mexico—Antiquities.   3. Indians of North America—Southwest, New—Antiquities.   4. Place (Philosophy)—Case studies.   5. Human ecology—Case studies.   6. Social archaeology—Case studies.   7. Ethnoarchaeology—Case studies.   8. Central America—Antiquities.   9. Mexico—Antiquities.   10. Southwest, New—Antiquities.   I. Bowser, Brenda J., 1957–   II. Zedeño, María Nieves.
  F1434.A85 2009
  970.01'1—dc22   2009003563

Cover photograph courtesy of Wendy Ashmore.

Contents

List of Illustrations   vii

Preface   ix

1. The Archaeology of Meaningful Places   1
   María Nieves Zedeño and Brenda J. Bowser

2. Biographies of Place at Quiriguá, Guatemala   15
   Wendy Ashmore

3. The Main Plaza of Monte Albán: A Life History of Place   32
   Arthur A. Joyce

4. Being in Place: Intersections of Identity and Experience on the Honduran Landscape   53
   Rosemary A. Joyce, Julia A. Hendon, and Jeanne Lopiparo

5. Mountains, Mounds, and Meaning: Metaphor in the Hohokam Cultural Landscape   73
   Stephanie M. Whittlesey

6. *Hopitutskwa* and *Ang Kuktota*: The Role of Archaeological Sites in Defining Hopi Cultural Landscapes   90
   Leigh J. Kuwanwisiwma and T. J. Ferguson

7. Negotiating the Imperial Landscape: The Geopolitics of Aztec Control in the Outer Provinces of the Empire   107
   Christopher P. Garraty and Michael A. Ohnersorgen

8. A Landscape of Gambles and Guts: Commodification of Land on the Arizona Frontier   132
   Michael P. Heilen and J. Jefferson Reid

9. Reconstructing an Ndee Sense of Place   149
   John R. Welch

10. Lost Cities, Prairie Castles   163
    Stephen H. Lekson

References Cited   181

Contributors   213

Index   215

Illustrations

Figures

2.1. Quiriguá Monument 5   16
2.2. Schematic map of Quiriguá floodplain settlement   17
2.3. Example of ditch exposure of ancient construction at Quiriguá   18
2.4. Map of Quiriguá site core   20
2.5. Plan of Quiriguá Locus 089   21
2.6. Quiriguá Monument 19   23
2.7. Plan of Quiriguá Group 3C-7   25
2.8. Quiriguá Pattern 3 as exemplified by Group 3C-2   26
2.9. Quiriguá Pattern 5 as exemplified by Group 3C-9   27
3.1. Map of Oaxaca   33
3.2. Photo of the Main Plaza of Monte Albán   35
3.3. Plan of the Main Plaza at Monte Albán   36
3.4. Formative period carved stones from Monte Albán   37
3.5. "Viborón" frieze from the North Platform at Monte Albán   37
3.6. Classic period carved stones from Monte Albán   40
3.7. VGPS residence and protective wall from Monte Albán's North Platform   43
3.8. Arroyo Group lintel painting from Mitla   46
4.1. Map of northern Honduras   54
4.2. Map of the Great Plaza of Cerro Palenque   57
4.3. Being in place at Cerro Palenque   58
4.4. Settlement in the central part of the Lower Ulúa River Valley   59
4.5. (a) Convergence of north–south axes of sites in the Lower Ulúa Valley   61
4.5. (b) Main orientational axes running through Travesía   62
4.6. (a) Plan of a "winter" ballcourt   66
4.6. (b) Plan of a "summer" ballcourt   67
4.7. Distribution of sites in the Oloman and Cataguana valleys on the Río Cuyumapa   68
5.1. Schematic map of Snaketown   82
5.2. Gila Butte   83
5.3. Canals located along the Gila River near Snaketown   84
6.1. The places and villages mentioned in Charlie Homehongva's 1955 narrative   92
6.2. Hopitutskwa symbolized by an encircling *homvi'ikya*   93
6.3. A field planted with a special strain of corn the Hopis have grown in the Southwest for more than a millennium   94
6.4. Hopi researchers in the Grand Canyon examining the archaeological remains of an ancestral village at South Canyon   96
6.5. Hopi researcher in the Grand Canyon inspecting granaries at Nankoweap   98
6.6. Boulder covered with petroglyphs at Tutuveni   100
6.7. Cultural landscape of Pasiwvi   103
6.8. Hopi rattle   106
7.1. Map of Postclassic western Mesoamerica   111

Illustrations

7.2. The south-central Gulf lowlands of Veracruz   112
7.3. The archaeological features of the provincial capital of Cotaxtla   113
7.4. Imitation Aztec III–style Black-on-Orange sherds from the Lower Blanco region   116
7.5. Examples of figurines from Cotaxtla   119
7.6. Examples of Aztec-style architectural tenons from Cotaxtla   120
7.7. Drawing of a *tecpilcalli*, or noble lord's house, from Sahagún   121
7.8. Middle Postclassic settlement patterns in the Lower Blanco region along the Blanco and Guerengo rivers   122
7.9. Late Postclassic settlement patterns in the Lower Blanco region along the Blanco and Guerengo rivers   123
8.1. Map of Sanford Ranch   133
8.2. The cognized landscape of Don Alonzo and Denton Sanford   146
8.3. Reconstruction of structures at Sanford Ranch   147
9.1. White Mountain Apache Tribe lands   152
9.2. Louie Zospah, White Mountain Apache Tribe Wildlife and Outdoor Recreation Ranger   153
9.3. Perry Tsadiasi, Levi Dehose, Harold Polingyumptewa, and Karl Hoerig   156
9.4. View to the west along Officer's Row at Fort Apache   158
10.1. Square Tower House, Mesa Verde   164
10.2. Manitou Cliff Dwellings   165
10.3. Kiva, Spruce Tree House, Mesa Verde   167
10.4. The Fort   169
10.5. The Fort wait staff   169
10.6. Bent's Old Fort, main gate   170
10.7. Bent's Old Fort, billiard room and laundry   171

Tables

4.1. Ballcourts in the Oloman and Cataguana Valleys   65
7.1. Presence/Absence of Major Basin of Mexico Aztec Decorated Pottery Types in Selected Archaeological Contexts in Near and Outer Provinces of the Empire   115
7.2. Aztec-Style Ceramic and Green Obsidian Counts from Three Surveys in the Outer Provinces of the Empire   117
7.3. *Comal* Percentages from the Area Just West of Callejón del Horno and Other Zones in the Lower Blanco Region   124
7.4. Ceramic Type Percentages from Middle Postclassic Collections by Types Only in Use During the Middle Postclassic Period and Those in Use During Both Middle and Late Postclassic Periods   125
7.5. Comparative Data from Three Zones in the Lower Blanco Region, Late Postclassic Period   126
9.1. Ndee Principles for Reconstructive Place Making   159

Preface

The Archaeology of Meaningful Places is the result of a shared and growing interest in redefining the theoretical and methodological tools needed to reconstruct the complex archaeological histories of people's relations with the places that constitute their natural and built environments. We originally addressed this concern at a Society for American Archaeology symposium in 2002; the collection of papers that resulted from fruitful discussions among symposium participants eventually grew to encompass two special issues of the *Journal of Archaeological Method and Theory* (2004) and an issue of *Expedition* (2004). The present volume includes two chapters developed from the original symposium papers and seven invited contributions. Such a prolific output demonstrates not only that a growing number of contemporary archaeologists are keenly engaged in the archaeology (or archaeologies) of place but also that the currency of this topic will endure for years to come.

Archaeologists who are interested in the relationship between people and place have a number of scientific and humanistic approaches at hand, from behavioral ecology to social theory and from geospatial modeling to phenomenology. While each of these approaches addresses human–nature relations from different theoretical and methodological standpoints, together they can contribute to a deeper understanding of human behavior and cognition as recorded in place. In 10 chapters, volume contributors thoughtfully integrate the results of scientifically oriented field research in Mesoamerica and the American Southwest and humanistic understandings of society and culture. The authors explore in detail the ways in which people assign meanings to the places they inhabit and the material forms these meanings may take. From this endeavor to join scientific and humanistic approaches, place emerges as a powerful and viable tool in the reconstruction and interpretation of the past as well as in the construction of social memory and cultural identity in the present.

The Archaeology of Meaningful Places is intended for archaeologists who are interested in incorporating place into their repertoire of conceptual tools, for readers who wish to delve into the tangible and intangible intricacies of people's interaction with their cultural and physical surroundings, and for those who are concerned with the impact of archaeological practice on the history and culture of descendant populations and other publics. We think the perspectives developed in the chapters to follow have great potential for stimulating theoretical and methodological advances in the archaeology of place. Furthermore, they can, and will, produce narratives and explanations of the past that both address the concerns and needs of the profession and satisfy the many public interests in archaeology.

We would like to thank James M. Skibo, editor of the Foundations of Archaeological Inquiry series, published by the University of Utah Press, and former press director Jeff Grathwohl for their invitation to undertake this book project and their encouragement. We are grateful to Peter DeLafosse, Glenda Cotter, and Reba Rauch at the University of Utah Press and Elisabeth A. Graves for finalizing publication of the book. We cannot express enough gratitude to the colleagues and friends who agreed to contribute to the book, readily responding to all queries and requests. Their patience and understanding greatly helped us see through the completion of this book.

As referees for the University of Utah Press, Mark Varien and an anonymous reviewer furnished useful comments on a draft of the book manuscript. Michael B. Schiffer and J. Jefferson Reid also read and commented on an early version of the introductory chapter.

The photograph of Quirigua Monument 19 that appears on the cover of this volume was graciously provided by Wendy Ashmore.

Finally, special recognition goes to Kacy Hollenback and Samrat Miller for their painstaking editorial assistance. Their youthful energy and computer skills saved us many hours of work and reduced our stress level by several orders of magnitude.

1

The Archaeology of Meaningful Places

María Nieves Zedeño and Brenda J. Bowser

*If place-making is a way of constructing the past,
a venerable means of doing human history,
it is also a way of constructing social traditions and,
in the process, personal and social identities.
We are, in a sense, the place-worlds we imagine.*
—Keith Basso, Wisdom Sits in Places

What is *place*, and why must archaeologists be concerned with it? In his groundbreaking book about language and place among the Cibecue Apache of Arizona, Basso (1996) demonstrates the intricate web of connections that exists among identity, trajectory, memory, and notions of the homeland. Place, in Basso's sense, is where history, both human and otherwise, happens and where knowledge gained by living history resides. What better concept, then, than place to organize the archaeological enterprise?

The Dictionary of Human Geography defines place simply as "a portion of geographical space occupied by a person or thing" (Johnston et al. 1994:442). According to Agnew (1987), a human place has three major elements: the locale, or setting(s) in which social relations are constituted formally or informally; the location, or geographic area encompassing the setting(s) for social interaction; and the sense of place. Thus, place is a juncture where environment, people, and meaning converge at multiple scales and, in the process, create a record of human behavior, perception, and cognition. The material record of human presence in a place is, in fact, archaeology's subject matter; economic, social, political, and symbolic meanings once ascribed to locales in the landscape may emerge in the process of reconstructing and interpreting people's pasts from the archaeological record.

Although the archaeology of place is a matter of current interest, it is not new to the profession; in fact, it may well surprise contemporary students of place that Lewis Binford was a modern pioneer in his recognition of the power and potential of this concept. In his article "The Archaeology of Place," he argues that

> until we turn our serious attention to the design of reliable methods for monitoring past conditions of interest, we will never be able to address interesting questions through the investigation of archaeological remains.... We must turn our analytical attention to the role of different places in the organization of past systems [1982:28–29].

Archaeologists have not lacked opportunities for developing intellectual frameworks that situate place and landscape as central to human histories. Take Waldo Wedel, for example. In his autobiographical article, "The Education of a Plains Archeologist," Wedel (1977:6) recounts the tremendous impact that taking classes from cultural geographer Carl Sauer—the venerable father of landscape studies—had on his view of human–nature dynamics on the Great Plains and on his explanations of continuity and change. In fact, Wedel is credited with having introduced principles of human ecology into Plains archaeology (Bamforth 1988:3). The anthropological community at large may never know just how profoundly influential were the frameworks set forth by Sauer (1925; who was in turn inspired by the cultural area studies of his University of California, Berkeley, colleague Alfred Kroeber) on generations of scholars wishing to expand horizons beyond the narrow confines of culture history and, more recently, of positivism. We do know, however, that it has taken many decades for anthropologists, and especially archaeologists, to ponder on place and landscape theories as they may apply to the reconstruction and interpretation of the past.

Although human ecology and cultural geography have had a great impact on anthropological theory since the 1930s (Steward 1955; Steward and Seltzer 1938; Wedel 1941, 1953), the positivism that accompanied the advent of the New Archaeology initially bypassed numerous aspects of human–nature dynamics for those most likely to create a conspicuous material record (Binford 1962). At that time, positivist geographers who favored quantitative tools of spatial analysis over the not-so-easily delimited and measured cultural landscapes also made important inroads in archaeological research (e.g., Clarke 1972; Hodder and Orton 1976). Landscape and place studies later regained popularity largely as a result of the humanistic geography of Cosgrove (Cosgrove and Daniels 1988), Jackson (1984), Pred (1984), and Tuan (1977), among others, and these concepts soon appeared in the anthropological literature in North America (e.g., Carmichael et al. 1994; Greider and Garkovich 1994; Rodman 1992; Walker 1991), Australia (e.g., Head 1993; Myers 1991), and Europe (e.g., Bender 1993; Ingold 1993; Tilley 1994). The influential anthropological work of Basso (1996) combined principles of ethnosemantics with geographic approaches to place.

Over the past 25 years, definitions and usages of place and landscape as conceptual tools for understanding cultural and social dynamics have evolved and expanded in unanticipated ways, as the essays in this volume and a number of topical reviews and critiques indicate (see Anschuetz et al. 2001; Ashmore and Knapp 1999; Fleming 2006; Norton 1989; Tilley 1994, 2004; Whittlesey 1998a, 2003; Zedeño 1997, 2000). Contemporary scholars attempting to set a broad range of intellectual and political agendas have also taken a keen interest in the concepts of place and landscape; these concepts also resonate with constituencies such as tribal communities, ethnic minorities, and many others whose pasts are investigated archaeologically. Here, 14 contributors argue compellingly that archaeology is about the meaning of place inasmuch as it is about the past and about material culture and environment; these place and landscape studies successfully integrate humanistic and scientific forms of inquiry, thus honoring the intellectual roots established by Sauer and his intellectual progeny.

In the broadest sense, this book is concerned with describing and explaining how particular places contain key elements for understanding the social worlds constructed, maintained, and modified by those who once inhabited them. This is achieved through the investigation of biographical, topographic, geopolitical, ideological, cosmological, and mnemonic facets of place, beginning with processes of place making and continuing with the development of networks among places and between places and broader landscapes. Diverse spatial and temporal contexts in two culture areas—Mesoamerica and the Greater Southwest—serve as the backdrop for nine chapters that show how place is an ideal starting point to begin unraveling the human past. Several authors further address the enduring significance of places of the past for contemporary peoples. Ultimately, the contributors champion the notion that place is a valid and useful analytic unit for describing, reconstructing, interpreting, and explaining the form, structure, and temporality of the meanings humans ascribe to their environment.

The book begins with a diachronic reconstruction of the Classic Maya community of Quiriguá (chapter 2), in which Wendy Ashmore demonstrates how alternative meanings of place can exist simultaneously and not always harmoniously. Celebration, alliance, domination, competition, and resistance are among the motives that may underlie place making; conflicting motives may in turn affect the relationships between singular places and social groups at several scales. Ashmore notes that meanings may be purposefully created or accrued through time and from distinctive interactions among places and people. The life histories of places such as Quiriguá, as they are built, maintained, modified, reconstructed, and abandoned or purposefully destroyed, can carry profound social and symbolic significance not only to the original dwellers but to those who may later visit or inhabit such places.

In chapter 3, Arthur Joyce traces the life history of the Main Plaza at Monte Albán, thus demonstrating how key components of a single place may be targeted to detect social and political change. This author utilizes archaeological, epigraphic, iconographic, ethnohistoric, and ethnographic data to explain the material and symbolic transformations of the plaza and their impact on practice, identity, memory, and power relations in this Oaxacan community. From this exercise, the Main Plaza of Monte Albán emerges as the epitome both of cosmic creation and of power "produced, experienced, maintained, and transformed through the practices of people." Joyce demonstrates that changes in relations of domination and subordination in complex polities are embodied in the biographies of monuments to social power and are informed by dominant ideologies.

Rosemary Joyce, Julia Hendon, and Jeanne Lopiparo unpack the process of emplacement of Classic Maya centers in Honduras (chapter 4). The authors treat *emplacement* as the body of structured and coordinated place-making actions that developed from shared cosmologies and geographies among interacting communities but that at the same time was interpreted uniquely at each community according to topography and cosmology. Emplacement is inferred from architectural, topographic, and cosmological dimensions of site layout along the Lower Ulúa River and tributaries, as they compare with highland Copán. The authors emphasize the interplay between shared principles and idiosyncrasies in settlement and ballcourt emplacement and its impact on the movement of people. Their argument clearly points to the importance of combining place and landscape scales of analysis in order to understand place-making practices from architectural layout.

In chapter 5, Stephanie Whittlesey explores the ideological landscape of the Hohokam of southern Arizona through cosmology, iconography, and the built environment. In her view, cultural landscapes reflect and symbolize ideology, values, and ethics, because they help naturalize social relations by making them appear inevitable. Whittlesey introduces the *mountain as a container of water* metaphor as the critical ideological link between Hohokam central places and the desert landscape; this metaphor allowed people to transfer ideological principles that were essential for the survival of a community's social world to younger generations. The author unpacks the mountain metaphor and other principles behind the organization of the pre-Classic central place of Snaketown through a multidimensional analysis of the cultural landscape.

Shifting the theme of place–landscape connections toward ethnic origins, group history, and identity, Leigh Kuwanwisiwma and T. J. Ferguson discuss the broad philosophical and spiritual concept of *Hopitutskwa*, or Hopi land (chapter 6). As a cultural landscape, Hopitutskwa encompasses myriad natural and cultural features as well as archaeological sites or "footprints" of the Hopi ancestors. The authors' discussion centers on interrelated concepts of place, scale, time, and context from the Hopi perspective, to highlight the important relationship among archaeological sites or places of the past, the homeland, and the people. As Kuwanwisiwma and Ferguson state, "The abiding connection Hopi people have with the material culture of their ancestors gives archaeology a deeply personal as well as intellectual meaning. Archaeology thus helps give focus to the comprehension of ancestral lifeways embodied in the monuments that constitute Hopi footprints on the landscape."

The next three chapters expand the focus and scale of place studies by emphasizing connections between imperial or national landscapes and places of local significance. In chapter 7, Christopher Garraty and Michael Ohnersorgen address the uneasy interaction between imperial rule and outer provinces of the Aztec Empire by looking at the ways in which rulers manipulated the landscape by altering public perceptions of social relations and meanings of place during times of upheaval. A geopolitical landscape perspective allows the authors to explain the juxtaposition of a central social order that co-opted provincial leaders and sacred places, imposed imperial symbols and ideologies, and rewrote economic policies, against the indigenous sovereignty of the imperial provinces of Cuetlaxtlan and Oztuma-Cutzamala in east and west Mexico, respectively. Here, identity, power struggles, assimilation, and resistance were expressed differentially in the construction and modification of local places and in the reproduction of provincial and imperial traditions.

In an exploration of nation–place relations on the western frontier, Michael Heilen and J. Jefferson Reid scrutinize the cultural, historical, and strategic contexts of land commodification in the American West (chapter 8). The place of choice, Sanford Ranch in southern Arizona, is illustrative of the relationships established between citizens and national forces in the process of settling the western frontier. By situating the trajectory of Sanford Ranch in a broad geographic scale and discussing its potential for success or failure in the ranching enterprise, the authors make it possible to appreciate just how diverse frontier experiences were and how every homestead possessed a unique life history and array of meanings even though they owed their existence to the national imperative to colonize and commodify country and people.

In chapter 9, John Welch lays out the historical and practical challenges of "reconstructing" senses of place at a time when meanings, names, and traditional cultural principles are disappearing alongside language among the White Mountain Apache, or Ndee, of Arizona. Welch introduces the Ndee concept of place whereby "land" and "mind" are a unity and memory and geography are inseparable. Not surprisingly, historical efforts to undermine this worldview by public and private interests in North America have resulted in actual land loss and concomitant erosion of tribal cultural values and knowledge. The author explains how contemporary White Mountain Apache people are revitalizing their sense of place not only by recognizing archaeological places and reconciling familiar landscape features with oral traditions but also by proactively restoring the environment as a means to assert their sovereignty over the ancestral homeland.

The volume closes with Stephen Lekson's essay on the dynamics of place in interpretive archaeology (chapter 10). Drawing comparisons from four public places—Mesa Verde Ruins, Manitou Cliff Dwellings, Bent's Old Fort, and The Fort restaurant on the outskirts of Denver, Colorado—Lekson points to the sliding scale of reality that permeates the interpretation of archaeological places by both scientists and the public at large. From a world heritage site to a privately owned replica of Mesa Verde's cliff dwellings, and from a carefully reconstructed frontier outpost to a popular restaurant fashioned in the likeness of that fort, fascination with all things archaeological runs through the public imagination and forces professional archaeologists to reconsider the cultural value of place irrespective of age or origin. Reflecting on the meaning each of these locales on the basis of criteria such as authenticity, context, and history, the author challenges readers to discover new senses of place; he convinces us that these archaeological places—whether real, relocated, reconstructed, or imitated—possess their own wisdom and deserve their own history.

In the remainder of this introductory essay we weave information and ideas from each chapter into a thematic overview where diverse lines of thought are integrated to reveal the multiple facets of meaningful places and to illustrate ways in which places may be approached archaeologically. We have framed our arguments on the archaeology of meaningful places within the methodological and theoretical positions upheld by the authors to highlight their individuality as well as their common intellectual goals and achievements.

Toward an Archaeology of Meaningful Places

The need for an archaeology of place that explicitly deals with the structure of the archaeological record was acknowledged as early as 1982 by Lewis Binford, but frameworks that integrate archaeological method with theoretical understandings of meaningful places have been slow to develop and operationalize (e.g., Adler 1996; Anschuetz et al. 2001; Ashmore 2002; Ashmore and Knapp 1999; Bowser 2004; Van Dyke and Alcock 2003; Whittlesey 1998a, 2003; Zedeño 2000; Zedeño et al. 1997). These newer frameworks have not as yet been widely adopted largely because of the analytic challenges posed by deriving meaning from archaeological places. The volume authors address these challenges by integrating empirical approaches to archaeological places with broadly based interpretations and reconstructions of meaning.

An archaeology of place, as Bowser (2004:1) defines it, is one that focuses on the ways in which people impart meaning—both symbolically and through action—to their cultural and physical surroundings at multiple scales and on the material forms these meanings may take. Its premise is simple: people create places through behavioral interactions with nature and the supernatural; they cognize their experiences by developing spatial referents for their actions through material modification and verbal and metaphoric inscription. On the basis of these cognitive processes, people develop senses of place and attachments to place that motivate, structure, and transform their interactions with the material world in patterned ways (e.g., Gould 1980; Myers 1991). Thus, the scrutiny of archaeological places as geographic or architectural referents of human behavior, perception, cognition, and history has the potential to reveal an untold wealth of cultural and social information.

An archaeology of place must address both natural and modified environments. "Natural places" are those locales in the landscape that, though not obviously a product of human modification, affect human behavior and are in turn modified through verbal and nonverbal inscription (Basso 1996; Bradley 2000; Jones 1998; Tilley and Bennett 2001; Whitridge 2004). Mountains, rivers, springs, quarries, lakes, conspicuous landforms, plants, and animals inform social and cultural practices. As Joyce and colleagues note in chapter 4, these natural places may affect the emplacement of architectural features and even entire towns or temples. Naming and the construction of natural metaphors and imaginaries (Whitridge 2004; Whittlesey, chapter 5) promote the preservation and transmission of knowledge by reference to singular places. An archaeology of natural places, therefore, considers nature's architecture as a fundamental conceptual resource for understanding cultural form (Tilley and Bennett 2001:335).

The concept of place as "built environment" is not new to social sciences; in fact, a great deal of archaeological, ethnographic, and geographic research has been devoted to the modification of the earth's surface by means of constructing facilities—houses, streets, public plazas, temples, monuments. Prehistoric and historical archaeology emphasizes the ways in which this built environment constrains or enhances social interaction and communication (e.g., Bender 1993; Cosgrove and Daniels 1988; Hirsch and O'Hanlon 1995; Jackson 1984; Lipe and Hegmon 1989; Matthews 2002; Parker Pearson and Richards 1994; Pauls 2006; Rathje and Schiffer 1982; Schiffer and Miller 1999; Tuan 1977). The theoretical writings of Foucault (1977) and Giddens (1984), in particular, have received a great deal of attention in spatial archaeology (e.g., Ferguson 1996; Nielsen 1995; Smith 1996). As cogently argued by Wendy Ashmore (chapter 2) and Arthur Joyce (chapter 3), approaches to architectural places can be productive when they focus on material biographies or life histories vis-à-vis social and cultural change. As a complement to biographies, emplacement can reveal the delicate balance of commonalities and differences in the architectural interpretation of overarching cosmologies (Joyce et al., chapter 4). Ideally, the archaeology of place should seamlessly integrate the natural and the built environments, as this is also an archaeology of people's historical relationships with nature.

Most recently, agency and materiality have further lent the archaeology of place a fresh focus by bringing forth issues of perception, practice, and memory. Each of these approaches underscores both individual and social dimensions of place, as well as the power of places and actors to influence one another and to mold or altogether alter the course of social history (e.g., Meskell 2003; Thomas 1993; Tilley 1994; Van Dyke and Alcock 2003). David and Lourandos (1999:107) and Lekson (chapter 10), for example, point out that history addresses not so much the nature and dynamics of outside realities as people's relationships with their surroundings, their social and physical environments as experienced, and cultural constructions and social memory. Hopi and Apache senses of place (Kuwanwisiwma and Ferguson, chapter 6; Welch, chapter 9) further indicate the inseparability of place, memory, and identity, highlighting the need to practice an archaeology of place that is responsive to alternative ontologies and alternative forms of history. Such practice could in turn allow a closer approximation to the meanings of past places and would foster the appreciation and preservation of cultural heritage and contemporary cultural values attached to it.

An archaeology of place also has a decidedly political facet: power struggles, contestation, displacement, opportunism, and resistance are common threads throughout this volume; many of these topics are articulated in detail by Garraty and Ohnersorgen (chapter 7), Heilen and Reid (chapter 8), and Welch (chapter 9). These authors unpack the intricate connections of places and the increasingly larger geopolitical landscapes, which may encompass a country, an empire, or a continent. By alternating scales of analysis, it is possible to bring forth the depth and extent of variability in place-making practices and meanings as well as the tapestry of local responses to ideological imperatives. To lose sight of this vast scale of observation and analysis is to completely misunderstand the potential of place for uncovering the workings of the world.

As is evident in several chapters, places and the landscapes that contain them are multilayered; each layer, in turn, represents a particular realm of experience and cognition. For example, in this multiethnic and multicultural world, given places and landscapes may be lived or understood in diverse and often contrasting ways (Rodman 1992); this much is true for the Aztec (Garraty and Ohnersorgen, chapter 7), the Arizona settlers (Heilen and Reid, chapter 8), the Hopi (Kuwanwisiwma and Ferguson, chapter 6), and the Apache or Ndee (Welch, chapter 9). Through current technological advances, notably geographic information systems, different natural and cultural "layers" can be visualized to facilitate the reconstruction and interpretation of place meanings.

In short, this is a challenging kind of archaeology, one that pushes the boundaries of scientific archaeological inquiry by seeking empirical approaches to subjective experience and combining humanistic and scientific methods. The goal of such an endeavor is not to sacrifice theoretical and methodological rigor for discursive flare but, rather, to cast the intellectual net wide enough to incorporate useful concepts and methods from many fields. An archaeology of place is, therefore, frankly and unabashedly multidisciplinary. Furthermore, as scholars we are generally aware of the larger power struggles in which our narratives of place are embedded globally (King 2003; Knapp and Ashmore 1999); thus our research must be cognizant of the fact that knowledge of distant places is accessible to everyone and can affect us all.

What Is a Meaningful Place?

At its simplest and most useful for archaeological pursuits, *place* is a discrete locus of behavior, materials, and memory—a meaningful locale, a product of people's interactions with nature and the supernatural as well as with one another. As noted above, the concept "place" encompasses a wide array of spatial categories, not the least of which are physiographic features such as caves, mountains, springs, ancient trees, and salient rock outcrops (e.g., Ashmore and Knapp 1999; Bradley 2000; Stoffle and Zedeño 2001a, 2001b); the sky; and the ocean bottom. Place becomes a material culture category by virtue of transformation through human activity (Agnew 1987; Bowser 2002:136–144; Carroll 2007; Zedeño 2000:106). Furthermore, *place* is distinguished from *space* by virtue of interaction, action, memory, and meaning (Carroll 2007; Low and Lawrence-Zúñiga 2003; Whitridge 2004). The recognition of a place's existence and its significance by the individual and the collective is what defines its meanings, outlines its historical trajectory, explains its connections with other places, and lays out its articulation with the broader landscape, whether tacitly or explicitly.

To illustrate, for the Hopi of Arizona or the Hidatsa of North Dakota, an eagle nest is not simply a domestic structure built by a parenting raptor. An eagle nest is a locus of religious activity because it contains a resource that is critical for the spiritual well-being and survival of the community. Among the Hopi, ownership of an eagle nest is determined by clan membership and inherited accordingly; the knowledge required to trap eagles and to use feathers belongs to clan and society and must be transferred through formal training (Fewkes 1900). In the case of the Hidatsa, the right to trap eagles must be acquired through visions, self-inflicted torture, and expensive purchase; it also has ties to clan membership and inheritance rules (Wilson 1928).

In both cases, eagle-trapping places may not exhibit measurable human modification except for the placement of perishable and nonperishable offerings or the construction of a trapping pit and a temporary structure or shelter nearby. Yet, for the members of these cultures, the eagle nest, as a place, conveys a clear sense of ancestral origin, ritual purpose, and social rights and obligations; provides a geographic anchor for identifying territorial identities within and between groups; and serves as a source of knowledge and moral lessons for the generations to come. Eagle nests or eagle-trapping pits continue to be used today as territorial markers, providing these groups with a means to symbolically assert ownership and use rights over lands that were lost to them in the nineteenth century. Human histories thus have a very strong spatial focus that lends a ready visual tool to memory and a sense of continuity and regeneration in the face of strife, destruction, or turmoil.

Place is distinct from *site* in that visible or measurable human modification is not a necessary and sufficient condition of place, whereas site is, by archaeological definition, an arbitrary category in archaeological systematics that contains material evidence of human activity (Binford 1982; Ebert 1992; King 2003; Rossignol and Wandsnider 1992). This important distinction does not imply that an archaeological place exists outside a material referent; rather, it suggests that human action, whether random, opportunistic, or purposeful, creates and modifies places and marks their significance in ways not always amenable to traditional archaeological analysis. In his critique of archaeological systematics, Binford (1982) advances the idea that place, as an activity locus, should be the unit of interest in archaeological research because it best captures the range of variation in human–land and human–resource interactions that characterized the organization of past cultural systems. He notes that site, as a typological unit, conflates meaningful variation into categories that tell less about the past than about archaeological typologies.

For Binford, a focus on assemblages, features, and resource zones, on the other hand, reveals far more information of interest than site typologies: "The facts of interest are the ways in which places are differentiated one from another" (1982:28–29). Although his emphasis on the economic organization of mobile hunter-gatherers would be seen today as overly narrow, his outline of method is both accurate and timeless. One may begin approaching place from an assemblage-centered methodology, as he proposes, and progressively expand the reach of the analysis to incorporate unmodified physiographic features, from plants and animals to prominent landforms and even the sky, seasons, sensory properties, and other elements of nature that could have influenced the life history and performance characteristics of particular places (Carroll 2007; Zedeño 2000). Inferences of meaning must thus be buttressed with sound archaeological data, historical documents, or ethnographic analogy (e.g., Bowser and Patton 2004; Brown 2004; Stewart et al. 2004; Whitridge 2004; Zedeño and Laluk 2008). Archaeologists are uniquely trained to analyze space, and thus they can move effortlessly from space to place without becoming burdened by essentialist site typologies.

Like contemporary approaches to landscape (Tress and Tress 2001; Zedeño 2000; Zedeño et al. 1999), the archaeological study of place today encompasses minimally five dimensions: spatial, temporal, formal, cognitive, and relational, as Whittlesey (chapter 5) illustrates in the Hohokam case. Likewise, volume contributors address each of these dimensions at multiple scales. Flexibility of scale is perhaps one of the most useful characteristics of place as a unit of analysis, as it allows the researcher to move from the bird's-eye view afforded by large-scale units, such as a river system, a mountain range, an empire, or a nation, to the single landform or architectural feature. By the same token, places may also be analyzed as discrete loci in their own right or as components of progressively larger units. As shown in this volume, multidimensional and multiscalar studies are the most effective at isolating place meanings.

Place, Memory, and Metaphor

Place is the repository of sequences of actions that, through time and repetition, become part of a people's "tradition." Such sequences of actions may be evident, for example, in the types of artifacts and features associated with multiple occupations of a given locale or in visibly consistent use practices that modify a place and its immediate surroundings according to its users' needs. If, through time, a place remains relatively undisturbed, then the artifacts, features, and modifications can become anchors of individual and group memories, of collective knowledge about land and history, and of moral lessons needed to maintain social cohesion. These landmarks are like pages in the history of a people (Zedeño 2000:107), as shown in the Ndee and Hopi cases (Kuwanwisiwma and Ferguson, chapter 6; Welch, chapter 9). Not surprisingly, the intentional destruction of meaningful places—for example, the bombing of the World Trade Center in New York City in 2001—is an effective means to alter or affect the cultural core, historical trajectory, and collective memory of a people (Meskell 2002).

Throughout history, individuals and societies have made places to initiate, enhance, celebrate, or commemorate people's interactions with one another as well as with nature and the supernatural (Joyce 2003; Joyce and Hendon 2000; Meskell 2003; Schama 1995; Tilley 1994; Van Dyke and Alcock 2003). An obsidian flake deposited at the base of a cliff, a copper nugget thrown into a lake, a pictograph, a stela, a plaza, a war memorial, a restaurant, and a mound are place forms that represent unique social orders and systems of thought, but all point to the universal need to create places that remind us and others about the experiences a human society has undergone and the knowledge it has acquired (Lekson, chapter 10). Beyond memory, many of these modifications attempt to secure the continuity of harmonious relationships with powerful forces of the universe (Brown 2004; Carroll et al. 2004).

Place making, therefore, is the power to "appropriate nature" (after Ingold 1986) and to "make culture" (after Tilley and Bennett 2001)—to develop bonds, make land our homeland, create order and negotiate power, integrate our practices and worldviews with those of others, and anchor experiences in the landscape by naming its features or by building our own, so that we can remember and learn from them in the future. Yet this purposeful exercise and the landscape modifications it leaves behind are but a sliver of the immensity of human action. People are continuously interacting with their surroundings and modifying them in unseen, unintentional, and unpredictable ways, and these interactions foster strong attachments to place even if they only last for short periods (Ingold 1993; Schiffer and Miller 1999; Thomas 2001). More often than not, it is this antlike work that exerts the greatest change. Why, then, do we appeal to a few places when we must remember our own history and teach it to others?

Whittlesey (chapter 5) states that a culturally constructed landscape is made of place metaphors that allow people to structure perceptions and social relations, to make people see connections they had not seen before, and even to predict the future. People do not need to remember and commemorate every place they have created because they have metaphors. As Whittlesey's analysis of Hohokam mound construction at Snaketown suggests, a single metaphor allows people to conflate redundant places or link complementary places and features from multilayered landscapes into one concept or suite of related concepts and tie it to a few key places or landmarks.

Origin and migration traditions are examples of how multiple time periods, multiple group trajectories, and separate geographies become conjoined through metaphor into a single story line and a single landscape, to which all members of the society can relate at a given time in their collective history (Zedeño and Laluk 2008; Zedeño et al. 2009). This phenomenon may explain why places are named and talked about selectively and, crucial for archaeological inquiry, why places are differentially used, marked, modified, reused, and abandoned (Binford 1982; Schroeder 2004). It is important, therefore, to identify and explain places as a means to understand cultural landscapes rather than address landscapes as monolithic units, for place is what gives texture and substance to people's relations with land and resources and with one another—the proverbial widening of horizons starts at one place and extends from there.

Place Biographies

Places would not be as useful for manipulating the social order if they were not constantly in the process of becoming. The transformation of a place into a landmark, for example, may involve a series of activities and interactions that crosscut various realms of individual and social life, from subsistence to ritual, and that accumulate, materially and mnemonically, through time (Zedeño 2000:106–110; Zedeño et al. 1997:125). The concatenation of diverse interactions of people and place generally produces landmarks with complex life histories not only in the extent of their material modifications but also in terms of accreted memories and metaphors attached to them. Ashmore (2002:1178, chapter 2) asks, *What happens to a place after it has been established and affirmed?* Life history analyses reveal that place biographies are typically punctuated by events or interactions originating from four inclusive sources of change: natural landscape evolution, natural catastrophes, change in user groups, and material modifications. Changes in physiography, sudden or otherwise, may drastically alter people/place interactions; consider, for example, the effect of known volcanic eruptions, droughts, and floods on societal change worldwide. Places may be changed physically and meaningfully to accommodate diverse ethnic identities and changes in the economic, social, and political standing of their users. Intriguingly, as Ashmore (chapter 2), Joyce (chapter 3), and Garraty and Ohnersorgen (chapter 7) write, places may be modified materially and meaningfully to maintain continuity or to destroy continuity, depending on the historical contingencies within which they are being used and remembered. Because places are not passive stages for human action, they, too, can influence social relations and social change.

In writing Quiriguá's biography, Ashmore (chapter 2) notes that places may acquire successive meanings from use over time, particularly in the face of cultural diversity among users. The biography of a place may be rewritten by inventing new associations with creation myths, by modifying appearance, by selectively memorializing or forgetting, or even by creating distance between the place and its users. Whether manipulated by a single individual, by a social sector, or by the entire group, places may thus evolve with the users, creating in the process a sense of continuity. Joyce's portrayal of Monte Albán's Main Plaza (chapter 3) is yet another example of dovetailing place evolution and social order, where a central place becomes the axis mundi or organizing principle by which a social group attempts to perpetuate itself even in times of political unrest. Yet, as Joyce suggests, changes in the social order, such as increasing control of a user group to the detriment of another, may in time cause the breakdown of organic connections among places and users, as in the case of Monte Albán. When continuity is sought, place as a whole incorporates elements of the past and the present to achieve a sense of timelessness and a seamless transition in the social order.

It is important, therefore, to take into account that a place may represent multiple trajectories that, through time, are conflated or obscured by the smoothing effect of continuity. As Gallivan (2006:87) notes, place biographies precisely help sort out memories and retell stories from alternative viewpoints, thus de-homogenizing history and enhancing the diversity of historical experiences, particularly in multicultural and multiethnic contexts. Garraty and Ohnersorgen (chapter 7) note that changes can also be imposed upon occupied places as an attempt to assimilate others or to end resistance, as seen in the outer provinces of the Aztec Empire. Intentional burial, burning, demolishing or effacing, and abandonment, as seen often in Mesoamerican and southwestern monuments, are all evidence of transformation both in the original fabric of a place and in social relationships.

Place Networks

Places do not exist in isolation, write Heilen and Reid (chapter 8). A place generally stands at the juncture of one or more socially constructed and sometimes conflicting landscapes; in fact, the meaning of a place often derives from its relative position within a network of other places across those landscapes (Rodman 1992). The significance of a place may be determined not only by its spatial, temporal, formal, and cognitive dimensions but also by its performance characteristics, that is, by its capacity to facilitate certain kinds of interactions—a relational dimension (Carroll 2007). This much is clear in chapter 4, where Joyce and her colleagues argue that the emplacement of Classic Maya centers, which responded to both overarching cosmological principles and the singularities of site location, was coordinated to facilitate the flow of people along a river system and between topographic zones and to enhance supracommunity participation in formal activities such as the ballgame.

The characteristics of place networks are in turn determined by the nature of people–place interactions. For example, places along a trail or a river, as is the case of the Lower Ulúa settlement system (Joyce et al., chapter 4), are connected sequentially by their geographic position relative to each leg of the trail and by the order in which people moving along it experienced places during a journey (Ingold 1993; Zedeño et al. 2008). On the other hand, the Main Plaza of Monte Albán is suggestive of a network of places established around a center point (Joyce, chapter 3), which is analogous (but scaled differently) to the networks established between the Aztec capital and the outer provincial centers (Garraty and Ohnersorgen, chapter 7) or between Washington, D.C., and the western frontier (Heilen and Reid, chapter 8). Such arrangements may be conceived as place networks or "systems of settings" (Ashmore 2002:1176), each with its own unique form and organizational structure.

To piece together people's histories from a place-making perspective it is necessary to address the ways in which places, by virtue of human action, become linked to one another to form a place network (Heilen 2005; Zedeño 1997, 2000). A network may encompass different types of places that complement one another in a single realm of action. To illustrate, a place network associated with food production not only includes fields and field houses, storage pits and processing locales, but also the places where shrines are built, prayers are made, offerings are given to propitiate rain, and harvest feasts are held. All of these places may or may not be geographically contiguous, purposefully arranged in a specific design, or even within the farmer's visual field, yet they are all intricately connected. Conversely, topographically similar landforms, such as buttes or hills, within a given visual field or geographic range may each articulate into widely diverging networks of places, actions, and memories.

Through time, places may accrue links to more than one network. Consider, for example, the Hopitutskwa—a land composed of multi-layered physical, social, and spiritual place networks that dates back to creation and has evolved since time immemorial. As explained by Kuwanwisiwma and Ferguson (chapter 6), each place within the *Tutskwa* conveys information about the geographic origin and ethnolinguistic identity of the Hopi clans, their ancestral homes, their migrations and places they visited, their arrival to the contemporary homeland, their ritual calendar, and the struggles to preserve their sovereignty in times of change and upheaval. Sites of different ages, including the eagle nests discussed above, act as compasses in the sense that they help situate people in time, place, and specific cultural context. The concatenations of places are *Ang Kuktota* or footprints that remind the Hopi who they are, where they came from, and what they must do to preserve their culture and society.

Yet another characteristic of places and place networks is the layering of meaning that occurs when places are used or experienced by different individuals or user groups. In the case of our hypothetical traveler, if a trail or a river runs across two territorial units, then each place along the trail will stand at the juncture of two distinctive networks—that of the traveler experiencing a foreign land and that of the territory's owner (Ingold 1993; Rodman 1992). Similar connections may be found among many other kinds of networks. Layered meanings are typical in complex or ethnically diverse societies that came to share the same landscape. The colonization of native lands in North and Central America by Europeans is perhaps the most significant example of layered meanings, but prehistory, too, offers numerous examples, such as the case of the Aztec Empire. Layered meanings that characterize place networks may be unpacked by scrutinizing place biographies to explain causes and consequences of change in users or in activities, and by progressively contextualizing relationships among places, until a sense of landscape begins to take form.

Place Logic

Golledge (2003:30) states that in the process of learning about places, people internalize knowledge by deliberately encoding environmental information so that it can be used to determine where one is at any particular moment, where other specific perceived or encoded objects are in the surrounding space, how to get from one place to another, and how to communicate spatial knowledge to others. Welch's examination of Ndee place making (chapter 9) demonstrates that the mode by which people encode place information into known categories of knowledge, create new categories, and later reckon these from memory is bounded by language as well as by cultural training and experiences (Levinson 1996:353), or what may be called "place logic"—a kind of cultural logic that orders the structure and meaning of places and their components (Stoffle and Zedeño 2001a). Place logic incorporates critical principles governing the formation of place networks or systems of settings (e.g., Joyce et al., chapter 4; Kuwanwisiwma and Ferguson, chapter 6). Individual and collective memories of place are generally inscribed or represented to others by appealing to elements in the place logic that help individuals contextualize unknown or newly experienced places by associating them with familiar ones.

Politics of Place

The study of place networks further allows one to understand change in the social and cultural milieu that is generally associated with the rise of conflict and its resolution. At the heart of human–nature interactions is the ability to make decisions about the nature and condition of a place (e.g., Agnew 1987; Bender 1993; Nielsen 1995; Smith 1996). To gain insights into the processes by which people gain or lose decision-making power, it is necessary to look at the broad landscape within which a place is being used, modified, or avoided. Although speaking from two unrelated and very distinctive geographic and historical contexts—the Northwest Ordinance in the western frontier and the Aztec presence in core and outer provinces—Heilen and Reid (chapter 8) and Garraty and Ohnersorgen (chapter 7), respectively, present strikingly similar arguments regarding conflict and change in the political landscape and the impact on singular people–place relations. Both essays strongly converge on the idea that times of upheaval and dramatic change provide the best opportunity for analyzing the ways in which landscapes are socially constructed and places are connected within a broader network. These authors focus on the effect of the imposition of land-based systems of thought by a dominant political force over a local population and on the strategies of resistance versus submission to the imposed system.

Two facets of human–land interactions within a geopolitical landscape are addressed in these chapters. The first facet, in the words of Garraty and Ohnersorgen, is rooted in sovereignty, or "a suite of cultural dispositions that tie a given group to a certain space, including indigenous identities, traditions, and long-standing social networks." Such interactions are anthropogenic dynamic constructions with culturally organized dimensions. As Heilen and Reid put it, these characteristics turn place and landscape into inalienable possessions—not necessarily immutable in quality but, rather, socially negotiated, scale dependent, and contextually variable. Thus a key to domination is to impose changes on the suite of cultural dispositions that govern human–land relations and define sovereignty. The second facet, therefore, derives from the "'geographical...perspectives'...of different governing units or factions involved in negotiating political landscape features such as political boundaries, locations and meanings of central places, and important loci of ethnic or religious identity" (Garraty and Ohnersorgen, chapter 7). Because of the volatile nature of geopolitical relations, particularly in times of conflict, such landscapes are generally contested within and outside the society that claims territorial and ethnic ownership. In Heilen and Reid's view, geopolitical landscapes are distinct from sociopolitical landscapes in that the former are readily commodified. At the juncture of two conflicting landscape ideologies, a place may be at once inalienable and commodified, for example, Mount Graham in Arizona, which is sacred to the Apache but claimed by the scientific community for the siting of high-power telescopes.

Garraty and Ohnersorgen explain that modes of control over a people's social order may be best achieved by disrupting their compass or the way in which they structure their relationships in reference to their surrounding landscape. Political control may be direct or indirect, territorial or hegemonic. The most archaeologically visible forms of control are directly territorial, whereby both sociopolitical and geopolitical landscapes are reconstituted rapidly and visibly by actions of the controlling power such as military invasion and government takeover, dismantling and replacement of public architecture, transplanting of immigrant enclaves, forced relocation of the local population, religious desecration (Walker 1995), and other such actions that disrupt and break down the local population's physical attachments to places. At the opposite end of the spectrum are indirect forms of hegemonic control involving the symbolic imposition and manipulation of symbols and identities, thus causing disruption but not necessarily destruction or replacement of the social order. Indirect imposition of political control is likely to reconstitute the geopolitical landscape in ways that are less visible archaeologically than direct territorial control (Schreiber 1992).

Place-focused analyses, such as those of Sanford Ranch in Arizona by Heilen and Reid and of El Sauce and Callejón del Horno in Veracruz by Garraty and Ohnersorgen, lend contextual depth and rich detail to broadly traced landscape approaches by revealing variation in specific forms of conformity or resistance to political control. Both studies, for example, show how overarching forms of control appear in frontier environments and how local populations react to the imposition of external power. The biographies of El Sauce and Callejón del Horno show a gamut of symbolic and practical acts of resistance by provincial elites and commoners to the imposition of an Aztec imperial order, as they appear, often subtly, in the material record. Garraty and Ohnersorgen point out that the responses of provincial elites to the Aztec presence also involved their strategic formulation of alliances with the Aztec dominant elites. In the Aztec case, the landscape remained a heavily negotiated but inalienable possession. On the other hand, Sanford Ranch's biography illustrates, on a small scale, the pervasive commodifying effect of hegemonic imposition of the Public Land Survey System upon a landscape previously inhabited by native communities that saw it as inalienable. Heilen and Reid state that the grid system was not simply a practical means for assigning allotments to immigrants and settlers of the western frontier but also a system of thought that effectively stripped local populations of their attachments to places within that grid. In short, these authors demonstrate that landscape and place theory can and should encompass the broadest possible temporal and spatial scale as well as the most diverse social and cultural manifestations, hence making this theory a powerful tool for the explanation of social change.

Persistent Places: Archaeology and People Today

A common assumption is that unused or abandoned places became "lost" to people at some point in their life histories, hence acquiring archaeological or "natural" status. This unfortunate assumption has prevented archaeologists from gaining insights into people's enduring relationships with the land (Nelson 2000). Not long ago, Schlanger (1992) coined the term *persistent places* to denote those archaeological sites that show evidence of having been reused or revisited after their official "abandonment." Her conceptualization of a persistent place opened the door for discussions about the meaning of this evidence and the concepts and methods needed to properly explain it (Ashmore 2002; Zedeño 1997). At the core of a persistent place (a place that would not go away) is the human need to rekindle memories of experiences lived and to maintain rights and fulfill obligations inherited from the ancestors. Welch (chapter 9), for example, speaks of the challenges posed by the need to "reconstruct" a sense of place in the White Mountain Apache Reservation in Arizona decades after many ancestral places have been negatively affected by the activities (or lack thereof) of Indian and non-Indian people and by state and federal legislation dictating the fate of reservation lands. Yet Basso (1996) was able to uncover the wealth of place-based knowledge that still exists among the Cibecue Apache and to alert this community as to the urgency of preserving this knowledge and reconstructing their sense of place.

The notion of a persistent place also brings about the realization that places are not truly lost or abandoned, except perhaps in the analytic mind of the archaeologist who must distance him- or herself from a study subject in order to maintain a measure of objectivity. Rather, the specific role of a place in people's interactions and its position in a place network or landscape may change to accommodate new social relations and cultural imperatives. Consider, for example, the extraordinary significance of the National Park System in the lives of the American people, where individuals of myriad ethnic and cultural backgrounds can find common ground in the stewardship of natural and cultural monuments and a welcome stage for teaching children about American history and heritage. This piece of commonsense wisdom is seldom formally translated into the analysis and interpretation of human–place relations in the past.

A common statement found in interpretive signs and brochures of archaeological sites and monuments reads: *Why did they leave? Where did they go?* (e.g., Widdison 1991). This statement has the effect of both imbuing ancient places with a cloud of mystery and keeping them outside the reach of ordinary people, including the descendants of those who once inhabited them. This exercise, too, disenfranchises communities whose social memories are anchored in archaeological places because it situates them at the same level as tourists and scholars—outsiders. Dispelling the myth that archaeology is about the vanished are the memories and experiences of the living, whose cultural logic is inextricably linked to meaningful places. Lekson's case studies (chapter 10) are illustrative of how people can solve this artificial separation between them and untouchable ancient monuments by reinterpreting them in other places and in their own terms.

What is a "meaningful" place, and to whom is a place meaningful? one may ask. Welch (chapter 9), Kuwanwisiwma and Ferguson (chapter 6), and Lekson (chapter 10) furnish a clear answer to this question: a meaningful place is that which reminds people of their past and teaches them how to cope with the present and plan for the future. That this was true in the past is evident in ancient places that were made, marked, or modified to guide individuals and societies in making decisions and in keeping a balance with their environment and with the cosmos (Joyce, chapter 3). When such a human–place relationship was threatened or lost, people reinvented themselves in their new environment or attempted to recapture their compass; often, they did both. The White Mountain Apache, for example, are deeply involved in land-management strategies that are in harmony with their ancient worldview but that respond to the realities and needs of modern reservation life. In these endeavors, Welch states, the Ndee rely heavily on their place-bound traditions and teachings as guidance for proper behavior. In a similar vein, the Hopi do not see "archaeological" places as relics of their past but as the homes of the ancestors, still inhabited and very much alive.

Engaging the Archaeology of Meaningful Places

Archaeology is the only social science that theoretically and methodologically disengages from its subject matter in order to study it. Yet, as Joyce and colleagues (chapter 4), Whittlesey (chapter 5), and Lekson (chapter 10) explain, the challenge posed by implementing the archaeology of place is to coherently integrate objective and subjective means of analysis for reconstructing ancient places and interpreting their meanings. This integration is particularly necessary when piecing together place networks and elucidating elements of place logic. Lekson's discussion of three kinds of places—public archaeological parks, re-created sites, and a popular restaurant that resembles a monument—and other volume contributions invite us to ponder the doubtful wisdom of total disengagement, which prevents scholars from addressing archaeological places as broadly and deeply as possible.

At a minimum, archaeologists can certainly learn how people created meaningful places and what the effects of their creations were even if specific meanings are not amenable to archaeological analysis. From the perspective of heritage, Lekson's comparative analysis of interpretive materials written by archaeologists, land managers, and the interested public reveals the dangers of disengaging from our study subject. A remedy may well be for archaeologists to rewrite archaeologies that grant places their rightful histories (e.g., Pauketat's [1998] reassessment of Cahokia or Gallivan's [2006] reanalysis of Powhatan's Werowocomoco) and that show the currency of place in our lives, both as archaeologists and as members of the public. Archaeological places, although a thing of the past, have the power to remind us, in the here and now, who we are, where we belong, and what belongs to us.

In this volume 14 scholars demonstrate not only that place is integral to understanding the historical trajectories of human societies but that it is indeed possible to take this concept to the field and return with a coherent and meaningful reconstruction of the past. The authors address place from a variety of perspectives including behavioral archaeology, anthropology, cosmology, phenomenology, contemporary social theory, geography, history, ethnohistory, and architecture. Collectively, these chapters emphasize the need to embrace theoretical diversity and multiple lines of evidence to develop an understanding of the significance of archaeological places. Without reducing the concept to fit into the fragmentary nature of archaeology, the authors succeed at anchoring their arguments on the material record of experiences, activities, meanings, and metaphors and at underscoring the enduring presence of the past in contemporary society.

2

Biographies of Place at Quiriguá, Guatemala

Wendy Ashmore

Places have meaning. Social theorists have documented this abundantly, and archaeologists know it from personal awareness as well as theory. Meaning is attached to a place because of the experiences people have there and because they relate those experiences to others. The accounts are often oral, but fortunately for archaeological inquiry, they can also take material form. Rock markings, building form, and monument location—all these are among the range of potential repositories for meaning. The challenge is discerning what the meaning is.

Better put, the challenge is discerning what the meanings are. Many cases have documented that meanings established at one point in time can change or be forgotten entirely (e.g., Barrett 1999; Blake 1999, 2003; Bradley 1987). Even when originally attached meanings seem to us to have endured, we should remain wary of assuming that kind of constancy. For example, the voluminous literature on Stonehenge and nearby Neolithic landscapes speaks to both continuities and shifts, evident most dramatically in their meanings for people today (e.g., Bender 1998; Bradley 1993; Parker Pearson and Ramilisonina 1998; Parker Pearson et al. 2006). Similar remarks can be made for ancient places elsewhere in time and location, such as earthworks of midwestern North America or the masonry buildings of Chaco Canyon (e.g., Ashmore 2007a; Buikstra and Charles 1999; Charles et al. 2004; Lekson 1999; Neitzel 2003; Van Dyke 2003). Materialization of meaning aids memory about a place, but as archaeologists recognize increasingly, it is no guarantee of permanence (e.g., Bradley 1987, 2003; Van Dyke and Alcock 2003).

The point I explore here, however, is that alternative meanings of a place can also exist simultaneously. Sometimes this involves differential experience and understanding, and sometimes it is the locus of active conflict and negotiation—for land claims, political sovereignty, communal identity, or other deeply meaningful reasons (e.g., Blake 2004; Joyce 2003; Low 2000; Mack 2004). Again, Stonehenge offers dramatic examples, as outlined vividly with respect to sometimes antagonistic encounters in recent years and even pitched battles over control of access as well as moral and legal ownership (e.g., Bender 1998; Chippindale 1986; Chippindale et al. 1990). As archaeologists appreciate more fully the diversity within ancient society, they also come to recognize multiple meanings embodied simultaneously in the process of creating places, whether monumental platform mounds at Cahokia (e.g., Pauketat 2000; Pauketat and Alt 2003) or peasant house compounds near Classic Maya Xunantunich (e.g., Robin 2002; Yaeger 2000). Competition, alliance, celebration, domination, and resistance are among the motives that can underlie such place making. And to the extent that such diverse motives shape creation of a single place, the people who use, or visit, or remember the place will view it as materializing different, often complicated or even contradictory meanings. Material structure records meanings, and practices

FIGURE 2.1. Quiriguá Monument 5 (Stela E), 8 m in height, is the tallest of an array of ruler K'ak' Tiliw's sculptural monuments flanking the south side of Structure 1A-3. Not all Quiriguá monuments are as imposing as the set shown here. Photograph by Wendy Ashmore, 1976.

inscribe them in social memory. Again, in examining the evidence of ancient societies, the challenge for archaeologists is discerning what those meanings are.

To bring the foregoing points together entails recognizing that places acquire life histories, or biographies, as people live in them and that these biographies may incorporate any of the kinds of alternative meanings just described. Places that are marked by buildings and other discrete architectural features accumulate histories as constructed elements are built, occupied, maintained, modified, partly or wholly dismantled, relocated, or allowed to fall to ruin. Each of the diverse acts is a chapter in the life history that can carry profound, potent social and symbolic meanings. Builders and users create some aspects of meaning deliberately. Other aspects accrue from events and experiences that occur in a place, such that the same place can mean different things to different observers, at the same or different times.

Multiple biographies of place are possible for the Classic Maya site of Quiriguá. Those based on material evidence from the most widely known portions of the settlement would focus on political meanings and, for reasons indicated below, particularly meanings attached to the reign of Quiriguá's long-lived and energetic eighth-century king, K'ak' Tiliw'. This chapter reviews that life history briefly and then treats two discrete areas within the settlement that are less often discussed. The goal of this essay is to suggest that the meanings implied in those two locales alternately punctuate and challenge what we might consider the principal narrative.

More specifically, Classic Quiriguá is best known from its compact Acropolis and spacious Great Plaza, the setting for grand portrait monuments and royal displays centered on K'ak' Tiliw'. Two other locales within the floodplain settlement materialize apparently divergent and complementary meanings in the local social landscape. Established in a relatively marginal part of the community around AD 800, Group 7A-1 commemorates the turbulent rule of K'ak' Tiliw', after his successors had repaired political ruptures his actions had caused. In contrast, from the fifth century through the ninth, the more centrally located Group 3C-7 was a focus of public gatherings involving offerings of blood sacrifice and enduring display of at least one early royal portrait monument. Indeed, it was the pivot and northern border of a large public plaza that complemented—or rivaled—the better-known Great Plaza.

Research at Quiriguá, Guatemala

Since the mid–nineteenth century, the world has known Quiriguá as a Lowland Maya center with spectacularly elaborate sculpture but usually little else that seemed worthy of much note (Figure 2.1). In 1910, the 30-ha setting for most of the freestanding stone monuments was set aside for

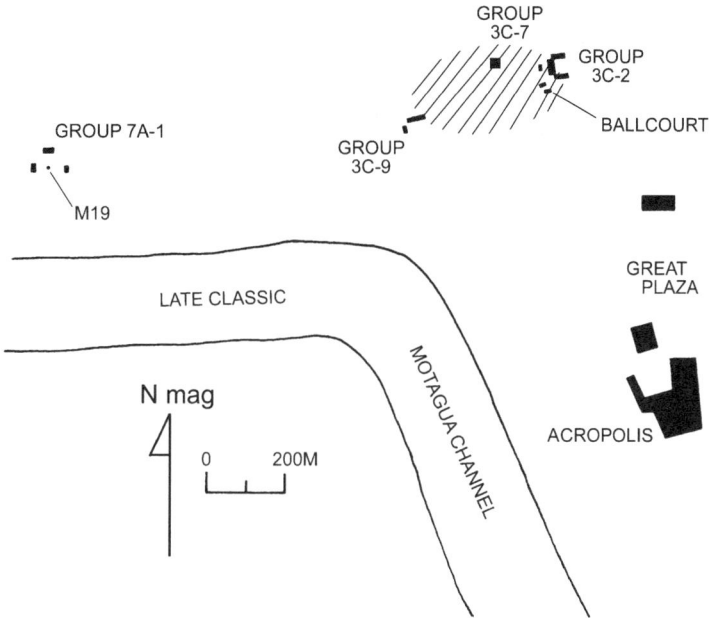

FIGURE 2.2. Schematic map of Quiriguá floodplain settlement, highlighting locations of the site core, Groups 7A-1, 3C-2, 3C-9, and 3C-7. Hachured space linking the last three elements approximates the inferred extent of Plaza 3C-1. Adapted from Ashmore 2007b:Figure 4.10, by permission of the University of Pennsylvania Museum.

protection as a national park, in the midst of plantations for bananas and other crops. After the bananas were killed by blight in the 1930s, the tall ceiba trees of the park stood as a dramatic isolate on a seemingly unbroken floodplain expanse. Despite intermittent research by multiple scholars since the 1880s, little remained known of the place other than its sculpture. In the mid-1970s, the Quiriguá Project of the University of Pennsylvania Museum sought to provide more systematic archaeological knowledge about the site and its surroundings through combined survey, excavation, artifact analysis, and renewed recording of sculpture (e.g., Ashmore 1981, 1984, 2007b; Sharer 1978, 1988, 1990; Sharer and Coe 1979). Models for designing the project's research and for interpreting its results were based firmly in processualist archaeological theory of the time.

Survey and excavation documented Quiriguá as a relatively small settlement (ca. 4 km²) on the northern floodplain of the Motagua River, occupied between at least the early fifth century AD and sometime in the ninth century (Figure 2.2).

Excavations were most intensive in the site core, the area of the protected park, in which architectural stratigraphy outlined an intricate sequence of civic construction and use (e.g., Jones and Sharer 1980; Jones et al. 1983). Outside the park limits, discovery and documentation were severely hampered by the natural accumulation of alluvial sediments, which had buried precolumbian remains under anywhere from a few centimeters to more than 2 m of earth. In 1977, however, commercial excavation of drainage ditches beyond the park incidentally revealed abundant Classic period artifacts and architecture. Although the ditch exposures were helpfully systematic in their regular spacing, they constituted an unusual sample of archaeological materials. Architecture, especially, was revealed for the most part as cross-section slices, from which construction orientations and plans were not always inferable (Figure 2.3). Limited opportunities for horizontal excavation clarified some cases; most remain conjectural (Ashmore 1981, 2007b). More dramatically, the ditch exposures attested

FIGURE 2.3. Example of ditch exposure of ancient construction at Quiriguá. Identification of a structure from the line of cobbles revealed in the ditch, foreground, was confirmed by clearing excavations, background. After Ashmore 2007b:Plate 7, by permission of the University of Pennsylvania Museum.

that extensive flooding by the Motagua River had damaged or destroyed parts of the settlement sometime in the seventh century.

Project research in the 1970s included investigations in the 2,100-km² expanse of the Lower Motagua Valley (LMV [Schortman 1993]). Among the striking findings of that inquiry was the isolation of Quiriguá with respect to "typical" Maya culture—or, more appropriately, to materialized customs of Classic Maya kings and nobles (e.g., Freidel 1979; Schortman 1989). The surrounding LMV sites were sufficiently different that Edward Schortman (e.g., 1986, 1989) posited that the royal court of Quiriguá—if not necessarily all of its subjects—constituted an intrusion of Maya among already resident populations of distinct identities. The location of Quiriguá in the southeast borderlands of the Lowland Maya world places it within a region of marked cultural diversity (e.g., Robinson 1987; Urban and Schortman 1986, 1988), and Schortman's inferences about Quiriguá ring true with increasing force. This point will be raised again later, with regard to the meaningful biography of the place.

After the close of project operations, Andrea Stone (1983), Matthew Looper (1995), and their mentor Linda Schele (1990a) undertook new epigraphic and iconographic studies of the sculptures and their hieroglyphic texts. Quiriguá's Classic period historical record now begins with the establishment of a royal dynasty in AD 426, under the auspices of neighboring Copán. Quiriguá's best-known ruler remains K'ak' Tiliw' (formerly known as Cauac Sky; reigned AD 725–785), the commissioner and subject matter of most of the site's famous stone sculptures. Indeed, K'ak' Tiliw's capture and beheading of the contemporary king of nearby Copán, in AD 738, is among the earliest deciphered and most widely known events in all of Classic Maya history. Until that point, Quiriguá had been politically subordinate to the larger and more widely influential Copán, and the rebellion sparked major upheavals in political order among the southeastern Maya and their non-Maya neighbors (e.g., Schortman and Nakamura 1991). By two decades after the death of the rebel king, however, relations with Copán had been reinstated, and at least some political ruptures had healed (e.g., Ashmore 2004a; Looper 1999, 2003; Martin and Grube 2000; Sharer 1978).

As large as the revolt and its aftermath loom in narratives about Quiriguá, available evidence suggests some intriguing alternative themes for a biography of the place as a whole. It is to those less orthodox materialized biographies that I now turn, highlighting how they have been discerned and their potential meanings for a diverse populace at Quiriguá.

Meaning in Spatial Organization

One goal for the 1970s settlement pattern study at Quiriguá was to understand the spatial organization of the place. Spatial models most prevalent at the time in archaeology, however, could not account for recurring arrangements of the most imposing architecture there. Combining structuralist approaches and city planning models (e.g., Fritz 1978; Rykwert 1988; Wheatley 1971) with interpretations of Maya iconography was more effective, collectively yielding a model of spatial grammar in which architecture was cast as a materialization of worldview. Specifically, I drew from work by Clemency Coggins (1980), Evon Vogt (1969), and others, including scholars working beyond the Maya area, to propose a model of civic planning among the Lowland Maya of Classic times (Ashmore 1989, 1991; Ashmore and Sabloff 2002, 2003). The model seemed to account for the distribution of monumental architecture in Tikal, Copán, and multiple other Classic Maya centers. More to the point here, it accounted for the arrangement of the principal architectural groups at Quiriguá, both in the site core and in the larger compounds of the adjoining settlement area. Initially, it also seemed fully consistent with the prevailing biography of place at Quiriguá.

Most succinctly, the model pairs an open, public area with a more secluded compound, juxtaposed along a north–south axis. Oft-discussed aspects of Maya worldview suggested meanings for the configuration. Royal portraits were carefully situated in the north, as were adjoining settings for public ceremony. All were thereby placed in locations that were simultaneously publicly prominent in the lived world and markers of the celestial realm (e.g., Ashmore 1989; Coggins 1980; Yorke 2006). The structured message was predominantly one of political legitimation, its meanings reinforced through public rituals and regal displays in arenas created explicitly for their performance.

The best-known expression of this plan at Quiriguá is the site core pairing of what are conventionally called the Great Plaza and the Acropolis (Figure 2.4). These are visually the most prominent spaces and buildings at Quiriguá and the locales most familiar to visitors in recent times—whether local visitors, tourists, or scholars. The same pairing of structures also occurs in other portions of the floodplain settlement, but these are now shrouded from view by banana trees (whose planting was the reason for the aforementioned ditch digging). Other nearby examples are documented on the opposite side of the Motagua River (Figure 2.5).

The Great Plaza and Acropolis visible today were shaped largely by directives from K'ak' Tiliw', before and after his tumultuous claim of independence. Observers since at least the late nineteenth century (e.g., Maudslay 1889–1902:6) have commented on the remarkable resemblance between Quiriguá's civic core and that of Copán, and most scholars now attribute the similarity to K'ak' Tiliw' having copied directly his former overlord's civic base, attempting to match or better the grandeur of the latter, to a degree that some consider excess or even unintended parody (e.g., Fash and Stuart 1991:163; Martin and Grube 2000:220–221).

What archaeologists call the "acropolis" at each site comprised an assemblage of residences and other buildings for the royal court. At both Copán and Quiriguá, inscriptions and architectonic sculpture indicate specific meanings for some particular buildings and open spaces (e.g., Fash 2001, 2005; Looper 1995). Quiriguá seems to have recalled and commemorated the fifth-century interment spot of its presumed dynastic founder (Sharer 2002), but its later kings and their builders expressed nothing even near approaching the veneration accorded Copán's founder, a veneration embodied in successive

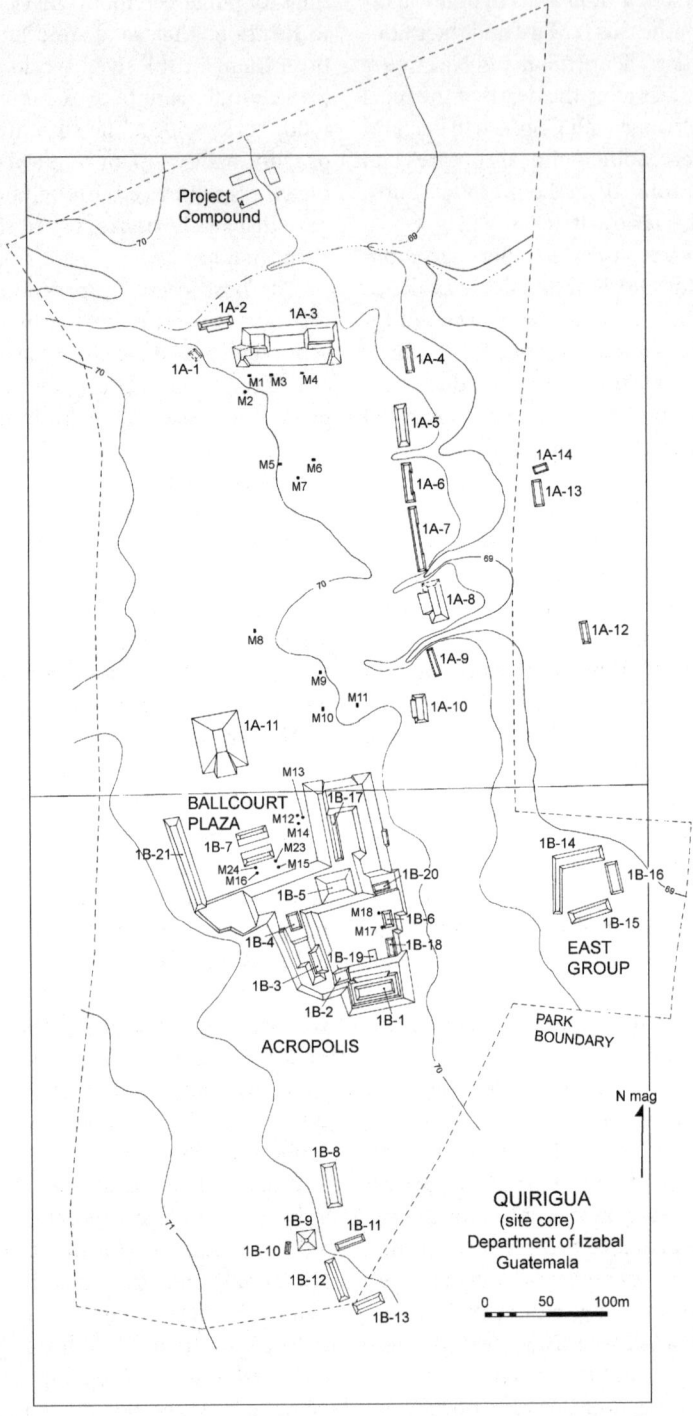

FIGURE 2.4. Map of Quiriguá site core. Stone sculpture monuments are designated by "M" and a number. Structure labels combine the map grid location with a number. Reproduced from Ashmore 2007b:Figure 1.4, by permission of the University of Pennsylvania Museum.

LOC. 089

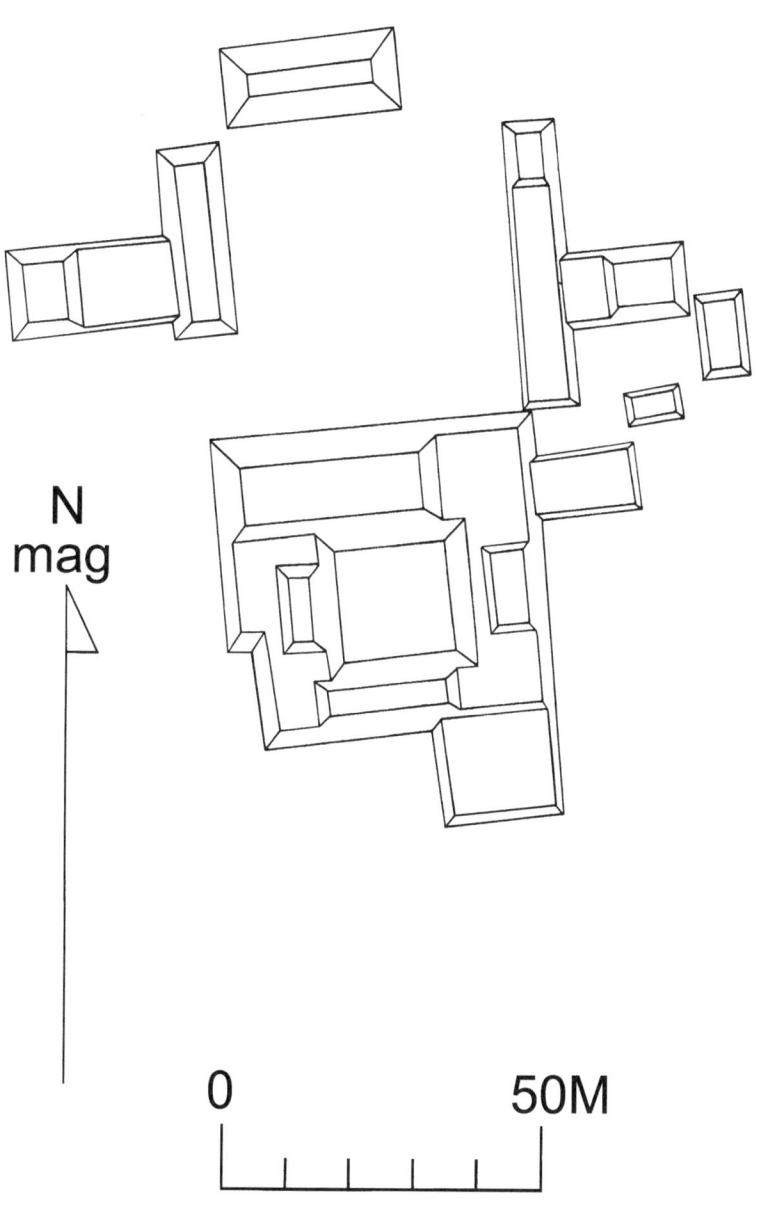

FIGURE 2.5. Plan of Quiriguá Locus 089, illustrating the juxtaposition of an open arena on the north with an enclosed compound on the south. Adapted from Ashmore 2007b:Figure 089.1, by permission of the University of Pennsylvania Museum.

constructions overlying and marking his tomb (e.g., Agurcia F. and Fash 2005; Sharer et al. 1999; Sharer et al. 2005; Taube 2004). The contrast is quite dramatic in scale and elaboration, manifest both in construction and in offerings associated with construction events. Such differential material expression is consistent with the relative standing of the two centers, their kings, and their founders within larger political and political-economic contexts.

The only Quiriguá sovereign who was accorded such honor, if still on a smaller scale, was K'ak' Tiliw'. As Sharer (1978:66) recognized early on, Structure 1B-2, likely a palace or other building of that ruler, remained open amid construction rising around it for several generations after the rebellious king's death. Such shrine-like recognition appears to parallel the treatment of Str. 10L-22 at Copán, the much larger "palace" of K'ak' Tiliw's defeated overlord. Importantly, however, K'ak' Tiliw's final resting place remains undiscovered, a point to which I return later.

North of the acropolis at each site, portrait stelae, elaborately sculpted and bearing long hieroglyphic texts, are arrayed across a spacious plaza (see Figures 2.1, 2.4). Such stelae are the hallmarks of royal portraiture at most Classic Maya sites. At Quiriguá, portraits of K'ak' Tiliw' visually dominate the Great Plaza, as do portraits of his earlier overlord (and ultimately, victim) in the corresponding Copán plaza. Only one certain and three possible stone sculptures, all quite small and none of them a stela, pertain to the earliest years in K'ak' Tiliw's reign. As part of Quiriguá's transformation after the rebellion in AD 738, however, he commissioned a series of very large stelae, reaching up to 8 m in height, as well as a huge platform (Platform 1A-1, subsequently obscured by flood deposits) on which to erect the last six of them (Jones et al. 1983; Sharer 1978; see Figure 2.1). On the final sculpture on the platform, Monument 7, a zoomorph in form, his successor recorded K'ak' Tiliw's death in AD 785.

That immediate successor, Sky Xul, governed Quiriguá for a decade or more and celebrated K'ak' Tiliw's long reign in text passages, construction, and spatial messages. Sky Xul's own portrait monuments are quite elaborate zoomorphs; notably, they neither take the stela form nor intrude on the platform tableau created by his famous predecessor. While the subsequent and final known king, Jade Sky, also kept K'ak' Tiliw's "palace" open and maintained the structured material expression embodied at Platform 1A-1, texts indicate that by AD 810 or before, he had reestablished the old Copán–Quiriguá relations that K'ak' Tiliw' had overturned.

The foregoing paragraphs present the prevailing biographical narrative for the place now called Quiriguá and the archaeological and epigraphic evidence supporting the meanings inferred for that life history. They largely omit discussion of eras preceding the rule of K'ak' Tiliw', for two reasons. The first is that construction and monuments from earlier times are more sparsely represented, partly because of sampling constraints and probably at least partly because of the seventh-century flood destruction cited earlier. The second reason, however, is that K'ak' Tiliw' rewrote the material biography of the place, acknowledging predecessors but emphatically stressing the new regime, its association with creation events, and its status on a par with—or newly superior to—Copán. The central meaning of the place became tightly bound up with this single, aggressively assertive king. As suggested earlier, however, I believe that there are other biographies, of varied time depth and subject reference, embodied in Quiriguá beyond the Great Plaza and Acropolis (Figure 2.2).

Group 7A-1 and Monument 19: A Place to Mark History and Diplomacy

This unimposing trio of mounds is located some 1,500 m west of the Great Plaza, along the eighth-century levee of the Motagua River (Ashmore 1980a). The group is distinguished principally by the presence of a single, text-bearing portrait stela, Monument 19 (known formerly as Stela S; Figures 2.2, 2.6). The stone monument drew Morley's interest, and he (1935:52–59) inferred that the compound was an outlier and predecessor to the site within what became the protected park. We now recognize, however, that Group 7A-1 is near the western extent of continuous eighth-century settlement remains. Although Morley thought it marked an early point in Quiriguá history, it is now known to be a late feature. Nevertheless, I suggest that Monument 19 remains a key to the identity and meaning of this specific place.

FIGURE 2.6. Quiriguá Monument 19. Erosion has obscured details both in the portrait of K'ak' Tiliw' and in the text on the other three sides of the stela. Photograph by Wendy Ashmore, 1976.

Although it is not the earliest sculpture assigned to the reign of K'ak' Tiliw', Monument 19 is the earliest known to follow the AD 738 rebellion and the first known instance where he adopted the royal Maya canon of stela erection, in AD 746. This stela-dedication date had been the basis for Morley's inference that the small group as a whole was earlier than the Great Plaza and Acropolis complex. Stelae that K'ak' Tiliw' dedicated only five and 10 years later, in AD 751 (Monument 8/Stela H) and 756 (Monument 10/Stela J), were both nearly double the 2.8-m height of his first, Monument 19, and were erected in the Great Plaza, the arena of his great, landmark victory—

the place where he had decapitated the hapless Copán king (Looper 1995, 1999, 2003; see Figure 2.4 for locations). Together, Monuments 8 and 10 have clear Copán counterparts in imagery, text, and location, which traditionally has been considered appropriate for "the first monument[s] erected after the Great Plaza was laid out" at Quiriguá (Fash and Stuart 1991:162).

Because it is earlier in dedication date, however, and was literally the first stela to follow the rebellion, Monument 19 plausibly deserved pride of place in the Great Plaza. Two pieces of archaeological evidence suggest that such a placement may have been the actual intent in AD 746. The first evidence is that the date on Monument 19 is inconsistent with the age that the stratigraphic context in Group 7A-1 implies. That is, the closest contemporary in hieroglyphic date, the taller Monument 8, was set simply into cobble and rubble fill, with no extra bracing (Stromsvik 1941:81, Figure 8a). At Monument 19, however, stone "cribbing" to brace the stela base closely resembled supporting foundations documented for Monument 9 (Stela I), dedicated by Jade Sky nearly 40 years later, in AD 800 (Jones et al. 1983:20, Figure 6.13a; Stromsvik 1941:82, Figure 25a). Although the limited available ceramics and architectural elements for other parts of Group 7A-1 are not chronologically definitive, they are compatible with the compound's establishment or refurbishing in the late eighth century (Ashmore 1981, 2007b; Jones et al. 1983:19), suggesting that Monument 19 was moved to Group 7A-1 in the decades after its dedication date.

A second, complementary piece of evidence helps account for the discrepant dates associated with the stela—as well as its seemingly counterintuitive location and its contradiction of Morley's earlier inferences. That evidence is Platform 1A-3, an unanticipated find in the eighth-century Great Plaza (Jones et al. 1983:10, Figures 6.3–6.4). This small stone platform's location, some 80 m west of Str. 1A-7, defined the northern vertex of a triangle with Monuments 8 and 10, and its highly fragmentary form is nonetheless reasonably interpreted as the masonry cap for a stela foundation. But no stela was encountered there. Although Monument 19 had its own cap and foundation in Group 7A-1, it seems most plausible that Platform 1A-3 marks the monument's original location, as the first of three stelae, set with consistent engineering in a structured arrangement in which the three royal portraits faced the eighth-century river channel, in K'ak' Tiliw's Great Plaza (see Figures 2.2, 2.4).

Taken together, then, the evidence from both the Great Plaza and Group 7A-1 suggests that Monument 19 was moved and reerected in a new location. If the inferred chronology is roughly correct, resetting followed K'ak' Tiliw's death by perhaps fewer than 20 years. Because Monument 19 was set in the center of a small, publicly accessible plaza, it seems a place where continued royal veneration could have taken place, with its somewhat removed location a diplomatic step by royal peacemaker Jade Sky, to allow commemoration of K'ak' Tiliw'. In Sharer's felicitous phrase, Monument 19 was the "stela of independence" (personal communication 2006). Local respects to the king and his threshold monument could still be paid, but in a more isolated location for its expression and thereby perhaps less offensive to visiting dignitaries from Copán.

In that regard, Group 7A-1 might parallel a memorial group at Copán (Group 8L-10) as a place to commemorate a venerable and sometimes controversial king—in the Copán case, honoring the very same king who had fallen victim to the Quiriguá revolt (Ashmore 1991). However, while the Copánec king who sponsored this memorial recognition of his assassinated predecessor also honored that sovereign in multiple other ways, Quiriguá's Jade Sky—at about the same time—distanced himself from his own, disruptive forerunner. Jade Sky's "distancing" was material and literal in the relocation of Monument 19, in contrast to more muted distancing in texts, where he alludes to the uprising, in Looper's reading, "as a thing of the past, engineered by a now defunct foreign power" (1995:193, 1999:276–277).

One last set of observations invites interpretation of Group 7A-1 more specifically as a royal funerary shrine. Martin and Grube indicate that, 10 days after his death, K'ak' Tiliw' was buried at the "'13 Kawak House,' a structure that has yet to be identified" (2000:222). Neither Morley's nor our excavations encountered any evidence of a tomb in exploration of the group, although excavations may have stopped short of an appropriate location, and the largest, northern structure had

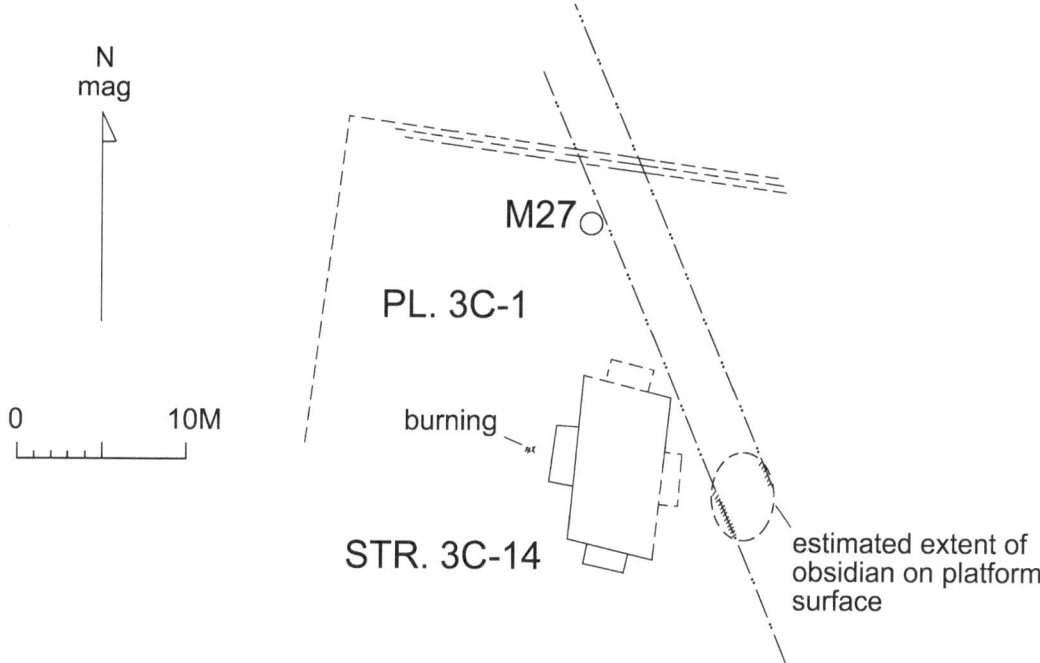

FIGURE 2.7. Plan of Quiriguá Group 3C-7, highlighting areas of obsidian and the most prominent burning; other burning (omitted from the figure) was also evident north and east of Str. 3C-14 and on its eroding summit. Paired diagonal lines at right indicate the line of the plantation ditch that exposed Monument 27, Platform 3C-1, and associated features. Adapted from Ashmore 2007b:Figure 3C.15, by permission of the University of Pennsylvania Museum.

been severely eroded and damaged by the time of our inquiry. Nevertheless, I offer the possibility that Group 7A-1 could have been the final resting place of K'ak' Tiliw', a meaningful placement for which relocation of Monument 19 perhaps provided closing accentuation. The group is certainly situated appropriately, at the western edge of the legendary king's capital, in the direction that signifies death.

Group 3C-7: A Place to Mark Continuity of Community

Thus far, the narrative has dealt with relatively shallow biographies, in the last centuries of Quiriguá's Classic period existence. Group 3C-7, however, offers another perspective, drawing on a deeper local history, dating back to at least the fifth century. Indeed, the kinds of recognition afforded this relatively modest complex seem to me to indicate its standing as one of the most important and enduring parts of the floodplain settlement (Figures 2.2, 2.7).

Multiple material traces, including large quantities of bloodletting implements, direct evidence of burning, and abundant broken censers, suggest that Group 3C-7 was the setting for ritual activities. I suggest that a central meaning and purpose to the rituals there was to foster or buttress dynastic and community stability, at least sometimes in response to both social turmoil and natural disaster. I further propose that this complex increasingly became a focus for civic gatherings having the same community-building goals. Before making that argument, I must first offer evidence for the existence of social challenges.

Social Tensions and Factionalism at Quiriguá

Social tensions plausibly would have characterized a local populace on whom rule by Maya outsiders had been imposed. As indicated earlier, Quiriguá texts and valley-wide material culture suggest such intrusion in AD 426 (e.g., Jones and Sharer 1980; Looper 1999; Martin and Grube 2000:216; Schortman 1986, 1993; Sharer 1978).

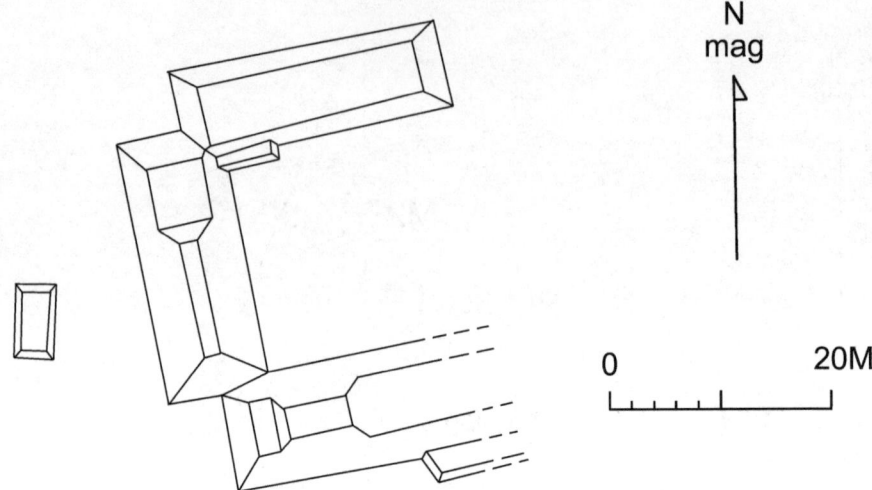

FIGURE 2.8. Quiriguá Pattern 3 as exemplified by Group 3C-2. Adapted from Ashmore 2007b:Figure 3.2, by permission of the University of Pennsylvania Museum.

However, local evidence lacks the hints at diplomatic assuagement that Traxler (2001, 2004) has discerned so skillfully for similarly intrusive governance at fifth-century Copán.

I suggest not only that factions existed in this early time frame but also that they persisted into at least the eighth century. In that later period, two mutually distinctive residential forms at Quiriguá suggest factional partitioning of local settlement, by the combination of their contrasting arrangements and their structured, mutually exclusive distributions on both sides of the Motagua (Ashmore 2007b). These forms are labeled Quiriguá Pattern (QP) 3 and 5 (Ashmore 1981, 1984; Sharer 1988). They are best recognized in relatively imposing assemblages of masonry buildings, presumably the domestic compounds of the most prominent local families (Figures 2.8–2.9). Reasoning from Schortman's interpretations, noted earlier, one might be tempted to equate tightly enclosed QP 3 groups specifically with "non-Maya" populations indigenous to the Lower Motagua Valley and valleys to its north and south (e.g., Orozco and Bronson 1991; Schortman and Nakamura 1991); the more open, directionally structured QP 5 could then be identified correspondingly as "Maya." However, I think Schortman would agree that such ascription oversimplifies matters. Each of these two domestic architectural patterns has parallels in the LMV as well as Copán, and precise origins of the layouts remain ambiguous. With regard to social composition, it is certain that Copán remained cosmopolitan, from at least the fifth century to the eighth century, including residents with distinct social heritages and material signatures, within some of the most elaborate precincts of the urban core (e.g., Group 9N-8 [Gerstle 1988]). At Quiriguá, it may be that ambiguity in interpreting residential forms reflects the intricacies of regional social diversity and its material expression, as well as local specifics of varied ancestry and political affiliations, especially among local royalty and nobility.

At any rate, after Maya dynastic kingship had been established in AD 426 at Quiriguá, three centuries of subsequent political subservience to Copán, not to mention presumable exaction of a growing tribute load, may well have worn on the internally diverse community at Quiriguá. K'ak' Tiliw's rebellion in AD 738 seems to have been a surprise to Copán, but the hieroglyphic evidence that it was sponsored by a distant enemy at Calakmul (Looper 1995) does not mean that the Quiriguá king lacked local backing. I have suggested elsewhere that the tribute load may have reached unbearable proportions by the time of the revolt, exacerbated by Copán's increasingly

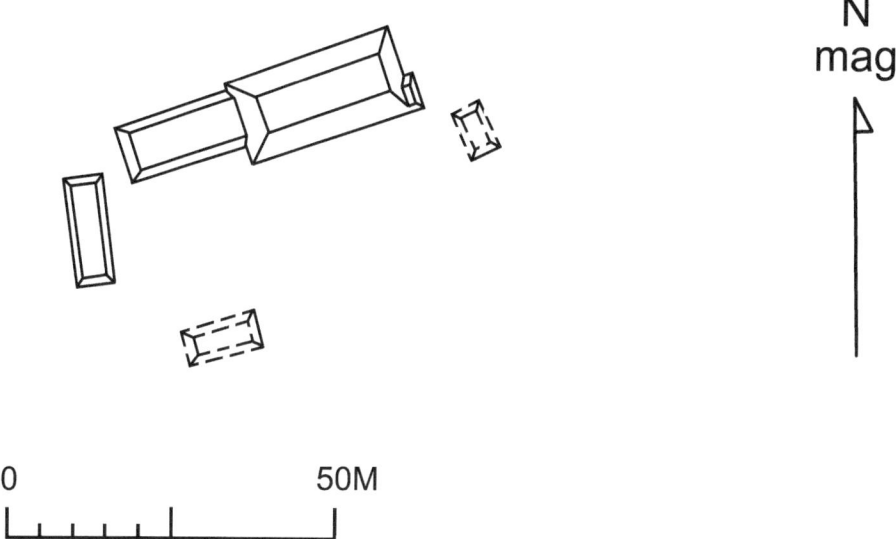

FIGURE 2.9. Quiriguá Pattern 5 as exemplified by Group 3C-9. Adapted from Ashmore 2007b: Figure 3.2, by permission of the University of Pennsylvania Museum.

desperate need for imported maize (Ashmore 2004a, 2007b; cf. Wingard 1996). In the mid–seventh century, the celebration of Copán ties on Monument 12 (Altar L) suggests that K'ak' Tiliw's own predecessor, "Ruler 5" (Martin and Grube 2000:217), may have set the stage for political crisis, in that he may have acquiesced initially to heightened tribute demands—partly in exchange for help rebuilding his own flood-ravaged community (Ashmore 2004a). If these political, economic, and fluvial developments are accepted as at least a partial array of stressful circumstances, what is the evidence for ritual response to them at Group 3C-7?

Rituals of Renewal and Termination

Motagua alluviation both damaged and protected the remains of Group 3C-7, until ditch excavation in late 1978 disclosed two fragments of a fifth-century stela (Monument 26) in the vicinity of a large, stone-walled, earthen platform (Platform 3C-1), on whose crushed-rhyolite surface rested a plain, disk-shaped schist "altar" (Monument 27). Monument 26 "dates...to 493, and mentions both a 'third' and a 'fourth king'" (Martin and Grube 2000:217) in the dynasty founded 67 years earlier under the aegis of Copán.

Although subsequent archaeological investigation failed to locate either the remainder of the stela or its erection spot, archaeological excavations did reveal Str. 3C-14, a small masonry platform, 9.5 m long and 4 m wide, atop the earthen platform. Like the steps of its underlying platform, the small structure was built with rhyolite blocks, and red-orange clay was used both as mortar and for floor surfacing. The resulting appearance is at least partly reminiscent of earthen platforms in the fifth-century Copán Acropolis that were "constructed of tamped, wet-laid clay, then 'plastered' with a layer of red-pigmented clay" (Carrelli 2004:119; Sharer et al. 1999; Sharer et al. 2005). It also is mirrored in early rhyolite-masonry buildings of the Quiriguá Acropolis, as well as the earliest, earthen constructions there (Jones 2007; Jones et al. 1983).

Just west of the center of Str. 3C-14, a stone-lined chamber housed an elaborate cache (Ashmore 1980b, 1981, 2007b; Ashmore et al. 1983; Sharer 1990). Contents of the cache included three pairs of pottery bowls placed lip to lip, in which were placed six pieces of carved jadeite, pieces of burned pyrite mirror, and bits of bone, cinnabar, and mercury, likely the product of the cache (and its cinnabar) having been burned. Similar ceramics and mercury were encountered nearly 2 km to the west, at the hilltop site of Group A, in the foundations of the only other fifth-century monument known from the Quiriguá area. The cache contents in Str. 3C-14 are unequaled at Quiriguá and recall many contemporary and often more elaborate jade-rich counterparts at Copán (e.g., Bell et al. 2004; Schele 1990b; Sharer et al. 1992).

Obsidian and Bloodletting

The most general index of ritual at Group 3C-7 is the strikingly large amount of obsidian there. As among other peoples of ancient Mesoamerica, Maya ritual often involved autosacrifice, using obsidian lancets to let blood (e.g., Schele and Miller 1986; Stuart 1984). Just east of Str. 3C-14, a dense, charcoal-laced deposit or series of deposits of obsidian blades, fragments, and blade-production debris littered Platform 3C-1. Because similar deposition was observed in exposures of different length on directly opposing sides of the modern ditch, they probably mark a single feature that extended originally across that 4-m expanse (see Figure 2.7). Surface collections alone in this circumscribed area yielded nearly 500 pieces of obsidian. More than three times as many additional pieces were recovered in excavation at the same spot. These are most likely the remains of bloodletting and its preparations. The activities the obsidian reflects took place within two centuries of the establishment of Group 3C-7, before the onset of Platform 3C-1's flood erosion and burial.

Burnt Offerings

Although the reason for bloodletting is not inherently clear, the fires and censer use on the same platform more specifically support the inference that these rituals were intended to foster or buttress dynastic and community stability. Karl Taube has written extensively about the association of "fire ritual and offerings [with] conjuring and communicating with gods and ancestors in both Teotihuacan and Classic Maya ritual" (2004:265; also Ramos G. 2006; Stuart 1998; Taube 1998, 2000). At Quiriguá Group 3C-7, besides the evidence of fire in the cache interior, discrete areas of burning were found in several open locations: in association with the obsidian deposit just described, on a surface of red-orange clay within 2 m west of Str. 3C-14, on the crushed-rhyolite surface of Platform 3C-1 north and east of the small surmounting structure, and—later—perhaps two lenses of burned material on its eroding summit (Ashmore 1981:813, 826, 2007b; Figure 2.7). These fire-related activities took place over a more extended period than that inferred for the bloodletting, a span whose likely extent is discussed further below.

Of equal importance, fire rituals also are implied by the presence of censers, as discussed explicitly by Stuart, Taube, and others. Censers from Group 3C-7 can be plausibly linked to cycles of life, death, and regeneration for the community, its king, and the cosmos. More specifically, censer fragments were encountered in three kinds of contexts: primary contexts associated with the Platform 3C-1 surface; deposition overlying the platform and structure after flood damage, while the locale was left open in disrepair; and from provenience lot 19M/27. The latter is a problematic ditch spoil recovery unit, retrieved by experienced personnel between archaeological field seasons shortly after commercial excavation of the modern ditch in late 1978. For reasons presented elsewhere (Ashmore 1981:846–847, 2007b), I believe that most lot contents likely came from Platform 3C-1 or nearby. Besides 18 obsidian blades and an equal number of fragments from blade-core reduction (i.e., additional likely bloodletters), those contents included 89 censer fragments, among which 21 were effigy forms (31 percent). Even acknowledging the problematic nature of this context, the proportion of effigy censers provisionally and suggestively recalls samples from site core contexts of public ritual related to royal performance and display near the ballcourt and Str. 1A-10 (Benyo 1979).

Perhaps Prudence Rice's categorical distinction between "image" (i.e., effigy) and "nonimage" censer forms is more fundamental for inference here. She suggests specifically that

> Of particular interest are Classic-period modeled image censers and censer stands, which are commonly recovered in contexts suggesting termination rituals, especially mortuary rituals accompanying the death of divine kings. The burning of incense ritually activates the sacred space of the structure, opening communica-

tion with the gods; the subsequent smashing of the censers deactivates it. These contexts of recovery support associations of these *incensarios* with broad cosmological cycles of life/death and regeneration, most strikingly with the parallel life cycles of the sun and the divine lord of the polity [1999:45].

Taube (1998, 2004) has inferred the metaphorical equation of censers and the red-painted buildings of Maya royal courts, buildings whose sequences of construction, demolition or burial, and replacement likewise relate to cycles of accession, death, and renewal of divine kingship. Often the buildings bear architectonic masks of stone and stucco, similar thematically to effigy censers, and as with the censers, smoke from burning incense often issued from their openings (e.g., Ramos G. 2006). Among the K'iche' Maya today, Linda Brown (2004:37) describes the importance of burning in specially marked places, transforming organic offerings there into smoke and thereby into a state appropriate for consumption by deities; smashing objects in related spaces terminates, expels, or otherwise marks transition in renewal of a positive state (e.g., quitting illness to reinstate health).

Although Str. 3C-14 lacks the grandeur of architectonic masks, I suggest that, together with its censers and other evidence of burning, the small structure fits within the range of buildings covered by Taube's inferences and that practices attested there are consistent with interpretations of ritual termination and renewal outlined by him, Rice, Brown, and others. I further suggest that the rituals that took place in all of Group 3C-7 specifically highlighted celebration of royal life and death, and by extension, of perpetual community regeneration, beginning in a period within 70 years after the local dynasty's founding. The death of K'ak' Tiliw' may have been among the events commemorated there, though likely not the only one. Although such rituals may have occurred in additional settings, this specific one was early, and, as I am about to argue, it was also particularly important and enduring.

Within the first century of Quiriguá's existence as a dynastic center of Maya society in AD 426, the low expansive platform and small surmounting structure had become, as just argued, a focus of public gatherings, involving display of at least one royal portrait monument, together with burning and offerings of blood sacrifice (see also Ashmore 1981:799–847, 2007b). The assemblage may have been, in turn, part of a larger fifth-century civic complex including a ballcourt (Group 3C-8 [Ashmore 1981:865–866, 2007b]), although most of the evidence for the other early buildings is confined to exposures low in the modern plantation ditch walls. (The putative ballcourt is approximately 125 m northwest of Group 3C-7, not marked on Figure 2.7.) Whatever their function, however, the structures of Group 3C-8 were, like those of 3C-7, built to impress viewers, their rhyolite masonry not only bound by a matrix of the distinctive red-orange clay but also likely having surfaces of the same material. In visual opulence as well as in overtly civic role, the precinct defined by these buildings and spaces complemented the earliest dynastic constructions of the Acropolis, nearly a kilometer to the southeast.

By some time in the seventh century, when the Acropolis was well established, Str. 3C-14 had begun to erode, and as hinted earlier, a sizable portion of Platform 3C-1 was washed away, arguably by flooding (Figure 2.7). In the aftermath, multiple episodes of flooding left sand that buried the platform, along with all but the highest parts of its small, summit structure. Flood sand deposits were traced continuously up to 200 m south of the structure and up to 100 m north and are at least roughly contemporary with massive deposits revealed in modern ditch exposures 75–100 m to the east.

Nevertheless, despite flood-wrought destruction of Platform 3C-1 in the seventh century, Group 3C-7 retained sufficient meaning and symbolic prominence for continued visitation through the ninth century. Evidence points to one or perhaps more termination rituals of some sort on the platform within a meter west of Str. 3C-14. Termination of one time span also heralds the beginning of another, and the material record suggests that people still came to this small semi-ruined building and still left smashed censers. If the imposition of a new dynastic rule at Quiriguá in AD 426 had indeed brought together local factions, as proposed earlier, locations such as this one could well have become emblems of the greater community, where community members' differences could be reconciled in shared ritual practices, if not necessarily smoothing entirely a faction-shaped heritage (e.g., Brumfiel and Fox 1994; Yaeger and Canuto 2000). Moreover, if the expanded tribute load posited earlier is correct, the importance of such a durable point of community identity should have increased, as stresses placed on the community grew. Damage from seventh-century floods plausibly would have intensified the importance of this survivor as a gathering place of the larger community and simultaneously may have removed some comparable venues for public gathering.

Civic Gatherings

There may be additional meanings to this place. Specifically, and on a larger scale, I believe that, by the eighth-century reign of K'ak' Tiliw', Group 3C-7 was the focus and perhaps the northern border of a civic gathering space left open to accommodate visitors (Figure 2.2). Each of the eastern and western boundaries of this space, Plaza 3C-1, was defined by masonry buildings in one of the two architectural forms inferred earlier as marking intracommunity factions, QP 3 (at Group 3C-2 [Figure 2.8]) and QP 5 (at Group 3C-9 [Figure 2.9]). The plaza so defined is a space virtually equal in expanse to the Great Plaza. Moreover, I believe that Plaza 3C-1 was central to community integration in a manner that complemented royal performances and display in the Great Plaza, celebrating community endurance as much as or more than dynastic authority or continuity.

Excavation evidence suggests large-scale food preparation in at least Group 3C-5 (Ashmore 1981, 2007b; Jones et al. 1983), and this would have supported feasting activities in the adjacent plaza. On the plaza margins, four substantial middens may be residues of festivals there (see Blitz 1993; Keller 2006; LeCount 2001). A scatter of some half dozen very small structures on its east and west edges might plausibly be service facilities related to public gatherings. Strs. 3C-9 and 3C-10 are relatively larger structures at the southeast edge of the proposed plaza but not as imposing as either Group 3C-5 or Group 3C-9. Together, Strs. 3C-9 and 3C-10 plausibly constitute a small ballcourt. Plaza 3C-1 may thus have epitomized community integration in many kinds of activities, celebrants gathering there under the gaze of what may have been the highest-ranked houses in the two proposed local factions.

No monuments of eighth-century Quiriguá rulers are known from this public space, unlike at the Great Plaza, where people gathered to learn of and celebrate the military feats and cosmic genealogies of K'ak' Tiliw' and his successors (Looper 2001). Although text and style references to local antecedents are common in Great Plaza monuments (Looper 1995, 2003), current evidence characterizes Plaza 3C-1 as a setting steeped more exclusively in early local history and community-wide meaning, apart from explicit celebration of any particular Late Classic king. Its festal gatherings fostered integration of the local populace, and the specific location commemorated rulers and times early in the history of the place, thereby marking continuity of community—perhaps expressed explicitly as continuity in the face of fluvial disaster and political upheaval.

Conclusion

As indicated at the outset of this chapter, multiple biographies of place are possible for Quiriguá. Although in the making since the 1880s, the reconstructed life history of the place prevailing today in most accounts began to emerge most clearly during and after fieldwork there in the late 1970s. Interpretive models, theoretical perspectives, and comparative evidence available at that time, however, virtually precluded the appearance of many of the ideas that current circumstances now encourage. The principal themes in Quiriguá's biography of place continue to be enriched and refined by further epigraphic and iconographic inquiry, as well as by comparisons with new archaeological finds at Copán and other sites. All of us who contribute to that narrative, however, still tend to focus on the meaning of Quiriguá as comprising a fairly linear dynastic history and, especially, on the meaningful impact of K'ak' Tiliw's reign.

Just as the meaning of the rebellion surely changed between the heady events of AD 738 and the rapprochement with Copán by AD 800, so too would the place associated with those occurrences have changed, in recollections, commemorations, and meaning. Moreover, individual members and groups in the Quiriguá community would have responded in different ways to the place and its meanings, including those associated with the royal house and those of nonroyal subjects and their families.

The biographies proposed here for Group 7A-1 and Group 3C-7 draw on all these kinds of insights. While they acknowledge the principal narrative, they append postscripts on the great king's life and offer prefatory and parallel accounts of factionalism and community building. Mindful of the interpretive cautions of Bradley (2003) and others, I offer these provisional biographies of places within the larger whole as chapters in a wider-ranging, more complicated life history of the place we now call Quiriguá. In that way they build on and complement other efforts to appreciate more fully the complexity of past lives and the places in which they were lived.

Acknowledgments

The Quiriguá Project of 1974–1979 was formed by contract between the Instituto de Antropología e Historia, Guatemala, and the University of Pennsylvania Museum. William R. Coe directed the research for the first two seasons, and Robert J. Sharer directed work over the final four seasons. Support was provided by the University of Pennsylvania Museum (Boyer Fund), the National Geographic Society, the National Science Foundation (BNS 7602185, 7624189, 7603283), the Ford Foundation, the Tikal Association, the Guatemalan Ministry of Defense, the Museum Applied Science Center for Archaeology (University of Pennsylvania Museum), the Department of Anthropology (University of Pennsylvania), Landon T. Clay, Alfred G. Zantzinger, and Dr. John M. Keshishian.

I sincerely thank Brenda Bowser and Nieves Zedeño for giving me the opportunity to contribute to this volume and for perceptive editing of earlier drafts. The chapter relies on findings presented most fully in a monograph published by the University of Pennsylvania Museum (Ashmore 2007b). I remain deeply grateful to my colleagues on the Quiriguá Project, prominently including Robert J. Sharer, Christopher Jones, David and Rebecca Sedat, Mary R. Bullard, Julie Benyo, John Weeks, Diane and Arlen Chase, and especially, Patricia Urban and Edward Schortman, who shared most directly the joys and frustrations of data collection and analysis and whose progressive insights on southeastern Mesoamerica have inspired me more than they know. Many people have shaped my thinking about space, place, and society in recent years, and with regard to ideas discussed in this chapter, I add thanks especially to Chelsea Blackmore, Jim Brady, Jane Buikstra, Clemency Coggins, Christina Halperin, Steve Houston, Angela Keller, Bernard Knapp, Matt Looper, Jerry Sabloff, Karl Taube, Sue Yorke, and two anonymous reviewers. Most of all, I appreciate Tom Patterson, for daily, wide-ranging discussions, critical feedback, and wonderfully relentless encouragement.

3

The Main Plaza of Monte Albán

A Life History of Place

Arthur A. Joyce

This chapter traces the 2,500-year life history of place of the Main Plaza at Monte Albán, from the site's founding through its major period of occupation as a political and religious center, its Postclassic and colonial "afterlife" as a place of creation, and its contemporary standing as a World Heritage Site, center of tourism, and symbol of Oaxacan and Mexican national identity. The ancient Zapotec city of Monte Albán was founded about 500 BC in the Valley of Oaxaca (Figure 3.1) and quickly grew into the first urban center in the southern Mexican highlands (Blanton 1978; Joyce 2000; Marcus and Flannery 1996). One of the first activities at the site was the construction of the Main Plaza precinct that housed politico-religious institutions and provided a stage for public ceremonies (A. Joyce 2000, 2004).[1] Monte Albán served as a political capital and sacred center until its collapse at ca. AD 800. The Main Plaza, however, did not remain static. It was continuously modified over its 1,300 years as an urban ceremonial and administrative center. After the collapse of the Monte Albán polity, when the majority of its population abandoned the site and its buildings turned to ruins, it continued as a sacred place for burying nobles and making ritual offerings. Despite the catastrophic impact of the Spanish conquest and the suppression of indigenous religious beliefs, documents and local myths show that indigenous people continued to believe in the sacred character of the Main Plaza well into the colonial period.

To examine the life history of place of the Main Plaza at Monte Albán, I integrate archaeological, epigraphic, iconographic, ethnohistorical, and ethnographic data. I follow Ashmore (2002:1178) in defining life history of place as the examination of people's recognition, use, and modification of a particular place over the full time span of its existence. I am interested in the history of material and symbolic transformations of the Main Plaza as well as the practices, identities, and power relations implicated in these transformations. I also consider continuities in meaning, arguing that throughout its life history, the Main Plaza was seen as a place of creation and a focal point for communal identity.

Theoretical Perspective

In this chapter, I consider how the life history of the Main Plaza at Monte Albán relates to changes in the interrelationship of meaning, practice, power, identity, and memory in the Valley of Oaxaca. The way people organize space and particularly how they conceptualize and alter ceremonial space are important aspects of structure that both shape and are shaped by social action (Ashmore 2002; Barrett 1999; Bourdieu 1977; Bradley 1987, 1993; Giddens 1979; Joyce 2000; Knapp and Ashmore 1999; Wheatley 1971). In Mesoamerica, recent archaeological research has shown that the architectural arrangement of ceremonial precincts at cities like Monte Albán, Teotihuacán, Copán, and Tikal materialized a shared view of

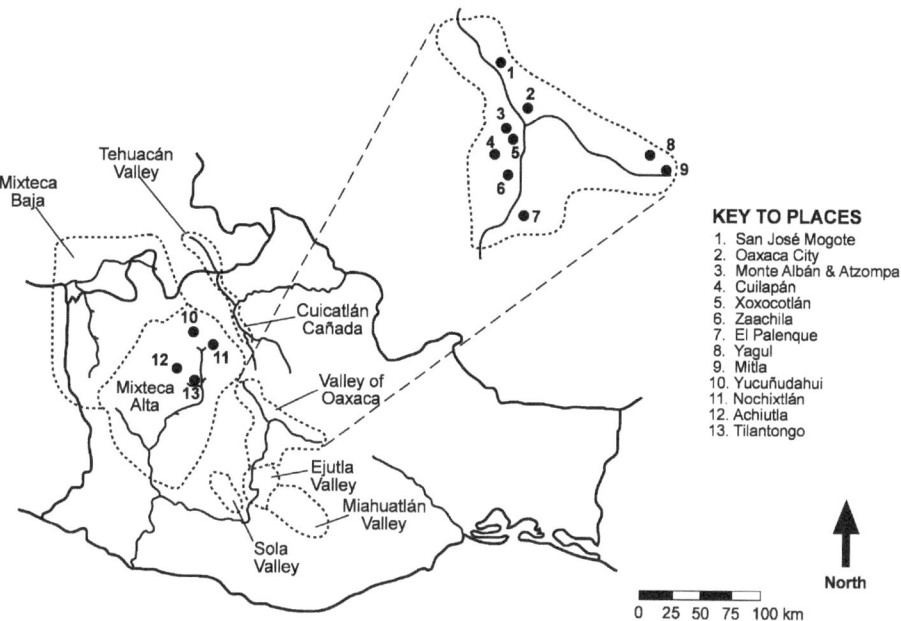

FIGURE 3.1. Map of Oaxaca showing sites and modern communities mentioned in the text.

the cosmos that was shaped by local political history (Ashmore 1991; Ashmore and Sabloff 2002; A. Joyce 2000, 2004; Love 1999; Schele and Guernsey Kappelman 2001; Sugiyama 1993). These ceremonial precincts were often seen as places of cosmic creation and served as axis mundi where cosmic planes of earth, sky, and underworld intersected. Pyramids, in particular, were viewed as sacred mountains (Schele and Freidel 1990:71–72). This sacred geography sanctified authority by positioning nobles as powerful intermediaries between commoners and the divine forces that created and maintained the cosmos. The creation, use, and alteration of monumental ceremonial spaces like the Main Plaza, therefore, embodied changes in power and relations of domination and subordination in the complex polities of ancient Mesoamerica.

The power of ceremonial precincts, however, was not derived just from the ideas that they embodied but was produced, experienced, maintained, and transformed through the practices of people (Ashmore and Knapp 1999; Bradley 1998). Rituals in temples and public plazas included sacrifice, ancestor veneration, processions, divination, and dance. Many of the ceremonies organized and performed by nobles reenacted the cosmic creation and were means of petitioning deities for fertility and prosperity on behalf of their people (Ashmore 2004b; Freidel et al. 1993; Joyce 2000). Religious practices were, therefore, in part ideological, creating a social contract where nobles performed the most important rituals, while commoners provided allegiance and tribute in return. The meaning and symbolism of ceremonial precincts, as well as the social practices carried out within these places, contributed to the production of social identities (Ashmore 2004b; A. Joyce 2004). By participating in emotionally charged ritual performances, people came to identify with their places in the social and cosmic order. In this chapter, I am particularly interested in how points of tension and conflict along status divisions were embodied in the Main Plaza, recognizing that other dimensions of social difference such as age, gender, and occupation were also important and should be further investigated.

As people move through, act in, and experience ceremonial centers like the Main Plaza they create social memory while inscribing social meaning on place (Connerton 1989). The physical arrangement and symbolism of buildings, plazas, courtyards, roads, and other architectural features channeled the movement and experiences of actors and therefore strengthened and focused memories. By manipulating space through the erection of physical or symbolic barriers around ceremonial precincts, elites restricted interaction between members of different groups to times and places of their choosing so as to control both the content and presentation of social discourse and the creation of meaning and memory (Hegmon et al. 2000; Hillier and Hanson 1984). Examples of the control of ceremonial space by elites include the initial construction of bounded monumental ceremonial spaces throughout Mesoamerica in the Middle/Late Formative period (Grove 1999; R. Joyce 2004; Love 1999; Ringle 1999), the construction of *sacbeob* or raised roads by the Maya to channel the flow of pilgrims into ceremonial centers (Ringle 1999), and the serpent wall surrounding and limiting access to the Mexica Templo Mayor precinct at Tenochtitlán (Brumfiel 1998; Hamann 2003a).

The ongoing use and alteration of monumental space transformed the meanings they embodied, although in ways that reflected the past, creating a life history of place (Ashmore 2002:1177–1179; Bradley 1998). Recently, John Barrett (1999) has described the creation of these life histories as involving the inhabitation of landscapes. Transformations of inhabited landscapes, including constructed monuments, involve the reworking of established meanings and the politics of their control. Even after their primary period of construction and use, monuments continued to hold meanings that were informed by their earlier histories (Bradley 1998; Sinopoli 2003), as exemplified by the Mexica performance of rituals at Teotihuacán, which they viewed as the place of the gods where time began. Bradley (1993) has referred to this as the "afterlife of monuments," recognizing that ruins and abandoned monuments remain a part of cognized landscapes even though periods of social disruption and abandonment enhance the opportunity for altering the meaning of ceremonial places (Knapp and Ashmore 1999:19).

The Main Plaza as a Political and Religious Center

Monte Albán was founded about 500 BC and within a few hundred years grew into the most powerful political and religious center in southern Mexico (Blanton et al. 1999; Joyce 2000; Marcus and Flannery 1996). By AD 200, the rulers of the city succeeded in overcoming their Oaxaca Valley rivals as Monte Albán became the capital of a complex polity that probably encompassed the entire valley. Settlement pattern research shows that at its demographic peak from AD 500 to 800, Monte Albán covered 650 ha with an estimated population of 15,000–30,000 (Blanton 1978:58). The city continued as the primary center in the Oaxaca Valley until its collapse at about AD 800, when the site was largely abandoned (Winter 2003).

Throughout Monte Albán's long history as a political capital, the Main Plaza precinct was the ceremonial-administrative center for the city and the Oaxaca Valley polity as a whole (Figure 3.2). In its final form, the Main Plaza consisted of a huge plaza measuring roughly 300 m north–south by 150 m east–west and bounded on its north and south ends by high platforms supporting numerous public buildings (Figure 3.3). The eastern and western sides were defined by rows of monumental buildings; a third row of structures ran north to south through the center of the plaza.

I argue that the Main Plaza was constructed as an axis mundi and a mountain of creation where people ritually petitioned deities for fertility and prosperity. Initially, the plaza was a place of community engagement in social practices, especially rituals, which contributed to the creation of a larger-scale corporate identity. Through time, however, nobles increasingly closed off and controlled access to the Main Plaza (A. Joyce 2004), transforming it from a largely public ceremonial space to an increasingly restricted elite residential area.

Communal Identity and Sacred Authority (500–100 BC)

Monte Albán was founded during a period of political crisis and conflict in the Valley of Oaxaca and beyond. Major political centers were in decline, like La Venta in the Gulf Coast lowlands and Chalcatzingo in the central Mexican highlands, while new political centers were emerging. In the century preceding the founding of Monte Albán, San José Mogote, the most powerful community in the Oaxaca Valley, lost population, and competitors may have raided the site's ceremonial

FIGURE 3.2. Photo of the Main Plaza of Monte Albán looking south with the North Platform in the foreground and the South Platform in the background. The North Platform's Patio Hundido is foreground right.

center, perhaps burning a temple (Joyce 2000; Marcus and Flannery 1996:121–135). Demographic changes as well as similarities in architecture, iconography, and mortuary practices indicate that people from the San José Mogote polity founded Monte Albán (Flannery and Marcus 1983a).

One of the first activities carried out at Monte Albán was construction of a Main Plaza precinct. The initial version, dating from 500 to 100 BC, consisted of the plaza itself, a western row of buildings, and much of the eastern half of the North Platform (Winter 2001:282–288). Even during its first few centuries, the scale of the Main Plaza far exceeded earlier ceremonial spaces in the Valley of Oaxaca, suggesting that the plaza was built to communicate with the otherworld in new and more powerful ways in response to the political crisis facing the site's founders. The hilltop location of Monte Albán also provided a defensive advantage during this period of conflict. Defensive concerns are suggested by the construction of a wall around the most vulnerable parts of the site by the Terminal Formative (100 BC–AD 200).

The symbolism and spatial arrangement of architecture and iconography suggest that the Main Plaza was founded as a place that symbolized the Zapotec cosmos, where rituals could be performed to reenact the primordial creation (A. Joyce 2000, 2004). The plaza was built on top of an imposing mountain that rises over 300 m above the valley floor, and it is likely that the entire ceremonial precinct was considered a sacred mountain of creation. The layout and iconography of the plaza resembled the quadripartite division of Mesoamerican ceremonial centers, which attached particular symbolic values to the cardinal directions and the axial center. At Monte Albán, as at many ceremonial centers, meanings assigned to the northern and southern directions were more clearly marked, with north representing the celestial realm and south, the earth or underworld (Ashmore 1991; Ashmore and Sabloff 2002; Sugiyama 1993). The eastern and western directions

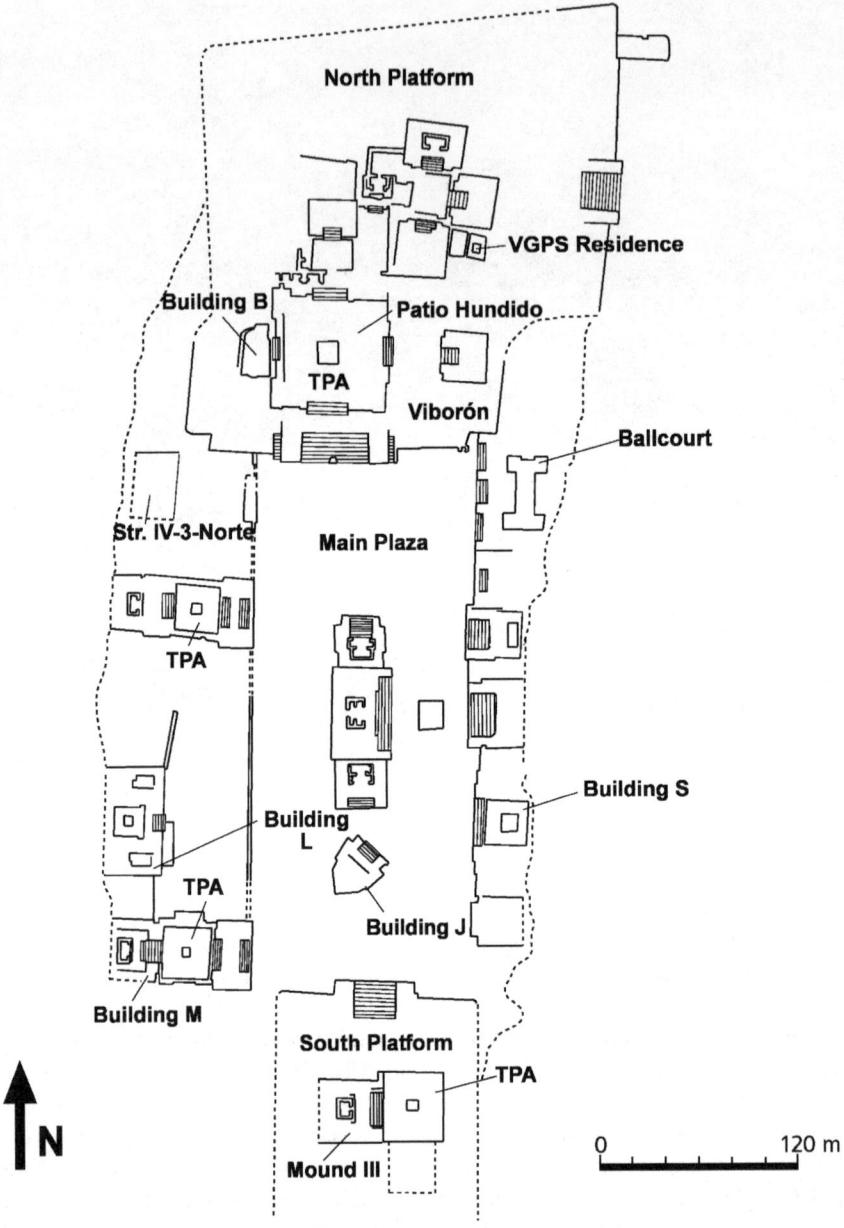

FIGURE 3.3. Plan of the Main Plaza at Monte Albán (TPA = temple–patio–altar complex).

may mark the rising and setting of the sun, respectively, while the axial center would represent the earthly world of the living.

The southern end of the Main Plaza contained iconographic references to sacrifice, warfare, ancestors, and earth or underworld. Building L-sub was the location of a gallery of carved stones known as the *danzantes* (Figure 3.4a) that in- cluded more than 350 monuments with references to warfare, human and autosacrifice, and invocations of ancestors for warfare-related oracular purposes (Scott 1978a; Urcid 2008). Mesoamericans believed that sacrificial victims went into the earth at death (Joyce 2000).

Conversely, north represented the celestial realm, and the plaza's northern monuments included iconographic references to sky, rain, and lightning. For example, a celestial reference is found in the stucco frieze known as the *viborón* or serpent (Figure 3.5) beneath the North Platform (Orr 1997). The frieze consists of a sky band with scrolls similar to the S-scroll rain cloud motif and serpentine figures resembling the Zapotec rain/lightning deity, Cocijo, with rain issuing from the figure's mouth. The frieze covers the sides of what appears to have been a sunken court. In Mesoamerica, sunken or enclosed plazas and ballcourts often symbolized interfaces between the world of the living and the sacred otherworld of deities and ancestors.[2]

The scale, accessibility, openness, and symbolism of the Main Plaza indicate that it was constructed as an arena where thousands of people of different social statuses and from different communities participated in public ceremonies. Until the Terminal Formative, the Main Plaza was open on its eastern side, making activities on the plaza accessible to commoners living on the terraces below. Ceremonies blended traditional rituals such as autosacrificial bloodletting, ancestor veneration, divination, and feasting with new practices like human sacrifice (Blanton et al. 1999:105–107; Joyce 2000; Orr 1997, 2001). The danzantes gallery with its depictions of sacrifice was constructed so that the images could be viewed during processions (Orr 1997). Sacrificial practices, especially human sacrifice, were particularly significant in contacting the otherworld, reenacting the cosmic creation, and renewing the world (Freidel et al. 1993; Joyce 2000; Monaghan 1990, 1994; Schele and Freidel 1990). In Mesoamerican creation stories, the current world was the result of a sacred covenant between humans and the gods whereby people petitioned deities for agricultural fertility and prosperity in return for sacrificial offerings. New religious cults are also indicated by the first

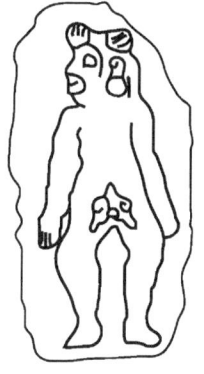

a.

b.

FIGURE 3.4. Formative period carved stones from Monte Albán: (a) danzante sculptures from Building L (redrawn from Scott 1978b); (b) Building J "Conquest Slab" (redrawn from Caso 1947: Figure 41; images not drawn to scale).

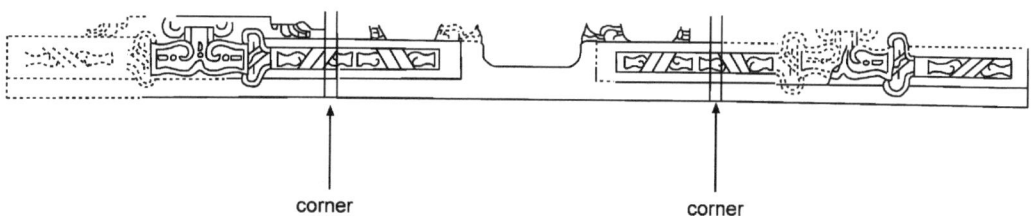

FIGURE 3.5. "Viborón" frieze from the North Platform at Monte Albán (redrawn from Urcid 1994b: Figura 7).

occurrence of effigy vessels depicting deities like Cocijo, the Old God, and the Wide-Billed Bird deity (Blanton et al. 1999:105–107; Winter 2001: 286–287).

The founding of Monte Albán, the construction of the Main Plaza, large-scale public rituals, and warfare were activities undoubtedly organized and led by nobles. Even before the founding of Monte Albán, the belief in nobles' religious authority, as well as their control over prestige goods and tribute, was a major aspect of their power (Grove and Gillespie 1992). An increasing association between elite residences and religious symbols and artifacts during the early years of Monte Albán indicates that nobles were gaining greater control of politico-religious ideas, practices, and institutions (Joyce and Winter 1996:36). Human sacrifice was a new, dramatic, and potent means for nobles to communicate with the divine and demonstrate both their power and their generosity to supporters. At Monte Albán, residences of the nobility were concentrated around the North Platform, creating an elite-ceremonial precinct that was spatially segregated from the rest of the community and which symbolically linked nobles and noble ancestors to the celestial realm.

Though nobles lived near the Main Plaza during the Formative, there were few explicit representations of local elites, and no high-status residences directly faced the plaza.[3] The emphasis was on public buildings, public spaces, and cosmic symbolism including images depicting sacrifice, warfare, and the celestial realm. The Main Plaza seems to have stressed the symbols of an emerging corporate identity while muting representations of rulers. The choice of an unoccupied hilltop in the middle of the valley for this new ceremonial center had the effect of distancing Monte Albán from traditional centers of settlement and politico-religious power, making the site a more effective symbol for new social formations. The initial construction of monumental buildings would have engaged people in emerging corporate structures, since it appears likely that labor was contributed voluntarily (Joyce 2000). The Main Plaza was visible for great distances so that its power as a sacred mountain and political center would have been present in the everyday lived experiences of people throughout the region.

The Main Plaza would have engaged people not just during public rituals but, in fact, would have continuously communicated aspects of dominant ideologies, although the plaza's accessibility presented possibilities for the discursive penetration of these beliefs as well (Hutson 2002).

Public ceremonies in the Main Plaza organized and led by nobles and participated in by large groups of commoners created powerful memories that bound people to the rulers, the symbols, and the new social order centered at Monte Albán. Public ritual performances contributed to the production of larger-scale corporate identities internalized in people's dispositions and externalized in social practices like contributing tribute, allegiance, and labor to the polity. Evidence suggests that warfare may have increased in scale at this time, which could also have united people behind rulers and ruling institutions (Joyce and Winter 1996). The creation of shared identities and alliances with people in other valley communities is indicated by the construction of public architecture, high-status residences, urns, and monumental art similar to those from Monte Albán in many sites during the Late/Terminal Formative (Marcus and Flannery 1996; Orr 1997; Spencer and Redmond 2001; Whalen 1988).

At the same time, the ritual performances and symbolism of the Main Plaza contributed to an increasing separation of noble and commoner identities. The special role that elites played as religious specialists dramatically reinforced their positions as mediators between commoners and the sacred. Monumental buildings would have served as stages elevating and separating nobles from the commoners on the plaza below. The separation of status groups would have been reinforced by the visibility of elite residences and the North Platform, symbolizing the linkage between nobles and the celestial realm. Elite identities were also symbolized by their control of exotic artifacts and knowledge such as urns, incense burners, hieroglyphic writing, and calendrics. The nobles' appropriation of religious ideas, spaces, and practices increased their power to attract followers, mobilize resources, defeat competitors, and interact with the sacred.

While people were increasingly incorporated into a larger-scale political formation, which by the Terminal Formative can probably be described as a state (Marcus and Flannery 1996), there undoubtedly were different degrees of compliance with the rulers, institutions, and practices centered at Monte Albán. Commoners and nobles in some parts of the valley actively resisted the emerging political structures and rulers of Monte Albán (A. Joyce 2004). For these people, the Main Plaza may not have been recognized as a sacred place and would have been viewed much differently than it was by those who willingly participated in ritual performances at Monte Albán. As Monte Albán's size and power grew, independence and resistance became increasingly risky. Spencer and Redmond (2001) have found evidence that the independent center of El Palenque was conquered by Monte Albán and a high-status residence and temple were destroyed by fire. As discussed in the next section, the rising power of the rulers of Monte Albán is also indicated by evidence that nobles began to exert greater control over the Main Plaza and the ritual practices carried out there.

Elite Appropriation of the Main Plaza (100 BC–AD 800)

By the Terminal Formative (100 BC–AD 200) and continuing through the Classic period (AD 200–800) the rulers of Monte Albán acquired political and religious authority over the entire Oaxaca Valley (Marcus and Flannery 1996). Elite appropriation of the Main Plaza was perhaps the most significant act in power consolidation. The Main Plaza became spatially segregated and increasingly controlled by the nobility as rulers shifted their focus away from rituals that emphasized communal identity and toward self-aggrandizement. The plaza was used less for large public ceremonies that engaged commoners and more as an elite residential precinct and an area for restricted ceremonies.

Early versions of the South Platform and the eastern row of buildings were constructed during the Terminal Formative, effectively closing off the Main Plaza (Winter 2001). The central row of structures was also built, which served to further restrict and channel traffic. Control of space was reflected at a smaller scale by the Zapotec two-room temple, where restricted rituals were carried out by Zapotec priests.

During the Terminal Formative, additions and alterations to the Main Plaza reinforced the basic themes of sacred geography (A. Joyce 2004). Building J in the southern end of the plaza continued the themes of sacrifice, warfare, and the underworld. During the Late Formative or early Terminal Formative, approximately 50 carved stone slabs were set in a monumental building whose original location is not certain, although it was probably in the southern end of the plaza because later in the Terminal Formative the slabs were reset in the walls of Building J (Urcid 1994a). These slabs have been interpreted as depicting places conquered by Monte Albán (Figure 3.4b). Many of the slabs depict the severed head of a captured ruler extending down beneath the terrestrial hill glyph with vegetation sprouting from the top of the hill sign. Part of the Building J program also included a representation of a local noble shown in the act of decapitation sacrifice (Urcid and Winter 2003:127). In the North Platform, the "viborón" court was built over, but an even larger sunken court, the Patio Hundido, was constructed in the southern end of the platform. Elite residences continued to be concentrated to the north of the Main Plaza, and by this time some were being constructed on the North Platform itself. Structure IV-3-Norte, located on the northwestern corner of the Main Plaza, was the first elite residence built directly on the plaza, although its entrance faced north rather than east onto the plaza (Barber and Joyce 2006). A ballcourt was built on the northeastern corner of the Main Plaza at what was probably the primary entrance point (Blanton 1978:63–66).

By the Classic period, Zapotec nobles throughout the Oaxaca Valley increasingly represented their personal power in portraits of themselves and their ancestors, rather than communal themes of cosmic creation and renewal (A. Joyce 2004). Depictions of nobles and noble ancestors were no longer restricted to the northern part of the plaza. Classic period monuments from the South Platform include a program of carved stones depicting a ruler presiding over bound war captives (Figure 3.6a; Urcid 1992:397–408), processional scenes commemorating living nobles and their ancestors (Urcid 1992:405), and a possible scene of divination by a Zapotec noble (Orr 1997:259). Other Classic period depictions of nobles or

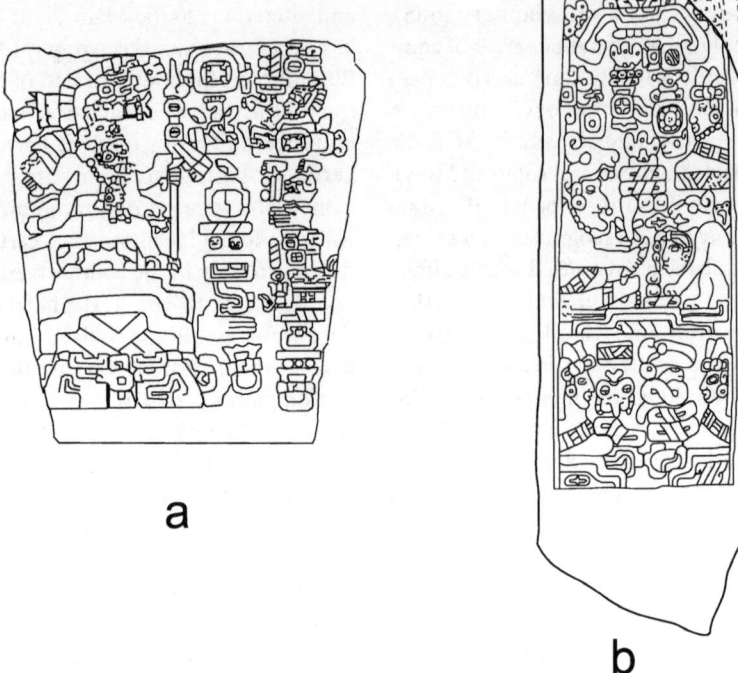

FIGURE 3.6. Classic period carved stones from Monte Albán: (a) South Platform monument showing a ruler (redrawn from Urcid 2001: Figure 5.30A); (b) Stela MA-VGE-2 (redrawn from Urcid et al. 1994: Figura 3A; images not drawn to scale).

noble ancestors have been found in the North Platform and other areas of the Main Plaza precinct (García Moll et al. 1986; Urcid 1994b, 2001; Urcid et al. 1994).

The Main Plaza increasingly became a focus of elite domestic activities and presumably was used less frequently as an arena for large-scale public ceremonies (Barber and Joyce 2006; A. Joyce 2004; Winter 2003). While elite residences continued to be concentrated on and around the North Platform, during the Early Classic period a high-status residence was built adjacent to the plaza just west of the South Platform. By the Late Classic this area included at least 10 residences, although no more than five were occupied simultaneously. Building S, the largest Late Classic elite residence, was built on the southeastern end of the plaza. An elite residence was also built on top of the 9-m-high platform of Building L, which had previously supported a temple (Winter 2003:109).

Other changes in the spatial configuration of the Main Plaza during the Late Classic involved both its external access and its internal layout. Blanton (1978:63–66) shows that by the Late Classic the plaza was largely closed off. People would have entered the plaza from highly restricted access points, enhancing the ability of nobles to monitor and control entry into the ceremonial center (Martínez and Markens 2004). The plaza itself was divided by the construction of temple–patio–altar (TPA) complexes. The TPA consisted of a temple elevated on a platform that faces a patio with an altar in the center. In most cases, access to the TPA was restricted either by building a wall around the patio or by constructing a sunken patio. Since the patios were far smaller than the Main Plaza, fewer people could have participated in ceremonies in the TPAs. Two TPAs were built on the west side of the Main Plaza, effectively segregating portions of the plaza, creating restricted ceremonial spaces.[4] Activities within the patio would have been hidden from the view of people outside. In addition to TPAs, the Late Classic also witnessed a major increase in the construction of two-room temples (Martínez 2002), which created additional restricted ritual spaces.

Another indication of the appropriation of ceremonial space by elites is the incorporation of a two-room temple into the Tomb 7 residence, a high-status house first constructed during the Terminal Formative (Martínez 2002). During the latter half of the Late Classic the western end of the residence was rebuilt as a two-room temple. The temple was built directly over a tomb that opened onto the patio, thereby associating the temple with the ancestors of the elite family that occupied the residence. This created one of the first architectural complexes in the region that formally united a high-status house with a public building (Barber and Joyce 2006:239).

The evidence indicates that the political practices of the nobility were focused less on elite–commoner relations and more on political relations among nobles. By the Late Classic, most newly carved stones at Monte Albán and other Oaxaca Valley sites were set in highly restricted locations. Genealogical registers depicting several generations of nobles, sometimes showing marriage scenes or rituals related to ancestor veneration, were the most common type of carved monument (Figure 3.6b). When found in situ, these carved stone slabs are mostly in tombs or other highly restricted locations (Urcid 2005). Similarly, painted murals that date largely to this period depict scenes of ancestor veneration and genealogical relations and are found in the most elaborate tombs in the valley, especially from several high-status residences north of the North Platform (Miller 1995). The concern with genealogy and ancestors, particularly in the context of tomb rituals, suggests that establishing genealogical linkages to powerful ancestors was crucial in negotiating and legitimating political power (Urcid 2005:147–154). The death of a ruler would have been a time of crisis and struggle over succession, requiring the establishment of genealogical relations and the renegotiation of alliances. Both TPAs and subpatio tombs may have been interfaces where restricted groups of elites contacted the sacred realm. The trend toward the construction of TPAs and restricted ceremonial spaces is found in administrative centers throughout the valley (Kowalewski et al. 1989:262–263).

Several explanations can be suggested for the shift away from large-scale public ceremonies and toward restricted ones. By the Classic period political authority and ideological principles in the Oaxaca Valley were well established. The institutionalization of political power may have lessened the necessity for large-scale ceremonies that engaged people in the symbols, rulers, and institutions of the polity. By the Late Classic the nobility had grown in size, and the social setting had become factionalized, with numerous subregional centers led by lesser nobles (Kowalewski et al. 1989; Lind 1994). Monte Albán itself was inhabited by various barrios, each led by an elite corporate group (Blanton 1978). The collapse of the Basin of Mexico state of Teotihuacán around AD 600 would have lessened the role of Monte Albán's rulers in negotiating relations with this powerful polity. Without the potential threat of Teotihuacán, local nobles may have asserted their independence and distanced themselves from Monte Albán's rulers (Blanton 1983; Urcid 2005:155). I have argued that these factors led to competition among nobles throughout the valley, which was negotiated ritually in highly restricted settings where genealogical relations and alliances could be worked out without undermining elite authority in relation to commoners (A. Joyce 2004:211). Nobles were able to maneuver for power through alliances and by strategic marriages allowing individuals to claim descent from several powerful ancestors through multiple lines of descent.

The appropriation of the Main Plaza by nobles would have inscribed new meanings on the ceremonial precinct. By the Late Classic the plaza was no longer primarily a public space that embodied the earlier corporate symbolism that signaled inclusion and the celebration of communal relations with the sacred. Instead, the plaza was increasingly residential as well as a ceremonial space for restricted rituals. Interaction with the otherworld was now focused around the sacred power of nobles, especially through contact with their ancestors. The construction of noble houses and the erection of portraits of rulers violated the earlier sacred geography, with its focus on cosmic symbolism, warfare, and human sacrifice. By the Late Classic, many of the earlier iconographic programs that communicated these themes, such as the danzantes and the Building J "conquest slabs," had been partially dismantled, reset in building foundations, and often plastered over (Caso 1938, 1939:173–174).

Nobles and commoners would have experienced the Main Plaza in very different ways. For nobles, the plaza was now both a ceremonial and a residential area. Noble families and perhaps retainers would have carried out their everyday domestic activities in and around the Main Plaza. The bulk of the plaza may no longer have been a liminal space for contacting the sacred realm, with TPAs creating restricted ceremonial spaces that were removed from everyday life and the domestic sphere. For commoners, the decrease in public ceremonies on the Main Plaza meant that they were less actively engaged in the kinds of dramatic ritual performances and shared experiences that created a sense of belonging and identity with the symbols, rulers, and institutions of the polity (A. Joyce 2004). If local nobles were actively competing and attempting to undermine the authority of Monte Albán, then central unifying symbols, especially surrounding the rulers of Monte Albán, would have been further weakened. The Main Plaza would have embodied an increasing separation, and perhaps tension, between the identities of commoners and rulers as well as between center and hinterland. Competition among the nobility and the disengagement of commoners from state ceremonies could have had the unintended outcome of weakening the allegiance of commoners and lesser nobles to rulers and ruling institutions, especially to the distant rulers of Monte Albán.

At the end of the Late Classic archaeological data suggest that the site's nobles were increasingly isolating themselves from the general population as people began to leave the city and as ruling institutions failed (Blanton 1978:100; Winter 2003). At this time, many of Monte Albán's elite residences were abandoned or were rebuilt on a smaller, more modest scale. Several new high-status residences were built in the Main Plaza precinct in very restricted locations, often protected by walls (Winter 2003:108–111). For example, the VGPS residence on the North Platform had a diagonal adobe wall that blocked the view of the house from people below (Figure 3.7). Residences throughout the site became increasingly enclosed and inwardly focused during the Late Classic, perhaps due to rising social tensions and divisions, especially between competing nobles and/or commoners (Hutson 2002:68–69; Winter 1974).

By AD 800 Monte Albán was in decline, with its people leaving the city and relocating to other parts of the valley. The causes of the collapse have been debated, although many researchers agree that factional competition was an important factor (A. Joyce 2004; Kowalewski et al. 1989:251; Lind 1994; Winter 2003:116). I argue that commoner disengagement was probably another key factor. When the social and political relations that linked Oaxaca Valley elites began to crumble in factional competition, commoners may have declined to support nobles, especially the rulers of Monte Albán. While the initial success of Monte Albán was a result of the engagement of commoners in rituals, labor projects, and military actions that came to be important symbols of the polity, its collapse may have been an unintended outcome of people's exclusion from many of these same symbolically, emotionally, and politically charged practices. Monte Albán would remain a sacred mountain until after the Spanish conquest, but it would never again be an important political center.

The Main Plaza as a Pre-Sunrise Place of Creation

During the Postclassic period (AD 800–1521) the area in and around the Main Plaza continued to be viewed as a sacred space where important rituals were carried out. The archaeological record demonstrates three different types of social practices in the Main Plaza precinct during the Postclassic (Herrera 2002; Winter 2003): (1) residential, as shown by the construction of a single house west of the South Platform; (2) defensive, as shown by the construction of a defensive wall over the South Platform; and (3) ritual, as shown by offerings and burials placed in earlier ceremonial structures. The evidence suggests that, like the ruins of other Classic period cities, Monte

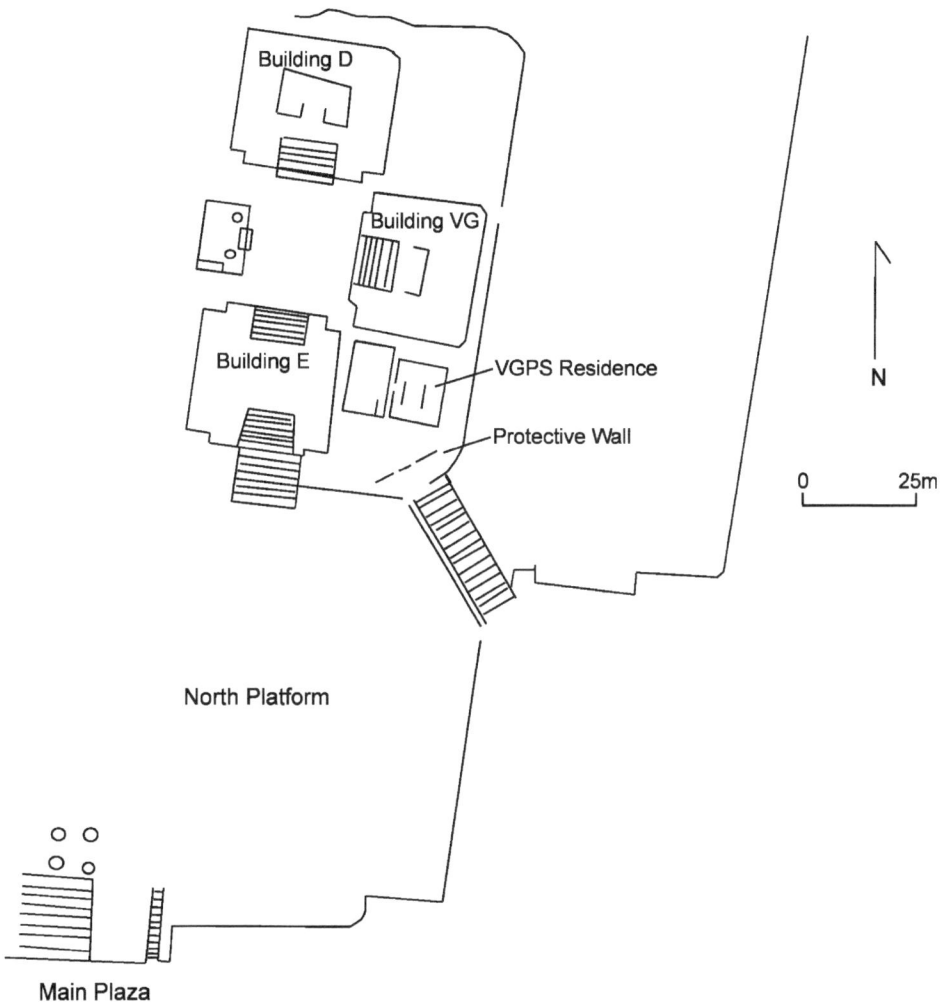

FIGURE 3.7. VGPS residence and protective wall from Monte Albán's North Platform (redrawn from Winter 2003:Figure 8.5).

Albán and especially the Main Plaza were remembered and celebrated as a place of creation where people continued to ritually contact the sacred realm (Hamann 2002). Colonial-period representations continued to depict the Main Plaza as a place of creation, and stories into the twentieth century viewed it as a place of powerful sacred forces.

Social Memory and the Early Postclassic Ritual Use of the Main Plaza (AD 800–1200)

During the Early Postclassic the Main Plaza precinct was largely abandoned. Winter (2003:114) excavated a single Early Postclassic residence in the area west of the South Platform where numerous Late Classic residences had been located. Ceremonial offerings indicate that people continuously returned to the Main Plaza to communicate with deities and ancestors using a narrowly prescribed set of ritual practices. Ritual deposits were relatively uniform both in content and in placement, with offerings left in reused tombs and TPAs (Herrera 2002). The most common objects in ritual deposits were miniature ceramic vessels, *penates*, and obsidian blades, all of which can be associated with death, sacrifice, and ancestors. Obsidian blades were used for autosacrificial bloodletting. Penates are small anthropomorphic stone figures that depict dead people with their eyes closed, possibly mummy bundles. Miniature ceramics were mostly utilitarian bowl and jar forms along with *sahumadores* (incense burners). Ethnographic data from Oaxaca indicate that miniature objects, including ceramic vessels, are used as offerings in mortuary rituals and as sacrificial offerings at sacred places such as caves, ruins, altars, mountaintops, and near prehispanic carved stones to petition deities for health and well-being (Bartolomé and Barabas 1982:230; Herrera 2002; Heyden 1975:345; Parsons 1936:314). The sacred places where miniatures have been left in the ethnographic present are all viewed as otherworld interfaces where deities and ancestors are contacted, like prehispanic TPAs and tombs. Sahumadores suggest the burning of incense as a sacrifice to the gods, as has been done from the colonial period to the present day (Ashmore, this volume; Brown 2004; Monaghan 1995:221).

Early Postclassic ritual deposits were recovered in TPAs in the North and South Platforms (Herrera 2002). Over 2,000 objects were recovered in fill over Building B, which constitutes the western side of the North Platform's Patio Hundido, the largest TPA at the site (Caso et al. 1967:399–403; Herrera 2002:351). In the South Platform TPA, thousands of objects were recovered above the altar and in the fill over the stairway and sides of Mound III, which, like Building B in the North Platform, made up the western side of the TPA. Offerings of miniature vessels were recovered from Building M, which formed the western side of a TPA on the southwestern end of the Main Plaza, and in the 7 Venado system south of the South Platform, which included a TPA (Herrera 2002:362–363). The offerings in the TPAs were not a single deposit but, rather, were the result of repeated rituals over the course of several centuries from the end of the Late Classic through the Early Postclassic (Winter 2003:115). In addition to offerings in TPAs, the contents of several subpatio tombs from Classic period residences around the Main Plaza were removed, and then offerings of miniature vessels and penates were left (Martínez et al. 2002; Winter 2003).

Offerings deposited in and around the Main Plaza show how memory and tradition produced continuities in meaning despite the disjunctive social changes of the Early Postclassic. The TPAs and tombs in which offerings were placed were considered interfaces to the sacred realm and were the most restricted and perhaps most sacred ceremonial spaces of the Late Classic, indicating that Early Postclassic ritual activities were based on social memories of the earlier uses and meanings of the site. In the case of the North and South Platform TPAs, Early Postclassic ritual deposits were left over an earlier sacred axis dating back to the Terminal Formative (Gámez 2002), suggesting an even deeper social memory. Oral and perhaps written histories would have transferred social memories of the ritual significance of TPAs and tombs through the generations. Ritual practices inscribed more permanent continuities in meaning and memory, with Early Postclassic offerings once again marking the plaza as a sacred place where sacrificial offerings were made to activate the sacred covenant and petition deities for fertility and prosperity.

Yet ritual practices also transformed memory and meaning in ways that reflected the new social order of the Early Postclassic. The high frequency of ritual offerings and the use of common objects such as miniature utilitarian ceramics and obsidian artifacts suggest that common people participated in the rituals. It may be that after the collapse of Monte Albán, commoners reclaimed the Main Plaza, which they had originally built and which they were increasingly excluded from during the Classic period. The removal of human remains from high-status tombs and their replacement with offerings seem more likely to have been carried out by the descendants of the tomb occupants and therefore by families descended from the Classic period nobility (Winter 2003: 115). At present it is difficult to assess the nature of Early Postclassic inequality (Oudijk 2002:75), although the data suggest that the social hierarchy may have been significantly reduced (Markens 2004:432–433). A reduction in hierarchy would be consistent with the impression that rituals on the Main Plaza were less restricted than they had been during the Classic period. The data indicate that despite the fragmented political relations of the Early Postclassic, the ceremonies on the Main Plaza referenced a shared history and identity as descendants of the ancestors who resided at the site.

The Late Postclassic: Nobles Reappropriate the Main Plaza (AD 1200–1521)

By the Late Postclassic the Oaxaca Valley was broken up into about a dozen independent polities, each ruled by a great house centered on a hereditary ruler (Kowalewski et al. 1989; Oudijk 2002; Pohl 2003a, 2003b). The political landscape was dynamic and factionalized, with the fortunes of polities waxing and waning depending on success in warfare and the establishment of marital alliances with other ruling houses. Prehispanic and early colonial-period documents record numerous such marriages, including several between Zapotec houses of the Valley of Oaxaca and Mixtec houses of the Nochixtlán Valley to the north.[5]

At Monte Albán a small community arose along the lower slopes of the site about 1 km north of the Main Plaza (Blanton 1978:101–103). While people were not living in the plaza, it continued to be treated as a sacred place where offerings were made and mortuary rituals carried out. Offerings continued to be left in TPAs, although fewer objects were left relative to the Early Postclassic (Caso et al. 1967:447–460).

A defensive wall built over the South Platform converted this area into a fortress like others found on hilltops above Late Postclassic communities such as Mitla and Yagul. These fortresses were places where surrounding communities retreated both during times of war against local enemies and when Aztec armies invaded. Ethnohistoric evidence shows that the Valley of Oaxaca was conquered and incorporated into the Aztec Empire during the last few decades before the Spanish conquest (Marcus 1983).

Noble and commoner identities were more clearly marked in ritual deposits and burials than they had been in the Early Postclassic. The focus of noble ritual returned to the area north of the North Platform. Several Classic period tombs in this area were reused for the interment of Late Postclassic nobles (Caso 1982; Winter 1995), and an offering of a mosaic mask and copper bells was left in the fill above the patio over Tomb 105 (Miller 1995:88–105). By far the most elaborate of the interments was in Tomb 7. The tomb itself was built as early as the Terminal Formative but was reused during the Late Postclassic to inter at least nine people. One of the most elaborate offerings ever discovered in the Americas, including hundreds of artifacts of gold, silver, copper, amber, jet, coral, shell, obsidian, turquoise, rock crystal, ceramic, and *tecali* along with more than a dozen bones carved with codex-style images (Caso 1982), accompanied these burials. The tomb was opened on multiple occasions during the Late Postclassic, probably for rituals and the placement of additional interments (Middleton et al. 1998). McCafferty and McCafferty (1994) make a strong argument that the tomb and its occupants were associated with the Mesoamerican Mother Goddess complex. The reuse of this particular tomb suggests the commemoration of a deeper memory of the significance of the architectural complex associated with Tomb 7. As discussed above, the Late Classic building above Tomb 7 was highly unusual in incorporating a two-room temple within a high-status residence (Barber and Joyce 2006:239). The interment of multiple individuals with one of the most spectacular offerings ever discovered in Mesoamerica shows that in the Late Postclassic this location continued to be viewed as a special place.

Beyond the area of the Main Plaza, flexed and seated low-status burials were intrusively interred in areas that were no longer occupied but which contain the remains of Late Classic residences (Caso et al. 1967:447; Martínez 1998:293–298). Like the reuse of tombs by noble families, it is possible that these interments represent claims to land through assertions of descent from important ancestors who resided at the site.

Monte Albán was therefore a site of fortifications, burials of powerful elites, and shrines, all of which are consistent with patterns recognized by Pohl and his colleagues (1997) for special locations on community boundaries depicted in Late Postclassic and early colonial manuscripts. The codices (indigenous prehispanic-style manuscripts) record the territorial claims of Late Postclassic polities, while boundaries shown on *lienzos* (colonial indigenous maps) record claims of important towns, often referencing territorial claims dating back to the prehispanic era. Boundaries are shown by a series of pictographs demarcating natural features such as mountains, rivers, and caves as well as fortifications, ballcourts, burial places, and shrines. Boundaries include neutral locations where people from competing polities met, such

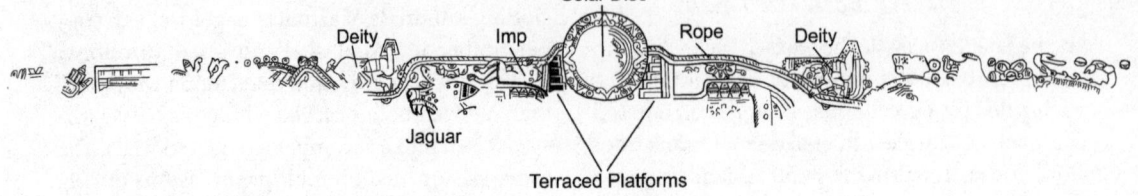

FIGURE 3.8. Arroyo Group lintel painting from Mitla (redrawn from Pohl 2005).

as border markets and sacred places. Ruined sites are also depicted as boundary locations and sacred places often inhabited by powerful deities, showing that Late Postclassic peoples saw ancient ruins as important elements in their cultural constructions of landscape (Hamann 2003b).

Late prehispanic and early colonial documents show some ruined sites as pre-sunrise places of creation (Hamann 2002, 2003b; Pohl 2003a). These places of creation were usually ruined hilltop sites that had major Classic period occupations like Monte Albán. In Mixtec belief, the creation of the current world began with the destruction of an earlier age following a cataclysmic war termed the "War of Heaven" by most codical scholars, though more appropriately interpreted as the "War with Earth, War with Rain" (Hamann 2002). The codices depict the war as fought by gods and Mixtec ancestors against rock-skinned stone men and rain-descending cloud men. The war ended in a sacred covenant between Mixtec ancestors and the gods of Earth and Rain. This covenant establishes cosmological debts to the gods, which are repaid through sacrifice. Through sacrificial offerings people petition the deities for agricultural and human fertility (Monaghan 1990). Following the establishment of the covenant, the current world began with the first sunrise of the new era and the founding of the major Late Postclassic ruling houses. In twentieth-century Zapotec and Mixtec myth, the first sunrise petrified the stone men inhabitants of the earlier age, which people often identify as prehispanic carved stone monuments (Hamann 2002:355; Parsons 1936:216, 454).

Unfortunately, codices that might have recorded Zapotec creation stories from the Oaxaca Valley did not survive the Spanish conquest. Pohl (1999, 2005), however, has shown that preserved portions of painted lintels from the palaces at Mitla record codex-like narratives of multiple creation sagas. The preserved section of the painted lintel on the Arroyo Group palace (Figure 3.8) records a Zapotec creation story similar to the first-sunrise narratives recorded in the Mixtec codices. The lintel features a celestial band broken by a large solar disk at the center of the composition directly over the doorway. The disk emerges from between two terraced temples, each set upon the back of a jaguar ornamented with flint knives. Two ropes are attached to the right and left sides of the solar disk and are grasped by deities that are descending from clefts in the sky. An implike figure, resembling the stone men of the Mixtec codices, grasps the rope to the left of the solar disk. Two ancestors beside a hill glyph that Pohl (2005) identifies as the place sign of Zaachila are further to the left, below the sky band.

The location of the creation event as two terraced temples from a "jaguar place" may reference Monte Albán's Main Plaza (Pohl 2002, 2005). People from the town of Xoxocotlán below Monte Albán knew the site as Cerro del Tigre, or Hill of the Jaguar (Bradomin 1955; Cruz 1946). Monte Albán is depicted as the Hill of the Jaguar in several eighteenth-century maps from Xoxocotlán and a colonial-period painting of the coat of arms from Cuilapan (Smith 1973:202–208; Whittaker 1980: 166–169). The Xoxocotlán map names 10 of the hills associated with Monte Albán. The Hill of the Jaguar represents the South Platform. As in the Arroyo Group lintel, the Cuilapan image shows a large sun rising over the Hill of the Jaguar, marking it as a place of creation. As late as the end of the nineteenth century, Castellanos (1989) was told that the Main Plaza was called Kehyik-anyi or "Plateau of the Sun" in the Mixtec dialect from Xoxocotlán. Whittaker's (1980:162) reporting of an informant's statement of seven caves/tombs below the Main Plaza is reminiscent of Mixtec and Aztec belief that the origin point from which their ancestors emerged was a place translated as "Seven Caves" or "Cave Seven" (see Monaghan 1995:210). Orr (1997:115–116) reports Zapotec informants who believe that carved stones from Monte Albán are examples of pre-sunrise giants that were turned to stone at the creation of the current world. Elsie Clews Parsons (1936:216) recorded myths of pre-sunrise stone people at Mitla in the early 1930s; one informant told Parsons that the stone people "lived here when the first sun came out. The ancient ones built the ruins before there was any sun" (1936:454).

The Mixtec codices date the time of the War with Earth, War with Rain and the dawn of the new era to the tenth century or the Early Postclassic (Byland and Pohl 1994:14; Hamann 2002). Several scholars have argued that the "War with Earth, War with Rain" is an account of the violent collapse of Classic period polities such as the one centered at Monte Albán, followed by the emergence of the smaller, fragmented polities of the Postclassic (Byland and Pohl 1994; Jansen 1998). The problem with this literal interpretation of the codices is that the timing of the war is a century or two later than the fragmentation of the Late Classic states. Data from highland Oaxaca (Markens 2004:432–433; Winter 2003), while still problematic, also suggest that Postclassic polities did not emerge directly out of the Late Classic political centers. The Early Postclassic appears to have been a time of reduced inequality, with ruling families having lost much of their wealth and power.

Instead, I argue that the codical creation stories are retroactive fifteenth- and sixteenth-century accounts of the collapse transformed by the political realities of the Late Postclassic. The codices as well as the creation stories on the Mitla lintels depict the War with Earth, War with Rain as occurring amid the ruins of Late Classic cities like Monte Albán. The war results in the destruction of an earlier, immoral age followed by the first sunrise of a new, moral, and properly ordered era and the founding of Late Postclassic royal houses (Hamann 2002; Pohl 2002). Hamann (2002:359–360) argues that these creation stories transformed memories of the collapse in ways that legitimated the authority of Late Postclassic nobles. The codices legitimated noble authority by showing that the royal houses of polities like Zaachila and Tilantongo had existed since the creation of the current world. Noble ancestors participated in the events of the creation and the formation of the sacred covenant that established the fundamental relations between people and the gods. The identification of the Main Plaza as a place of creation represents a second appropriation of the ceremonial precinct by the nobility, although in this case it was an appropriation of the plaza's past to legitimate political relations in the Late Postclassic present.

In the fragmented and contentious political landscape of the Late Postclassic, Monte Albán brought together nobles and commoners from different communities both physically and symbolically (Pohl et al. 1997:227). As a pre-sunrise place of creation, Monte Albán allowed for wider kinds of integration through shared rituals and perhaps as a neutral marketing location and fortress for defense against common enemies. As a place of creation, the Main Plaza embodied a shared origin and ancestry of Zapotec peoples throughout the valley, although one that legitimated noble authority and internalized distinct elite and commoner identities. That the Zapotec creation at Monte Albán is portrayed on one of a series of painted lintels at Mitla, which also include depictions of Mixtec and Tolteca-Chichimeca creation stories, reflects an even wider identity shared among Late Postclassic nobles (Pohl 1999, 2002).

Colonial Period to the Present: The Main Plaza Goes Global (AD 1521–2006)

Despite the massive depopulation and cultural disruptions resulting from the Spanish conquest, the Xoxocotlán maps and the Cuilapan coat of arms show that well into the eighteenth century the Main Plaza was being depicted as a place of creation, embodying indigenous religious belief and social memory of the prehispanic past. Colonial maps from Xoxocotlán and San Juan Chapultepec (now part of Oaxaca City) show that Monte Albán continued to be identified as a boundary location (Smith 1973:202–210). Continuity with the prehispanic past suggests resistance to the suppression of indigenous belief by Spanish colonial authorities.

During the eighteenth and nineteenth centuries scholars interested in the prehispanic past such as Guillaume Dupaiz, Eduard Muhlenpfordt, Désireé Charnay, William Henry Holmes, and Eduard Seler visited Monte Albán and wrote about the site. Recognition of indigenous peoples and the prehispanic past did not emerge as an important aspect of a Mexican national identity until the independence movement of the early nineteenth century (Fowler 1987:233–234). Following independence, however, concepts of indigenous culture and history declined in representations of state identity. It was not until the revolutionary period of the first two decades of the twentieth century that *indigenismo* reemerged as a major aspect of Mexican national identity. The promotion and appropriation of indigenous culture and history by the Mexican state involved idealizing the prehispanic past and emphasizing the continuity of past and present Mexican peoples.

Part of this reemphasis of the indigenous past involved sponsoring the first large-scale systematic archaeological projects in Mexico, beginning with Manuel Gamio's excavations at Teotihuacán. To their credit, many archaeologists of the period, such as Gamio and Alfonso Caso, recognized the devastation of the Spanish conquest. In the mid-1920s, Gamio suggested that Monte Albán should be the focus of archaeological explorations, and he arranged with the nearby towns for the area of the Main Plaza to be ceded to the state. In late 1931, Caso began major excavations. With the discovery of Tomb 7 in early 1932, Monte Albán burst onto the world stage, with the Western press traveling to the site to view the excavations and interview Caso (Benítez 1993:34). Paramount Studios shot a short film of the tomb, and Caso quickly authored a report, which appeared in the October 1932 issue of *National Geographic Magazine*. Caso continued fieldwork at Monte Albán with his colleagues Ignacio Bernal and Jorge Acosta until 1958. Part of Caso's work involved reconstructing the Main Plaza and opening the site as a major tourist center.

Beginning with Caso and continuing to the present, archaeological research has reinterpreted Monte Albán from the perspective of twentieth- and twenty-first-century scholarly archaeologies, and the site has become a focus of debate on problems such as state formation and collapse, early urbanism, and ancient empires (e.g., Blanton et al. 1999; Caso 1932; Flannery and Marcus 1983b; Joyce 2000; Joyce and Winter 1996; Marcus and Flannery 1996; Robles 2001a, 2001b; Winter 1989). The interpretations of archaeologists have been reinscribed onto the site through reconstruction and reconsolidation, primarily in and around the Main Plaza. The opening of the site to tourism has allowed people from much of the world to experience and interpret Monte Albán. Groups ranging from politicians, to scientists, to New Age spiritualists as well as indigenous Oaxacans now claim the site as a symbol of their diverse identities.

Archaeological projects in and around the Main Plaza have brought archaeologists and local Zapotec people together, where they have exchanged ideas about the nature, history, and meaning of the site. Caso recounts a story told shortly after the discovery of Tomb 7 that shows how his work was viewed by indigenous people in the context of the sacred qualities of the site:

> It is related that one night, when I was in the central plaza of Monte Albán, a well of crystal water opened up at the foot of one of the monuments, and in the middle of it floated a red vessel made from a gourd shell, inside of which was a gilded fish. Instead of being frightened by this marvel, I caught the jug and the fish within it; whereupon the fish informed me of the location of the treasure in Tomb 7 [1932:496].

In a curious parallel, objects used in the foundation ceremonies depicted in the Mixtec codices include both gourd vessels and fish. Since Caso's work in the 1930s, Oaxaca Valley Zapotecs, especially from the communities of Xoxocotlán and Cuilapan, have been hired as workers on archaeological projects, thereby reflecting the contemporary power relations of Oaxaca. The descendants of the builders of the Main Plaza are now the workers excavating and reconstructing the site under the direction of scholars trained in Western, scientific archaeology.

Monte Albán and especially the Main Plaza continue to be recognized by local people as places with sacred properties. Archaeologists have found evidence of recent ritual activities such as the remains of sacrificed chickens, foodstuffs, votive candles, and modern ceramic vessels (Caso 1932:493; Orr 1997:115–117; Marcus Winter, personal communication 2003). The South Platform in particular is identified as a "place of the devil" where people go to trade their souls for money (Orr 1997:117–119). Looter's trenches dug into structures on the South Platform are viewed as sacred caves, and archaeologists have found evidence of curing rituals within the trenches. Monte Albán also continues to be a boundary site, with local communities contesting ownership of the land with each other, the state government, and archaeologists. Monte Albán is a symbol of indigenous identity and resistance, which includes the use of archaeological research by indigenous scholars (de la Cruz 2004).

Increased tourism and the engagement of the site in processes of globalization, however, have begun to further broaden the appropriation of Monte Albán in ritual activity and identity formation. In 1987, stressing continuity between the prehispanic past and the present, the archaeological site of Monte Albán, along with the colonial city of Oaxaca, was inscribed onto the U.N. Educational Scientific and Cultural Organization World Heritage List as a place of "outstanding universal value." In August 1987, Monte Albán was the scene of New Age rituals conducted to celebrate the "Harmonic Convergence" marking the culmination of a cycle of history. Today Monte Albán is simultaneously a symbol of indigenous identity and history, Mexican national identity, worldwide human achievement, and New Age spiritualism.

Conclusions

Since the founding of Monte Albán at ca. 500 BC, the Main Plaza has gone through a complex history of construction, use, modification, abandonment, reuse, and reconstruction that has been continuously inscribed onto the buildings, ritual deposits, tombs, burials, and other historical traces at the site. The life history of the plaza embodies transformations in sociopolitical relations, ideology, and identity in the Valley of Oaxaca and beyond. The plaza has been a symbol of new social orders and of the collapse of old ones, demonstrating the complex ways in which meaning is inscribed in the spatial relationships and symbolism of architectural and archaeological remains. Yet the history of the Main Plaza should not be viewed simply as a passive reflection of changing social relations. As people moved through the plaza or viewed it from afar, their experiences with its meaning and symbolism as well as the practices carried out there were important aspects of social structure internalized as memory and disposition.

A consideration of the life history of place focuses attention on the ways in which power relations were inscribed in and reinforced by the symbolic and spatial patterning of the Main Plaza. The Main Plaza's life history makes clear that throughout its time as the ceremonial center of a political capital, the plaza embodied the power of rulers and ruling institutions. The evidence also suggests that there were other ways of experiencing the plaza beyond those of the nobles who increasingly appropriated the ceremonial precinct for their own aggrandizement. Conflict among Oaxaca Valley polities in the first few centuries after the site's founding indicates that many people in the valley were resisting incorporation by Monte Albán. As they defended their community against the forces of Monte Albán, the people of El Palenque must have viewed the ceremonial precinct, visible on a distant hilltop, in a very different way than people engaged in ceremonies on the Main Plaza. Monte Albán's success in defeating competitors in the Oaxaca Valley and beyond was in part due to the emphasis on communal affiliation and engagement in symbolism and ritual practice in the ceremonial center. By the Classic period, however, commoners were increasingly excluded from the Main Plaza and were less engaged in the kinds of large-scale public rituals for which the plaza was initially constructed. Some commoners and lesser nobles may have come to experience the transformation of the Main Plaza into an embodiment of elite aggrandizement as a symbol of the neglect of moral responsibilities of the rulers of Monte Albán (Jansen 2004:135).

Despite the collapse of Monte Albán as a political center at ca. AD 800, the Main Plaza continued to be viewed as a sacred mountain of creation where important rituals were carried out. The life history of Monte Albán exemplifies points made by scholars such as Barrett (1999) and Bradley (1993, 1998) that ruined monuments do not simply disappear from the landscape but are reinterpreted in their afterlives. Early Postclassic people who traveled to the Main Plaza to make ritual offerings moved through the center of a once-powerful city that was abandoned and falling into ruin but still held sacred power through its associations with the otherworld, including the presence of the ancestors who had once inhabited the site. The Main Plaza seems to have once again been accessible to commoners, embodying the less hierarchical identities of the Early Postclassic. By the Late Postclassic social practices, reflecting a fragmented and increasingly competitive political landscape, transformed the plaza into a boundary site that brought together people from multiple communities in the valley both physically and symbolically. Ritual practices mediated interpolity conflict and reproduced a broader social identity that reflected common historical ties to Monte Albán. This shared history and identity was also reflected in the belief in the Main Plaza as a pre-sunrise place of creation. The plaza once again embodied elite authority, not by reference to the cosmic symbolism of buildings that housed rulers and ruling institutions but, instead, by reference to the ruined buildings of an earlier creation that was destroyed in the first sunrise of a new era that established the ruling dynasties of the Late Postclassic.

The representation of the Main Plaza as a pre-sunrise place of creation continued into the colonial period despite massive depopulation, forceful oppression, and the suppression of indigenous religious beliefs and practices. Depictions of Monte Albán as a place of creation no longer legitimated the authority of nobles but, rather, symbolized indigenous identity and resistance to European acculturation and oppression in part by referencing the prehispanic past. Over the past century Monte Albán has been claimed by other constituencies, becoming a symbol of Mexican national identity, the advance of archaeological science, worldwide humanistic achievement, and New Age spiritualism. The diverse views of Monte Albán held by these groups embody contemporary struggles: local–global, indigenous–colonialist, modernism–postmodernism, among others.

The Main Plaza has embodied change and transformation, but it is also possible to recognize long-term continuities in the meanings ascribed to the plaza. From the founding of Monte Albán, the evidence indicates that the Main Plaza was viewed as an axis mundi where the sacred covenant could be enacted and the cosmic creation could be reenacted in powerful ways. Another aspect of the long term may ironically involve a kind of continuity through disjuncture in indigenous discourses on disruptive social change. As argued by several scholars (Byland and Pohl 1994; Hamann 2002; Jansen 1998), Mesoamerican peoples invoked the past to explain the disjunctive break in power relations represented by the Classic period collapse. The royal houses of the Late Postclassic legitimated their rise to power in part by appropriating the past and explaining their origins in the cataclysmic destruction of an earlier era and the first sunrise of a new age. The life history of Monte Albán records an even earlier disjunctive break in social relations, that of the founding of the site at ca. 500 BC. Like the Classic-to-Postclassic transition, the social crisis of the late Middle Formative saw a dramatic break with the past, as represented by the movement from valley floor sites and the founding of Monte Albán, the development of new religious beliefs and practices, and the construction of the Main Plaza (Joyce 2000). The dramatic social changes that accompanied the founding of Monte Albán may have been explained by reference to a cataclysmic creation event inscribed in the sacred geography of the Main Plaza that also served to legitimate the authority of rulers by associating them with the creation and renewal of a new era. The Middle-to-Late Formative and the Classic-to-Postclassic transitions may therefore represent a kind of continuity in indigenous discourses on disjunctive social change in the framework of cyclical views of time and history.

The continuity in the meaning and symbolism of the Main Plaza supports Hamann's (2002) arguments concerning structures of the long term in Mesoamerican tradition. Drawing on Sahlins (1996), Hamann argues for long-term continuity in the interconnected ideas of cyclical time whereby past eras have been destroyed in world-transforming cataclysms creating a new social order, a transformation accompanied by the creation of sacrificial original debts to the divine. Hamann (2002:367) takes issue with recent criticisms of the idea of structures of the long term by social theorists focused instead on disjuncture and the pliability of cultural meanings to strategic manipulation, especially under conditions of colonialism and modernity. Contra Hodder (2002), Hamann's view of structures of the long term rejects essentialist positions that see long-term structures as fundamental and unchanging (e.g., Braudel 1980).

The life history of the Main Plaza shows that while views of creation and the sacred covenant have persisted, the social practices that reproduce these continuities in meaning as well as their social and political significance have changed dramatically through the centuries. The social and political significance of the Main Plaza has also changed radically (A. Joyce 2004). The plaza has at various times embodied communal power, the divine authority of the Classic period nobility and later on the Late Postclassic royal houses, and still later, resistance to Spanish colonialism. Given the power of the symbolism of the Main Plaza, it has also been a site of struggle, whether involving tension between a traditional communal ethos and aggrandizing nobles of the Classic period, between competing royal houses of the Late Postclassic, or more recently between social constructions of indigenous and national identities. As a site of struggle, the Main Plaza has been strategically transformed both physically and symbolically to advance particular interests, as when the hilltop was first converted from a natural to a cultural monument (Joyce 2000) and when it was increasingly appropriated by Classic period nobles.

Yet, through the *longue durée* of the Main Plaza's life history, it has persisted as a place of creation and a material symbol of enduring ideas concerning cyclical creation, sacrifice, and sacred debt. These ideas and the practices that reproduce them have been dynamic and changing, but a central theme has persisted. Factors that account for these enduring structures include the ways in which they were materially inscribed in art, architecture, offerings, and burials; how they were embedded in varied relational fields; and perhaps their sacred qualities. The recent history of the Main Plaza indicates, however, that even these long-term structures may now be undergoing change. While more isolated communities in the Mixteca Alta have maintained traditional beliefs that represent Hamann's (2002) long-term structures (see Monaghan 1990, 1995), Zapotec peoples in the Oaxaca Valley have in recent years been subjected to more intensive forces of globalization, including access to television, the Internet, tourism, and migration. It is my impression that these processes are contributing to the increasing transformation of indigenous discourses on Monte Albán as Oaxaca Valley Zapotecs engage with alternative discourses, including those of scientific archaeology. Regardless of the present state of structures of the long term, the Main Plaza of Monte Albán has continued for its 2,500-year history as a powerful symbol of indigenous identity in the Valley of Oaxaca.

Acknowledgments

I would like to thank Doug Bamforth, Cathy Cameron, Linda Cordell, Jim Hester, Byron Hamann, Scott Hutson, Steve Lekson, Robert Markens, Cira Martínez, Payson Sheets, Javier Urcid, Marcus Winter, and two anonymous reviewers for input on earlier drafts of this chapter. I would also like to thank Brenda Bowser for her helpful editorial suggestions. During the writing of this chapter I was supported by an American Council of Learned Societies/Social Science Research Council/National Endowment for the Humanities International and Area Studies Fellowship and a Faculty Fellowship from the Council on Research and Creative Work, University of Colorado at Boulder.

Notes

1. I examine the civic-ceremonial center of Monte Albán, which I refer to as the Main Plaza precinct. The precinct includes the Main Plaza proper, the buildings immediately surrounding the plaza, and the area north of the North Platform, which includes the highest concentration of high-status residences at the site as well as additional public buildings. I term this area the Main Plaza precinct because the plaza was its focal point.

2. Many researchers assume that sunken courts, especially ballcourts, are associated primarily with the underworld. Recent iconographic and epigraphic studies have shown, however, that sunken courts are more broadly associated with, and were seen as, opening into diverse aspects of the otherworld (Freidel et al. 1993:350–355). It is not surprising, therefore, that the earliest sunken courts at Monte Albán are associated with the northern part of the Main Plaza, with its references to the celestial realm.
3. A possible residential structure of unknown date has been identified beneath System IV in the northwestern end of the Main Plaza (Javier Urcid, personal communication 2006).
4. The two TPAs that created restricted ceremonial spaces in the Main Plaza had patios enclosing 625 m^2 in the case of System IV and 784 m^2 for System M. In contrast, the Main Plaza covers 45,000 m^2.
5. A marital alliance between a Mixtec prince of Yanhuitlán and the daughter of a Zapotec king resulted in the immigration of a large group of Mixtec peasants into the Valley of Oaxaca to work the land of the prince. They settled in lands at the southern base of Monte Albán, and after the conquest their descendants moved to the towns of Cuilapan and Xoxocotlán, where they produced a number of important documents that refer to Monte Albán as a sacred site and a community boundary (Smith 1973).

4

Being in Place

Intersections of Identity and Experience on the Honduran Landscape

Rosemary A. Joyce, Julia A. Hendon, and Jeanne Lopiparo

Spatial analyses are a fundamental part of archaeology. At the scale of the site and the region, spatial distributions have been the subject of intensive settlement pattern analysis and, more recently, have become the data for landscape studies. This shift in terminology from *settlement pattern* to *landscape* involves more than a superficial relabeling. Where settlement patterns offer evidence of large-scale processes linking groups of humans with their geomorphological and ecological contexts, landscape is more securely focused on a human perspective, taking into account what Ashmore (2002) has felicitously called the "dispositions and decisions" involved in making place. To shift our attention from settlement pattern to landscape, and thence to place, is thus to undertake a transition from seeing sites as indirect evidence of processes originating elsewhere to seeing locales as part of the material through which processes of place take shape. Places are not merely the evidence that something happened; they are the thing itself in the process of happening (Pred 1984:282).

A place-based perspective complicates our task as archaeologists, making it less feasible to interpret mapped data without taking into account other kinds of information for which we are only beginning to develop methods of inquiry. As Tim Ingold argues,

> A place owes its character to the experiences it affords to those who spend time there—to the sights, sounds and indeed smells that constitute its specific ambience. And these, in turn, depend on the kinds of activities in which its inhabitants engage. It is from this relational context of people's engagement with the world, in the business of dwelling, that each place draws its unique significance [1993:155].

At the same time, archaeologists may be in a particularly strong position to trace some of the factors that contribute to the formation of place, particularly the experiences that specific material conditions encourage or allow and the histories of human engagement that are a large part of most analyses of place. As Margaret Rodman argues, places "are not inert containers. They are politicized, culturally relative, historically specific, local and multiple constructions.... Places have multiple meanings that are constructed spatially" and hold "physical, emotional, and experiential realities...at particular times" (1992:641). In this chapter, we explore what a shift from a concern with higher-order processes to human-scale decisions and dispositions involved in making places does to our understanding of a specific body of data from the Late to Terminal Classic period in northwest Honduras (roughly AD 500–1000).

Beginning with the kinds of maps that traditionally have offered us the material for macroscale analyses of process, we show how putting these patterns into appropriate temporal frames allows us to view them dynamically. We suggest ways in which a human-scale perspective from a specific position in place allows us to understand mapped relationships as orientations of human

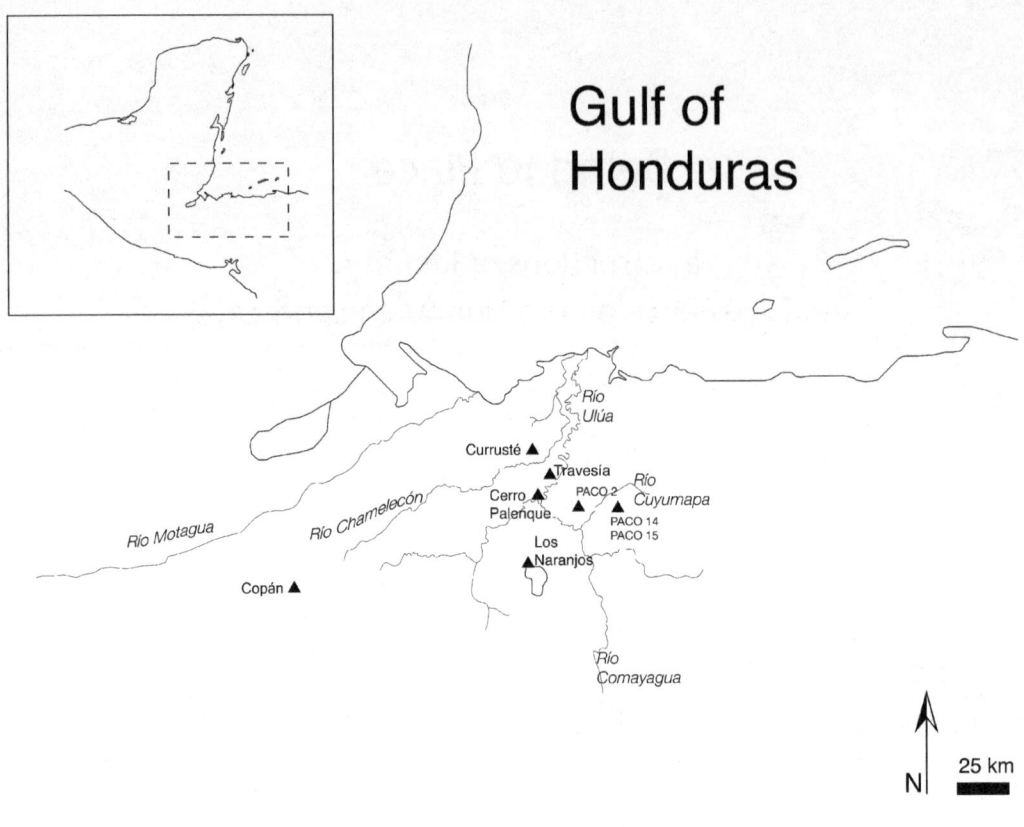

FIGURE 4.1. Map of northern Honduras showing sites discussed: Copán, Cerro Palenque, Currusté, Travesía, Los Naranjos, PACO 2, PACO 14, and PACO 15. Courtesy of Rosemary A. Joyce.

action. Putting the places we are talking about in this kind of lived context brings us to consider how even orientations that look the same may differ experientially. We advocate a combination of traditional map-based approaches and ground-level historicized consideration of how apparently similar places can be distinguished. In this we follow the suggestion of geographer J. Nicholas Entrikin:

> We understand the specificity of place from a point of view, and for this reason the student of place relies upon forms of analysis that lie between the centered [subjective, experiential] and decentered [objective, transcendent] view; such forms may be described as narrative-like syntheses [1991:3, cited in Rodman 1992:642].

We begin with a long-noted comparison between the Classic Maya center Copán, located in western highland Honduras, and Cerro Palenque, the largest known settlement in the history of the Lower Ulúa Valley of north-coastal Honduras (Figure 4.1). We then move out from Cerro Palenque to encompass the local landscape within which it is sited, considering relationships of different centers in the valley to the same points of geographic reference. Our consideration of valley-wide spatial patterning introduces an element of time, specifically seasonal time, with the annual solar cycle providing an indispensable part of the orientation of people in this shared spatial context. We further examine relations of temporality and place through a description and discussion of the distribution of places with ballcourts along the drainage of the Río Cuyumapa, upstream from the Lower Ulúa Valley.

We show that Cerro Palenque, the largest settlement in the Lower Ulúa Valley during the

Terminal Classic period, shares features in plan that are typical of contemporary Classic Maya settlements but that in local context are significantly different. The dominant north–south axis of the site, superficially a point of identity with Classic Maya sites, is better understood as a vector of movement toward the south, a direction experientially marked by upward movement that reverses the Classic Maya association of south with down and north with up. A valley-wide tendency for north–south site axes to be skewed exemplified at Cerro Palenque turns out to result from residents in different locations building with reference to shared geographic points of reference. The dominant reference point is a pathway leading toward a major mountain south of the valley. At Travesía, a second large site, east–west positioning in relation to events in the solar cycle as they were visible on the horizons is combined with this regionally shared southern orientation. Multiple architectural complexes along the Cuyumapa River, upstream from the Lower Ulúa Valley, also employed orientations that on one level conform to shared events of the annual solar cycle. But at the same time, these places were sites of distinctive form and likely seasonal use by populations of different size and scope.

In the course of the essay, we move from discussion of site maps to human actions, from settlement pattern to human inhabitation of place. The sites we discuss become less easily disentangled from each other, from their histories, and from the other bodies of information that we use to understand what we first document through maps. In the final section, we come back to a consideration of the broader implications of a shift to a concern with place, arguing that by engaging with our data in this way we have learned to understand factors with clear relevance to explaining why settlements developed over time in certain ways and not others.

From Site Planning to Being in Place: Cerro Palenque

In her discussions of principles of Classic Maya site planning, Wendy Ashmore (1987, 1989; Ashmore and Sabloff 2002:204) compares Classic Maya Copán to other sites from Honduras. These other Honduran sites differ notably from Copán. In them, archaeologists have found no evidence of stone portrait monuments or texts, hallmarks of the political visual culture of Copán. Cerro Palenque on the Lower Ulúa River, where we conducted two distinct phases of research in the 1980s and 2000s, is one of these other sites (Hendon 2002, 2007; Hendon and Lopiparo 2004; Joyce 1991; Joyce and Hendon 2000; Lopiparo et al. 2005). As a starting point for our examination of place making in western Honduras, Ashmore's influential formulation of a general model of site planning and its application to Cerro Palenque serve to highlight the intertwined challenges of making sense of site plans and relating them to the social and political contexts in which they were created.

The fundamental thesis proposed by Ashmore (1989, 1991:200; Ashmore and Sabloff 2002:202) is that Maya elites undertook construction projects guided by cosmological principles, intended to create site centers that mimicked key aspects of the world making that initiated creation, according to Maya belief. Some of these cosmological principles are widely shared in the Americas. These include the concept of the cosmos as having multiple layers and the identification of four directions on the horizontal plane as different in character from each other. While European colonizers routinely assimilated the four horizontal world directions to the cardinal points of the compass, abundant evidence suggests that for peoples of Mesoamerica, the four world directions were lines, not points: intercardinal points defined the corners of the horizontal plane of the world in which humans lived. For the Maya specifically, and likely for other Mesoamerican peoples, the corners of the horizontal plane were delimited by the extreme north and south points reached by the sun on the horizon during its annual seasonal cycle, at the winter (south) and summer (north) solstices (Aveni 1980). A vertical dimension was also delimited by the movement of the sun, with the highest point of the daily solar round (zenith) defining an extreme upward point and the contrasting extreme downward point (nadir) occurring when the sun was conceived of as traveling below the plane of the earth. For Mesoamerican peoples, these two points placed the sun in the middle of a plane above the terrestrial at mid-day and below the terrestrial at mid-night, either as the sole additional planes in a stacked conception of the cosmos or as part of a stack of multiple planes. As Ashmore (1991) and others (Coggins 1980) have noted, Maya peoples systematically linked directions on the horizontal terrestrial plane with those of the vertical axis, so that the northern and southern edges of the horizontal plane came to stand for the upper and lower planes through which the sun cycled every day.

Multiple templates generated in keeping with these shared cosmological principles can be identified at different Classic period Maya sites such as Tikal, Copán, and Seibal (Ashmore and Sabloff 2002). In Honduras, Ashmore (1987, 1989) drew attention to resemblances of settlement centers at sites farther east to the site plan of Late Classic Copán. These other Honduran sites, which include Cerro Palenque, are smaller in size than Copán and have no evidence of the personalization of political authority evident in the use of written texts and portrait sculpture at Copán. Nonetheless, they share features of site planning that suggest a worldview shared with the more stratified polity centered at Copán. In Copán's Main Group, a north–south axis relates secular space composed of enclosed courtyards on the south to more ceremonial, open plaza space on the north (Ashmore 1991). At the point where these two sectors join, a pair of buildings with mirror-image profiles, oriented north–south, form an architectural transition between these two kinds of space. This is the main ballcourt of Copán, an example of one of the diagnostic specialized building forms of Mesoamerica. Drawing on the abundant iconography and written texts available at Classic Maya sites like Copán, Ashmore (1989, 1991:200) has argued that the emphasis on the north–south dimension relates to Maya concepts of the north as celestial, associated with ancestors, and of south as terrestrial or even associated with the underworld. By implication, similar understandings would have underwritten the construction of sites in Honduras where no iconography or texts exist but whose plans share the same axiality, juxtaposition of architectural features, and ballcourt position.

The features that make Cerro Palenque seem comparable to Copán are a shared emphasis on a north–south axis and a ballcourt on the south end of a large ceremonial plaza, with residential architecture south of that. Indeed, the plan of the central plaza of Cerro Palenque (Figure 4.2) seems very much like the plan of Copán's Main Group. While the relative location of the ballcourt is switched from the east to the west side of the main plaza, the similarity of the two plaza plans is reinforced by the presence of a central platform in both. There is, of course, a major difference in scale, especially of the structures in the Cerro Palenque southern residential group when compared to the courtyards and pyramids south of the ballcourt at Copán. As well, although the orientation of the Cerro Palenque ballcourt is basically north–south, it is skewed to the east. Nonetheless, the north–south axiality and the zoning of secular living space and more ceremonial spaces joined by a ballcourt are striking parallels in these site plans.

Necessarily left out of plan-based approaches to comparing sites are a host of other features that can only be experienced on the ground. Both Copán and Cerro Palenque are located along the course of the major river in their respective valleys, but the settings are otherwise quite different. At Copán, the Main Group lies directly on the river floodplain with the flanks of the surrounding mountains rising up and creating an enclosed valley approximately 25 km^2 in area. Cerro Palenque sits on the highest ridges and peaks of a set of hills rising 100 to 200 m above the union of the Río Comayagua and Río Blanco with the Ulúa River, with a visual prospect down into the floodplains (Figure 4.3). The Ulúa River is much larger than the Copán River, and the Lower Ulúa Valley is a vast tropical floodplain (about 2,400 km^2) through which it meanders. The much larger scale of the Lower Ulúa Valley makes it impossible from Cerro Palenque to see all the edges of the valley. In contrast to the encircling highlands that enclose Copán, at Cerro Palenque, the views are of walls of mountains east and west, with an open frontier on the north, where the river enters the Caribbean, and more distant mountains on the south that are seasonally visible or obscured by clouds.

Settlement in the Copán Valley was concentrated in a 1-km^2 area centered on the main architectural group, which originally probably occupied 15 to 20 ha along the river (Webster 1999: 16, 20). In the Late Classic Copán Valley, only this centralized settlement zone included a ballcourt. The original ballcourt here was rebuilt in

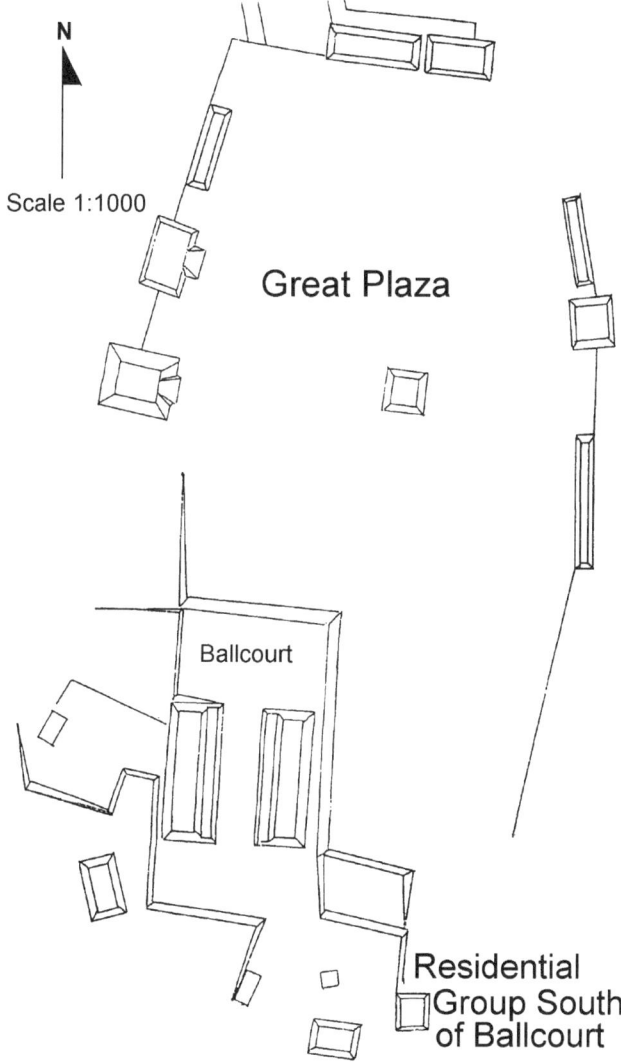

FIGURE 4.2. Map of the Great Plaza of Cerro Palenque. Based on original by Rosemary A. Joyce; courtesy of Julia A. Hendon.

the same position multiple times over the centuries beginning before AD 400 (Webster 1999:18). At the end of the continuous span of occupation of the Copán Main Group, in the ninth century a second ballcourt was constructed a short distance away, still within the central concentration of buildings, maintaining the monopoly by the residents of this central place on this form of architectural feature.

In contrast, even though Cerro Palenque was the single largest settlement in the Lower Ulúa Valley in the Classic period, it was not the center of valley settlement distribution or political organization even at its peak. Approximately 500 Classic period sites have been identified in the Lower Ulúa Valley, distributed along the major and minor watercourses. Most of these were individual agricultural hamlets forming almost continuous distributions along streams and river levees (Figure 4.4). At regular intervals along the eastern and western mountain edge and along the main rivers, groups of larger buildings, many including

FIGURE 4.3. Being in place at Cerro Palenque: view across the valley from the southwest, across the peak of Cerro Palenque toward the mountains on the eastern horizon. Photograph by Russell Sheptak.

ballcourts, formed small and medium clusters of more specialized architecture.

Cerro Palenque was originally only one among many smaller central places in this distribution. The original Classic period settlement was formed by clusters of buildings on the highest hilltops constructed prior to AD 700 (Joyce 1991). This area of the site did not incorporate a ballcourt. By AD 850, new construction projects on lower ridges in the hills extending north expanded the settlement to its maximum extent of 3 km², including adding the main plaza with its large ballcourt, increasing the number of buildings in the contiguous site zone to over 500 structures. This was twice the number of buildings in the largest centers previously developed in the Lower Ulúa Valley, although only about half the size of the 1,035 structures recorded and one-third to one-quarter of the projected number of structures that once occupied the 1-km² area of central Copán (Webster 1999:20–21). While the growth of Cerro Palenque suggests a change in the nature of central places in the Lower Ulúa Valley, already existing agricultural hamlets continued to be occupied in the ninth and tenth centuries, maintaining a settlement pattern oriented toward the waterways of the valley that was not centered on Cerro Palenque. Although the picture is less clear for the small and large centers of the Classic period, there was at least some period of time during which many of these centers continued in use as Cerro Palenque grew to its maximum size.

From the perspective of mapped distributions of architectural features, Copán and Cerro Palenque initially look similar. In their broader topographic contexts, they are quite different. On closer examination, even their shared emphases on cosmological orientation may be a point of distinction between them. Ashmore (1991) demonstrates that at Copán, the orientation of the Main Group extended out to encompass other groups of architecture. These other architectural groups were occupied by people with strong social, ritual, and political connections to the patrons of construction of the architecture of the Main Group. Together, the Main Group and these other groups sketched out a larger-scale cosmogram particularly emphasizing the north–south dimension. In this schema, north was the most significant direction, associated with the upper plane of the cosmos, with the solar zenith, and with ancestry.

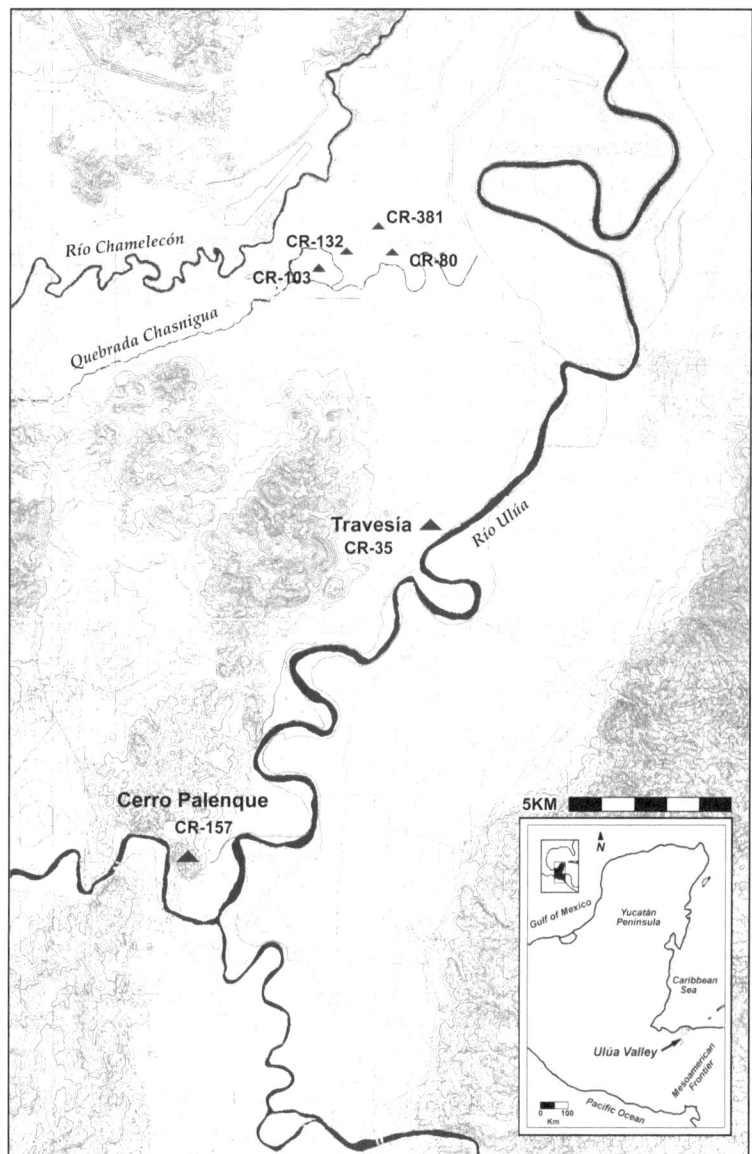

FIGURE 4.4. Settlement in the central part of the Lower Ulúa River Valley including the central places Cerro Palenque and Travesía. Sites CR-103, -132, -381, and -80 are part of a continuous distribution of settlement along the subsidiary streams Quebrada Chasnigua and Quebrada Mantecales. Courtesy of Jeanne Lopiparo.

At Cerro Palenque, the orientation of structures turns inward toward the original settlement on the peak of the southern hill, the tallest topographic feature at the site (Joyce and Hendon 2000). As the settlement zone physically expanded during its late surge of growth, it did so within clear boundaries defined by ravines on the north and the enclosing Ulúa River course that traversed the other three sides of the hills. While there is a strong north–south axis at the site, it is best understood as an orientation toward the Cerro Palenque peak at the south end of the site, as a directional vector. Groups of residential structures were arrayed in rectilinear layouts that often left the side facing the Cerro Palenque peak unobstructed, creating a visual orientation toward the south. Even the main plaza actually is best understood as part of a broader layout directed south toward the oldest settlement on Cerro Palenque's peak. Placed in the context of the complete site map, the main plaza lies at the southern end of a series of terraces descending from the northern edge of the site. These terraces end in a ramp joined to the main plaza by a pair of raised stone walkways. Although the walkways can be viewed as conduits for traffic in either direction, the cobble ramp is relatively steep and difficult to climb up, suggesting a preferential pattern of movement down from the terraces, from north to south.

While both Copán and Cerro Palenque share north–south axiality in plan, at Cerro Palenque this is a direction that extends south from the north. In fact, north–south axiality in the Lower Ulúa Valley as a whole is best understood in terms of a shared directional vector through which people oriented themselves to the south and in which south was an upward direction.

Being Emplaced: The Geomantic Landscape of the Lower Ulúa Valley

While the axis of the main plaza at Cerro Palenque is roughly north–south, it is actually skewed to the east. Jeanne Lopiparo (2003, 2004, 2006, 2007) notes that skewing of site orientations to the east is the norm in the Lower Ulúa Valley, even though the precise orientations vary from site to site. She has shown that communities in the Classic period Lower Ulúa Valley that were otherwise independent of each other organizationally coordinated their place-making actions through an orientation toward shared physiographic points of reference. These practices, which she compares to the construction of *ceques* in Andean South America, *emplaced* Ulúa Valley settlements in a meaningful spatial and seasonal context that was shared throughout the valley even though it was not the product of centralized control. *Emplacement* here has the sense of involving "a hierarchic ensemble of places: sacred places and profane places: protected places and open, exposed places: urban places and rural places" (Foucault 1986:22). The orientation of settlements toward marked features of the landscape did not simply echo or express preexisting emplacement; it produced it. As the builders of central places oriented them to the same features, they incorporated those features in their extended sense of place.

Each of the settlement centers with complexes of mapped architecture in the Lower Ulúa Valley has a basically rectilinear plan. Sites constructed at the same time in a relatively small area show quite substantial differences in orientation. The divergence from due north ranges from 17°E at Currusté to 28°E at Travesía. Lopiparo (2003, 2004, 2006, 2007) shows that the orientations of the different centers converge on the most imposing mountain in the region, located at the south end of the valley (Figure 4.5a). The south-facing orientations of Ulúa Valley centers toward this imposing mountain are inherently local forms of place making. As at Copán, the emphasis on a north–south axis may be based on an understanding of the organization of cosmic space in which a vertical axis is transformed onto a horizontal plane. But the axial orientation of the Lower Ulúa Valley is not abstract but lived, not general but specific. It reverses the poles of the north–south axis shared by many Classic Lowland Maya centers to the west. In the local geomantic system of the Lower Ulúa Valley, south is experientially up, as the landscape rises toward the interior highlands and the focal mountain itself rises above the surrounding area.

These spatial orientations are echoed at Cerro Palenque, where the southern orientation leads up to the highest local peak. It may not be an accident that the vector extending south from Travesía, one of the largest of the Late Classic centers, extends directly across the peak at Cerro Palenque itself. The architecture of the original buildings constructed on the peaks of Cerro Palenque in the Late Classic period is closely related to that of Travesía and suggests that the original small center at Cerro Palenque was built as a subordinate to the larger center at Travesía (Joyce 1991:124). At both sites, cut-stone blocks were used to construct buildings covered in a thick coat of white plaster. Cut-stone slabs were worked into sculptural ornaments for the buildings at both sites, including distinctive stepped geometrics with pairs of pierced circular motifs. No other known site in the Lower Ulúa Valley has any of these architectural or sculptural characteristics. Like Andean

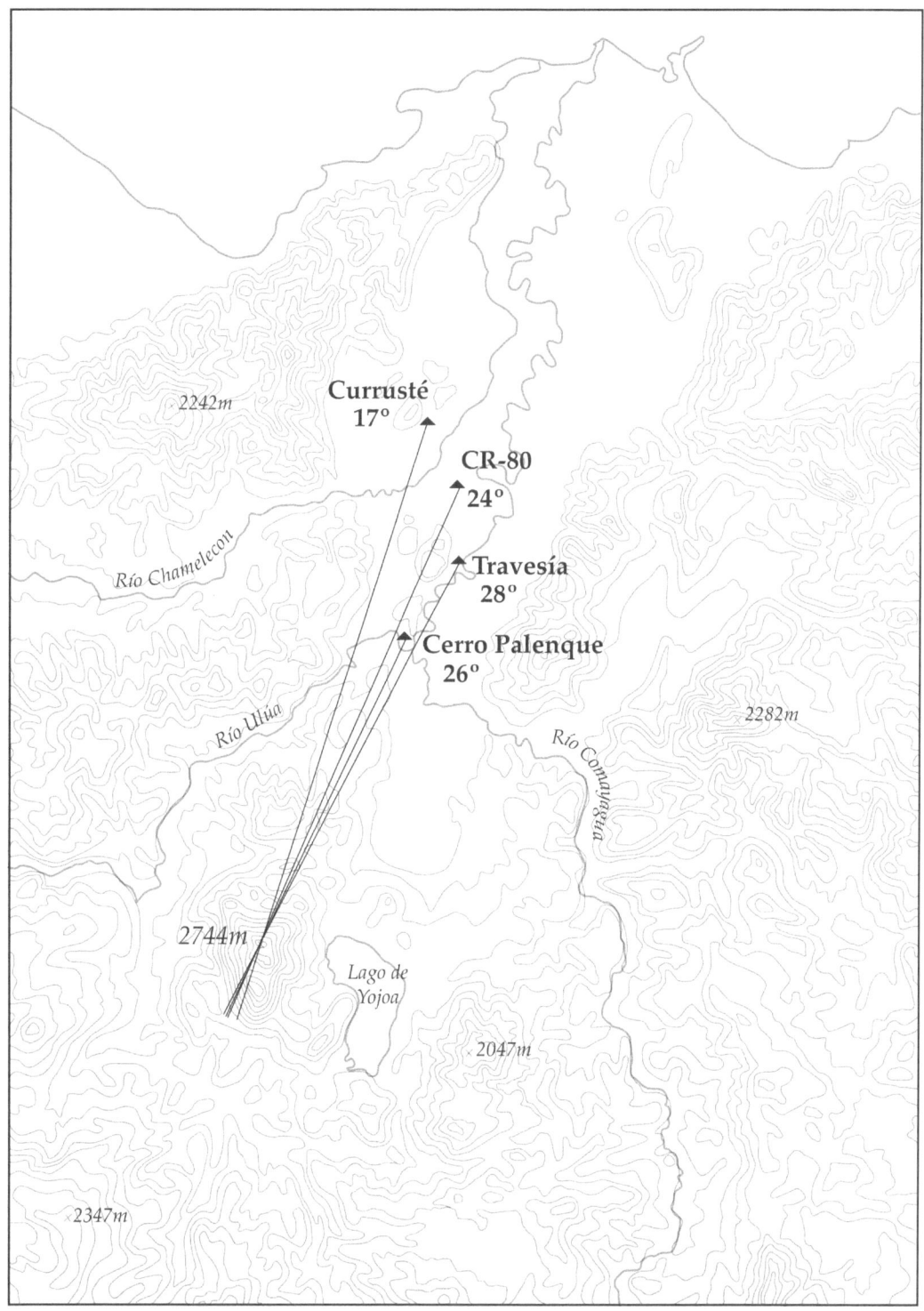

FIGURE 4.5a. Convergence of north–south axes of sites in the Lower Ulúa Valley on the Montaña de Santa Barbara. Courtesy of Jeanne Lopiparo.

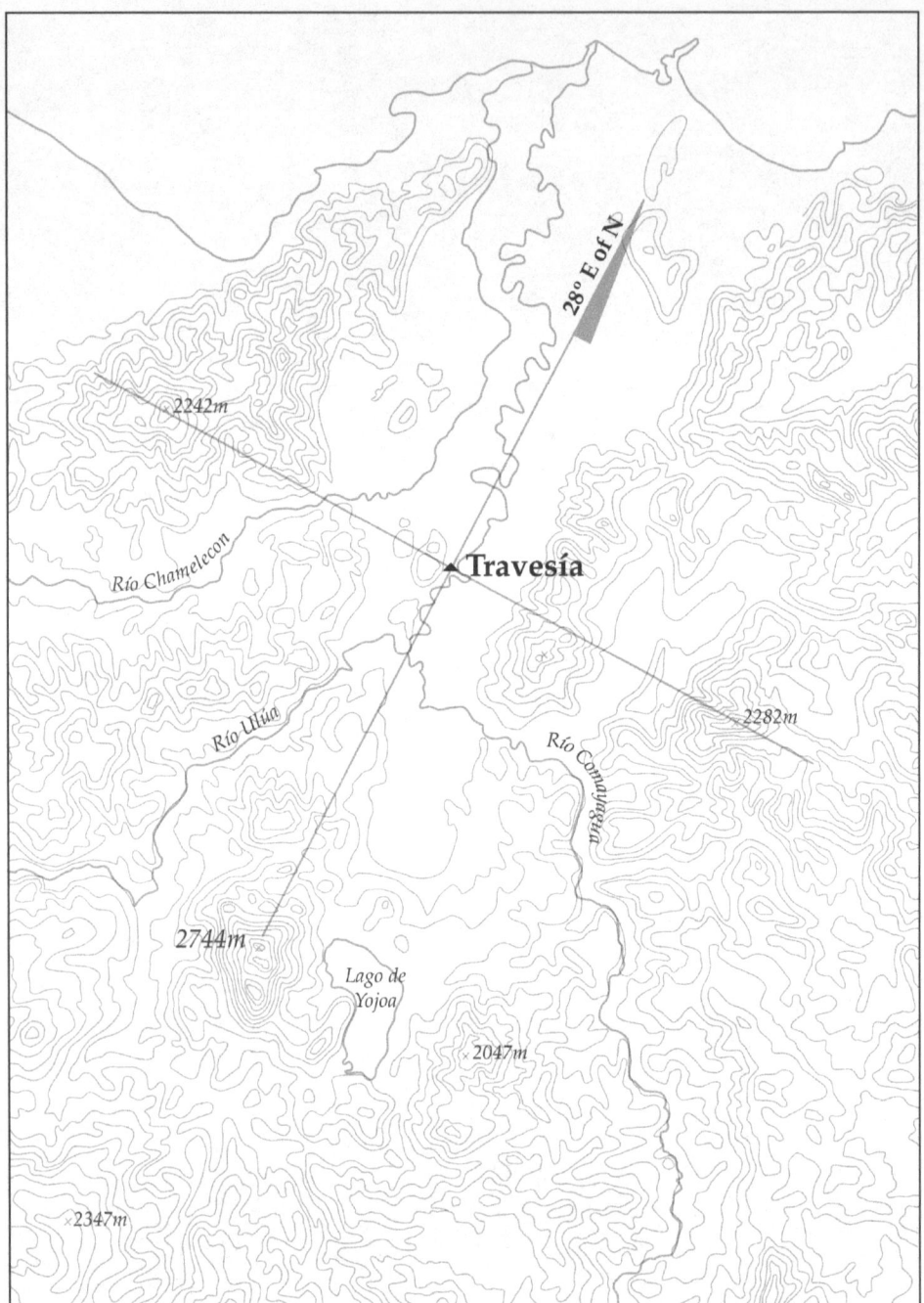

FIGURE 4.5b. Main orientational axes running through Travesía. Courtesy of Jeanne Lopiparo.

ceques, larger-scale vectors of orientation in the Lower Ulúa Valley were likely produced through many local acts of orientation extending between intervisible points, in this case, from Travesía toward the peak of Cerro Palenque, which looms on its southern horizon at even the cloudiest points in the year. As with the ceques, to understand these orientations, we need to consider how the places where they originate would have been related to the places toward which they were directed.

This southern mountain often has cloud cover long before rains descend to the Lower Ulúa Valley itself. As rain falls on the highlands, residents of the valley experience the outcome in rises in stream volume and changes in the color of the water, as sediment from the highlands is carried downstream. It is this network of streams that formed the main means of communication from one settlement to another in the valley. At the time these settlements were occupied, travel to the southern mountain most likely would have followed the course of the Río Blanco that joins the Ulúa River just south of Cerro Palenque. This river originates as the Río Lindo in the uplands around Lake Yojoa, a basin formed when volcanic eruptions built up barriers to downhill drainage. The headwaters of the Río Lindo create a major waterfall where they cross the edge of this lava flow, and there a group of large buildings arranged in a rectangle form a small Late Classic center today called Pulhapanzak. Transforming the map into a path we find the landscape: "In the landscape, the distance between two places, A and B, is experienced as a journey made, a bodily movement from one place to the other, and the gradually changing vistas along the route" (Ingold 1993:154).

If we consider the orientations of sites to the landscape from the perspective of experiences of place making grounded in a specific locality, then we can also begin to understand the broader patterns of site plans in a region as products of history and agency. Lopiparo (2003, 2007) has demonstrated that the main architectural group at Travesía was simultaneously oriented to other landscape features along a perpendicular east–west line (Figure 4.5b). The east–west axis of Travesía intersects the tallest mountain peak visible on the eastern horizon and crosses the mouth of the canyon of the Chamelecon River visible as a pass in the mountains on the west. When the site was inhabited, the particular points intersected on the east and west horizons would have been the locations of sunrise and sunset on the winter solstice.

The builders who placed this architectural group in the floodplains of the Lower Ulúa Valley in the Late Classic period effectively centered the entire cosmos on Travesía. They made it the pivot where a shared regional "vertical" axis extending to the southern mountain bisected a winter solstice path of the sun aligned to significant landscape features in a way only possible at this particular place. Though these are mobilizations of understandings of astronomical and seasonal phenomena shared with the builders of Lowland Maya sites to the west, like Copán, they gained their local meaning through local experiences and local actions. As Bruce Owens, citing Robert Levy (1990:616), argues, this kind of emplacement is "a powerful device for turning accident and history into structure, for trying to escape the contingencies and consequences of history, for trying to capture change, to make change seem illusory within an enduring order" (Owens 2002:305), an order that may be evident in maps. But, as Owens adds, "if we examine the places and spaces between the cardinal points, outside the cosmological grids, and locate them in the temporal flows of purely human making, we encounter a kind of chaos whose coherence lies in the contingencies of the creation and transformation of each of its parts" (2002:305). A final Honduran example demonstrates how keeping the emphasis on the local context in making the move from documenting settlement patterns to understanding the production of place can lead to a better model of the more chaotic processes through which places were created.

Making Place: Ballcourts in the Cuyumapa River Valley

Ballcourts oriented along north–south axes were incorporated in the major architectural groups at Copán, Cerro Palenque, and Travesía. In each case, they were located at a point of transition from a more open plaza area surrounded by tall platforms to a more enclosed courtyard with more secular, residential or palace uses. At all three sites, the open plaza area features a central platform that reinforces the identification of the plaza with the horizontal plane in which the four world directions are the sides of a space unfolding around a central axis of a vertical plane. The relative placement of architectural features varied in each case: at Copán, the ballcourt was southeast of the main plaza, north of the courtyards of the Acropolis; at Cerro Palenque, the ballcourt was on the southwest edge of the Great Plaza, just north of a major residential group; and at

Travesía, where the enclosed courtyards are on the north, the ballcourt was placed on the northwest edge of the open plaza area. Yet, despite these differences, we can imagine that the ballcourts had similar experiential significance at each of these sites, visible to those allowed access to the open plaza and under the patronage of those with privileged access to the courtyards.

Quite different understandings of the experience of place are required to make sense of a series of ballcourts documented in the Cuyumapa River Valley, located on a small tributary of the Comayagua River upstream from Cerro Palenque in the uplands of the mountains on the eastern edge of the Lower Ulúa Valley. There, Julia Hendon and Rosemary Joyce directed multiyear settlement pattern research in the 1990s (Joyce and Hendon 2000). Among the 66 mapped architectural clusters (made up of 511 individual structures) in this 165-km² area, were at least six ballcourts (with a probable seventh disturbed by construction before our research). Although ballcourts are not uncommon in Honduras, this is an unusual density of these features.

Ballcourts can be conceived, as Susan Gillespie (1991) has argued in detail, as spaces of transition between cosmological realms. Ballcourts are part of some of the earliest large villages in Mesoamerica, dating as early as 1500 BC (Hill and Clark 2001). Throughout their 3,000-year history, ballcourts are understood as architectural settings for athletic competitions using balls made of native rubber. Visual and literary works spanning much of the history of ballcourt use suggest that commonly, two teams competed to move the ball through the alley formed by the two flanking structures and into an end zone, which could be open or enclosed by architectural features. The same visual and literary sources associate the movement of the rubber ball through the space of the court with the movements of the major planets, although the details of such associations may have varied over time and from place to place (Cohodas 1991). In ballcourts, factions representing sides of different cosmic, political, and social dualities could come together and be placed in a hierarchy of winners and losers.

Mesoamerican ballcourts varied in the orientation of their playing alley; in the length and width of the alley, delimited by the flanking structures; and in the internal profile of those flanking structures, which probably affected the manner in which the ball was moved between players as it was struck off the differently angled surfaces. These variables show significant regional and chronological patterns, suggesting that there were shared approaches to the playing of ballgames within regions at particular points in time (Borhegyi 1969; Quirarte 1977; Scarborough 1991; Smith 1961). Within these taxonomies, the Late Classic ballcourt at Copán is typical of ballcourts from a wide area of the Late Classic Maya lowlands and western Honduras, including the ballcourt at Travesía (Joyce 1991:137).

The ballcourt at Cerro Palenque is most closely related to ballcourts at the site of Los Naranjos on Lake Yojoa (Joyce 1991:69). The Los Naranjos and Cerro Palenque ballcourts, built or at least remodeled after AD 800, share distinctive features with contemporary Terminal Classic or Early Postclassic ballcourts from sites in the Maya highlands of Guatemala. The plans of these ballcourts can be seen as an elaboration of the earlier Copán ballcourt plan achieved by adding a low bench inside the playing alley, changing the angles of the walls and thus presumably the way the game was played (Joyce 1991:137). The many ballcourts mapped in the Oloman and Cataguana valleys formed by the Cuyumapa River are generally comparable in plan to the Copán ballcourt and to related ballcourts throughout western Honduras, but some have features that recall the variations from this plan seen at Cerro Palenque and Los Naranjos.

Dissertation research has explored evidence for activities in and around several ballcourts in the Oloman and Cataguana valleys and in residential compounds adjacent to one in the Oloman Valley (Fox 1994, 1996; Fung 1995a, 1995b). This research suggests that with the exception of one ballcourt used in the Late Formative/Early Classic period, the ballcourts and associated residential structures visible on the surface along the Río Cuyumapa all were in use in the Late to Terminal Classic. This makes them contemporary with ballcourts in use at Cerro Palenque and Travesía. Distinctive pottery from Cerro Palenque was in fact present in the Río Cuyumapa sites, and pottery from that area was noted in the Lower Ulúa Valley sites (Lopiparo et al. 2005). Yet the orga-

TABLE 4.1. Ballcourts in the Oloman and Cataguana Valleys

Type of Ballcourt	Ballcourt Site	Orientation of Alley (°)	Alley Length (m)	Alley Width (m)
"Summer" ballcourts	PACO 2	9.5	24	11
	PACO 15	35.5	27	9
	PACO 14	52	29	9
	PACO 9	?	16?	9?
	Average		26.67	9.67
	SD		2.52	1.15
"Winter" ballcourts	PACO 5	105.5	45	22
	PACO 17	106	31	15
	PACO 11	?	32	7
	Average		36	14.67
	SD		7.81	7.50

Note: Dimensions of ballcourts are rounded to the nearest meter. Two ballcourts were mapped under conditions that make some data incomparable to the other ballcourts presented here. PACO 9, a possible ballcourt associated with a single large mound, had been bulldozed before reconnaissance, and all data must be considered highly uncertain. The length and width measurements are not included in the average and standard deviations calculated. A tentative orientation of 88° has previously been published. At PACO 11, contemporary farmers occupying the land to claim use rights were not comfortable with our undertaking instrument mapping; pacing produced acceptable data on length and width of the ballcourt alley, included in the calculations here. Alley orientation is still uncertain. It was previously published as 163°.

nizational patterns of the Cuyumapa sites are almost entirely unlike those of the neighboring region. Notably, ballcourts are extremely varied in size, shape, orientation, and articulation with other architectural features.

As we have noted previously (Joyce and Hendon 2000), settlement features in the Oloman and Cataguana valleys are distributed continuously along watercourses. Larger structures that are found do not form the focus of settlement distribution, and in this, the region is comparable to the central part of the Lower Ulúa Valley. All of the ballcourts are part of such larger architectural groups, which have two observable patterns. In one, a ballcourt is placed adjacent to a single large platform. The large platform may be located at one end of the ballcourt alley or perpendicular to the alley but always is farther west than the ballcourt alley. In the second pattern, the ballcourt forms part of a large plaza bounded by multiple tall platforms. Examples of plaza-located ballcourts were located on the north or south sides of the groups in which they were found.

While there was no standard size or orientation among these ballcourts, their orientation was not entirely random. These ballcourts fall into two classes, alleys oriented roughly east of north and those oriented east of south (Table 4.1). All of the ballcourts that were part of plaza groups, regardless of their specific placement in the plaza, were oriented toward the southeast. These ballcourts also have longer alleys (Figure 4.6a). All of the ballcourts that were constructed in groups with a single flanking mound to the west were oriented east of north (Figure 4.6b). The southeast orientations are more regular, and two are quite close to the expected sunrise direction on the eastern horizon at winter solstice. The northeast orientations, in contrast, are less tightly clustered, but they still are close to the corresponding summer solstice sunrise direction on the eastern horizon.

Though clearly not constituting the kind of architectural solstice observatories well known in Mesoamerican sites, ballcourts in the Cuyumapa drainage were apparently oriented in seasonally differentiated directions. Rather than seeing these as flawed implementations of astronomical observatories, we view them as part of landscape production by the farming population. As

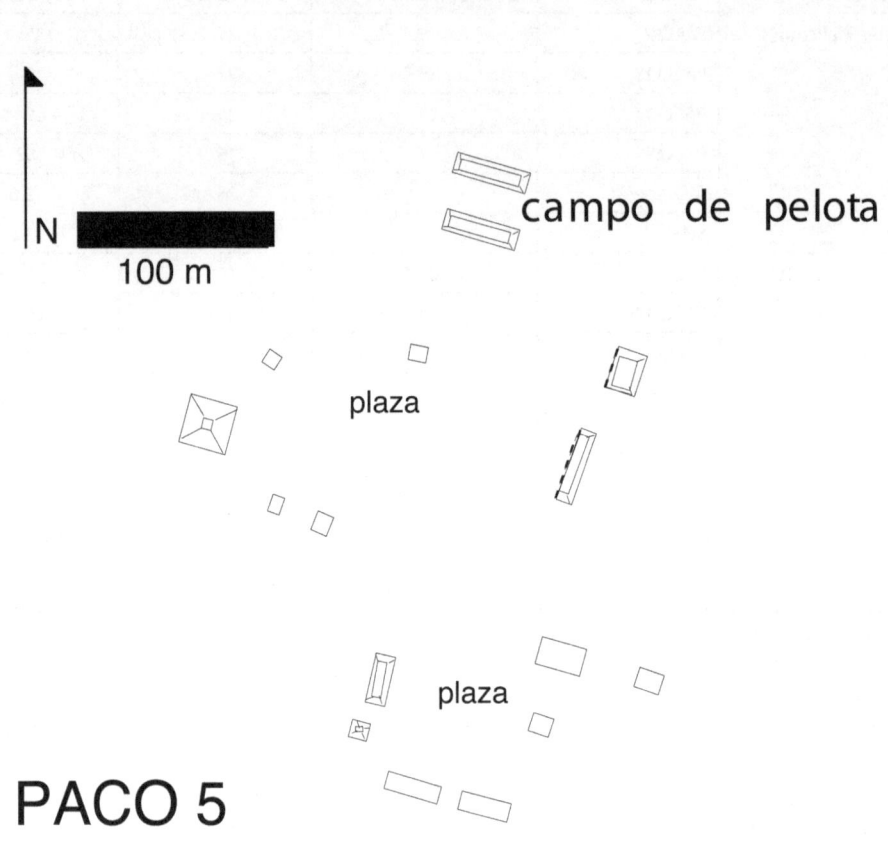

FIGURE 4.6a. Plan of a "winter" ballcourt (PACO 5) oriented southeast, part of a plaza group, with larger dimensions, and located downstream on a major river. Courtesy of Rosemary A. Joyce and Julia A. Hendon.

Ingold says, "We resonate to the cycles of vegetative growth and decay, not to the earth's revolutions around the sun, even though the latter cause the cycle of the seasons" (1993:163). When we map the distribution of the apparent "summer" and "winter" ballcourts it is notable that the more varied summer ballcourts are all located on minor tributary streams (Figure 4.7), whereas the winter ballcourts not only have longer alleys and form part of larger plazas but are located centrally on the major rivers.

The Cuyumapa ballcourts, if used seasonally, would have segmented the landscape differently at different times of the year. For the farmers who occupied most of the buildings we recorded, the annual cycle was the cycle of farming. The spring was the time of field preparation in anticipation of the first rains, clearing new land, and planting. The summer solstice comes when the fields have been established and plants are growing, a time when intensive weeding and cultivation are at a maximum. The summer ballcourts located upstream on small tributaries would have been accessible to local farmers without requiring them to travel far from their own fields.

Winter ballcourts were located at points on major rivers that could be reached by larger numbers of people, but at the cost of traveling farther from home fields. At the time of the winter solstice in December, crops planted in late spring would have already matured, and their harvest should have been completed. The rains would

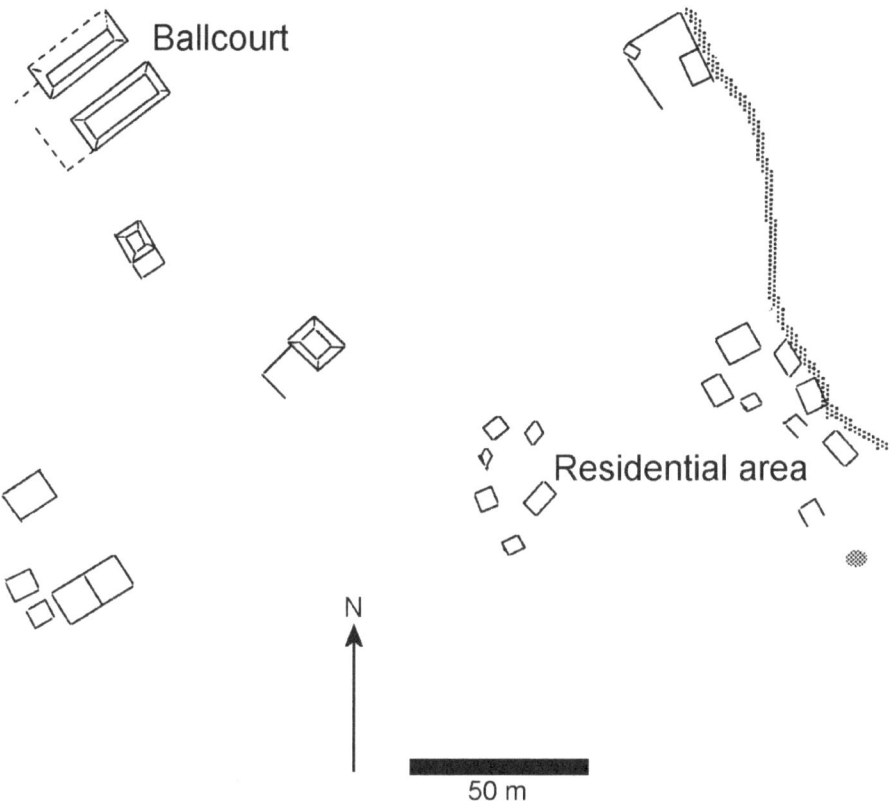

FIGURE 4.6b. Plan of a "summer" ballcourt (PACO 14, San Juan Camalote) oriented northeast, with an open plan, with smaller dimensions, and located upstream on a tributary. Courtesy of Rosemary A. Joyce and Julia A. Hendon.

have decreased from their peak in early fall. This is the time when winter festivals could draw on the bounty of harvest.

If the Cuyumapa ballcourts saw seasonal use in the fashion suggested by both their location and their orientation, activities held in these places may have drawn on overlapping communities of participants. What people did in these locations created different kinds of locales. This is what Ingold (1993) captures in his discussion of the way lived activities form *taskscapes*, lived spaces archaeologists approach through their solid remains. If we are interested in the projects that brought together "the paths of two or more people or of those persons and tangible resources, such as buildings, furniture, machinery, and raw materials" (Pred 1984:281), we must reinstate the movements of people in these places: "The forms of the taskscape, like those of music, come into being through movement...the taskscape exists only so long as people are actually engaged in the activities of dwelling" (Ingold 1993:161).

A person who took part in summer solstice games at a local ballcourt might travel downstream for the winter solstice events at a larger winter ballcourt. Visitors to some of the summer ballcourts demonstrably participated in ritual burning of incense and partook of food and drink presented in beautifully crafted bottles and bowls (Fox 1994). Based on analogies with ethnohistorically described use of ballcourts elsewhere, John G. Fox (1994, 1996) has suggested that other, more ephemeral actions likely took place near or in ballcourts, not only matches of games played with a rubber ball but also likely other games and dances. The formation of competitive factions, the teams that competed in games, was common to the events that historically took place around ballcourts. Such factions were often composed of visitors from local or more distant places. As

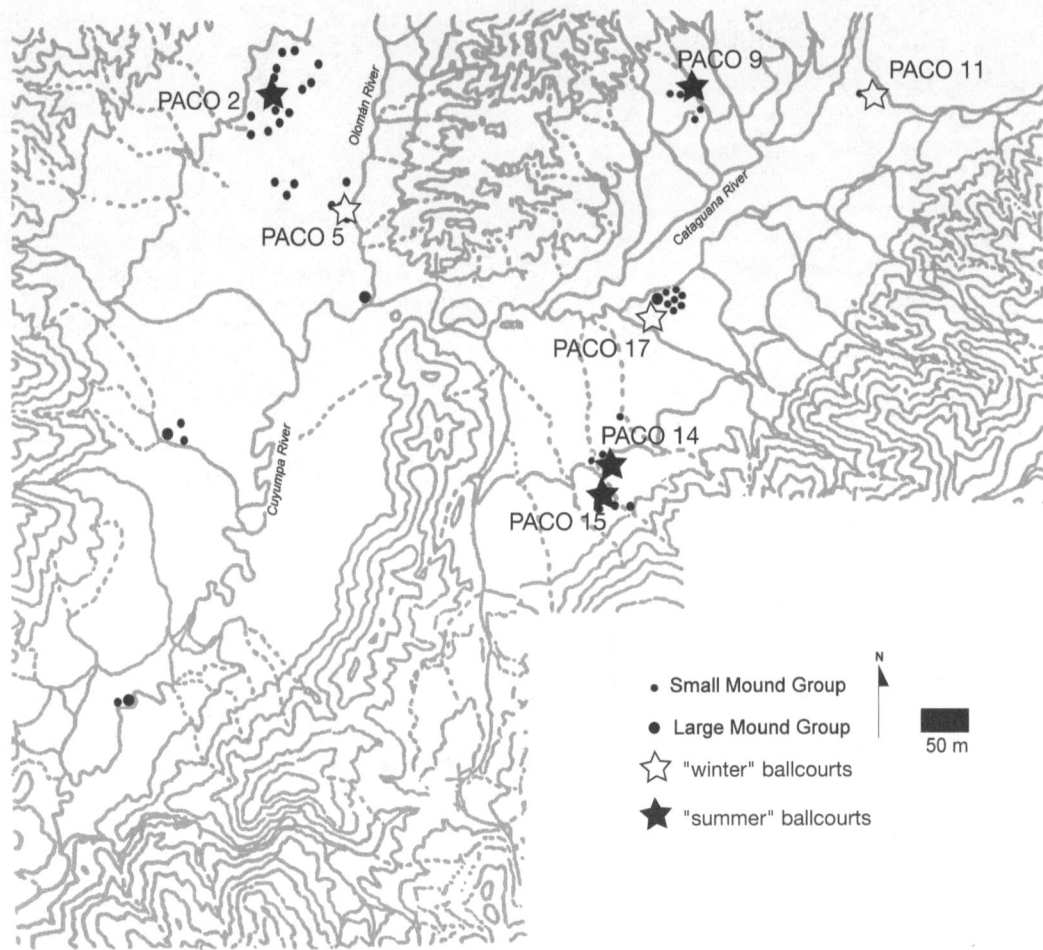

FIGURE 4.7. Distribution of sites in the Oloman and Cataguana valleys on the Río Cuyumapa showing locations of winter and summer ballcourts. Courtesy of Rosemary A. Joyce and Julia A. Hendon.

places in process, both summer and winter ballcourts would have been sites where different groups emerged through the identification of people with each other as team members and supporters.

The kinds of places formed at these localities were the product of specific and probably shifting groups of people; at different points in the year, these localities would have been very different kinds of places. The summer ballcourts, with their less formal architectural settings, may have been important as everyday points of reference for people residing in the area. Their open plans would have allowed them to be used for informal games by local children learning how to play and for practice by teams planning to compete in games held there or elsewhere. Although the length of ballcourt alleys varied widely, most were about the same width, which may have allowed participants who practiced in summer ballcourts to hone skills to use when they entered winter ballcourts.

On the occasions when summer ballcourts were the sites of formal competition, they likely attracted larger and more diverse groups of spectators as well as teams of competitors. Among those present would have been the leaders of the rituals, whose traces remain as incense-burning vessels, whether these were elders of locally resident families or individuals with recognized status as ritual specialists. Food and drink would have been prepared and served by some people acting as hosts. Christopher Fung (1995a, 1995b) has identified evidence for more intensive labor investments in tasks including the grinding of food in the residence closest to one summer ballcourt, a likely candidate for the residence of the hosts of such events. It is possible that most of those participating in events hosted at summer ballcourts lived not far from these places.

Winter ballcourts, attached to major plazas with multiple large-scale structures and located on the main rivers, may have witnessed larger and more diverse groups of participants. Some of those attending might have come from areas where a local summer ballcourt was available and thus may have had ideas about what to expect. Others in attendance may have come from farther afield, from sites in the Lower Ulúa Valley or other neighboring areas from which we have identified imported pottery. Their expectations about events at ballcourts would rest on their own local experiences, which may well have been different from those of local residents. The experiences created by the mix of people drawn from the wider Cuyumapa region, or even beyond, would potentially have made these sites more cosmopolitan places when they were in use.

When they were not the focus of active crowds of players, dancers, gamblers, cooks and servers, and feasting guests, winter ballcourts may have been sites of greater inactivity than summer ballcourts ever witnessed. Summer ballcourts are located in the midst of small residential groups, and the pulse of life around them would never have been still. Winter ballcourts tend to be peripheral to centers of population. Attached to enclosed plazas, they would have been more easily subject to controlled access. Groups of children who did wander into a winter ballcourt thinking to practice their skills would have faced a longer, perhaps more daunting, alley framed by more substantial architecture, including cut-stone sculpture.

As lived spaces, ballcourts cannot be understood by considering only their plans, however much we might intuit from their size, shape, and orientation. They were given their specific character by the actions of those who lived around and traveled to them. They simultaneously shaped multiple landscapes for participants with different historical relations to them. Ballcourts were multilocal (Rodman 1992), multiple landscapes for participants with different historical relations to them, different places formed by the same features. From the point of view of hosts and local performers, they were all central places in landscapes. They also were central places for local guests. But local hosts and guests agreeing in viewing these as central places would still constitute the same locality as two subtly different places. For those hosting or performing, the place was a center from which renown would travel outward. For local guests, the same place was a site for gathering in a dispersed network of social relations. Insofar as performers and hosts were from the same local area, the ballcourts they shared would be heterotopias (Foucault 1986), simultaneously a point of ingathering for networks of social allies and the point of a vector aimed outward, perhaps in specific directions.

The very same places seen as central by local participants were experienced very differently by visitors from farther away. For such nonlocal visitors, traveling to a distant locality for a specific event, these places may have been sites on the edge of geographic knowledge, peripheries reached by leaving home behind, at the very least, points on a journey. This effect, while somewhat independent of actual distance, may have been especially salient for those who came from places where ballcourts were always oriented north–south, such as the Lower Ulúa Valley, or where ballcourts were not used, such as neighboring regions to the south and northeast. Not just distant or peripheral, the ballcourts to which they traveled were uncanny places for such visitors. Yet, at the same time, for visitors who came to perform as players or dancers, these places occupied the same position as they did for local performers, as centers of reputation projected outward.

As their likely seasonal use reminds us, these ballcourts were also places produced in time. Experientially, during the lifetime of people who participated in events at these places, the nature of participation would change—and hence the character of the place. Young children might be carried to the ballcourts, viewing events there before being able to understand them. Older children might practice their ball playing and dancing in preparation for events where they were able to participate. Over the course of a life, the overlay of repeated experiences would form a background of expectations that became part of the fabric of the place for each participant. Idiosyncratic associations, although for the most part inaccessible to us today, would have been part of this process, as participants remembered not just games in general but the game they won, not dances in general but the dance where they shone.

These ballcourts were different places throughout the year and throughout the sequences of events orchestrated when they were formally in use. If our understandings of ballcourt symbolism and use are accurate, when ritual specialists were burning incense as part of formal sequences of events, ballcourts became points of connection with supernatural realms and the beings that inhabited them, openings on the vertical axis leading to the underworld and upperworld, perhaps most important including solar beings. When players were engaged in a game in the alley, these became central stages, arenas surrounded by spectators visually focused on the action taking place but also taking part in a swirl of peripheral wagering and side conversations. When the games ended and the dancing began, perhaps winding through the alley, perhaps taking advantage of the terraces and plazas around the ballcourts, the ballcourts became part of the background for people eating, drinking, playing music and singing, dancing, and engaging in all the other activities that marked such celebrations.

Ballcourts also had longer-term histories, obscured by the practice of renovation in place that itself was part of the process that produced the memory of their histories. In the Cuyumapa River Valley, the unique case of the ballcourts at PACO 14 and 15 gives us more of a sense of such history. These two ballcourts are built within a few hundred meters of each other on the slopes along the same small stream, the Quebrada Camalote. PACO 15 is closer to the level terrain of the valley floor. Here, excavations confirmed early construction and use, from the end of the Middle Formative into the Early Classic (Fox 1994). Following that, despite evidence from nearby residences of continued occupation, the ballcourt seems to have been left intact and unaltered but also accumulated no new evidence of use. Instead, a new ballcourt was built uphill at PACO 14. Cached vessels in this ballcourt date to the end of the Late Classic or the Terminal Classic, making its latest use contemporary with other known ballcourts and with the latest residential occupation along the Quebrada Camalote. These two ballcourts are almost exactly the same size. Where they differ is in precise orientation. Although both are oriented east of north, the later ballcourt is 20° different in orientation and comes closest to the actual orientation of the summer solstice sunrise. It is tempting to think that perhaps the builders here adjusted the orientation to better match such a cosmological template. But these two ballcourts also are oriented along sloping terrain, and it is quite likely that the microlocal context led to the adjustment of orientation. With the size of the ballcourt alley allowing the people of the region to continue to practice ballgames in the same way as they had for centuries, the creation of the uphill ballcourt while the original ballcourt was maintained downhill explicitly made this a locale where ballgames could be seen to have a history.

Implications: Moving Through the Honduran Landscape

Margaret Rodman reminds us that "for each inhabitant, a place has a unique reality, one in which meaning is shared with other people and places. *The links in these chains of experienced places are forged of culture and history*" (1992:644). Archaeologists are in an extraordinary position to trace such chains, through the residues of the repetition of actions in specific locations and the relations of identity and distinctions between places in their fixed and mobile features. To do so unavoidably involves engagement with what Rodman calls multilocality, the multiplicity of places that exist in the same location due to the distinctions among the human actors who occupy them and through occupying, give them form. While daunting, the goal of representing multilocality is not an impossible one to address. Following Ingold (1993:162), we have tried to shift from thinking of landscape as purely visual to understanding it as the product of movement. That leads us to begin to see difference where a map without motion persuades us to imagine identity.

In the Lower Ulúa Valley, we can now see the map at the macroscale of site and region as a product of movement in a particular direction, not simply of a visual orientation. Our exploration of the specificities of the ballcourts along the Río Cuyumapa extends this understanding from the scale of the individual building to the macroregion linking the ballcourts in this area to those downstream in the Lower Ulúa Valley. What joins these places together is not merely the cartographic grid: it is the actual movement of people through the landscape. That movement is shaped by the "previously sedimented array of cultural and social practices" in the places the moving body traverses (Pred 1984:285). But as Pred (1984:282) argues, the actual paths that lead people through places and the specific projects they engage in are always open-ended; this *way* of viewing place is universally applicable, but specific applications will always be historically contingent.

Ballcourts, sites of formally patterned rhythmic movement, make it impossible to avoid thinking about movement as central to the making of place. In a much debated contribution to thinking about place, Michel de Certeau (1984:115–130) describes the movement of human subjects as producing experiences of space and associating them with histories, as taking the map and through practice giving it a specific reality. In his formulation, "The street geometrically defined by urban planners is transformed into a space [*espace*] by walkers" (de Certeau 1984:117). To account for such actively constituted locales requires taking account of "vectors of direction, velocities, and time variables" because espace is "composed of intersections of mobile elements...actuated by the ensemble of movements deployed within it"; it is "the effect produced by the operations that orient it, situate it, temporalize it, and make it function in a polyvalent unity of conflictual programs or contractual proximities" (de Certeau 1984:117). While critiqued for adopting an overly textual approach to the activation of espace and dwelling too much on the individual and antistructural aspects of spatial practice, de Certeau's argument is productive for an understanding of the social nature of the body practices employed by the moving subject who makes place, practices simultaneously patterned and unique (Morris 2004).

It is no accident that the places that coordinated different paths, and through that coordination facilitated the large-scale projects that produced the patterns we can map at regional scales in Honduras, were places where formal movement was sedimented in the landscape. Beyond their cosmological meanings, and the political, social, economic, and ritual functions they may have had, the ballcourts built by residents of farming hamlets and towns in the Lower Ulúa and Cuyumapa river valleys made places in the past as much as they make places for us today. But to understand the effects of these acts of place making, we have to reinstate them as places in motion. We need to see orientations as vectors along which not only vision but sound, movement, and other sensory experience moved: As processions moved along the stone walkways at Cerro Palenque, or through ballcourts at any of the sites we discussed, how far did the noise spread? Where did the smoke from the burning incense reach? We need to put the places we model into action at multiple scales, not only spatial but temporal. We need to consider whether some places were "moving faster" than others: What difference is there between a place that develops over one or two generations, as Cerro Palenque's main plaza did, and one where place is a product of centuries, as at Copán? We need to do this because the mere fact of buildings being laid out or built does not explain how the construction and use of buildings in general or in specific instances mobilized people into action, making them part of larger social groups undertaking the projects that shaped particular places as villages, towns, and cities.

Our discussion has followed the suggestion that places will likely be best represented by a combination of objective and subjective analyses, a narrative synthesis of map and experience. Places are more than the patterns we can see in two dimensions. They must be understood as in process in time. Even places that are very formally planned and that suggest coordination may be experienced quite differently through time and as they become the centers of Ingold's (1993) "taskscapes," the lived rhythms of peoples' lives. Taking the map as a place to begin, we can arrive at the identification of some of the principles that may have governed the making of place by differently situated actors who inhabited the buildings, remade them, and passed on to their successors traditions of building and being in place at a particular location, occupied as a series of locales, each with its own senses of place.

Acknowledgments

This chapter draws on data from a project in the Cuyumapa Valley codirected by Joyce and Hendon, independent projects by each at Cerro Palenque in the 1980s (Joyce) and 2000s (Hendon), and a separate field project initiated and directed by Lopiparo in the central Ulúa Valley. These projects were undertaken with the permission and support of the Instituto Hondureño de Antropología e Historia. We wish to particularly acknowledge the support of Lic. Carmen Julia Fajardo and the late George Hasemann, former Jefes de Arqueología; the late Lic. Juan Alberto Durón, Jefe Regional del Norte; and institute representatives and workers on our projects, without whom there would be no data to discuss. Funding for these projects was provided by grants from the National Science Foundation, the Wenner-Gren Foundation for Anthropological Research, Harvard University, and the University of California, Berkeley. We would like to dedicate this work to the memory of the late Allan Pred, an inspirational and generous colleague and teacher.

5

Mountains, Mounds, and Meaning

Metaphor in the Hohokam Cultural Landscape

Stephanie M. Whittlesey

The concept of cultural landscapes is a potent paradigm for understanding the relationships between people and their natural and social environments. The study of cultural landscapes embraces the cognitively constituted processes by which people assign meaning to the environment, turning spaces into places. As such, it can be defined as a holistic anthropology of place (Whittlesey 2003). Although it has tremendous potential, the cultural-landscapes approach has been little used in the U.S. Southwest, particularly in archaeological studies. This may stem from contemporary archaeology's positivist and materialist bias, which tends to shy away from models based on cognition, perception, and belief. Regardless, the universality of the cultural landscape in past and contemporary societies indicates that it probably is a uniquely human approach to the land and its resources, the culmination of our evolutionary heritage. The relationships among humans and their physical, biological, and social environments play a key role in adaptation and perhaps in evolution. As Flores has expressed it, "Diversity in human culture just may be almost as important to adaptation and evolution on earth as we have long believed ecological diversity to be" (1998:36). If we are to model human–environment relationships with any validity, archaeologists must come to terms with cultural landscapes.

Because they are created through culture, cognition, perception, and language, cultural landscapes reflect and symbolize ideology, values, and ethics. "Ideology takes social relations and makes them appear to be resident in nature or history, which makes them apparently inevitable," Leone (1984:26) has observed. Landscape also reflects social organization and political order. Public spaces often are rich in symbols and images that remind people of their civic duties and responsibilities (Jackson 1984; Mrozowski and Beaudry 1990:189). Because of the embedded character of landscape and culture, the cultural landscapes of the past are a rich source of information about concepts and phenomena that are inherently difficult for archaeologists to construe, such as ideology.

This essay explores the ideological dimension of an ancient cultural landscape created by the Hohokam of central and southern Arizona. It examines a significant landscape feature, the mountain, as a cultural metaphor. Central to cosmology, iconography, and the built environment, the mountain metaphor was replicated in many aspects of Hohokam life. It illustrates well the intertwining of the sacred and the everyday in Hohokam culture.

After summarizing the approach to cultural landscapes used in this analysis and the role of conceptual metaphors in archaeological studies, the essay introduces the Hohokam culture, the natural environment, and the important Hohokam site of Snaketown. Next, the essay considers the mountain metaphor in Mesoamerican religious life and parallel concepts in Hohokam iconography, the built environment, and the sacred landscape. The significance of natural landscape features in creating Hohokam central places is underscored. The chapter concludes with a discussion of the need to consider cultural landscapes as a unitary whole.

Cultural Landscapes

Although its origins are decades old, stemming from the seminal notions of cultural geographers such as Carl Sauer (1925) and John B. Jackson (1984), only recently has the cultural-landscapes approach enjoyed a renaissance in archaeology (Anschuetz 1996; Anschuetz and Scheick 1998; Ashmore and Knapp 1999; Bender 1993; Cosgrove and Daniels 1988; Ezzo and Altschul 1993; Fairley 2003; Hirsch and O'Hanlon 1995; Knapp and Ashmore 1999; McClelland 1991; McClelland et al. n.d.; Stoffle et al. 1997; Whittlesey 2003; Whittlesey et al. 1998; Yamin and Metheny 1996; Zedeño 1997; Zedeño et al. 1997; Zedeño et al. 1999). Because it builds upon the basic ecological theory and the interdisciplinary environmental studies that have guided archaeology since its inception, the concept is eminently suited to archaeological investigations.

The principle underlying the cultural-landscapes approach is simple but powerful: human beings do not passively "adapt" to their physical, natural, and social environments. Rather, people actively shape these environments through perception, cognition, and behavior. The cultural landscape is simultaneously the product of nature and human interactions with nature, and therefore it is a seamless blending of nature and culture. According to Knapp and Ashmore, "Landscape is an entity that exists by virtue of its being perceived, experienced, and contextualized by people" (1999:1). As Jackson has written, a landscape "is a space or a collection of spaces made by a group of people who modify the natural environment to survive, to create order, and to produce a just and lasting society" (1995:43).

Landscape is a word with multiple meanings, as a number of authors have pointed out (e.g., Stoddart 2000; Thomas 2001). The cultural-landscape approach used here differs from other applications. In anthropology, landscape often is used as a metaphor to categorize social, political, and ideological relationships (e.g., Bender 1993; Low and Lawrence-Zúñiga 2003). Cultural geography, historical architecture, and landscape architecture employ other versions of landscape, expressed well in John B. Jackson's numerous influential works. Archaeologists often use landscape as a framework to approach ancient human–environment relationships on a regional scale, employing geographic information systems, geoarchaeology, and multidisciplinary environmental studies to model settlement patterns (e.g., Rossignol and Wandsnider 1992; Stoddart 2000).

By contrast, the view of cultural landscapes used in this essay emphasizes that cultural landscapes not only are created by people but largely are created by the evanescent characteristics of *culture*. Landscape does not mean only topography and environment or passive adaptation to the environment. Greider and Garkovich provide a useful definition of cultural landscapes as

> the symbolic environments created by human acts of conferring meaning to nature and the environment, of giving the environment definition and form from a particular angle of vision and through a special filter of values and beliefs. Every landscape is a symbolic environment. These landscapes reflect our self-definitions that are grounded in culture [1994:1].

The ways in which people perceive places and conceptualize their environments are learned and transmitted via culture and language. By naming and identifying topographic and biological features, people establish and maintain their identities. In a fundamental way, names create landscapes (Basso 1996; Tilley 1994). Therefore, a cultural landscape can be defined as a cognized environment that has been created by cultural perceptions (Whittlesey 2003). Perceptions determine how we interact with the environment, how we exploit and preserve it, and the ways in which we shape it and in turn are shaped by it.

The building blocks of the cultural landscape are the physical, biological, and social environments; human beings and their culture; and the interactions that take place between people and environments (Whittlesey 2003). The features of the physical, biological, and social environments, hereafter abbreviated as "the environment," provide the raw materials for building a cultural landscape. The environment provides the range of opportunities, or what Rapoport (1989:78) calls environmental qualities—attributes that can be seen as desirable or undesirable, as advantages or constraints. Social organization, culture, and cognitive processes take these materials and delimit the almost limitless possibilities the environment offers into a uniquely cultural construction.

Humans construct a modified environment that in turn shapes us. Human–environment interactions are neither passive nor unidirectional. Moreover, not all of the modifications resulting from interactions are beneficial or benign; some activities have unintended, harmful consequences. Some affect the ability of the environment to sustain its human inhabitants, forcing behavioral change or perhaps requiring people to abandon settlements and regions. As Gussow has expressed it, "Landscape is more than a passive backdrop to human events—it is a stage on which we move. The objects and forms on that stage shape our actions, guide our choices, restrict or enhance our freedom, and in mysterious ways even predict our future" (1995:225). Cultural landscapes therefore are dynamic, constituting multiple times and multiple places and embodying change and transformation as well as continuity and sequence (Knapp and Ashmore 1999:18). Landscape must not be seen as a static phenomenon but as a series of moments or perspectives, recognized most accurately as a process (Hirsch 1995:23).

Most importantly, the cultural-landscapes approach does not separate the natural and human worlds. Early conceptions of cultural landscape (e.g., Sauer 1925) defined cultural and natural landscapes as different things. Later scholars, including Jackson (1984), have made it clear that the dichotomy is false. Landscape is a *unity* of people and environment; humans are a part of nature, not apart from it (Flores 1998:36; Thompson 1995). The concept of cultural landscapes investigates what Yi-Fu Tuan has called the "interconnectedness of the natural and humanly constructed worlds" (quoted in Thompson 1995:xi).

We can study cultural landscapes within a convenient heuristic framework of landscape dimensions (Whittlesey 1998a, 2003). The *cognitive dimension* describes the ways in which people view the environment and model their interactions with it. How we perceive the environment determines how we interact with it and ultimately how we treat it. "In interacting with their physical environment," Crumley and Marquardt write, "people...make decisions and expend energy according to their own mental models of how the world operates" (1990:73).

The *formal dimension* refers to physical characteristics and properties—the tangible modifications and changes to the environment that humans create during their interactions. Landscape can be defined as "the material manifestation of the relations between humans and the environment" (Crumley 1994:6). In the process of living with the land, in their daily activities required for survival, people use the environment, build things upon it, and modify it in numerous ways. This principle ensures that cultural landscapes have a concrete, material aspect that enables archaeologists to investigate them. As van Dommelen points out, "Landscape always retains its materiality and omnipresence, no matter how embedded or interwoven it is in other domains" (1999:284). Because of this, landscape "can be understood as material culture" (van Dommelen 1999:284; see also Jackson 1984).

The *historical dimension* focuses on the life histories of cultural landscapes that embed layers of human activities in the land. The landscape is both medium for and outcome of action and previous histories of action (Tilley 1994:23). Schama (1995) has suggested that landscape is memory, fixing social and individual histories in space. Reinforcing the materiality of landscape, Inglis reminds us that landscape is "the most solid appearance in which a history can declare itself" (1977:489). The archaeological record is the outcome of human–environment interactions over time; in this sense, it is a layered record of the cultural landscapes of the past. The history of human–environment interactions also can be read in the environmental history of any place where humans have lived or worked.

The *relational dimension* focuses on organization, linking humans and the environment at a variety of scales. These connections may be behavioral, social, or symbolic, and they may or may not leave physical traces. The organization and scheduling of activities in space are relational aspects of cultural landscapes with which archaeologists are familiar and are central to settlement pattern studies (Thomas 1973, 1974, 1981). The relational dimension can be accessed through spatial analyses of sites, trails, nonsite phenomena, isolated artifacts, line-of-sight connections, signaling locations, and other archaeological data (Stoffle et al. 2000; Thomas 1993; Tilley 1993). Such analyses can assist in identifying important landmarks that may have no human modifications.

The *ideological dimension* incorporates the ways in which people assign meaning to their environment and their interactions with it. Rapoport (1990:42) underscores that people shape and interact with their environment through meaning, and this principle holds over time and among cultures the world over. Postmodern perspectives visualize landscapes as cultural images, the verbal or written representations of which provide texts of meaning (Daniels and Cosgrove 1988; Head 1993; Knapp and Ashmore 1999). To access meaning, we read the material images apparent in the formal dimension.

Anschuetz and Scheick provide a concise and elegant definition of landscape that illustrates the interaction of landscape dimensions, which I have added to this quotation:

> Through their daily activities, beliefs and values [the cognitive dimension], communities transform their physical surroundings into meaningful places based on particular patterns of morphology and arrangement [formal dimension]; through their physical modifications [formal dimension], the intimacies of their experiences and the sharing of their memories [relational dimension and historical dimension], they reshape the natural settings contained within their geographical spaces to legitimize the meanings bestowed upon the landscape [ideological dimension] [1998:5].

The Role of Metaphor

A brief comment about metaphor and the role it plays in cultural-landscapes studies is in order. In Mesoamerica and among the Hohokam, the mountain represents a conceptual metaphor, which enables one thing to be understood and experienced in terms of another (Ortman 2000:614). Basso (1990:55) explains that metaphors appear to violate linguistic roles in presenting an expression that is either patently false or conceptually absurd (Carnap 1955:47). A metaphor asserts that one thing is something else (Percy 1958:81). Metaphors therefore hold the ability to surprise us, to structure the perceptions of individuals in unanticipated ways, and to make them see associations they have never before beheld (Basso 1990:58). Moreover, as cultural symbols, metaphors impose order and meaning on "that elusive entity sometimes known as the 'real world'" (Basso 1990:58).

Although expressed most commonly in language, metaphors are revealed in the structure of ritual; events in sacred narratives; and the production, form, and use of artifacts (Ortman 2000:614). Ortman (2000), Ortman and Bradley (2002), and Tilley (1999) have argued convincingly that metaphors are encoded in material remains. Ortman (2000:614) makes the important point that metaphor is a matter of thought as well as poetic language. Thought precedes and shapes language as it does other forms of communication. Conceptual metaphors "form the foundations of cultural understandings, and are created and transmitted among beings with fundamentally poetic minds" (Ortman 2000:614).

Metaphor therefore plays as important a role in cultural landscapes as it does in language (Basso 1990:53). As cultural texts, landscape metaphors can be read; like other elements of the cultural landscape, they provide a reservoir of information about ideology and cosmology, including those aspects of style and aesthetics in the built environment that Reese-Taylor and Koontz (2001) label cultural poetics. In addition, if conceptual metaphor is a common denominator underlying language and material culture (Ortman 2000:640), inferring ancient metaphors from cultural landscapes and the built environment may allow us to trace historical continuities among linguistic, ethnic, and cultural groups.

For example, building on Tewa language constructs and cultural concepts, Ortman and Bradley (2002:74–75) argue that the ancestral Puebloan village of Sand Canyon Pueblo expressed a container metaphor. The canyon-rim village was built in a natural enclosure, and its construction mirrored larger regional conceptions of community. The village served as a setting for ritual performances, communal feasts, and shared food storage. Sand Canyon Pueblo was, literally and figuratively, the center place of the local community.

In the Mesoamerican and Hohokam worlds, mounds symbolized the natural landscape features of mountains and volcanoes. By extending and reinforcing powerful natural metaphors, these constructions become metaphors in and of themselves (Ortman 2000; Tilley 1999:76). As the following introduction to Hohokam culture and environment suggests, the mountain itself was a metaphor: it was viewed as a container of water.

The Hohokam and the Site of Snaketown

The Hohokam occupied the river valleys and foothills of central and southern Arizona between about AD 800 and 1150. Archaeologists have long debated the origin of the Hohokam, their relationship to preceding and succeeding peoples, and the chronology of their culture history (Dean 1991; Di Peso 1956; Haury 1950, 1976; Schiffer 1982). Many archaeologists agree that the Hohokam immigrated from a homeland somewhere in northern or west-coastal Mexico and represent what might be labeled a northern-frontier Mesoamerican society (Gumerman and Haury 1979; Haury 1976; Kelley 1966; Meighan 1999; Preucel 1996; Wallace et al. 1995; Whittlesey 2003). Although the topic remains controversial, some archaeologists also restrict the notion of the Hohokam to the time during which the ballcourt ceremonial complex centered their cultural system—the time labeled the pre-Classic period in Hohokam time-space systematics (Reid and Whittlesey 1997). The changes that took place at the beginning of the Classic period, around AD 1150 or 1200, were pervasive and extensive (e.g., Haury 1945). Whatever the cause, Hohokam culture was transformed. This chapter restricts discussion to the Hohokam pre-Classic period.

A consensus is emerging that what archaeologists recognize as Hohokam was a medley of processes and phenomena, rather than a discrete ethnic entity or a regional system, as Wilcox (1979) has labeled it (Whittlesey 1998b). The ballcourt complex, a ceremonial system of probable Mesoamerican origin, may have represented a cult to which people of diverse ethnicities and cultural affiliations belonged, much like the Southern Cult of the U.S. Southeast (Waring 1968; Waring and Holder 1968). Those who brought the cult to southern and central Arizona might have been "ethnically" Hohokam. They occupied the Middle Gila River Valley along one of Arizona's most predictable and least destructive rivers.

The natural landscape was at once forbidding and nurturing (Whittlesey 2003). The Hohokam inhabited the Basin and Range physiographic province and the Sonoran Desert ecosystem. Mountain ranges separated deep, alluvial basins through which several important rivers flowed in prehistory, including the Gila, Salt, Santa Cruz, and San Pedro rivers and many secondary streams. The Sonoran Desert is the greatest of North America's desert ecosystems. A desert of remarkable biodiversity (Dimmitt 2000), it is characterized by diverse cactus and leguminous trees, representing a so-called arborescent desert. Rainfall is limited, averaging less than 10 inches in most of the Phoenix Basin and slightly more in the Tucson Basin. Precipitation is biseasonal, falling in thunderous summer storms and gentle winter rains. The Sonoran Desert is hot as well as arid, with an extreme temperature range, low humidity in most seasons, and high evaporation rates. The number of sunny days and frost-free days created a long growing season, perhaps enabling two crops to be harvested. The Hohokam solved the desert's problem of aridity with innovative water-conveyance and -conservation systems (Fish 1995) and water-conserving cultigens and semicultivated plants, such as agave.

The Hohokam made their living by an inventive combination of irrigation agriculture, floodwater farming, and exploitation of the desert's more fruitful wild plant resources, such as cactus and mesquite (Fish 1995; Fish and Nabhan 1991; Gasser and Kwiatkowski 1991). Maize, several varieties of beans, cotton, and tobacco were cultivated; agave, little barley, and amaranth were semicultivated staples, along with a variety of weedy species that inhabited fields. Hohokam canal systems, built entirely by hand without metal tools or draft animals, were sophisticated engineering constructions that often were refurbished and used by Arizona's historical-period farmers (Ackerly et al. 1987; Breternitz 1991; Dart 1989; Doyel 1991; Nials et al. 1989).

The Hohokam built settlements composed of pit structures arranged in clusters sharing outdoor space, called courtyard groups (Howard 1985). Larger settlements contained outdoor communal areas or plazas and exhibited an organizational structure based on directional orientation and concentric placement of dwellings around communal features (Gladwin et al. 1937; Haury 1976; Wilcox et al. 1981).

Ballcourts—oval, earthen constructions typically oriented north–south or east–west—marked the locations of important villages (Wilcox and Sternberg 1983). Although their precise function is debated, most archaeologists agree that the Hohokam played a version of the Mesoamerican ballgame in these enclosures. As well as serving as theaters for enacting important myths, celebrating celestial events, and coordinating the agricultural calendar (Wilcox 1991), ballcourts may have played a role in the control and distribution of irrigation water, much like the Balinese water temples described by Lansing (1991; Whittlesey 1998b).

The Hohokam prepared their dead for the afterlife with a complex, protracted ritual involving cremation of the deceased, personal belongings, and offerings. The ritual involved multiple steps and may have included postcremation working of the remains, curation, and burial of separate skeletal elements in a manner suggestive of ancestor veneration (Haury 1976). Ritual destruction of offerings accompanied burial events (Haury 1976). Dwellings and their contents, including food remains, often were burned, either as part of the mortuary rite (Huntington 1986) or as a separate rite of purification and termination.

Hohokam artwork was highly distinctive, unlike that produced by contemporaneous prehistoric cultures of the U.S. Southwest. Pottery included red-painted buff ware and shiny, schist-tempered plain ware, the latter used for domestic purposes. Pottery containers, particularly painted ware, were made in exotic shapes that included tripod vessels, bowls with widely flaring rims, effigy vessels, and censers. Painted pottery was decorated with life-forms (see Haury 1965, 1976) or repeated, small elements and geometric patterns resembling basketry or textiles. Stonework and shell ornaments were shaped in or carved with lifelike zoomorphic and anthropomorphic figures. Similar images characterized Hohokam rock art (Bostwick 2002; Wallace and Holmlund 1986). The shell-manufacturing industry was strongly developed; marine shell from the Gulf of California was worked in specialist communities and distributed widely (Howard 1993; Marmaduke and Martynec 1993).

An innovative approach to farming the desert, a mixed subsistence strategy, and an outstanding ability to make the stark and thorny desert bring forth crops allowed the Hohokam to expand into many different regions in central and southern Arizona. Colonies of Hohokam with close ties to the Phoenix Basin were established in the Tonto Basin and other locales in central Arizona (Haury 1932; Stark et al. 1995; Vanderpot et al. 1994; Weed and Ward 1970). One of the most distinctive regional expressions of Hohokam culture was located in the Tucson Basin, where floodwater irrigation was emphasized and a local ceramic tradition developed (Doelle and Wallace 1991). Indigenous groups participated in the Hohokam ballcourt–cremation ceremonial complex, which spread throughout southeastern Arizona, through central Arizona, and as far north as Flagstaff (Wilcox 1991; Whittlesey 1998b).

Hohokam culture has been investigated with an overarching empiricist and materialist framework that has emphasized environmental adaptation and has often adopted a rather deterministic stance. There has been little room for cultural landscapes in this framework. Significant synthetic works (e.g., Gumerman 1991) have emphasized the desert as context and the role of the environment in determining the shape of Hohokam culture. This theoretical framework has been so overwhelmingly dominant that all archaeological cultures found in the Sonoran Desert typically have been labeled Hohokam, regardless of other material and economic characteristics.

Perhaps the single most important Hohokam site is Snaketown, located in the middle Gila River Valley on the Gila River Indian Community south of metropolitan Phoenix and a few kilometers downstream of the community of Sacaton, Arizona. It was excavated by two different expeditions separated by three decades. In 1934–1935, archaeologists of the Gila Pueblo Archaeological Foundation, a private institution headed by Harold S. Gladwin (Reid and Whittlesey 1997), were the first to investigate Snaketown. The site was selected after a series of wide-ranging surveys in search of the limits of the Red-on-Buff culture, as it was called at that time for its characteristic pottery. Snaketown lay in the center of the regional distribution of red-on-buff ceramics, had not been vandalized, and was enormous, covering more than a square mile in extent. Clearly its research potential was great. The Akimel O'odham (Pima) people who lived nearby called the site by a Pima term meaning "The Place of the Snakes" or "Many Rattlesnakes" (Russell 1908:23), hence its English name. The Gila Pueblo work resulted in a major descriptive monograph (Gladwin et al. 1937) that became a landmark in southwestern archaeology and was the standard by which the Hohokam were known for decades. The work establishes the Hohokam ceramic sequence and chronology and describes architecture, mortuary practices, and material culture (Reid and Whittlesey 1997).

Emil W. Haury directed the 1934–1935 fieldwork and was the primary author of the 1937 monograph. In 1964 and 1965, he returned to Snaketown to revisit the site under the auspices of the National Science Foundation. His avowed purpose was to address critiques that had been leveled at the original Snaketown research by garnering fresh, new data. This work resulted in a second major monograph (Haury 1976) that verifies the original cultural-historical sequence and provides additional descriptive information.

The Hohokam chronology has long been (and continues to be) a controversial and much-debated topic. Ceramic information and stratigraphy indicate that Snaketown was occupied from the Pioneer period through the Sedentary period, or throughout the entire pre-Classic cultural sequence. Current information dates these periods between about AD 300 and 1150 (Dean 1991). The first expedition located 173 pit structures, of which 40 were excavated; the second expedition identified 165 pre-Classic pit structures (Wilcox et al. 1981:115). There were 60 mounds, numerous extramural features, wells, cemeteries, and crematories where the deceased were prepared for the afterlife.

Site structure and inferred population changed greatly during Snaketown's occupation (Haury 1976; Wilcox et al. 1981). Wilcox et al. (1981:145–146) suggest that trash mounds first appeared during the Snaketown phase (there is no way to know if these were deliberate constructions or gradual accumulations) and that the large ballcourt was built during the Gila Butte phase. The number of houses and inferred population grew gradually from the Pioneer through the Colonial periods but increased sixfold during the Sacaton phase, the time of greatest population density (Wilcox et al. 1981:195).

Regardless of how archaeologists view Snaketown, it remains the largest Hohokam site excavated to date, and its site structure, which appears to be cosmologically oriented, its numerous ceremonial features, and its many cemeteries and crematories suggest that Snaketown may have been a focal point of Hohokam religious life as well as a densely populated residential settlement. As Wilcox et al. note, "Snaketown must have been regarded as a sacred place" (1981:209). I will explore some of Snaketown's more unusual features in subsequent sections.

The Mountain Metaphor: A Cultural-Landscapes Approach

To understand the mountain metaphor in Hohokam culture, it is necessary to comprehend something of Mesoamerican belief and ceremonial systems. Scholars concur that an overarching cultural and belief system stretched from Panama to northern Sonora and Chihuahua, if not farther north (Willey 1973:154). Cosmology, spiritual themes, deities, cults, ritual behaviors, iconography, and symbolism were replicated throughout this vast region. The Mesoamerican religious and ritual complex was sophisticated and extraordinarily complex, the product of centuries of philosophical speculation and ritual practice (Griffith 1992:9). Overarching elements included a cosmos that was divided in vertical and horizontal dimensions and was presided over by a pantheon of deities, many of them representing powerful natural forces, such as wind and rain. A consistent suite of themes structured the spiritual and everyday worlds, including ancestor veneration, purification, sacrifice, death and rebirth, and transformation. The sacred aspects of landscape symbolized these themes and provided a setting in which cosmological events were replicated, the gods were petitioned, and sacrifices to ensure harmony and balance in the cosmos were enacted.

As a people whose probable homeland was in northern or west-coastal Mexico, the Hohokam shared in the pan-Mesoamerican phenomenon that Preucel has labeled "the Mesoamerican worldview" (1996:125). It is likely that many elements of this worldview were transmitted to the U.S. Southwest long before the Hohokam arrived in southern Arizona. A cult devoted to bringing rain may have arrived during the Archaic period along with domesticated plants and cultivation techniques. Regardless, the Hohokam brought with them a distinctive worldview, a set of religious beliefs and practices, and a recognizable iconography that had no previous parallels (Whittlesey 2004).

Perhaps the most important phenomenon in the Mesoamerican and Hohokam worlds was the mountain. It was a central, vital metaphor in the natural world and in the built environment, representing layered cosmological concepts, symbolism of natural forces, and ritual behaviors. It is difficult to find a single entity more powerful or more evocative. The mountain was universally viewed as the generator of clouds and the source of springs, lakes, streams, and rain (Brady and Ashmore 1999:126; Burland and Forman 1975:26; Vogt 1981). Its hollow heart held water as well as maize and other treasure (Brady and Ashmore 1999:126; van Zantwijk 1981). As such, mountains were described metaphorically as containers or vessels in which water was stored (Berlo 1992; Broda 1991:84; Townsend 1992a:181). The mountain therefore symbolized the most vital natural element to an agricultural people heavily invested in maize cultivation and living in an arid land. The mountain was the home of the rain gods, played a crucial role in ceremonies designed to bring rain, and was mimicked in the built environment. As Ortman (2000) has emphasized, the expression of this conceptual metaphor in material culture, ritual structure, and myth (as well as in language) indicates that the mountain metaphor was deeply seated in ancient cognition and thought. Following the convention established by Lakoff and Johnson (1980), we can express the mountain metaphor as A MOUNTAIN IS A CONTAINER OF WATER. I find it intriguing that a similar metaphor characterized Sand Canyon Pueblo—A COMMUNITY IS A CONTAINER—and pottery containers shared numerous perceptual and experiential properties with canyon-rim villages (Ortman and Bradley 2002).

The meaning of the mountain metaphor in Mesoamerican religious beliefs is clear. Because of its connection to rain, the mountain was home to Tlaloc, the ancient rain/storm/earth god. According to Townsend (1992b:114), the name was derived from the Nahuatl world *tlalli*, meaning "earth," and the suffix *oc*, implying "something lying upon the surface." The latter alludes to the familiar sight of clouds collecting around mountain peaks during the rainy season. The cult dedicated to Tlaloc is one of the oldest that can be identified in the iconography of ancient Mexico, appearing by the Late Preclassic period (800–300 BC) in the Puebla-Tlaxcala region (Weaver 1981:106). Tlaloc and his female counterpart and consort, Chalchiuhtlicue, governed the Tlaloque, spirits of mountains and powerful weather phenomena (Miller and Taube 1993:166–167). The Tlaloque were associated with the cardinal directions and dispensed beneficial and destructive moisture.

In considering the role of the mountain metaphor in the Hohokam belief and ceremonial system and their cultural landscape, the dimensions of cultural landscapes presented above are adopted as a framework for discussion.

Cognitive Dimension

Worldview, Tuan has written, "is a people's more or less systematic attempt to make sense of environment" (1977:88). Cosmologies attempt to answer questions of human beings' place in nature, construct order from chaos, and arrange people and nature in harmonious ways. In Mesoamerican cosmology and among the Hohokam as well, vertical space was divided into three segments (the "upperworld" or heaven, the "middleworld" or earth's surface, and the underworld [Cohodas 1975]). Mediation among the upperworld, middleworld, and underworld was a key activity necessary for community survival (Cohodas 1975; Gillespie 1993; Gossen 1986). The mountain played a central role in cosmological structure, representing one of several pathways between the vertical dimensions. Caves and mountains were linked closely; the cave was the entrance to the mountain, and both were connected to the underworld (Townsend 1992a:178). This connection meant that mountains were thought to be the homes and meeting places of the ancestors, who dwelled in watery domains, and therefore linked living communities with the ancestors (Brady and Ashmore 1999:128). Rituals and sacrifices to the ancestors often were conducted in cave and mountain settings. Sacrifice was viewed as an act of paying debts to Tlaloc (Sahagún 1953; Townsend 1992b), and because of the connections among Tlaloc, mountains, and rainfall, ceremonies and sacrifices to Tlaloc were carried out on mountain peaks at the beginning of the rainy season (Schaafsma 1999:167).

Horizontal space was divided into four segments representing the cardinal directions (Preucel 1996:125) and center, the fifth direction. Each direction was associated with specific symbols and colors; deities were expressed in the sacred number of four (Miller and Taube 1993:150). Directional and color symbolism also applied to mountains and mountain deities. The horizontal dimension was connected to the vertical dimension and the solar year. Balance was achieved by rotation of the various directions about the center, the earth's surface (Preucel 1996:125).

Concepts of replication, redundancy, and duality permeated Mesoamerican cosmology (Miller and Taube 1993:30). Dualities—male and female, fire and water, day and night, moon and sun, earth and sky, zenith and nadir, wet and dry—punctuated worldview (Joyce 1991; Miller and Taube 1993:81) and were exemplified in the benevolent and malevolent aspects of many deities. In these pairings, Mesoamerican peoples recognized the essential interdependence of opposites (Markman and Markman 1992:198).

Duality and directional and cosmological symbolism can be seen in the settlement layout of Snaketown. The village was laid out according to the cardinal directions, and its most important ceremonial constructions were placed according to these directions and in multiples of two (Figure 5.1). One small and one large ballcourt were located east and west of the ring of mounds, respectively. The ballcourts were laid out on an east–west axis, with the smaller one expressing the eastern direction and the larger, the western direction. This duality was paralleled by platform mounds, which were laid out on a north–south axis. The larger mounds and most of those capped with caliche expressed the southern direction, most notably the large, caliche-capped Mounds 38 and 39 that were located south of the plaza. Smaller mounds and those built mainly from dirt containing little trash expressed the northern direction and were situated north of the plaza (Wilcox et al. 1981:135–137). Snaketown also had two concentric habitation zones consisting of house clusters, an inner zone and an outer zone (see Figure 5.1).

During the Pioneer and Colonial periods, the orientations of pit structure entryways had a bimodal distribution (east or south); during the Sedentary period, the entryway orientations were divided among the four cardinal directions (Wilcox et al. 1981:162). The alignments of ballcourts and the central modes in domestic architecture orientation matched closely (Wilcox et al. 1981:209). Wilcox et al. (1981:218) point out that multiple dualities can be observed in Snaketown's ceremonial architecture: high/low, large/small, ballcourts/platform mounds, inner/outer.

Snaketown was structured on the central plaza, the center or middle place of the settlement; mounds ringed the plaza, and architectural features were located farther outward in the concentric structure. Overall, this layout could reflect the Mesoamerican quincunx, the equal-armed cross or Greek cross. This symbol represented space and time, unifying the earth and the cosmos, the daily and the calendrical cycles (Hunt 1977:248; McAnany 1995:85; Séjourné 1976). Its center was a fifth point representing the axis mundi or center of rotation. The peculiarly square contour line of the plaza (see Figure 5.1; Wilcox et al. 1981:Figure 30) suggests that the entire settlement represented a square within a circle.

Replication and redundancy—of metaphors, iconographic images, and many other elements—created a multilayered cultural landscape. For example, the structure of the cosmos was repeated in the everyday world, where cosmological concepts were mirrored in numerology, the sacred landscape, art, and ritual performances. This principle can be seen readily in the Hohokam cultural landscape. Natural features with paramount significance were mimicked in the built environment; symbols were repeated in multiple contexts. As we will see, even small fragments of a sacred topographic feature were incorporated in the pastes of ceramic containers.

Richards (1996) has suggested that houses, tombs, and henge monuments in Neolithic

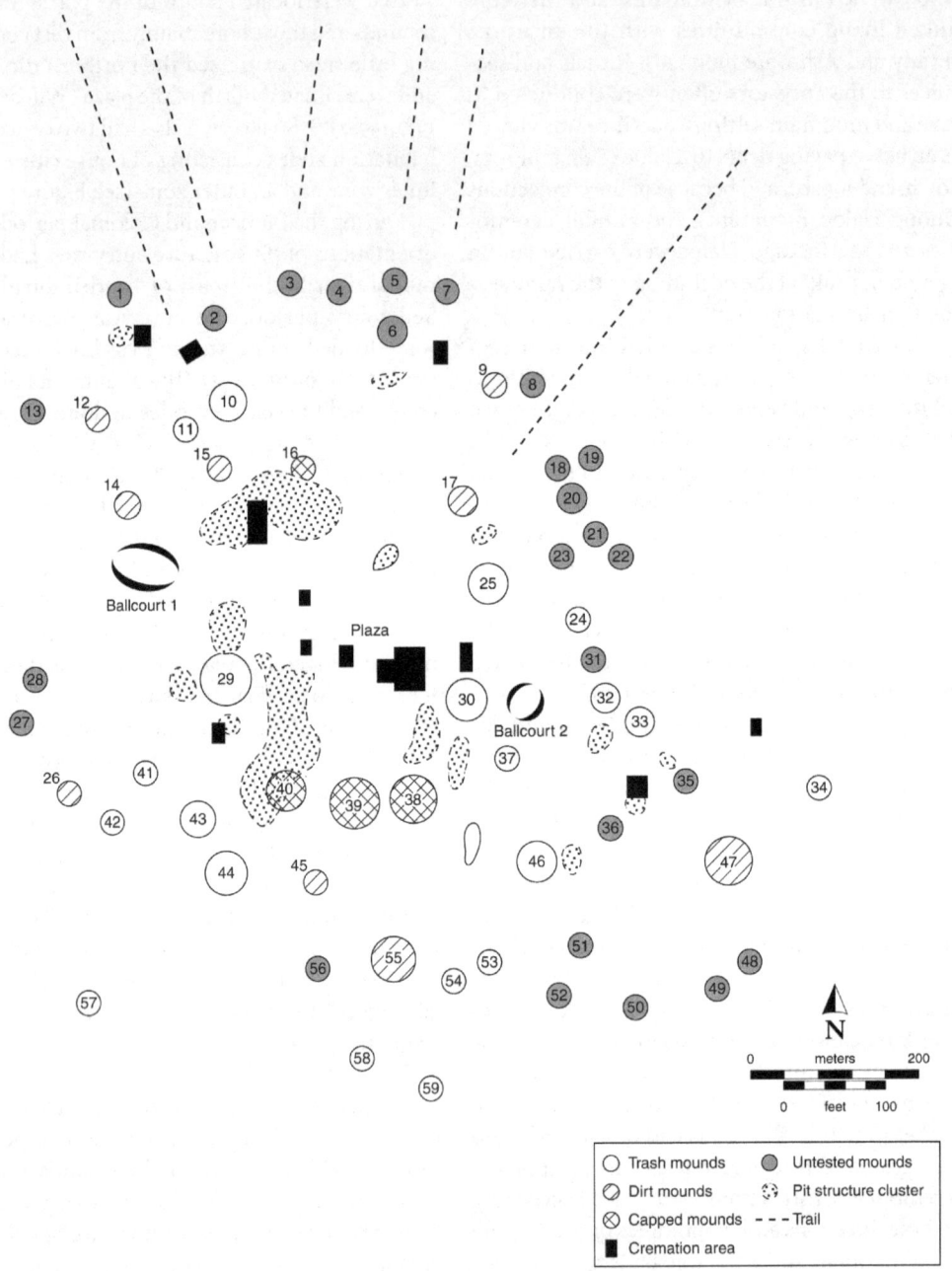

FIGURE 5.1. Schematic map of Snaketown showing the central plaza, various types of mounds, architectural features, cremation areas, and trails. Prepared by Peg Robbins and William Olguin, Statistical Research, Inc., Tucson.

FIGURE 5.2. Gila Butte, view looking north. Photograph by Stephanie M. Whittlesey.

Orkney were aspects of a single cosmological scheme drawing on the natural forms of the land. Frazer (1998) has hypothesized further that the places where megalithic monuments were constructed were marked as sacred before the tombs were built. We can see both principles in operation at Snaketown. The mountain metaphor apparently defined its location and reinforced its central religious and ritual functions. Snaketown was located 5 km (3 mi) from Gila Butte, a topographic eminence also called Double Butte. This feature, standing some 152 m (500 ft) above the Gila River on its north bank, was characterized by twin peaks separated by a low saddle (Figure 5.2). The southern peak also was capped with dual crests. Representing one of the region's outcrops of hard and durable metamorphic stone, Gila Butte forced the river to curve around its base.

Remarkably, Haury (1976:123) has postulated that one diversion point for the major irrigation canal sprang from the foot of Gila Butte (Figure 5.3). This canal watered the ancient fields that were located between the village and the peak (Haury 1976:Figure 8.3). Water—the substance of life—therefore literally flowed from Gila Butte, and the metaphor A MOUNTAIN IS A CONTAINER OF WATER was reinforced on a daily basis for the residents of Snaketown. A common Mesoamerican aesthetic trope, that of Snake Mountain (Schele and Kappelman 2001), holds rather extraordinary similarities to Gila Butte and its irrigation canal. Coatépec, or Snake Mountain, was a central landmark in Aztec creation stories. In their great migration from Aztlan to Tenochtitlán, the Aztecs stopped at Snake Mountain, on which they built a temple to their patron god, Huitzilopochtli. Huitzilopochtli built a ballcourt at the base of the mountain containing a hole or "skull place" from which water flowed. The Aztecs dammed up the hole to create a well of water, forming a lake at the base of Snake Mountain to provide water for cultivation and sustenance (Schele and Kappelman 2001:31). Schele and Kappelman (2001:47) suggest that cultural landscapes modeled upon the ideals of Snake Mountain (and its companion in myth, Sustenance Mountain) can be traced back into the Formative period of Mesoamerica. It would not be surprising to find this trope expressed at Gila Butte and Snaketown.

By virtue of its iconographic connections, the natural landscape feature of Gila Butte was transformed into a metaphor of extraordinary significance to the Hohokam. Gila Butte represented a powerful symbolic combination of duality, the

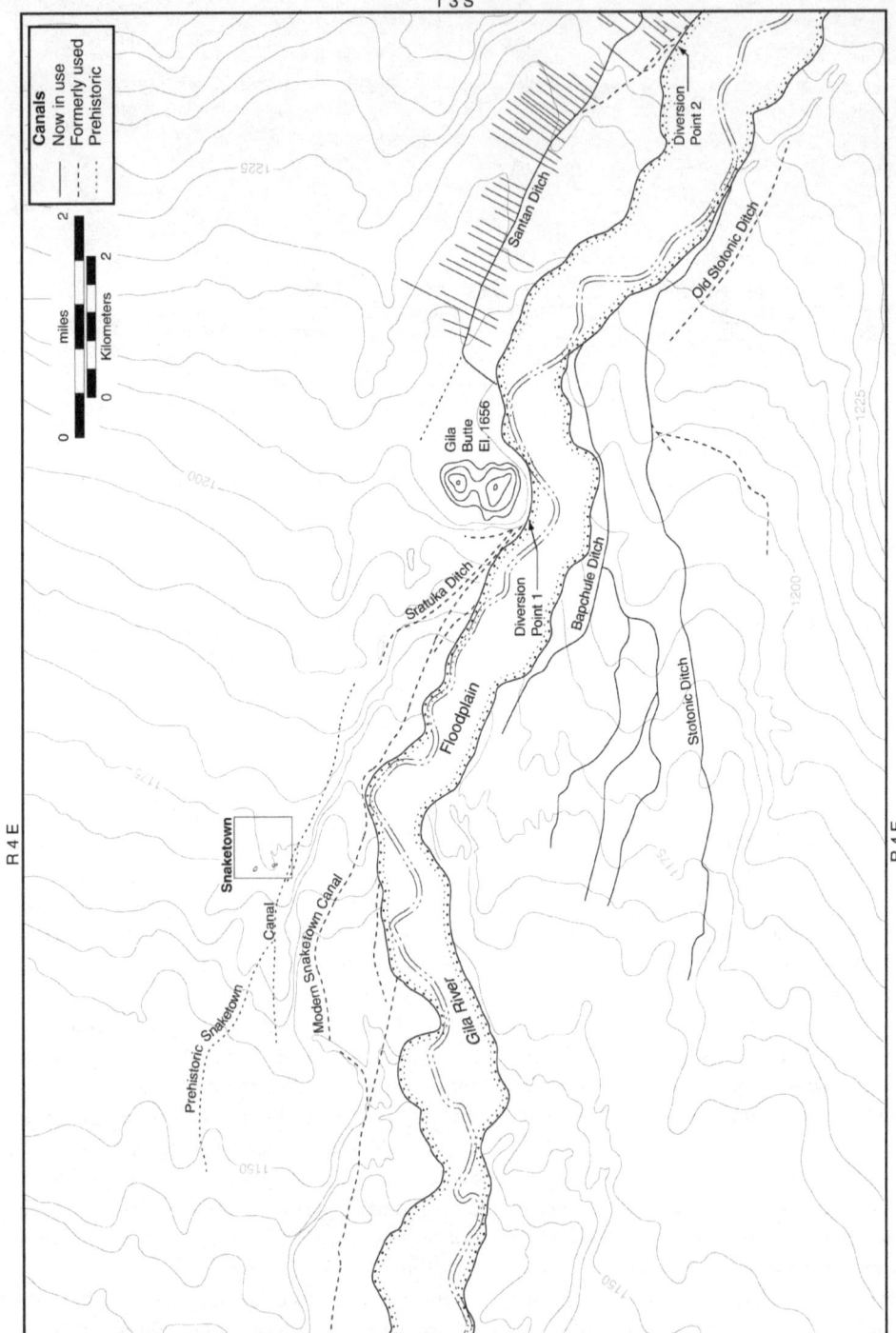

FIGURE 5.3. Canals located along the Gila River near Snaketown. Note Gila Butte. Prepared by Peg Robbins and William Olguin, Statistical Research, Inc., Tucson.

sacred number four, the mountain, and its water-giving abilities. As the religious center of the Hohokam world, Snaketown likely was interpreted as a center place because of Gila Butte, which represented a powerful natural symbol. The construction of ritual features and dwellings celebrated and reinforced the symbolism. The public projects themselves came to identify a sacred place in the landscape, legitimated community rights to the land, and possibly linked leaders to sacred patrons. Such means, Grove and Gillespie point out, metaphorically convert "nature and wilderness to culture and community" (1992:18). As we will see next, the built environment repeated and enhanced physical environmental symbols through architectural mimicry.

Formal Dimension

Monuments can be viewed as a means of reconfiguring and enhancing natural landscapes. The built environment is a microcosm of the landscape, a context in which relationships between people and land are clarified and dramatized (Bradley 1998; Thomas 2001:178–179). In Mesoamerica, the built environment replicated significant topographic features that held deep iconographic meaning. Mounds and pyramids were artificial sacred spaces that symbolized mountains and volcanoes (Miller and Taube 1993:28), thus becoming conceptual metaphors themselves.

Bostwick (1992:81) has suggested that pyramids such as the Great Pyramid at Tenochitlán symbolized the divisions of the universe. They were marked with sculpture identifying them as aquatic realms and linking them to the supernatural world (Miller 1984; Sugiyama 1993). Temples had similar parallels, representing natural caves (Markman and Markman 1992:413; Schele and Freidel 1990). Symbolizing the axis mundi, caves were represented metaphorically in the centers of Mayan villages (Redfield and Villa Rojas 1962:114; Vogt 1976). As in the natural landscape, temples and mounds were conjoined because of their linked symbolism. Mounds or pyramids and temples typically were constructed as a complex with profound meaning and ritual power.

The metaphor of Snake Mountain, or Coatépec, depicted in the Aztec migration epic was extended into the built environment via the temple. Schele and Kappelman (2001:35) observe that the Templo Mayor at Tenochitlán was a twin structure with shrines devoted to Tlaloc and Huitzilopochtli. Serpents decorate the bases of the balustrades and undulate across the frontal platform. Schele and Kappelman write, "The Templo Mayor was, as in the image from the *Codex Azcatitlan*, the human-built version of Snake Mountain. Moreover, the construction and conceptual organization of the Templo Mayor dramatically illustrates the paradigms articulated in the Coatépec myth" (2001:35). Associated structures, such as the ballcourt, and ritual events that took place in the temple precinct reenacted mythic events and reinforced the paradigmatic nature of the Coatépec myth (Schele and Kappelman 2001:36).

Similar processes of architectural mimicry were fundamental in the Hohokam built environment. The mountain was replicated in the form of trash mounds and artificial mounds. Sixty mounds were built at Snaketown, more than at any other Hohokam site. Although some were used solely for trash disposal, others were artificially capped, and some were wholly artificial. One of the most intriguing artificial platform mounds is Mound 16, a round, flat-topped edifice (Haury 1976:84–92). Built of clean adobe and caliche plaster, it was repeatedly refaced and resurfaced, perhaps in renewal ceremonies. A setback in the sloping face served as a step for priests or other officials to climb to the top. The last surface was associated with a series of postholes encircling the mound and likely representing a palisade. Another artificial platform, Mound 39, had a long history of construction and use, and the geographic center of the mound was shifted by translocating the original mound mass (Haury 1976:83).

Moreover, the concentric organization of mounds at Snaketown may have expressed cosmological concepts. The large, caliche-capped mounds and most of the dirt mounds were located in different rings around the plaza. The smallest mounds constructed primarily of household refuse were located on the periphery (see Figure 5.1; Wilcox et al. 1981:138, Figure 31). One of the largest mounds at Snaketown, Mound 29, faced Ballcourt 2 across the central plaza. During the Sedentary period, a 38-m-wide corridor connected Mound 29 and Ballcourt 2 (Wilcox et al. 1981:138). Two large pit structures facing the corridor contained evidence for specialized, community use. Did this mound–ballcourt complex reflect a myth, such as Snake Mountain, in the built environment? Did it provide a ritual context for reenacting myths? We have no way to know for sure, but the parallels between Snaketown and Mesoamerican ritual complexes with their associated iconography are vivid and strong.

Monuments further reorganize the materials of the landscape itself (Thomas 2001:179). Construction materials may hold symbolic significance as well as serving expedient purposes (Parker Pearson and Ramilisonina 1998). Hohokam monuments transposed the stone of the mountain peak into the native earth of the platform mound. The persistent opposition of earth and the heavens, representing sky, clouds, and rain, in the built environment and Hohokam iconography may be another example of the principle of duality and balance.

More humble aspects of the built environment also mimicked the sacred mountain. Hohokam residential units typically were associated with uncapped trash mounds. Such mounds served to demarcate and separate precincts within larger villages, ringing and enclosing clusters of courtyard groups (Elson 1986:53; Henderson 1987; Wallace 1995:790–791; Whittlesey 2004), and also were associated with smaller residential settlements. At large settlements, mounds tended to be placed relative to the cardinal locations and were located east, west, north, and south of house clusters (Wallace 1995:Figure 15.8).

The trash mound was more than a simple place for disposing refuse. By their location, trash mounds had a prominent place in Hohokam social identity, representing the kinship relations that structured house clusters and courtyard groups and separating kin groups in larger settlements—symbolically separating "us" from "them." Ancient Mesoamericans associated mountains with the ancestors. We can see in the humble trash mound, as a construction mimicking mountains and by means of its location next to a residential group, a complicated metaphoric link among the living and their ancestors, who helped to bring rain and restore balance to the world. At many Hohokam sites, human burials were interred in or near trash mounds. This was the case with Sedentary period sites in the Tucson Basin, at which discrete cemeteries typically are not found (Huntington 1986; Wellman and Dart 1996:51). As Becker (1988) has argued, all interments—caches, inhumations, cremations—represented earth offerings (see also Moholy-Nagy 1978; Pohl 1983:94). Because they symbolized an important landscape feature, trash mounds also may have been the locale for rituals (Preucel 1996:127).

In addition, facilities for group food preparation, such as *hornos* (earth ovens) and rock-filled roasting pits, were located on the perimeter of residential areas near trash mounds. Communal food preparation and feasting associated with mortuary rites, descent-group ceremonies, and ancestor-veneration rituals would have served to emphasize the connections among the living and the dead, feeding the ancestors as well as their living descendants.

Strong parallels are evident in Mesoamerican societies. McAnany reports that because ancestors were buried within house compounds, residences were in effect a type of domestic mausoleum: "Residences and their circumambient spaces were the repositories of ancestral remains. As such, these places were potent links to the past as well as important items of inheritance. Maya expressed their genealogies not only in hieroglyphic script but also in the physical use and reuse of places" (1995:8). The Hohokam lived in similar fashion. They resided in the same spaces season after season and generation after generation, rebuilding homes and constructing new dwellings as the needs of domestic groups changed but holding the central courtyard more or less constant (Whittlesey 2004). They buried their dead near their dwellings, linking the living and the ancestors. Land was "clearly not simply soil, but rather an entity always fused with the ancestors, under whose joint authority the living are placed" (de Coppet 1985:81). Household residents would have been reminded on a daily basis of their connection with the earth (Brady and Ashmore 1999:131). In this way, the sacred and dwelling landscapes merged (van Dommelen 1999).

Relational Dimension

Technology is one of the primary ways by which people interact with their environment and therefore offers one measure of the relational landscape dimension. We can see a number of connections among landscape metaphors, architectural constructions mimicking mountains, and material culture. Alone, the convergence of numerous prehistoric trails upon Gila Butte would be sufficient to indicate the importance of this landscape metaphor. More importantly, metamorphic stone from the butte was quarried (Rafferty 1982). The highly micaceous schist was crushed to make pottery temper (Walsh-Anduze 1993) and used to fashion palettes, ceremonial items that were employed in conjunction with censers in ritual acts involving the burning of mineral substances (Haury 1976:288; Hawley 1965).

Use of schist as temper is especially intriguing. Schist has no obvious value in increasing a container's strength or porosity, and most Hohokam ceramics also contained sand-sized inclusions that either were collected from washes or were present in clay when it was mined. Although plain ware and some red-ware pottery contained considerable schist, resulting in a sparkling, glittery surface, even painted pottery contained small quantities of the material. It is possible that the glittering surface of plain-ware pottery symbolized water or perhaps stars (Doyel 1992; Whittlesey 1998b). Regardless, schist may have been a crucial emblem of Hohokam identity. One is reminded of similar actions on the part of Aboriginal peoples of Australia. Stone quarry sites hold sacred significance as the resting places of the ancestors. Quarrying stone for axes is, therefore, quarrying the bones of the ancestors, and the axes retain the power of the source (Tilley 1994:53). Hohokam painted containers containing schist fragments were used as cremation urns and mortuary offerings and in other ritual activities; the micaceous plain-ware ollas served as storage containers for agricultural products and water. The importance of Gila Butte schist is underscored by the fact that ceramic containers were made in quantity at Snaketown, perhaps by craft specialists, and then distributed widely. Thus, the Hohokam carried pieces of the sacred mountain with them as they settled throughout central and southern Arizona. Whereas these notions are certainly speculative, the redundancy and multilayered character of the symbolism are striking (see Ortman and Bradley 2002). The symbolism of Gila Butte, pottery containers, and schist combine in a mutually reinforcing way.

Historical Dimension

Various lines of evidence indicate that Snaketown was a central place for hundreds of years. As Wilcox et al. (1981:201) have noted, Snaketown lies in the center of the Phoenix Basin. A system of trails connected it to settlements located to the north. Although site layout was altered with the addition of dwellings and ceremonial facilities through time, there is some indication that cosmological and ideological concepts structured site layout from the beginning. The central plaza remained stable through time, for example, and the earliest, large houses appear to have been arranged with reference to the cardinal directions.

Throughout its history, Snaketown was sustained by irrigation farming. There is some dispute concerning the age of irrigation. Haury (1976) believed it began during the Vahki phase of the Pioneer period, whereas Wilcox (Wilcox and Shenk 1977:180–181; Wilcox et al. 1981:204) thought that irrigation was not established until later in the Pioneer period. Regardless, the water flowing from Gila Butte surely was a primary factor promoting settlement at Snaketown and marking it as a regional ceremonial center. Snaketown was abandoned at precisely the time that the Hohokam ceremonial complex appeared to dissolve, leaving a vacuum for other religious and ideological traditions to fill (Doyel 1980:35; Haury 1976:327, 338; Wilcox et al. 1981:210). Later, after a century or so of abandonment, small, dispersed hamlets were established west of Snaketown (Wilcox et al. 1981:212). Perhaps the Snaketown aura lived on, even after abandonment.

Ideological Dimension

Because of the vital role of perception and cognition in creating cultural landscapes, each landscape component has meaning. Redundancy in landmarks, repetition in decorative themes, architectural mimicry, and other material expressions of landscape indicate meaningful patterns. We may not always be able to assign precise meanings to such patterns, of course, but we can certainly determine that they embody meaning.

The aridity of the natural landscape and the importance of rainfall to Hohokam farming systems has been stressed. As an agricultural people wholly invested in the cultivation of a suite of plantfood staples, rain would have been considered the source of life itself. Surely, it must have focused Hohokam religion and ritual. By comparison with Mesoamerican ideology, the mountain symbolized rain and clouds to the Hohokam. Platform mounds and mountain peaks therefore may have served as locales for conducting ceremonies dedicated to a rain god, such as Tlaloc, and for petitioning the ancestors to help bring rain, health, and abundance to the community.

There is no direct evidence that Hohokam platform mounds and peaks such as Gila Butte symbolized rain and were used for rain-bringing ceremonies, but logic suggests that this was the case. Most platform mounds have no evidence that dwellings or other architectural features were built atop them, and they also lack domestic facilities such as hearths. They were not used as residential localities (Downum and Bostwick 2003). Haury draws similarities between Hohokam and Mesoamerican mounds in suggesting that "the idea that an elevation was a proper place for ritual practices, phased construction, the use of a step or steps, and modification of the form of the mound by shifting the geographical center, possibly in response to a concept related to calendrical cycles, are explicit reminders of southern [Mesoamerican] ties" (1976:93).

Moreover, other landscape features clearly were used for ritual activities. Springs in southern Arizona typically were marked with petroglyphs (Wallace and Holmlund 1986), and caves served as locations for more elaborate offerings. Caches of offerings were left at cave shrines, such as Double Butte Cave in the Santan Hills (Haury 1945) and a locale near Casa Blanca containing shamanistic items described by Pima ethnographer Russell (1908:256). Red Cave, located in the Whetstone Mountains in southeastern Arizona (Ferg and Mead 1993) was an important cave shrine. This four-chambered cave contained offerings including more than 300 sherd discs placed within a rimstone basin of water or in the red mud on the cave floor.

Hohokam iconography does not depict mountains per se, but the natural forces of which the mountain was emblematic, such as rain, clouds, and other sources of moisture, are pervasive and redundant in Hohokam iconography (Whittlesey 2003). Waterbirds and reptiles evocative of water are depicted on pottery, stone objects, and shell ornaments. I have discussed the possible water symbolism of micaceous schist-tempered pottery. Geometric elements representing abstract depictions of clouds, such as terraced elements, also appear on pottery.

Conclusion

By nature, archaeologists are taxonomists, because classification is the means by which we order our data. We classify material objects, architectural features, site types, stages of sociopolitical integration, and more. We also try to classify cultural landscapes. Cleere (1995:65–66), for example, specifies criteria for recognizing three kinds of cultural landscapes: "clearly defined" landscapes, "organically evolved" landscapes, and "associative cultural" landscapes. Knapp and Ashmore (1999: 10–13) identify "constructed landscapes," "conceptualized landscapes," and "ideational landscapes." Chapters in Ashmore and Knapp's (1999) edited volume address the "sacred landscape," the "mythical landscape," and the "industrial landscape."

Such classifications reduce the effectiveness of the cultural-landscapes approach, as van Dommelen (1999:283) points out so succinctly. The landscape is a unity of past and present, sacred and profane, cosmology and nature, ancestors and the living. Landscape "is an extraordinarily encompassing notion" that embraces what van Dommelen (1999:284) calls the "multiplicity" of landscape. We should explore how different activities meet and merge in the cultural landscape through the relational and historical dimensions, rather than attempting to classify an evanescent phenomenon that inherently is not amenable to classification. All aspects of human life meet in the cultural landscape.

The ancient Maya offer an excellent example of the multiplicity of cultural landscape. Among these people, archaeologists would have great difficulty defining a "sacred landscape" and separating it from a "domestic landscape," because the sacred and secular were intertwined so closely. Like other Mesoamerican peoples, the Maya possessed a sophisticated and deeply embedded concept of ancestor veneration. It was a highly pragmatic practice that "drew power from the past, legitimized the current state of affairs (including all the inequities in rights and privileges), and charted a course for the future" (McAnany 1995:1).

Accordingly, the Maya incorporated the ancestors into the world of the living by placing them in domestic contexts—under house floors, in residential shrines, and within funerary pyramids (McAnany 1995). Mortuary rites were protracted and included transgenerational occupation and refurbishing of the household compounds in which the dead were interred, successive interment in pyramids and ancestral shrines, and display of skeletal parts and ashes (Coe 1956; Tozzer 1941). The cycle of death and rebirth was played out in the continual refurbishing of funerary pyramids, which were razed, rebuilt, remodeled, and refaced (Coe 1956:388; McAnany 1995:51–52).

We can see similar processes operating among the Hohokam. The natural landscape, the sacred aspects of the built environment, and the domestic landscape, or what Zedeño (1997) calls "living space"—habitation activities and the built environment necessary to shelter from the elements—were intertwined. Natural topographic features were invested with extraordinary cosmological and ideological significance. One especially powerful feature, Gila Butte, was an important factor prompting the settlement of Snaketown and its development into the center place of the Hohokam world. The organization of mounds, dwellings, and facilities in the built environment was a deeply meaningful reflection and reinforcement of cosmological principles and symbols. Monuments and the natural features they mimicked were interdependent ritual structures. Mounds represented mountains, and the humble trash mound—a seemingly domestic, even profane feature—also was a profound symbol and a likely locale for ritual acts. The ancestors were interred with the living and often were buried near trash mounds. The whole was a multilayered construction with intertwined themes, iconography, and functions.

The usefulness of a cultural-landscapes approach in deriving meaning from Hohokam material culture and interpreting Hohokam prehistory is clear. No other theoretical paradigm has proved more effective in teasing out those elements that were profoundly influential in shaping past lives and also are difficult for archaeologists to infer. Other archaeologists may find the approach equally useful and help us toward a more thorough understanding of the past.

Acknowledgments

Thanks are extended to Nieves Zedeño, one of the innovators of the cultural-landscapes approach in southwestern anthropology, for the invitation to contribute to this volume. I appreciate her assistance as well as help from Brenda Bowser. Peg Robbins and William Olguin of the Publications Department at Statistical Research, Inc., prepared the illustrations. I am grateful to two anonymous reviewers who offered kind words and constructive suggestions. Jeff Reid provided useful comments on a draft of the essay. Any errors of substance or interpretation are my own.

6

Hopitutskwa and *Ang Kuktota*

The Role of Archaeological Sites in Defining Hopi Cultural Landscapes

Leigh J. Kuwanwisiwma and T. J. Ferguson

In its broadest philosophical and spiritual sense, *Hopitutskwa*—Hopi land—encompasses all the land the Hopi people and their ancestors traveled through, lived on, and were buried in during the long migration from the place of origin to *Tuuwanasavi* (the earth center) on the Hopi Mesas. As a cultural landscape, Hopitutskwa is defined by many features, including landforms associated with deities and historical events, rivers, springs, trails, shrines, and what the Hopi people call *itaakuku*, our "footprints." These footprints are the archaeological sites that were created and used by Hopi ancestors. In this essay, we examine how Hopi people use archaeological sites to help define the cultural landscape of Hopitutskwa. We pay particular attention to the interrelated concepts of place, scale, time, and context that are needed to explain the cultural importance archaeological sites have for the Hopi people.

Hopitutskwa

Tutskwa is the word for "land" in the Hopi language (Hopi Dictionary Project 1998:678; Seaman 1985:144). *Hopitutskwa* thus means "Hopi land" (Whiteley 1989:1). The concept of Hopitutskwa is deeply rooted in the Hopi religion. After the Hopis emerged into the Fourth Way of Life, they encountered the deity Màasaw in the Grand Canyon. Màasaw was the guardian of the earth, and he gave them a digging stick and a bag of seeds so that they could live as humble and hardworking farmers. They made a spiritual pact with Màasaw, wherein he agreed to let the Hopis use his land if they would act as stewards of the earth (Ferguson et al. 1993:27; Malotki and Lomatuway'ma 1987:67–73). This land is symbolized by a *tuwvota*, or shield design, that conceptually signifies *tuuwaqatsi*, the earth, and the four worlds the Hopis have experienced.

The geographic extent of *Mastutskwa* or Màasaw's land (Malotki and Lomatuway'ma 1987:68; Swanton 1952:352) was described by A. M. Stephen in the 1890s using information collected during discussions in Hopi kivas. According to Stephen,

> Masau first traveled south, then circuitously to the eastward until he reached his starting point. He called this area his land. The exact limits are unknown, but it is surmised he started from a point about where Fort Mohave now is situated, thence south as far as the Isthmus of Panama, skirted eastward along the Gulf of Mexico and northward by the line of the Rio Grande up into Colorado, thence westerly along the thirty-six parallel or thereabouts to the Rio Colorado, meandering along its tributaries and so on southward to his starting point at Fort Mohave. This was Masau's land originally, the land of the Hopituh [1929:55–56].

Following divine instructions, the Hopis continued their migrations until, after many generations, each clan arrived at its rightful place at Tuuwanasavi on the Hopi Mesas. Each clan brought with it the knowledge and right to use the shrines and resources in the area the people migrated from. By fulfilling their pact, the Hopis earned the right to use Màasaw's land; Mastutskwa became Hopitutskwa. From a Hopi perspective, Hopi land and religion are inseparable (Kuwanwisiwma 2002; Whiteley 1989:55–56).

In the words of Andrew Hermequaftewa, of the Tsorsngyam (Bluebird Clan) of Shungopavi,

> Our religious teachings are based upon the proper care of our land and the people who live upon it. We must not lose the way of life of our religion if we are to remain Hopis.... The Hopi land is the Hopi religion. The Hopi religion is bound up in the Hopi land.... The Hopi lives and protects his land by worshipping, by praying, by fasting, according to the plans and instructions of Maasau [1953:4–5].

Hopitutskwa is thus first and foremost a religious concept essential to the practice of religion in all of the Hopi villages on the three Hopi Mesas. In geographic terms, Hopitutskwa includes all of the lands where the Hopis have placed their footprints and for which they act as stewards according to their pact with Màasaw.

In 1955, the Bureau of Indian Affairs held a series of hearings on the Hopi Reservation regarding tribal and federal governance. Tutskwa was a topic many Hopis discussed, providing insights into the range of Hopi beliefs about their land. Andrew Hermequaftewa gave a broad definition of Hopi lands, stating,

> Our land is divided among our shrines [that] are established in the various directions for the purpose of prayer altars where we are to offer our prayers. The land which we considered as our land was from shore to shore. We were given the privilege of using all the waters for the springs; such law was given to us in its completeness.... These shrines are marked at San Francisco Peaks, Navajo Mountain, and at a place they call Salt down south at Zuni [in Bureau of Indian Affairs 1955:86].

Charlie Homehongva discussed the internal dynamic of how a unified tribal claim to Hopitutskwa was derived from the many separate entitlements of individual villages (Figure 6.1). He recounted a meeting held at Orayvi where the representatives of all of the Hopi villages met to consider the land. As he described it,

> So they said "Loloma"—he was chief at Old Oraibi—"You designate your area first." Loloma designated as a starting point Navajo Mountain. He said that will never go away. Then it followed the ridge on to the Grand Canyon up to the point where there was a spring that leads up near the route that goes to Supai Canyon and that was the road he designated for himself. And then they turned to Seetpella, the representative from Shungopavy. He designated the area up and around Williams—that is now Williams, Arizona. From there he went south to Turquoise Lakes and also included San Francisco Peaks because that was their eagle hunting area. That was the area he designated. It came then next to Sipaulovi's turn. Takanilsie—he was the spokesman for that village. He continued from where Shungopavy left off, taking in the mountain ridge south of Winslow over to the Woodruff mountains. Then came Mishongnovi's turn and its representative was Tawimoke. He designated the area from the Woodruff mountains on east to the Salt below Zuni and said that Salt area there was to be held open for both Sipaulavi and Mishongnovi so that they could get their salt there. From that point they came north to a place on this side of Ganado which they called Red Point. There they drew a plaque on the rocks. Then came Walpi's turn. Their spokesman was Iss. He continued the line from Red Point on the north to a point beyond Burnt Corn. That was the area he chose for his people. Following came Beeva, a representative of the Tewa village. He continued from that point and joined the land again at Navajo Mountain. This was the land that they designated for themselves to be used by their people [in Bureau of Indian Affairs 1955:148–149].

Ritual acknowledgment of Hopitutskwa is affirmed through a religious pilgrimage to eight shrines associated with ancestral villages and petroglyphs (Figure 6.2). The area demarcated by these pilgrimage shrines is conceptualized by Hopi cultural and religious leaders as the "plaza"

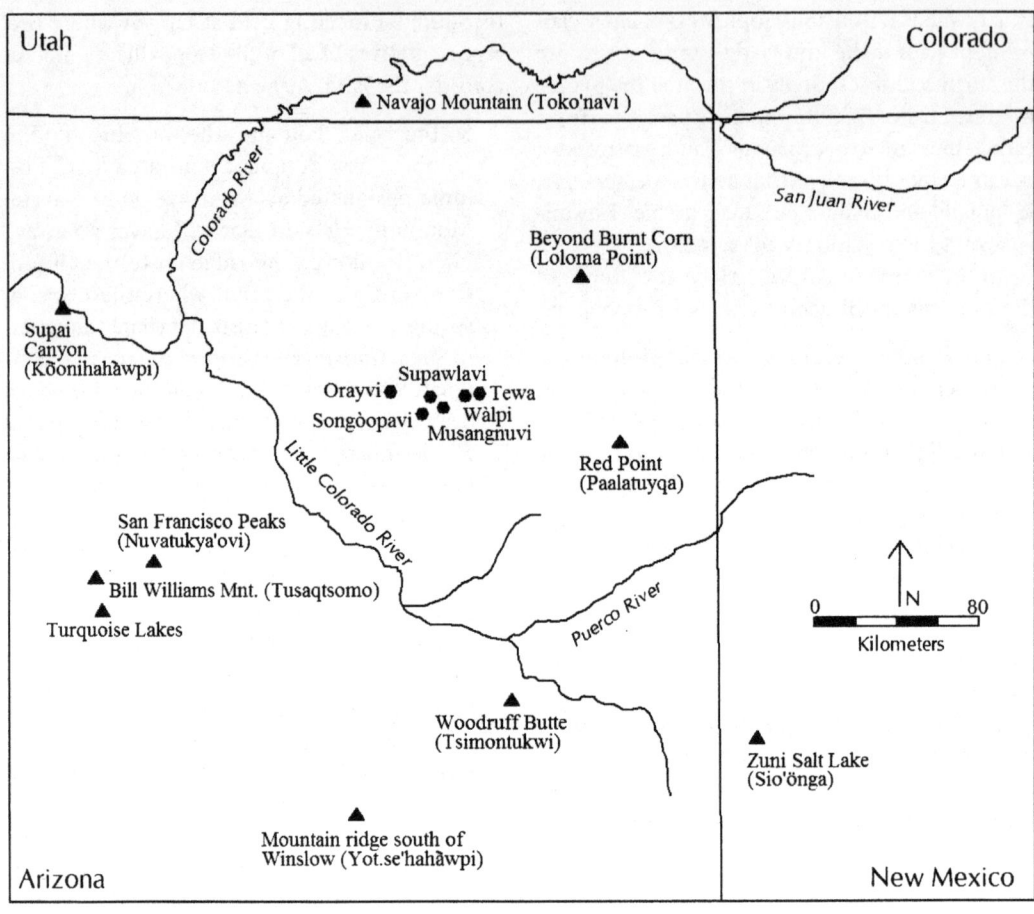

FIGURE 6.1. The places (triangles) and villages (circles) mentioned in Charlie Homehongva's 1955 narrative designate Hopi land in the nineteenth and twentieth centuries.

of Hopi lands. The delineation of Hopitutskwa is thus perceived not as a boundary but as a *homvi'ikya*, a term that derives from two words (Jenkins et al. 1994). *Hooma* is the sacred cornmeal that Hopis use for prayer offerings; *vi'ikya* is a route or place, an actual geographic designation of something. *Homvi'ikya* therefore refers to a route literally used in the offering of the prayer meal. The shrines visited on the Hopitutskwa homvi'ikya are used to pay homage to the entire domain of stewardship and the full extent of Hopi lands, including lands that lie far beyond the area encircled during the pilgrimage. The ritual depositing of prayer feathers and sticks in addition to ceremonial smoking concludes each stop at a shrine.

Ang Kuktota

Concepts of Hopitutskwa are communicated through kiva talk and ritual discourse associated with ceremonial activities. These verbal descriptions are mapped onto the geography of the Southwest through the apprehension of the kuktota, or footprints, that Hopi people encounter as they travel across the land. *Ang kuktota*, literally, "along there, make footprints," was an integral part of the covenant the Hopi people made with Màasaw (Loma'omvaya and Ferguson 1999). The Hopi were instructed to leave their footprints as evidence that they had fulfilled their spiritual obligations. As Hopi clans migrated throughout the Southwest and beyond, they settled in various places where they established themselves

Defining Hopi Cultural Landscapes

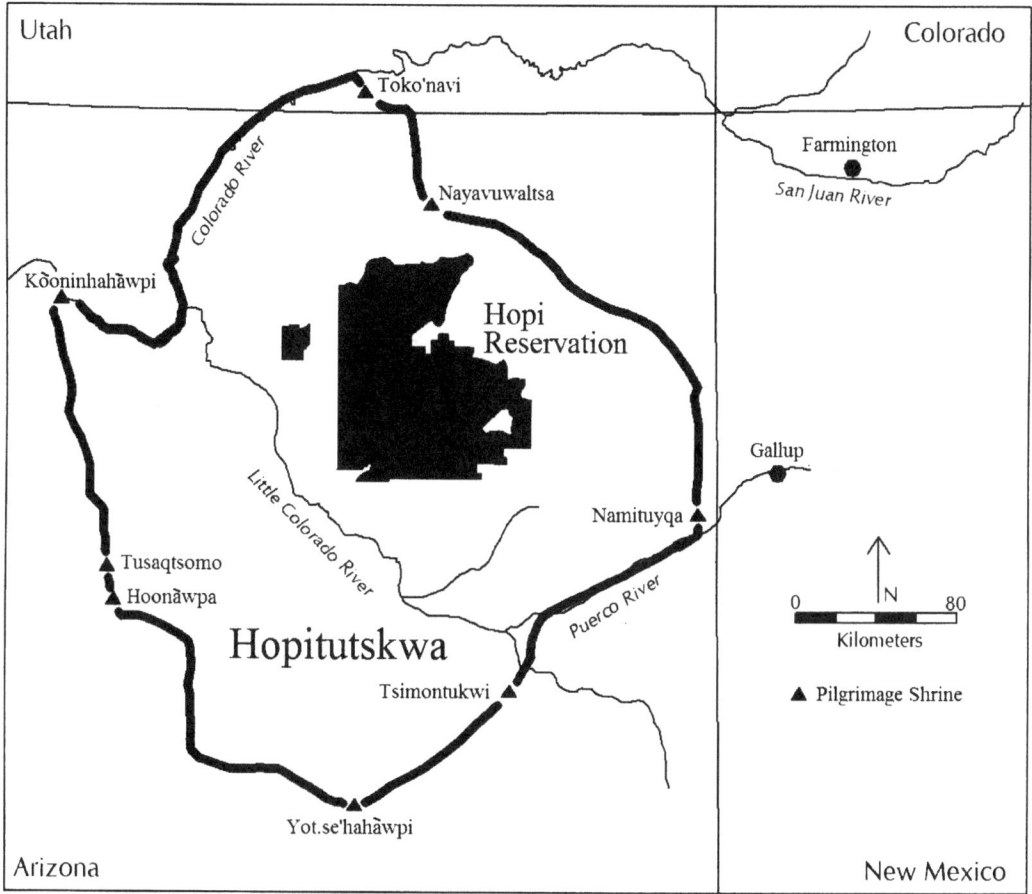

FIGURE 6.2. Hopitutskwa symbolized by an encircling *homvi'ikya* (pilgrimage route) used to pay homage to the larger cultural landscape demarcated by Hopi footprints associated with origin and migration.

by cultivating and caring for the earth (Figure 6.3). During these migrations the Hopis came to know and ritually use many springs, pilgrimage trails, and shrines. In addition, as the Hopi ancestors migrated, they left behind the graves of their relatives, ancestral villages, petroglyphs, potsherds, and other material culture as kuktota, physical evidence that they had vested the land with their spiritual stewardship and fulfilled their pact with Màasaw.

Hopi ancestral footprints today are represented in the archaeological record of the Southwest. They constitute monuments on the landscape because they are enduring physical markers of the existence of Hopi ancestors, fixing social memories in a tangible and perpetual form in time and space. As monuments, Hopi footprints provide prima facie evidence for the migration of Hopi clans and the successful fulfillment of the spiritual responsibilities of land stewardship. Hopitutskwa is thus recognized by individual tribal members in the footprints left by their ancestors, and these footprints provide a means for Hopi people to directly and personally experience their history.

The idea that ancestral archaeological sites are monuments or "flags" that mark Hopitutskwa is pervasive in Hopi culture (Banyacya 1966; Hopi Tribe n.d.; Lomayaktewa et al. 1971; Widdison 1991:32; Yava 1978:71). For instance, in a letter to President Harry Truman in 1949, Hopi leaders stated, "This land is a sacred home to the Hopi people.... Our flag still flies throughout our land

FIGURE 6.3. A field, cultivated in the drainage of Dinnebito Wash in 2004, planted with a special strain of corn the Hopis have grown in the dry deserts of the Southwest for more than a millennium. Photograph by Stewart B. Koyiyumptewa; courtesy of Hopi Cultural Preservation Office.

(our ancient ruins)" (Talahaftewa [and Others] 1949; Geertz 1994:441–446). This letter was signed by the "hereditary Hopi Chieftains of the Hopi Pueblos of Hotevilla, Shungopovy, and Mushongnovi" and includes a list of 20 other Hopis who supported the statement.

Hopi leaders continue to articulate the belief that archaeological sites are monuments of Hopi history. Tribal Chairman Ferrell Secakuku, for example, explained in remarks at the 1993 National Interagency Wilderness Conference that

> Hopis do not view cultural resources, such as ruins, as abandoned or as artifacts of the past. To a Hopi, these villages were left as is when the people were given a sign to move on. These homes, [kivas], storehouses, and everything else that makes a community, were left exactly as they were because it is our belief the Hopi will someday return. Our people are still there. Today the Hopi designate these ruins as a symbol or their sovereign flag. Potsherds are left in abundance, usually broken into small pieces with the trademarks showing. These are the footprints of the occupants. Hopis believe that ruins should remain untouched because when anything is taken it breaks down the value of holding the village in place.... Hopi prophecy recognizes these cultural resources as part of today's living culture. They indeed should be protected for the future of our people [1993:9].

Members of the Hopi Cultural Resources Advisory Task Team, an advisory council sponsored by the Hopi Cultural Preservation Office, continue to express the same view. For instance, Dalton Taylor, from Songoopavi, explains that

> those old folks are the ones telling me that someday these ruins and broken pottery are going to be really something to our people. The late-comers, you know, once they establish a home they exploit the land so far around the

village and claim it. So they used to tell me, that Pahaana [Anglo-Americans] when they capture another town they put their flag up. And that's our flag, the ruins, they left those ruins to stand for us so that we can get our land up to that area one day [in Ferguson 1998:266].

Mr. Taylor thinks that burial sites and ancestral villages are to the Hopis what the Star-Spangled Banner is to other Americans. In one interview he said, "I was told not to forget these ancestors.... Even though (the ancestors) are dead, they're still holding onto the land" (Schill 1993:13). For the Hopi, ancestral sites are important because they are both monuments and the location of ancestral graves. These are inseparable. Hopi cultural advisers think of archaeological sites as monuments of Hopi history embedded in, and giving cultural meaning to, the landscape.

From an anthropological perspective, as Clemmer observes, "the Hopis identify their ancestral dwelling places as much by symbols etched into rock and architectural ruins as by clan legends and traditions. In a sense, knowledgeable Hopis 'read' an archaeological landscape with reference to the fundamental principles of their cosmological system" (1993:86). In this cosmological system, the *kiikiqo*, or ancestral settlements of the Hopis, represent the realization of the spiritual plans of their ancestors.

Hopi Footprints in the Cultural Landscape of Öngtupqa

Archaeological sites in Öngtupqa, the Grand Canyon, provide an example of how Hopi footprints are used to compose a cultural landscape. The historical and cultural connection between the Hopi and ancient ancestral villages in the Grand Canyon have long been recognized by archaeologists. Schwartz has concluded that the archaeological record indicates that the prehistoric Puebloan people who left the Grand Canyon "moved east and became part of the ancestral line of the Hopi Indians, profoundly influencing the development of Hopi cosmology" (1989:67). He suggests that the variety seen in Hopi oral traditions derives from the fact that many different prehistoric groups migrated to the Hopi Mesas. In discussing this relationship, Schwartz concludes that,

like many groups, the Canyon Anasazi probably mixed into early Hopi society and culture, contributing their share of rites and deities to Hopi religion. For historically, references to the Grand Canyon as a sacred place are woven throughout Hopi cosmology and ceremonial practices. The reconstruction of the religion of any prehistoric culture is difficult, at best, but suggestions of what impact the Grand Canyon Anasazi may have made on the Hopis can be found in four separate but related areas: the Hopi myth of emergence, their deity Maasaw, their journey to the earth's navel, and some of their customs associated with death [1989:69].

The Hopi today use ancestral archaeological sites in the Grand Canyon to cognize a vital cultural landscape associated with traditions of Hopi origin, migration, and spirituality. These archaeological sites include shrines, ancestral villages, graves, agricultural features, roasting pits, artifact scatters, trails, and petroglyphs. These sites provide a palpable sense of place and history, which are acknowledged and interpreted by Hopi tribal members when they visit Öngtupqa. The objective and phenomenological aspects of this landscape were documented in research undertaken in the Grand Canyon with Hopi cultural advisers during five river trips between 1991 and 1995 (Ferguson 1998). Unattributed quotations of Hopi advisers in this chapter derive from this research.

Ancestral Villages

The Hopi believe that the "ruins" in the Grand Canyon that archaeologists and the general public think of as remnants of the distant past are still inhabited by the spirits of Hopi ancestors (Figure 6.4). Given this belief, Ferrell Secakuku has said, "My recommendation to the [Hopi] Cultural Preservation Office is that we not call them ruins, since they're a part of a living culture.... I'd like to call them ancestral villages" (Schill 1993:13).

Anthropologists have also described how the Hopi believe that their ancestors are associated with archaeological sites in the manner depicted by Secakuku. In writing about the Hopi, for instance, Eggan has observed that

FIGURE 6.4. Hopi researchers in the Grand Canyon examining the archaeological remains of an ancestral village at South Canyon. Photograph by T. J. Ferguson, October 2, 1993.

archaeological sites, representing the former homes of particular clans, are sacred areas that are visited periodically to make offerings to ancestors, with requests for aid in growing crops. Nearby ruins are visited in connection with particular ceremonies to notify the deceased relatives buried there that the ceremony is in progress and the dead should do their part [1994:14].

Hopi cultural advisers who have conducted research in the Grand Canyon report that they feel the presence of their ancestors while traveling through Öngtupqa and visiting the *Hisatsinom* (ancestral Hopi) villages found there. For instance, in describing a river trip through the Grand Canyon, Walter Hamana from Orayvi reported, "Like I said, I'm never alone. I have that feeling all day, every day, I have that feeling." The knowledge that their ancestors watch them while they are in Öngtupqa imbues Hopis' expeditions to the canyon with a powerful spiritual aspect. Hopi ancestral sites are prevalent in the Grand Canyon—the Hopi Tribe has identified

235 of them—so Hopi people constantly feel the presence of their ancestors as they travel through Öngtupqa.

Ferrell Secakuku, from Supawlavi, has discussed the reverence that contemporary Hopi have for ancestral archaeology, stating,

> The Hopi way of measuring the value of cultural resources and other so-called artifacts is not in terms of money. Rather it is their importance for life today and their future destiny. The future of the Hopi is a great burden to them because we must live a life of spiritual meditation and humbleness in order to take this corrupt world, which will get worse, into the better world. Yes, we believe in the fifth world and our spiritual integrity must be strong to keep our ruined villages alive. Our houses, [kivas], and our shrines at the ruined village perimeters must be kept warm and active. We rely on our spiritual ancestors who passed this way and are still there to receive the messages [1993:9].

Hopi cultural advisers report that the ancestral Hisatsinom archaeology in the Grand Canyon is important to them personally, even if they do not physically visit these archaeological sites (Ferguson 1998:254). As Simon Polingyumptewa from Hotvela explained, "Those things are still important to us old people who believe and respect them." Hopi footprints in the Grand Canyon are important because they signify to tribal members who they are descended from and, in so doing, provide an emotionally satisfying physical connection to the places formerly occupied by Hopi ancestors.

Graves of the Ancestors

Hopi footprints in the Grand Canyon gain cultural significance from the fact that Hopi ancestors are buried in many of the archaeological sites. In this regard, Jerry Honawa from Hotvela said, "There are reasons for all of these ruins, down there. There are reasons for people being left there.... Their souls are there; those are the beginning of the first of the migrations." Expressing a similar idea, Milland Lomakema from Songoopavi said, "Even if I don't go to these ruins, people who lived before us live in those areas, and we respect them. If they bury them right there on those sites, we respect them because they lived here before us."

The disturbance of ancestral graves in the Grand Canyon (and elsewhere) is of concern to the Hopi because these are the final spiritual resting place for deceased relatives. Death is profound in the Hopi belief system because while the *hiqwsi'at* (breath) of the deceased is released into the spirit world, the corporeal body remains in the ground to continue its final, physical journey to become one with the earth (Ferguson et al. 2001). Any disturbance of the final physical journey is a desecration. Öngtupqa has particular salience with regard to death because it is the final destination for the *hiqwsi*, or breath spirit.

The elements of archaeological monuments that give cultural meaning to the landscape are inseparable from the graves associated with them. As explained by Abbott Sekaquaptewa from Hotvela,

> They are the monuments of our territorial domain. This is what I have been taught by the old people. They are there for a purpose. And that is to show that, if you get rid of the monument, then there is nothing to show that this is a territorial boundary of the pueblo clans. The other thing is that they left primarily old people when they moved on, but of course always with some younger people to look after the older people. The reason they left older people was because they did not have the strength to make another move to reestablish themselves. The other reason is that in time their spirits would be the guardians of those places...because their spirits, although they are not residing in the remains anymore, they continue to return there, and they abide in the general area where these sites are located. And that's the purpose. They are the guardians of those ancient places [in Ferguson 1998:266].

Agricultural Areas and Granaries

Hopi ancestors are believed to have occupied the Grand Canyon because of its abundant water resources and long growing season (Ferguson 1998: 263–264). Hopi people who today visit the archaeological remains of granaries in Öngtupqa, such as those found at Nankoweap, find pumpkin seeds and corncobs within these features (Figure 6.5).

FIGURE 6.5. Hopi researcher in the Grand Canyon inspecting granaries at Nankoweap. Photograph by T. J. Ferguson, April 28, 1994.

These cultigens are still important crops at Hopi, and along with the corn-grinding tools found at ancestral villages, they provide obvious evidence that Hopi ancestors were farmers, just as they are described in Hopi traditions. Some Hopi believe that their ancestors left seeds at Nankoweap and other granaries as a symbolic act because they expected other clans to come in and use the area after they left. This was done to honor the spiritual instructions the Hopi received to leave things for the people who would follow them. Even today, some Hopi farmers bury a jar of seeds in the field house at their farm for their descendants who will come later.

Hopis conducting research in the Grand Canyon pointed out that the growth of particular plants marks areas of productive farmland. The presence of sandy soil with stands of *suwvi* (saltbush) or *teeve* (greasewood) or the presence of *sivapi* (rabbitbrush) on any soil indicates a place that has farming potential. In the Grand Canyon, these areas are often located near ancient villages, reinforcing the cultural associations between ancestors and farming.

Roasting Pits and Cooking Pits

"Roasting pits" are a common archaeological feature in the Grand Canyon. The classic morphology of these pits was understood by Hopi cultural advisers in relation to archaeological formation processes, that is, the ring of discarded fire-cracked rock surrounds a center with larger stones marking the location of the pit. In the Hopi language, these features are called *tumqöpqö*. *Tum* derives from the word *tumowa*, which means "flat, hard rocks"; *qöpqö* means "oven." *Tuupe'* means "to cook." Hopi cultural advisers thought that most of the tumqöpqö in the Grand Canyon were used for baking agave. However, they suggested that these features may have also been used for roasting meat from small game or for heating stones that would be covered with sand to provide a warm sleeping platform. Similar pits are used for these purposes at Hopi, as well as for processing piñon pinecones with heat to release the nuts from them. Cooking pits represent a substantial investment of labor and thus an intensive use of the environment.

In considering cooking pit sites in the Grand

Canyon, Hopi research participants discussed whether these features may have more than functional meaning. The Hopi view these features as another example of the footprints their ancestors were instructed to leave on the landscape. Thus, at the same time that they embrace utilitarian explanations for archaeological sites, the Hopi imbue these features with additional, more culturally meaningful explanations relating to their pact with Màasaw.

Shrines, Offering Places, and Pilgrimage Trails

There are many Hopi shrines in Öngtupqa where sacred offerings are deposited. These shrines are situated in places determined by deities in ancient times, and they thus play an essential role in the Hopi religion. Most Euro-Americans view religious places such as churches or shrines as symbolic of a universal being. For the Hopi, however, as Vernon Masayesva explains, "Places and things here on earth often are more than symbols. God may actually be present in places or things here on earth" (1994:94). Masayesva notes that one way to protect native religious rites is to protect American Indian shrines.

Archaeologists have described the various types of physical construction associated with Hopi shrines near the Hopi villages (Adams 1986:47; Fewkes 1906, 1910:558), and these descriptions also apply to shrines in the Grand Canyon. Some shrines have no physical attributes other than prayer sticks deposited in the earth. Other shrines are marked by a single distinctive stone or by an enclosure of stones with an opening to the east. Some shrines are located in caves or natural depressions in a boulder. The most elaborate shrines are sealed stone vaults containing symbolic representations of supernatural beings, waterworn stones, or fossils. Some shrines have offerings associated with a particular spiritual purpose. For instance, a warrior's shrine contains netted shields, bows, and arrows, whereas an eagle shrine may contain painted wooden fetishes representing eagle's eggs. Some shrines are used to store ceremonial paraphernalia. Springs are used as places to deposit prayer offerings, and they are thus considered by Hopis to be shrines.

Hopi cultural advisers pointed out that every Hopi settlement has a plaza with a *pahoki*, or shrine for depositing the prayer feathers that spiritually integrate the life of the village (Ferguson 1998:255–258; see also Fewkes 1906:360; Frigout 1979:568). Ancestral villages, even those in "ruin," are living things. These shrines are believed to be present at archaeological sites in the Grand Canyon even if their archaeological expression may not be visible on the surface. In the Grand Canyon, Hopi cultural advisers believe, shrines are also located outside of the boundaries of archaeological sites as mapped by archaeologists. These outlying shrines may be interpreted as simple "rock piles" or cairns by archaeologists, who thus undervalue their true significance. In addition, some cultural advisers considered archaeological sites themselves to be shrines because they are places where ancestors are buried with offerings.

Hopi shrines and offering places in Öngtupqa range from subtle natural features to well-constructed architectural forms. From the Hopi perspective, the most important element of these shrines is a spiritual value determined by religious factors, not the physical expression of shrines as archaeological sites. Shrines in Öngtupqa are associated with the spiritual aspects of emergence, migration, manhood initiation, death, rainfall, fertility, and other important aspects of the Hopi religion (Eggan 1994:11–14).

The shrines in Öngtupqa are connected with a pilgrimage trail that leads from the Hopi villages to the Hopi Salt Mine in the Grand Canyon (Eiseman 1959, 1961; Ferguson 1998:151–214; Fewkes 1906:352–353; Simmons 1942:232–246). This trail, more than 128 km (80 mi) in length, is marked by 37 shrines and named places, including a shrine where clan marks were left by the pilgrimage participants; shrines where prayer offerings were ritually deposited; shrines associated with Hopi deities; and shrines where water, pigments, and salt were collected for ritual use at Hopi. The Salt Pilgrimage to Öngtupqa is associated with the Third Mesa Wuwstim ceremony, but the pilgrimage trail was also used for ritual purposes by religious leaders from other Hopi villages. The pilgrimage route and its associated shrines provide a physical and spiritual connection that ties together the cultural landscapes of the Hopi villages and Öngtupqa.

FIGURE 6.6. Boulder covered with petroglyphs at Tutuveni marking the clan affiliation of Salt Pilgrimage participants. Photograph by T. J. Ferguson, July 15, 1992.

The Hopi place a great cultural importance on their shrines, in the Grand Canyon and everywhere else they occur. As former tribal chairman Abbott Sekaquaptewa stated, "The most important thing is the shrines. The elders say that the shrines are our standards—the way white people raise flags over their territory. Without our shrines, our inheritance, we simply cannot continue as Hopis" (in Page 1982:626).

Trail Markers

Hopi cultural advisers working in Öngtupqa noted that trail markers occur at intervals along Hopi trails in the Grand Canyon (Ferguson 1998:258). These cairns or rock piles are constructed to visually mark the route of trails. Hopis on pilgrimages to the Grand Canyon would also pick up rocks and place them on rock piles for ceremonial purposes. In addition, offering places and shrines that may look like cairns will also mark trails. A regional perspective is needed to correctly interpret "rock piles" by tracing their linear connections in a regional context.

Petroglyphs and Pictographs

The generic Hopi term for petroglyphs and pictographs is *tutuveni*. *Peeni* (or *peena*) is glossed as "writing," so the Hopi term *tutuveni* is interpreted to mean "their marks" (McCreery and Malotki 1994). Hopi cultural advisers noted that they interpret rock art by reference to Hopi teachings (Ferguson 1998:259–262). The petroglyphs and pictographs along the Salt Pilgrimage trail, and in the Grand Canyon, are therefore fascinating and meaningful aspects of the archaeological record that Hopis value greatly as the signs of their ancestors.

Petroglyphs are one of the most important elements of the archaeological record used by Hopi people in defining cultural landscapes. This is because petroglyphs embody iconographic elements that mark the occupation of land by specific clans (Bernardini 2005a:93–116). The Hopi inscription of clan symbols is well documented at Tutuveni, one of the series of shrines associated with the Salt Pilgrimage trail to the Grand Canyon (Bernardini 2005b; Colton and Colton 1931; Ferguson 1998; Michaelis 1981). Here, for centuries, Hopi religious practitioners have stopped on the way to the Grand Canyon to carve a petroglyph depicting the *wuuya* (totemic symbol) of their clan (Simmons 1942:232–246). More than 2,000 individual petroglyphs representing 33 Hopi clans have been placed on cliff faces and freestanding boulders at Tutuveni. If an individual was repeating the pilgrimage, he would carve his clan glyph next to the one he had previously made, producing a wonderful sequence of repetitive images (Figure 6.6). One such sequence of glyphs documents that members from the Corn Clan made 16 pilgrimages along the Salt Trail. Other sequences contain fewer individual glyphs, and a number of single glyphs indicate that many Hopi men were only privileged to make a single pilgrimage as part of their Wuwstim initiation into manhood.

Similar to the petroglyphs at Tutuveni, there are several pictographs of clan totems at the Hopi Salt Mine, painted with hematite obtained from another nearby shrine. Taken together, these petroglyphs visually confirm that Hopi clansmen have repeatedly performed their ritual responsibilities associated with Öngtupqa. The images pecked into or painted on rocks serve as important monuments and shrines marking the route of the pilgrimage trail and provide a powerful historical connection between the performance of ancient and contemporary Hopi ceremonies.

Hopi petroglyphs dating from the period AD 1300 to the present have also been recorded in the Glen Canyon stretch of the Colorado River. Foster (1954:15) and Turner (1963:27–28) observe that petroglyphs in Glen Canyon are similar to symbols associated with Hopi rituals and clans. For instance, the Water, Snake, and Reed clans have ethnographically documented totemic symbols similar to the petroglyphs in Glen Canyon. Petroglyphs in Glen Canyon provide evidence of a direct cultural and historical relationship between its ancient occupants and the modern Hopi. Turner (1963:5–6) concludes that these petroglyphs are linked to revisitation of the canyon by Hopis, an interpretation supported by the presence of Hopi yellow ware sherds.

The Hopi, like archaeologists (Adams 1986:20–21), recognize that prehistoric and historic petroglyphs and pictographs indicate long-term Hopi use of the landscape. These petroglyphs "demonstrate and validate the Hopi claim to aboriginal presence in the Four Corners area" (Leigh Jenkins, in Widdison 1991:32). Many Hopi advisers interpreted the petroglyphs in the Grand Canyon as clan marks created during the migration of Hopi ancestors (Ferguson 1998:259–262). Glyphs of spirals, called *potaveni*, are a common symbol depicting Hopi migration (Malotki and Lomatuway'ma 1987:28), and this migration symbol implies that clans were present (Fewkes 1897:3). In addition to clan totems and migration symbols, Hopis also interpret some painted handprints as symbols made by clan leaders to mark the lands under the stewardship of their clan. Other, often isolated handprints signify other meanings, perhaps boundary markers for the use of land associated with agricultural activities.

Some petroglyphs in the Grand Canyon are thought to be symbolic images tied to human land uses or ritual practices rather than representations of clan signs. A petroglyph of a rabbit, for instance, may be a clan symbol, but it may also simply represent a successful hunt or even the spirit of the depicted animal. The knowledge needed to interpret the power and meaning of petroglyphs as cultural symbols is not universally shared at Hopi, so there are often multiple interpretations of petroglyphs. People from different villages may have different interpretations of a glyph based on esoteric knowledge specific to their community. Some Hopis think that petroglyphs are supposed to remain a mystery and that some petroglyphs may simply be children's creations. Other petroglyphs and pictographs may just be rock *art* and not ritually meaningful symbols. Variation in individual knowledge about the meaning of petroglyphs introduces a personal element into the cognition of cultural landscapes.

The ambiguity of some petroglyphs fosters discourse about them among Hopi people. During fieldwork in the Grand Canyon, cultural advisers often spent considerable time discussing petroglyphs, asking each other what they meant, and sharing traditional stories that these images brought to mind. Hopi men thus learned from one another while talking about the archaeological elements of the landscape (Ferguson 1998:261). The sharing of information between tribal members is an important component of the interpretive dynamic that unfolds when petroglyphs are encountered on the landscape. The glyphs represent the past, but their contemporary interpretation makes sense of the present.

Regardless of interpretative issues, it is clear that the petroglyphs and pictographs in the Grand Canyon are meaningful for many Hopi people. In describing a river trip he made with Bureau of Reclamation and National Park Service officials, for instance, Ferrell Secakuku, the chairman of the Hopi Tribe, reported,

> And when I went to see the petroglyphs I already recognized it right away. Because

knowing what I have learned from my uncles, that we do have some places down there that we have stayed as we traveled the river. You have probably heard about the Tiyo...but there are other times that we went down through there. And these are the places where, I guess, we rested for several days. And these are the places where we stayed to recuperate and then, then also gain, gather food from the other, from the top, and then we went on. But this place was definitely a Snake Clan place were it has a snake petroglyphs on there. And then it also have a petroglyph of the Lizard Man. And much of the Horny Toad.

And then it also had migration pattern there. And then that is what I explained as being the four worlds and then how I explained that to them. And that's what we believe then, that is still the basis of our culture and our religion and that is what we practice during this Men's Ceremony that we call the *Wuwtsim*. And then I explained to them about the different societies, the four societies that we have—the One Horn, Two Horn, the Singers, and [the Wuwtsim] [in Ferguson 1998:261].

For Hopi people, the petroglyphs and pictographs in the Grand Canyon provide definite evidence that their ancestors inhabited this area in the past. Whether they were produced as clan marks, as ritual symbols, or for other purposes, in the Hopi worldview these petroglyphs mark ancestral sites. As Dalton Taylor from Songoopavi said, "What our old folks tell us to look for if we ever go to any ruins or sites is a circle like a plaque. A spiral. Look for that, if you find it that tells you our people was there" (in Ferguson 1998:262).

Reading the Landscape of Öngtupqa

During fieldwork in the Grand Canyon, Hopi men who had not previously traveled along the river corridor readily interpreted the cultural landscape of Öngtupqa. The location of shrines in relation to the striking topographical features of the canyon; the presence of mines where salt and pigments have been procured; the historical association between Hopi ancestors and ancient archaeological sites; the presence of potsherds, grinding tools, cooking features, and agricultural fields—all of these are recounted in Hopi traditions. When these archaeological features are encountered in the Grand Canyon, the Hopi understand their ritual and historical associations in relation to the natural environment and the religious teachings they are entrusted with (Loma'omvaya et al. 2001). Origin, migration, stewardship, life, and death are all evident in the setting and composition of ancestral archaeological sites in the Grand Canyon. Archaeological sites augment the natural grandeur of Öngtupqa, helping to define a powerful cultural landscape central in Hopi cosmology and history.

Place, Scale, Time, and Context in the Archaeology of Cultural Landscapes

As archaeological sites, kuktota constitute discrete places on the land. They occupy a geographic space that can be physically bounded by architectural remains, artifact scatters, and other features. In Hopi thought, however, these sites are inextricably associated with the surrounding region. The culturally meaningful scale needed to interpret kuktota thus far exceeds the boundaries of archaeological sites as delineated by artifact scatters and architecture. Furthermore, as elements of cultural landscapes, archaeological sites need to be interpreted in sets rather than in isolation. A regional scale is thus needed to comprehend kuktota.

For example, the Hopi Cultural Preservation Office recently collaborated with Desert Archaeology, Inc., in an investigation of 40 archaeological sites in the right-of-way of U.S. Highway 89 north of Flagstaff, Arizona (Ferguson and Loma'omvaya 2000). This project area lies northeast of the San Francisco Peaks, in a landscape that overlooks the Little Colorado River Valley and a complex of archaeological sites within Wupatki National Monument. With the help of Hopi cultural advisers, we were able to place these archaeological sites in a broad ethnohistoric context, with Nuvatukya'ovi (the San Francisco Peaks) and Wupatki anchoring one end of the cultural landscape and the Hopi Mesas anchoring the other. We found that the history of the relatively small archaeological sites within the project area could only be understood in relation to the trajectories of clan migrations, the Hopi deities that are associated with various landforms, and the routes across the project area

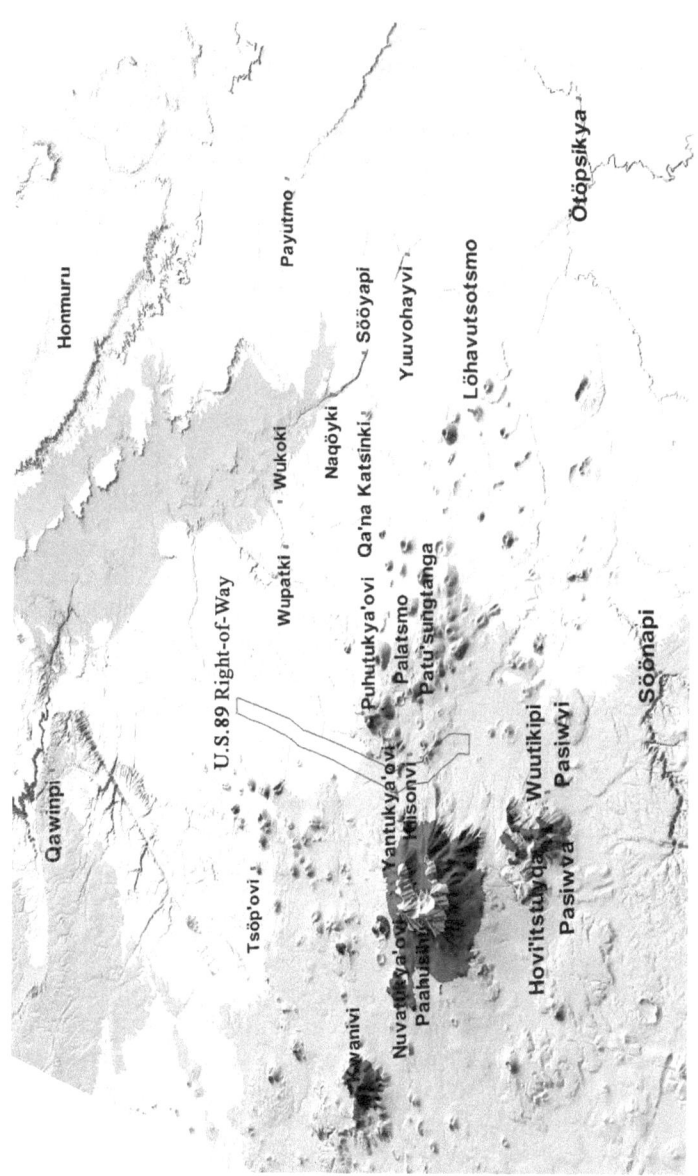

FIGURE 6.7. Cultural landscape of Pasiwvi needed to understand archaeological sites along a road right-of-way near Flagstaff. The area depicted in this figure encompasses more than 8,000 km².

Hopi people travel during religious pilgrimages to the San Francisco Peaks (Figure 6.7). Visiting the small archaeological sites in the project area recalled the larger patterns of Hopi history, and in the Hopi view these small sites can only be comprehended by considering their role in the region as a whole.

This region, more than 8,000 km² in size, constitutes Pasiwvi, a place name derived from the Hopi words *pasiwni* (intent, plan, design) and *pasiwta* (be finished, completed). *Pasiwvi* is sometimes translated as the "meeting place" or "the place of making decision" (Hopi Dictionary Project 1998:394). *Pasiwvi* simultaneously signifies a specific pueblo, a geographic region, and an epoch. Its conceptualization thus combines spatial and temporal elements, and the interpretation of Pasiwvi is dependent on narrative context. As a place name, *Pasiwvi* is applied to Elden Pueblo, but it also applies to the region surrounding Nuvatukya'ovi, including the archaeological sites in the U.S. 89 study area. It is in the region encompassing these sites that clans came together to receive and deliberate over spiritual instructions on how to conduct migrations and be Hopi. Pasiwvi is thus a place of great thought, where Hopi ancestors met and contemplated their spiritual covenant with Màasaw to leave their footprints on the land and serve as earth stewards. After clans migrated from Pasiwvi to the Hopi Mesas, Hopi people traveled back to the area to make religious offerings, for example, at shrines located at archaeological sites. The trails used during these pilgrimages are linear archaeological sites that provide a physical connection between Nuvatukya'ovi and the Hopi villages, and their use provides an opportunity for new generations of Hopi people to revisit ancestral villages and thus, experience Hopi history.

While hundreds of ancestral sites are known by Hopi names, such as Yupköyvi (Chaco Canyon) and Tawtoykya (Mesa Verde), many thousands more are unnamed but nevertheless important in Hopi history. As contemporary Hopi people encounter the footprints of their ancestors, new place names are created, and these often refer to prominent features of the land. Hopi cultural advisers came to know Nankoweap in the Grand Canyon, for instance, as Patatpela or "Red Cliff" (Ferguson 1998:307). This name provides a meaningful way to recall the ancestral sites at Nankoweap when they are described to people who have not directly experienced them. These place names thus operate at various scales, sometimes encompassing both a single site and a group of closely related sites in their natural setting.

As discussed, Hopi people interpret petroglyphs and pictographs as signs left by their ancestors throughout the Southwest. Clan symbols, handprints, and depictions of ritual figures provide a visual medium embedded in the land that connects contemporary Hopi people with their ancestors. In addition, Hopis who examine petroglyphs and pictographs often trace them with their fingertips or match their hands to them, providing a tactile dimension to the physical connection they experience. As with other types of archaeological sites, it is necessary to see petroglyphs in relation to their surrounding physical setting in order to put thoughts together and interpret them. The geophysical placement of images on rocks and the scale of the surrounding landscape are both essential attributes of petroglyph sites.

Time is implicated in archaeological sites because they represent a series of places occupied by clan ancestors in an earlier era, a period between emergence and the establishment of the Hopi villages. This underscores the historicity of ancestral sites. While Hopi people appreciate and make use of chronological data provided by scientific archaeology, in Hopi theories of the past the spatial geography recounted in traditional clan histories is more important than time as an absolute, linear scale. The location of archaeological sites on the landscape carries meaning in relation to accounts that describe the directions various clans traveled as they set their footprints on the land, and this directionalism entails a relative temporal sequence in which a series of sites is sequentially occupied, leading to the founding of the various Hopi villages. The Tonto Cliff Dwellings in central Arizona, for instance, were occupied by Hopi clans during their journey from Palatkwapi (the "Red Land of the South") to the Hopi Mesas (Ferguson and Loma'omvaya 1999:73–120). The spatial placement of Wukoskyavi (Tonto Basin) between Mexico and Hopi is as important in Hopi concepts of the past as the absolute dating of the site by archaeologists to the fourteenth century (Fox and Dean 1996).

The context of archaeological sites within the Hopi belief system is an essential element of the cultural landscape. Ancestral villages that have fallen into ruin are not dead places whose only meaning comes from scientific values. The Hopi ancestors who lived in these villages still spiritually occupy these places, and these ancestors play an integral and ongoing role in the contemporary Hopi ceremonies that bring rain, fertility, and other blessings for the Hopi people and their neighbors throughout the world. Kuktota—footprints—are thus part of the living legacy of the ancestors, and they play a vital role in the religious activities essential to the perpetuation of Hopi society. Ancestors and sacred objects were buried in ancestral villages, and the Hopi thus treat these places as shrines. Hopi people visiting an ancestral site feel a deep reverence for both the place and the surrounding landscape of which it is a part.

Navoti and *Wiimi*: Archaeological Sites, Cultural Landscapes, and the Phenomenology of Hopi History

Much of Hopi history is phenomenological inasmuch as it is apprehended subjectively through the personal experience of archaeological sites and cultural landscapes. At a personal level, many Hopi people transcend the factual knowledge and assumptions derived from scientific archaeology to allow a pure intuition of history to be directly experienced based on spiritual purpose, intention, and respect for ancestors. This experience is tempered by an individual's understanding of *navoti* and *wiimi*. Navoti is a historical understanding derived from experiences handed down by ancestors to their descendants. Wiimi includes sacred artifacts and the knowledge of how to use them properly in religious ceremonies and rituals. Wiimi is an essential part of the archaeological record, often having been ritually deposited by Hopi ancestors engaged in religious activities in the ancient past. Together, navoti and wiimi provide both the means to know the past and the ability to invoke the power of the ancestors in the present through ritual offerings and ceremonies (Loma'omvaya and Ferguson 1999). The propitiation of ancestors through prayers based on navoti and wiimi is key to maintaining Hopi culture and life. In Hopi thought, the meaning of the past is what it contributes to life in the present.

Places and landscapes have the power to recall the past in a direct fashion (Küchler 1993; Morphy 1995). Cultural landscapes thus encompass land and human experience. Within these cultural landscapes, archaeological sites help situate people in historical time and space. Cultural landscapes thus provide a conceptual framework for historical knowledge. Archaeological sites are enduring features on the land, and as a result cultural landscapes can be sustained for long periods without direct physical use. Hopi people encountering cultural landscapes for the first time have the ability to draw upon navoti and wiimi to share the past with their ancestors. In this way, archaeological sites and cultural landscapes are used to construct contemporary social identities.

Archaeological sites thus provide insight into the connection between the Hopi past and present that confirms navoti as historical experience. The veracity of navoti is not in question, but Hopi people take note when archaeological data are found to support descriptions of life embedded in navoti. Many elements of ancient material culture, especially ritual objects and iconography, serve to confirm the historicity of wiimi. The historical association with Hopi ancestors is reinforced when Hopi people discover ritual artifacts in the archaeological record that are identical to wiimi still in use in Hopi ceremonies. The abiding connection Hopi people have with the material culture of their ancestors gives archaeology a deeply personal as well as intellectual meaning. Archaeology thus helps give focus to the comprehension of ancestral lifeways embodied in the monuments that constitute Hopi footprints on the landscape.

Conclusion

We conclude by observing that Hopi conceptions of cultural landscapes find expression in diverse media that operate at many different levels of meaning. For instance, Hopi conceptions of cultural landscapes are reified in the rattles given to young boys in sacred dances. Many of these

FIGURE 6.8. Hopi rattle symbolizing elements of the cultural landscape. Photograph by T. J. Ferguson, November 11, 2001.

rattles incorporate symbolism that invokes the spiritual leadership of the ancestors in Hopitutskwa (evidenced by footprints), the area of the Hopi heartland, Màasaw's land (with its corn, plants, and life), and the migration of clans that led to the founding of Hopi villages (Figure 6.8). Hopis witnessing dancing in the plaza of their village are focused on the performance of their religious activities, but the rattles connect them with cultural landscapes that extend to the full extent of Hopitutskwa. When not being used in ceremonies, these rattles are often displayed on the walls of Hopi houses, where they serve as a daily reminder of how navoti and wiimi link Hopi footprints, history, and cultural landscapes.

7

Negotiating the Imperial Landscape

The Geopolitics of Aztec Control in the Outer Provinces of the Empire

Christopher P. Garraty and Michael A. Ohnersorgen

Landscapes are dynamic cultural constructions (Anschuetz et al. 2001) that encompass not only the natural environment but also the broader physical, social, and political milieus in which people live. Landscapes encompass physical and natural properties as well as humans and the ways they conceptualize, experience, and symbolize the landscape (Fisher and Thurston 1999). Landscapes, therefore, have culturally organized dimensions that are shaped by human activities, beliefs, and values (Ingold 1993). As arenas for human activity, landscapes in turn structure and organize perception and action (Anschuetz et al. 2001:161; cf. Bourdieu 1977). Human interaction with the landscape is therefore one of continual negotiation and mediation (Knapp and Ashmore 1999): "The landscape is never inert; people engage with it, re-work it, appropriate and contest it. It is part of the way in which identities are created and disputed, whether as individual, group, or nation-state" (Bender 1993:3).

The spatial-temporal dimensions of land use have driven numerous distributional and historical studies of landscapes, including settlement pattern studies (Anschuetz et al. 2001; Ashmore 2002; Fisher and Thurston 1999; Knapp and Ashmore 1999). We perceive landscapes as social and symbolic constructs instilled with social meaning and collective memories (Alcock 2001). Perceptions of landscape are thus crucial to social reproduction, and landscape studies are well suited to address issues of sociopolitical change: "Landscape is 'integral to both the reproduction and contestation of political power' (Duncan 1990:3), a direct reflection of human-conceived boundaries and administration, and also of spatial perceptions, belief systems, power and conflict" (Thurston 1999:662).

Bender (1999:633) and Alcock (2001) suggest that periods of major social change, such as state formation, urbanization, and political upheavals, should constitute an important focus of landscape studies. It is during such times that new attitudes toward the physical world are forged, as are new social, cultural, and political relations with the land and with other people. Thurston (1999:661) makes a similar point, referring to periods of major political upheaval as "critical junctures" when social institutions are particularly vulnerable and when society can be dramatically reshaped through combinations of force, threat, terror, and the creation of false consciousness. In Mesoamerica, the Aztec conquest of outer provincial areas and the spread of a Late Postclassic world system of economic and stylistic interaction (Berdan and Smith 2003) represent exactly this kind of major upheaval to perceptions of social and political relations, and we examine the ways these relations were reinvented to satisfy imperial goals and how populations reacted to create new landscapes of social and political power.

In this chapter we suggest that imperial rule in the outer provinces of the Aztec Empire effected a transformation of the landscape by altering public perceptions of social relations and the meanings of place. We adopt a geopolitical landscape perspective to evaluate landscape changes in the imperial provinces. Briefly, geopolitics can be defined as the study of the ways in which political entities perceive national and international spatial arrangements (e.g., community borders, "global" resource access) and how these perceptions are mobilized for strategic or economic advantage (Cohen 2003; O'Tuathail 1996; Parker 1998). Imperial interactions with provincial populations reflect the degree to which subject populations accepted, rejected, or resisted an imperial (international) presence juxtaposed against the retention of local *sovereignty* over space and social landscape divisions. Sovereignty is here defined as a suite of cultural dispositions that tie a given group to a certain space, including indigenous identities, traditions, and long-standing social networks (after Kuus 2002).

To control provincial populations and ensure tribute receipts, Aztec imperial leaders actively sought to redefine geopolitical landscapes through military threat, co-optation of provincial leaders and sacred places, imposition of imperial symbols and ideology, market expansion, population reorganization, tribute, and the manipulation of economic and land-use patterns (Smith 2001). However, empires do not simply arise from the political initiatives instigated by imperial leaders but from the actions and initiatives of both imperial leaders and subject populations (e.g., Balkansky 2002). For example, some local elites voluntarily allied themselves with ancient imperial regimes to bolster their authority and to cement control over their subject constituencies. Other elites may have resisted the imperial presence or only reluctantly accepted imperial rule, perhaps because imperial demands brought about a reduction in tribute receipts for themselves, limited their governing authority, or both.

Many provincial commoners also benefited from market opportunities introduced by integration into an international market arena or, in some cases, from the restructuring of land-tenure systems by imperial leaders. Still other commoners actively resisted imperial rule, knowing that they would have to shoulder greater responsibility for added tribute demands or incur other forms of socioeconomic changes that could effectively alienate some commoners from local economic institutions, such as local marketplaces. Overall, different factions and "interest groups" in subject polities likely saw a number of different benefits and costs to alliance with, or resistance to, imperial regimes. Conceptions of the landscape under Aztec rule, we argue, were constantly renegotiated, as imperial leaders fine-tuned their strategies for maintaining control and provincial populations fine-tuned strategies to exploit, resist, or cope with the imperial regime. As a result, what we refer to as imperial practices—that is, the outcomes of core-subject interactions rather than core-centric imperial strategies—reflect the interactions and ongoing *social negotiations* among imperial and local agencies (Brumfiel 1992). We follow Brumfiel's definition of social negotiation as the "conflicts and compromises among people with different problems and possibilities by virtue of their membership in different alliance networks" (1992:551).

We begin our study with a brief discussion of the concept of geopolitical landscape. We then outline its applicability to the Aztec Empire. We explore changes in the geopolitical landscape on the outer provinces of the Aztec Empire, drawing mostly upon recently collected surface data from the Gulf Coast of Mexico, specifically from the imperial province of Cuetlaxtlan.[1] For comparison, we also draw on data from another outer imperial province, the Oztuma-Cutzamala region of the State of Guerrero, west Mexico (Silverstein 2000, 2001).[2] We conclude that the imperial rule at the outer provinces reflected a variety of imperial-instigated landscape shifts. Cotaxtla, the provincial capital of Cuetlaxtlan, strongly resisted imperial rule, which necessitated overt tactics designed to suppress the traditional sociopolitical importance of the center. The center shows evidence for a fairly strong imperial presence that included the installation of imperial and military officials, possible colonists, and a program of imperial-style art, architecture, and ritual practices. In addition, surface data from a probable Cotaxtla hinterland in the Lower Blanco River region reveal the replacement of a pre-imperial Middle Postclassic (AD 1200–1350/1400) center, El

Sauce, and the founding of a new Late Postclassic (AD 1350/1400–1520) center at Callejón del Horno in a previously uninhabited (or lightly inhabited) area (Garraty and Stark 2002). This relocation might indicate a deliberate strategy to symbolically divorce Callejón del Horno from the governing establishment previously centered at El Sauce. This shift, along with the adoption of Aztec-style pottery as media for expressing elite status, suggests a possible suppression of pre-imperial elite practices and institutions.

Defining the Geopolitical Landscape: Local Sovereignty and International Networks

We frame our study of Aztec imperial practices in terms of a *geopolitical landscape*. We use Cohen's (2003) framework for studying geopolitics because it provides a suitably flexible framework for the present analysis. According to Cohen,

> [Geopolitics is] the analysis of the interaction between, on the one hand, geographical settings and perspectives and, on the other hand, political processes. The settings are composed of geographic features and patterns and the multilayered regions that they form. The political processes include forces that operate at the international level and those on the domestic scene that influence international behavior. Both geographical settings and political processes are dynamic, and each influences and is influenced by the other. Geopolitics addresses the consequences of this interaction [2003:12].

Cohen's broad framework can be broken down into a nearly limitless array of themes and topics. Important in this definition is Cohen's mention of "geographical settings and perspectives," which point to the variable agencies of different governing units or factions involved in negotiating political landscape features such as political boundaries, locations and meanings of central places, and important loci of ethnic or religious identity (2003:23). Many modern geopolitical studies (Blouet 2001; Kuus 2002) address the struggles of small nation-states to retain local sovereignty and "border maintenance" in the face of pressures from economic globalization (e.g., intrusions of multinational corporations) and international confederations (e.g., NAFTA, the European Union). Studies of ancient imperialism and state expansion involve similar themes. State formation and state expansion *necessarily* concern conflicts between expansionist state agencies seeking to promote broad regional integration and the means they employ to undercut local or domestic interest groups seeking to retain local sovereignty and native traditions (Gailey and Patterson 1987; Patterson 1991). Many of these conflicts relate to the political understanding and manipulations of landscapes and territorial borders. The ways that domestic and "international" agents differently define, maintain, contest, and breach the cognized political landscape divisions and place designations can be conceived as processes of social negotiation (Brumfiel 1992).

The phrase *geopolitical landscape* may seem redundant, since the control and contestation of physical space and landscape features are implicit in the definition of geopolitics above. For our purposes, however, we use the term *geopolitics* to refer to the processes inherent in socially negotiating the political meanings of space. The geopolitical landscape, then, represents the culmination of these processes, that is, their physical consequences and the archaeological patterns that reflect them. The benefit of the geopolitical landscape approach adopted here is that, by definition, it considers the multitude of agencies and interactive processes involved in defining the diverse means the empire used to consolidate power over a massive expanse.

From a geopolitical landscape perspective, we argue below that the paucity, or abundance, of Aztec-related material culture in the outer provinces of the empire does not so much reflect imperial strategies but, rather, the outcomes of negotiations among imperial and subject populations. In other words, the degree to which the imperial presence was communicated through material media (e.g., Aztec goods, architecture) can be viewed not only in terms of imperial strategies but also in terms of the degree to which local populations and interest groups willingly allied and affiliated themselves with the imperial regime. As a result, provincial administrative practices were shaped by many local particularities that changed over space and time, likely resulting in a patchwork of administrative strategies that will be revealed as provincial locations are examined more closely (Berdan and Smith 1996; Ohnersorgen 2006).

The Aztec Geopolitical Landscape: Imperial Efforts to Weaken Sovereignty in the Outer Provinces

Ancient expansionist states, as well as modern ones, had to contend with the problem of how to circumvent local traditions, ethnicities, identities, and desires to retain sovereignty and realign local interests to comply with state interests (Brumfiel 2000; Gailey and Patterson 1987). The Inca policy for confronting this problem was to resettle entire communities hundreds of kilometers away from their homelands (*mitmaq*); perhaps one-quarter to one-third of the subject population of the Inca Empire was subject to resettlement in distant, unfamiliar places (D'Altroy 2002; Patterson 1987, 1991). Group sovereignty is closely tied to the landscape (Kuus 2002), and thus the Incas undermined local sovereignty by alienating groups from their homelands and from the spatial focus of native histories, identities, and meanings. State formation at Teotihuacán also may have involved massive resettlement of rural communities in the burgeoning metropolis, where subject populations could be more easily monitored and taxed (Millon 1981; Pasztory 1997; Sanders et al. 1979). Resettlement is a costly means of subverting local sovereignty, however, since it requires a large policing force to monitor the resettlement process and ensure compliance.

The Aztecs generally employed a less costly, noninterventionist policy. If imperial leaders received the tribute or strategic assistance they demanded from a subject polity, they generally left local traditions and sovereign borders intact. Hicks (1994) explains that the imperial regime employed an extensive spy network to gather intelligence about internal political factions in a given polity or region. Aztec emissaries then sought to forge alliances with the factions they perceived as potentially friendly to imperial interests. Local factions and leaders in provincial territories probably differently perceived the costs and benefits of alliance versus contestation to Aztec rule. Berdan and Smith (1996; Smith 1986; Smith and Berdan 1992) emphasize that many local elites benefited enormously from alliance with the imperial regime, since they had the imperial force to back up their heightened tribute demands. Many also benefited by gaining access to interregional market exchanges, which were a major source of elite revenues in the core of the empire in the Basin of Mexico (Blanton 1996; Hassig 1985) and probably in the outer provinces as well. The fostering of common interests among elites throughout the imperial domain formed a strong basis for imperial consolidation (Smith 1986), which Berdan and Smith (1996) call the Aztec "elite strategy."

Although less costly, the Aztec noninterventionist strategy necessitated a delicate touch, in that it largely rested on the ability of Aztec leaders to extract tribute and labor without alienating local elites and undermining their sovereignty. For this reason, the elite strategy was not always effective, and many elites resisted imperial demands (Berdan and Smith 1996:210–211). Some local leaders were reluctant to cede tribute and land to imperial overlords but did so to evade the risks entailed by *not* complying with imperial demands. As such, many had to live with the constant threat of removal from office or additional imperial demands (Berdan and Smith 1996:215). The Aztec regime viewed military conquest as a less desirable, more costly alternative to alliance building (Hassig 1984, 1985), and it generally refrained from implementing more direct means of control, such as military occupation, colonization, or regime changes, unless deemed necessary.

The extent to which imperial forces intruded on local sovereignties was tailored to specific contexts, contingent upon the cooperation of local elites, preexisting ties to other states (especially to enemies of the empire, such as Tlaxcalla and the Tarascan state [see Figure 7.1]), and the importance of a given province to imperial economic and strategic interests. For example, Boone, discussing regional manuscript-painting styles and annalistic methods, discusses "the uneven quality of Aztec political and cultural influence" (1996: 205). Provincial elites near the imperial core in the Basin of Mexico generally adopted Aztec painting styles and annalistic methods, but acceptance was spotty in outer provinces. Mixtec lords (southeast of the basin), although subject to imperial rule, were unwilling to adopt these practices (Boone 1996). Conversely, elites in other

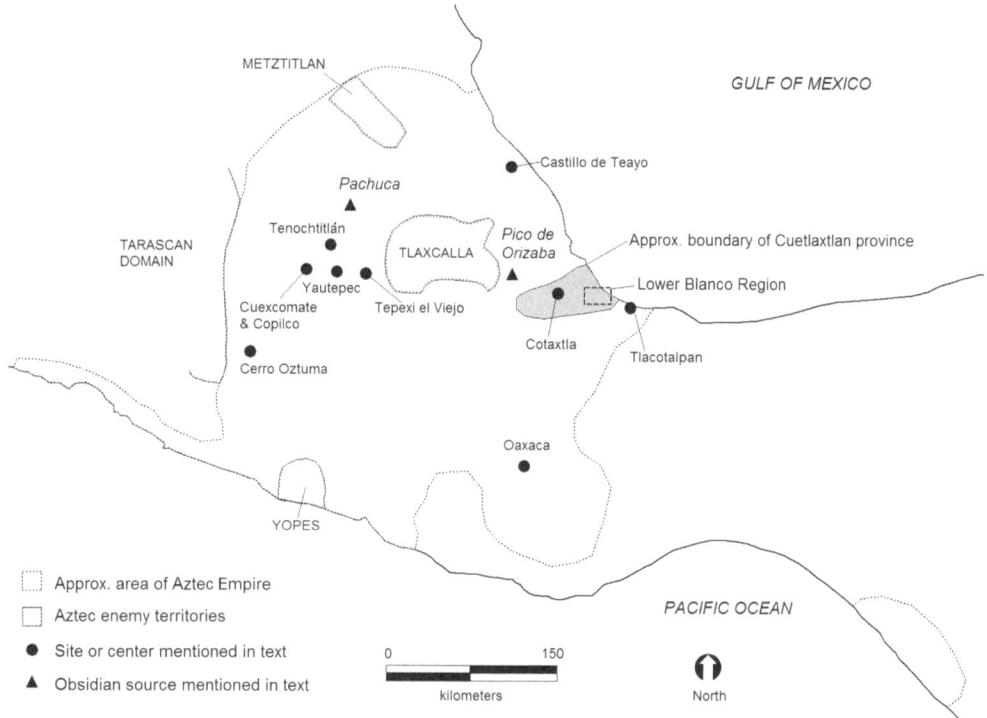

FIGURE 7.1. Map of Postclassic western Mesoamerica showing approximate boundaries of the Aztec Empire, enemy territories, and the major sites, regions, and obsidian sources mentioned in the text. The Cuetlaxtlan provincial borders are approximated from a map created by Berdan et al. (1996) but expanded slightly to include the Lower Blanco region (see text).

outer provinces—in the northern Gulf Coast, for example—accepted them.

Boone's (1996) example is instructive about how interaction between elites in the core and provincial areas socially negotiated the imperial presence and how this negotiation process shaped the geopolitical landscape of the empire. Some provincial elites openly adopted imperial styles and goods to communicate their allegiance to the imperial regime. Others forged alliance with the empire (possibly under duress) but sought to retain local sovereignty in styles and traditions. The importance of a conquered region to imperial interests and the military or economic power of some polities probably provided leverage for some elites in the outer provinces to negotiate retention of sovereignty. The Aztec regime always maintained at least a cursory presence, however, by placing imperial tax collectors, or *calpixques*, in subject provinces (Carrasco 1999; Hicks 1992). Beyond this, the materialization of an imperial presence would have been a matter of social negotiation—first, between imperial and local elites and second, between local leaders and their constituencies, with whom they shared a common history and ethnic identity (Brumfiel 1994). In the remainder of this essay, we consider archaeological evidence for social negotiations of the meanings of place in the outer provinces of the empire.

Archaeological Survey and Surface Collection in Cuetlaxtlan, Veracruz, Mexico

Cuetlaxtlan is located in the lower western basin of the Papaloapan River in south-central Veracruz (Figure 7.1). The Papaloapan River, one of the largest in Mexico, drains into a confluence of tributaries on the southern Gulf Coast. One of these tributaries, the Blanco River, courses into a delta-distributary zone, demarcated by the split of the Blanco and de las Pozas rivers, before it drains

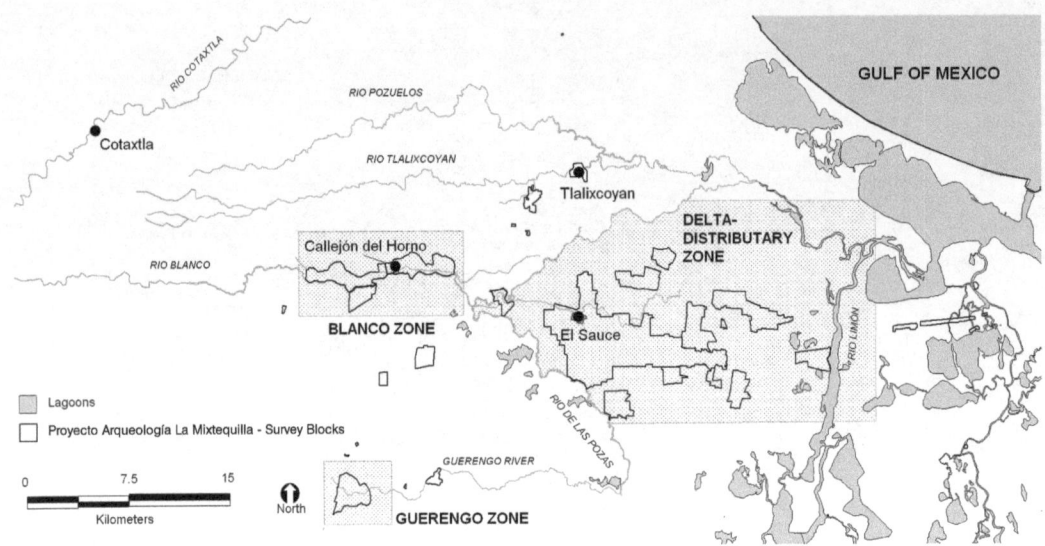

FIGURE 7.2. The south-central Gulf lowlands of Veracruz showing the approximate locations of Cotaxtla and the Lower Blanco region survey areas.

into a complex of estuarine lagoons and mangrove along the coastal plain (Figure 7.2). The Blanco delta-distributary zone was a favored region of prehispanic settlement (Stark 1999), largely because its moist, low-lying soils (0–20 m above sea level) are amenable to recessional agriculture (Speaker 2001; Stark 1999). Farther west are the Cotaxtla River and its distributaries, which drain into the Gulf of Mexico just south of modern Veracruz City.

The Aztecs first conquered Cuetlaxtlan in the late 1450s or early 1460s, at which time it was strongly allied with Tlaxcalla, an enemy state of the Aztec Empire (see Ohnersorgen 2006:8–13). This affiliation helped fuel rebellion, and several Aztec rulers ultimately claimed conquest of the capital, Cotaxtla. The Cuetlaxtlan province extended from the coast at least into the foothills of the eastern Sierra Madre, where Cotaxtla is located. In contrast to the low-lying, relatively wet coastal plain, the piedmont zone is semiarid, and the terrain is rough and broken by bedrock hills and small arroyos. Historical documents and Aztec tribute records attest to the wealth of natural resources in the Cuetlaxtlan province (e.g., Acuña 1985; Berdan and Anawalt 1992; Durán 1967; Paso y Troncoso 1905–1906). Cotton, cacao, tropical feathers, animal skins, seashells, fish, and shellfish were available in the province and ultimately attracted the interest of the Aztecs (Berdan and Anawalt 1992:Folio 49r; Berdan et al. 1996:128, 286; Durán 1967, 2:183).

The Gulf Coast data sets used for this study come from two intensive survey and surface collection projects along the Blanco and Cotaxtla drainages (Figure 7.2). The first of these, the Cotaxtla Archaeological Survey, was conducted in 1998 and included intensive systematic survey, mapping, and surface artifact collection at Cotaxtla (Figure 7.3; see Ohnersorgen 2001, 2006:6–8). The survey focused on the center itself, which occupies a 1.85-km² mesa top overlooking Río Cotaxtla. The second survey project, the Proyecto Arqueológico La Mixtequilla (PALM), directed by Barbara Stark, covered 99 km² of noncontiguous survey blocks in the Lower Blanco region.[3] Since the project began in the mid-1980s, PALM survey crews have made over 2,000 collections from various mound features and other surface concentrations. The PALM survey complements the Cotaxtla survey, since it adds a broad, hinterland dimension to the archaeological study of Aztec imperialism in the Gulf lowlands. The PALM survey also adds a chronological dimension to this study that is not yet possible at Cotaxtla (Garraty and Stark 2002:7–9). The survey

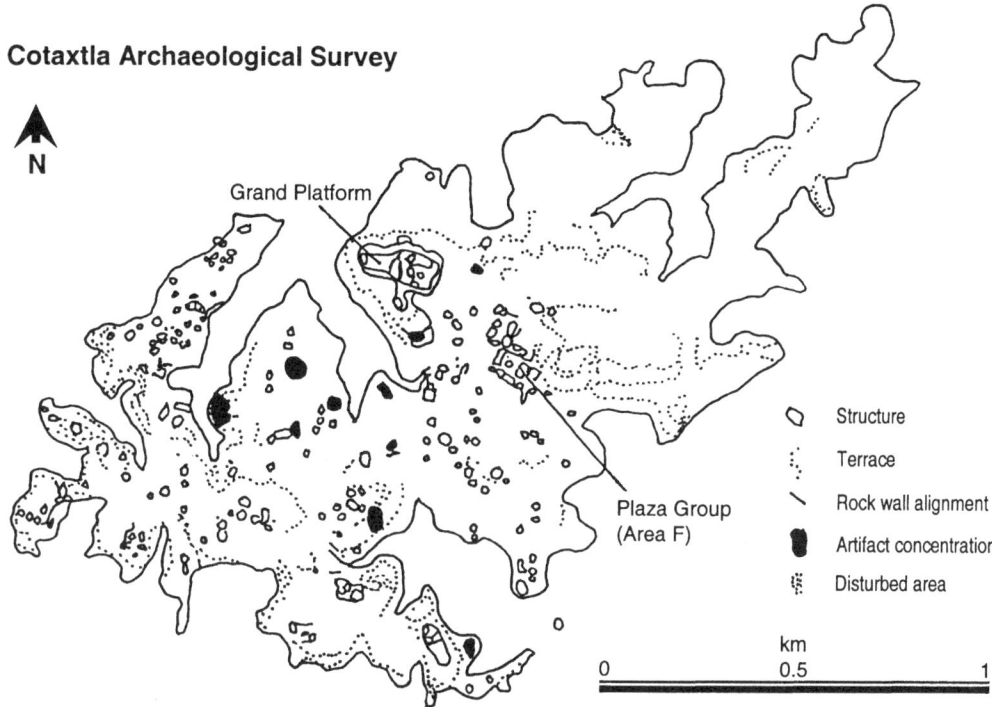

FIGURE 7.3. The archaeological features of the provincial capital of Cotaxtla. © 2006, Elsevier; reprinted with permission.

area includes two Postclassic sites: a Middle Postclassic center, El Sauce, in the delta-distributary zone, and a Late Postclassic center, Callejón del Horno, upstream along the Blanco River.

Colonial records do not indicate the precise geographic limits of the Cuetlaxtlan province. We therefore are compelled to *indirectly* infer whether Cuetlaxtlan included the Lower Blanco region. The region was situated between two known provincial subject towns (Tlalixcoyan and Tlacotalpan) and therefore would have been vulnerable to imperial rule (Stark 1974). In addition, Garraty and Stark (2002) suggest that the Lower Blanco region was likely subject to imperial rule based on assemblages of Aztec-style pottery types in percentages comparable to those from known provinces (Smith 1990). Cotaxtla, ca. 24 km northwest of Callejón del Horno, is the nearest provincial center to the region. Both Carrasco (1999:317) and García Márquez (1998) identify the town of Tlalixcoyan (ca. 15 km northeast of Callejón del Horno) as a subject of Cotaxtla, and Callejón del Horno is located closer to Cotaxtla than Tlalixcoyan (ca. 35 km away). The next-closest named provincial center, Tlacotalpan, is more than 50 km east of Callejón del Horno along the Papaloapan River (Figure 7.1) and was part of a neighboring imperial province (Tuxtepec). Skoglund et al.'s (2006) compositional study of Late Postclassic pottery from Cotaxtla and the Lower Blanco region suggests pottery exchange between the two areas, which may attest political ties as well. In sum, both geographic and archaeological evidence suggests that Callejón del Horno and the other settlements in the Lower Blanco were likely part of Cuetlaxtlan.

Interpreting Material Evidence in the Outer Provinces

The material evidence from the outer provinces presents a number of interpretive difficulties, with the pottery chronology foremost among them. The chronology of the Late Postclassic period in much of western Mesoamerica is typically defined as ca. AD 1350–1519 and is defined mainly by the presence of Aztec III–style Black-on-Orange pottery

(Umberger 1996; Umberger and Klein 1993). The initial use and spread of Aztec III–style pottery may predate Aztec rule (ca. AD 1430), however, by as much as 80 years (Umberger and Klein 1993: 324–325). Thus, the presence of Aztec-style pottery and other goods cannot be taken as wholly diagnostic of Aztec imperial presence in the region, since it could have been trafficked prior to the founding of the imperial regime. ("Aztec-style goods" here refers to materials specifically associated with the imperial heartland in the Basin of Mexico.) A related problem is that, as Smith and Berdan (2003) point out, a world system of commercial exchange and international stylistic interaction encompassed much of western Mesoamerica prior to the empire. Aztec III–style pottery vessels appear in some areas outside of the basin prior to the advent of imperial rule (M. Smith 1987, 1990; Umberger and Klein 1993). This presents an equifinality problem related to determining whether the presence of Aztec-style material remains in provincial areas indicates imperial presence or pre-imperial trade (Ohnersorgen 2006:5–6; Stark 1990).

We suggest that the presence of Aztec-style goods at Cuetlaxtlan was *most likely* a reflection of imperial activity and not pre-imperial interaction. First, Cuetlaxtlan's alliance with Tlaxcalla may have prevented its participation in pre-imperial networks of interaction with the basin. Although some exchange crossed enemy borders (Smith and Berdan 2003), it is unlikely that Aztec pottery types would have reached Cuetlaxtlan in such quantities prior to its integration into the Aztec regime. In fact, in an event leading up to Cotaxtla's initial conquest, Cuetlaxtlan lords, at the urging of their Tlaxcallan allies, ordered the murder of Aztec merchants in the region (Alvarado Tezozomoc 1944:122–123; Durán 1967, 2:177–183). In addition, if exchange accounted for the presence of Aztec types in areas outside of the imperial core in the Basin of Mexico (Smith 1990), we would expect exchange of a fuller repertoire of Aztec-style pottery in areas within the boundaries of the world system (Garraty and Stark 2002:28–29). Yet only a limited number of Aztec-style pottery types have been recovered in the Lower Blanco region and Cotaxtla (Table 7.1). Especially notable is the lack of Aztec-style *Guinda* (mainly Texcoco Black-on-Red and Texcoco Black-and-White-on-Red) in Cuetlaxtlan, since it is abundant in Middle and Late Postclassic assemblages in the basin (Garraty and Stark 2002).

The dearth of Aztec-style pottery in Cuetlaxtlan is striking when compared against site assemblages from the provinces nearer to the imperial core (Table 7.1).[4] Sites located near the core generally include a nearly complete inventory of Aztec decorated types from the basin (Table 7.1). In contrast, primarily Black-on-Orange ceramics (imports and imitations) were collected from the three regions located in the more distant areas listed in Table 7.1 (Oztuma-Cutzamala and Cuetlaxtlan), along with very low quantities of one or two other basin types. It seems unlikely that only a small subset of basin types would be sold in distant places or reach distant areas through down-the-line exchange. Also, Skoglund et al.'s (2006) compositional study revealed that most of the Aztec-style pottery from Cotaxtla and the Lower Blanco region was made from local clays, which suggests that some individuals in the area established a deliberate affiliation with imperial-style material goods. We cannot rule out the possibility that local pottery producers made imitation Aztec-style pottery prior to the founding of the empire, but it seems more likely to us that the presence of imitation pottery precipitated the local elites' desire to materialize their connections to the imperial regime (Garraty and Stark 2002).

In sum, the nearly complete replication of the Aztec-style decorated pottery type inventory in the provinces nearer to the imperial core suggests pottery exchange with polities in the Basin of Mexico (Smith 2003). Furthermore, the presence of Middle Postclassic Aztec II Black-on-Orange pottery in some of these nearby areas (Table 7.1) suggests that economic interaction with populations in the basin had begun before the imperial formation. The nearby polities were likely involved in a pre-imperial, pan–central Mexican regional interaction network (M. Smith 1987; Smith and Berdan 2003). However, the reduced inventory of basin pottery types, the predominance of imitation Aztec-style pottery in the Cuetlaxtlan and Oztuma-Cutzamala regions, and the lack of Aztec II–style Black-on-Orange in the outer provinces do not support the idea of a long-standing pottery-exchange relationship between

TABLE 7.1. Presence/Absence of Major Basin of Mexico Aztec Decorated Pottery Types in Selected Archaeological Contexts in Near and Outer Provinces of the Empire

Major Basin of Mexico Aztec Decorated Types	Near Provinces				Outer Provinces		
	Yautepec, Morelos	Capilco, Morelos	Cuexcomate, Morelos	Tepexi El Viejo, Puebla	Oztuma-Cutzamala, Guerrero	Lower Blanco Region	Cotaxtla
Aztec II Black-on-Orange	+	–	–	+	–	–	–
Aztec III Black-on-Orange	+	+	+	+	+	+	+
Imitation Aztec Black-on-Orange	+	+	+	+	+	+	+
Texcoco Molded Censers	+	+	+	+	–	+	+
Aztec-style *Guinda*	+	+	+	+	+	–	–
Fabric-Marked Salt Containers	+	+	–	–	–	–	?[a]
Chalco-Cholula Polychrome	+	–	–	+	–	–	–
Aztec Spinning Bowls	+	+	+	–	–	–	–
Xochimilco Polychrome Jars	+	–	–	–	–	–	–
Source	Olson 2001	Olson 2001	Olson 2001	Gorenstein 1973	Silverstein 2000	Garraty and Stark 2002	Ohnersorgen 2001

Note: Olson (2001) reports type percentages from a selection of excavated lots from three sites in Morelos. Capilco and Cuexcomate are rural provincial sites in Morelos. Yautepec was a provincial center in Morelos. Gorenstein (1973) excavated a single unit at the Tepexi El Viejo, an imperial fortress site in central Puebla. Silverstein (2000, 2001) reports collections from intensive surveys of the Oztuma-Cutzamala region of Guerrero, which included the provincial center and fortress of Cerro Oztuma.

[a] A very small number of fabric-impressed sherds were recovered during surface collection at Cotaxtla. Although they are visually similar to Texcoco Fabric-Marked examples illustrated by Smith (1992:385), they have not been subjected to compositional analysis to determine their origin.

FIGURE 7.4. Imitation Aztec III–style Black-on-Orange sherds from the Lower Blanco region. Upper two rows are rims from interior-decorated vessels. Bottom row includes basal sherds and slab supports. Collection numbers, from left to right: 1566, 1386, 848, 1751, 1380 (upper row); 1380, 1624, 59 (middle row); 1719, 1006, 338, 336 (bottom row). Courtesy of Barbara Stark.

these distant regions and the basin prior to imperial rule.

This result in no way is meant to challenge the idea of a pre-imperial world system. We simply want to emphasize that the greater political stability afforded by the Aztec expansion probably laid the groundwork for expanded international trade and interaction after ca. AD 1430. Indeed, the expansion of commercial avenues of exchange was one of the principal goals of the empire (Berdan 1988, 1994). In this context, trade goods were probably exchanged more widely between the imperial core and the outer provinces. The growing power and influence of the empire also probably created more demand for imperial-affiliated goods in subject areas, as argued below, which also could have increased the volume of core-periphery exchanges.

Imperial Co-Optation of Centers and the "Elite Strategy"

We suggest here that the provincial centers came to symbolize and manifest Aztec imperial rule in the outer provinces. The signification of Aztec affiliation at these centers, however, could reflect either the imperial co-optation of local elites or the desires of local leaders to affiliate themselves with imperial traditions. The most reliable archaeological indicators of Aztec presence in the outer provinces are Aztec-style pottery and green obsidian (Figure 7.4). As stated above, most of the Aztec-style pottery types reported from archaeological contexts in the outer provinces are Aztec III Black-on-Orange vessels, mostly local imitations (Table 7.1). Visually distinctive green obsidian derives from the Pachuca source in southern Hidalgo, just north of the Basin of Mexico, and was probably traded throughout Mesoamerica by commercial traders from the basin or surrounding areas (Braswell 2003; Smith and Berdan 2003). Smith (1990) analyzed large-scale distributions of these two material classes to evaluate the nature of Aztec exchange in Postclassic Mesoamerica and found that these goods typically occur in known imperial provinces. Also, in the Oztuma-Cutzamala region, Silverstein (2000) analyzed distributions of several material classes—including pottery, obsidian, metals, ground stone, pipes,

TABLE 7.2. Aztec-Style Ceramic and Green Obsidian Counts from Three Surveys in the Outer Provinces of the Empire

Site	% of Aztec-Style Ceramics		Green Obsidian Counts per 100 Sherds	
	Central Area	Noncenter Areas	Central Area	Noncenter Areas
Cotaxtla, Grand Platform[a]	3.5	.4	4.7	6.8
Callejón del Horno[b]	5.3	1.6	40.9	19.1
Cerro Oztuma, Guerrero[c]	6.6	1.2	7.2	1.3

[a] Ceramics data are based on total rims from systematic surface collections comparing the Grand Platform to other areas of the site (Ohnersorgen 2001). Judgmentally placed collection units on the Grand Platform, not included in this analysis, yielded percentages of Aztec ceramics up to 14 percent, and the platform contained more than half of all Aztec ceramics collected. Obsidian data are based on counts of green obsidian per 100 rim sherds in systematic surface collections comparing the Grand Platform to other areas of the site (Ohnersorgen 2001). The higher count away from the Grand Platform is skewed by a blade-production area near the platform, where the green obsidian frequency was 46.4 per 100 rim sherds. Given its proximity to the Grand Platform, as well as its abundance of green obsidian, this workshop may have been under state (Aztec) control.

[b] Ceramics data are summarized from Garraty and Stark 2002:Table 7, PSC cluster #1, and include Late Postclassic unmixed set collections (rims only) in the center of Callejón del Horno and its immediate environs ("central area"; n = 1,490 rims). "Noncentral area" collections are all Late Postclassic unmixed-set collections outside of this cluster (n = 2,230 rims). Data are based on counts of Aztec III–style Black-on-Orange and Texcoco Molded censers. Percentages were calculated relative to rim totals from Late Postclassic unmixed set (see Garraty and Stark 2002:7–9). Obsidian data are based on counts of green obsidian pieces per 100 rims using the same criteria as above (PSC cluster #1 collections vs. all other Late Postclassic collections).

[c] Silverstein (2001:Table 2) compares ceramic data from the Aztec fortress at Cerro Oztuma ("central area") to two local Chontal sites, Ixtepec and Totoltepec ("noncentral areas"), based on intensive surface collections. Aztec ceramics are defined as Aztec III, Aztec III/IV, and imitations (no mention of Texcoco Molded). Percentages were calculated relative to sherd totals per site, which presumably includes rims and body sherds. Obsidian data are summarized from Silverstein 2001:Table 3, calculated relative to sherd totals reported in his Table 2.

and censers—and found that "only Aztec ceramics and obsidian have an unequivocal spatial correlation to the imperial boundary" (2000:229). Green obsidian and Aztec-style pottery goods are thus likely the best archaeological indicators of imperial presence (keeping in mind the caveat of equifinality noted above).

The Aztec-style pottery and green obsidian distributions from Cotaxtla, the Lower Blanco area, and the Oztuma-Cutzamala region are summarized in Table 7.2. In the three areas, Aztec-style pottery and green obsidian distributions are highly concentrated in "central areas." In the Lower Blanco and Oztuma-Cutzamala regions, Aztec-related goods occur in higher proportions in the local centers, Callejón del Horno and Cerro Oztuma, respectively. Cotaxtla adds another level of detail, since it shows a strong concentration of Aztec-style pottery at a specific locus within the provincial center, the Grand Platform, which probably was part of the principal imperial-affiliated civic-ceremonial core of the center (Ohnersorgen 2001, 2006). Although green obsidian is not particularly frequent in collections on Cotaxtla's Grand Platform, an immediately adjacent terrace housed an apparent obsidian blade workshop, where more than three-fourths of all the obsidian collected from the site was recovered. Collections on this terrace yield a high frequency of green obsidian of 46.4 pieces per 100 rim sherds. Given its proximity to the Grand Platform, it may have been associated with the imperial government at Cuetlaxtlan (Ohnersorgen 2001, 2006).

Citing the high frequency of local imitations and the centralized distributions of Aztec-style decorated pottery in the Lower Blanco region, Garraty and Stark (2002) argue that Aztec-style pottery may have been used as serving wares during elite-sponsored feasts or public events. If so, they may have been widely recognized as imperial objects by the general populace of Cuetlaxtlan and may have become a form of "political capital" for expressing Aztec affiliation. The Aztec-style goods in the smaller centers away from the provincial capital probably reflect the elite strategy (Berdan and Smith 1996) that the Aztecs used to cement interelite relationships in the imperial domain. Imperial leaders actively sought to attach local elites' political and economic aspirations to those of the imperial regime and create a self-conscious, panregional class of elites with vested interests in the ongoing prosperity and stability of the empire (Berdan and Smith 1996; Smith 1986).[5] At Cotaxtla, the high frequencies of Aztec-style sherds in central areas may not so much reflect elite co-optation as the physical presence of imperial governing officials and possible colonists at the center (see below). Local elites at Cotaxtla maintained little loyalty to their imperial overlords and rebelled on several occasions. According to documentary sources, local leaders were executed and replaced after one rebellious episode, and they remained hostile to imperial officials up to the time of Spanish contact. Pottery thus may still have been a symbol of imperial rule at Cotaxtla, but less a medium for locals to express affiliation.

After the conquest, the local populations of these places probably viewed the centers—as well as certain civic-ceremonial structures within those centers—as principal foci of imperial culture and practices, especially among the elites. The co-optation of elites and local and regional centers thus likely affected a major shift in the geopolitical landscape of the outer provinces, as argued below. Although Aztec-style pottery and green obsidian are primarily concentrated in central places, their distribution is not *exclusive* to them in any of the three survey areas. Aztec-style goods were probably commercially available to any consumers who wished to purchase them. However, probably more elites than commoners purchased Aztec-related goods in order to tap the symbolic value attached to them. Elites and imperial officials residing in the centers probably were wealthier and had greater means to purchase imported Aztec-style pottery, commission local potters to manufacture imitations, or both.

The Geopolitical Landscape of Cotaxtla
Imperial Colonization and the Shifting Ethnic Landscape

Another imperial transformation that would have had profound effects on local perceptions of the geopolitical landscape was the formation of new ethnic communities in the Gulf lowlands brought about by immigration and colonization. Community formation involves networks of closely interacting individuals concentrated in, or associated with, a particular territory. This association with a physical location provides a community with a sense of place or sense of affiliation with place (Anschuetz et al. 2001:181). It is a major component in how people interrelate with their environment to create their landscapes (Anschuetz et al. 2001:180). Local perceptions of the landscapes would have been markedly disrupted as foreign ethnic communities were introduced, claimed or staked out territories and resources, and were accommodated into existing social and economic frameworks. As an imperial strategy, colonization is effective in disenfranchising local populations from their territory and resources (i.e., from their physical landscapes) and, thus, from their sovereign identities and social practices.

Ethnohistoric and archaeological evidence supports the presence of highland enclaves or colonists at Cotaxtla. Imperial leaders maintained a calpixque at Cotaxtla after its initial conquest in ca. AD 1460 through the time of Spanish conquest in 1521 (Alvarado Tezozomoc 1944:122–123, 142–148; Durán 1967, 2:177–183, 197–203; Paso y Troncoso 1905–1906, 5:9).[6] Carrasco (1996:494) mentions that Aztec calpixques also were installed in two subject towns in the Cuetlaxtlan province, Mictlancuauhtla and Tlalixcoyan, and that Aztec *teyacanque* (bosses) were placed throughout the province. The installation of such officials probably involved small supporting entourages or enclaves. Military support for imperial officials may have involved larger groups of colonists. Cotaxtla housed a garrison of imperial soldiers (Torquemada 1943, 1:162) and was reportedly fortified (García Icazbalceta 1943, cited in Berdan and Anawalt 1992, 2:123). A second garrison was established at Otapa, a subject town of unknown location within the province. Although it is not known how large Aztec garrisons were, they must have been of sufficient size to maintain control or at least provide a convincing threat.

The establishment of Aztec enclaves or colonies is infrequently mentioned in ethnohistoric documents (Umberger 1996:152–159). Nor is there much corroborating archaeological evidence to indicate the presence of colonists in provincial areas, a problem that stems in part from a lack of archaeological research as well as from the destruction of sites and an Aztec tendency to supply colonists with local resources, rendering colonial-affiliated remains nearly invisible. Umberger (1996:152) argues that the resettlement of imperial officials and colonies in distant provinces was more significant than has been generally assumed. She (1996:155–156) describes several accounts of Aztec colonists in the Gulf lowlands, including an episode when Emperor Moctezuma II allegedly relocated 8,000 families from the Basin of Mexico to the Gulf lowlands after disease had decimated local populations (see also Herrera 1952:211–212; Stark 1990:266). Colonial chronicler Diego Durán (1967, 2:244) also observed survivors of families that migrated out of the basin during the great famine of the 1450s. Unfortunately, colonial accounts generally do not provide data on the specific locations of the colonists' settlements, although Umberger considers Cotaxtla a likely candidate. Linguistic evidence suggests that Aztec colonists were in Cuetlaxtlan. At the time of Spanish contact, Nahuatl was a prevalent language in the Gulf lowlands, and many provinces, including those neighboring Cuetlaxtlan, were bilingual or multilingual (Berdan et al. 1996:121, Table 5-4). Cuetlaxtlan, however, was monolingual in Nahuatl, which may indicate a stronger Aztec presence there.[7]

Neighboring provinces show organizational similarities to Cuetlaxtlan, suggesting a broader transformation of the landscape brought about by imperial political reorganization. Tochtepec, Cempoala, Quauhtochco, Xalapa, Misantla, and Tochpan each commanded a number of subject towns headed by local lords. Aztec officials, typically calpixque or governors, were stationed in at least one location in each of these provinces, with the exception of Cempoala (Berdan et al. 1996: 287). Like Cuetlaxtlan, these neighboring provinces also had Aztec garrisons or fortifications (or both), and Quauhtochco and Cempoala were particularly well fortified.

Archaeological evidence from Cotaxtla also suggests the presence of Aztec colonists. One line of evidence comes from figurines recovered by surface collections (Ohnersorgen 2006:18, 20). Most figurines from Cotaxtla are a flat, mold-made variety that was common in the Gulf lowlands at the time. Out of 60 figurine heads from this type,

FIGURE 7.5. Examples of figurines from Cotaxtla showing the characteristic hairstyle seen on Aztec figurines from the Basin of Mexico. © 2006, Elsevier; reprinted with permission.

12 (20 percent) are a subtype depicting a female with a characteristic hairstyle/headdress consisting of two knob-like projections (Figure 7.5) that resembles a variant of Aztec-style figurines found in the basin (especially Parsons's [1972] Type IA figurine heads; see also Millian 1981). Miller (n.d.) suggests that additional Aztec-style figurines may also be present in the Cuetlaxtlan region. These figurines were found in scattered areas associated with residential features and are notably absent from civic-ceremonial structures. The figurine evidence may suggest that Aztec domestic rituals occurred in some Cotaxtla households. Given the generally stable nature of domestic ritual practices (cf. Pool 1992; Santley et al. 1987), the figurines provide some support for the notion of Aztec residents, possibly soldiers or colonists. The presence of Aztec-style figurines could also indicate the widespread adoption of a foreign, possibly Aztec-affiliated religious ideology at Cotaxtla, rather than colonists. The presence of Aztec-style architectural remains (see below) might also support the notion of Aztec colonists.

Materializations of Imperial Ideology at Cotaxtla: Art and Architecture

We argue that state ideology and imperial imagery played important roles in the maintenance of imperial control and further effected a transformation of the geopolitical landscape of the outer

 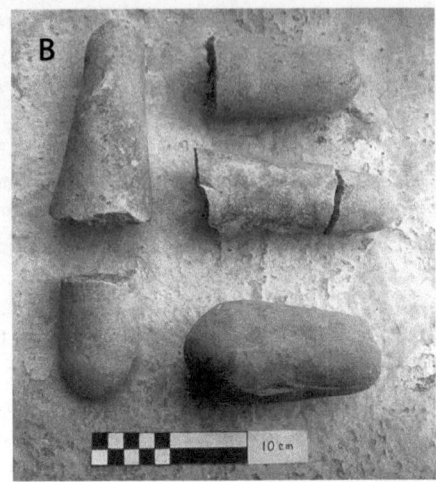

FIGURE 7.6. Examples of Aztec-style architectural tenons from Cotaxtla: (a) basalt tenons; (b) fired ceramic tenons. © 2006, Elsevier; reprinted with permission.

provinces. Imperial ideology was materialized in various media to reinforce new sociopolitical relationships and devalue the traditional significance of place. Given their permanence, high visibility, and impressiveness, architecture and sculpture are particularly well suited to express state ideology. In examples from many parts of the world, powerful expansionary states invested in imperial-style art and architecture in provincial locations as a form of legitimization and an expression of political dominance (e.g., D'Altroy 1992; Goldstein 1993; Moore 1992; Morris 1995; Schreiber 1992).

Aztec imperial-style art and architecture are rare in provincial locations outside the Basin of Mexico, suggesting that these media were used very selectively (Umberger 1996; Umberger and Klein 1993). Aztec officials and colonists often used existing houses and palaces or commandeered locals to provision them, so that new constructions were built in local styles (Umberger 1996:162). Umberger (1996) observed only three examples of Aztec-style architecture outside the basin. In one of these cases, Cerro Oztuma, Aztec colonists reportedly constructed and occupied a fort and other structures in the surrounding communities (Alvarado Tezozomoc 1975:527; Durán 1967, 2:351–355; Paso y Troncoso 1905–1906, 6:113; Silverstein 2001). In the Gulf lowlands, the main pyramid at Castillo de Teayo in northern Veracruz and the main pyramid at Quauhtochco, near Cotaxtla, are readily recognized as Aztec-style constructions (Medellín 1952; Miranda 1998; Solís 1986; Umberger 1996:164–166). Castillo de Teayo is noteworthy for a sizable corpus of Aztec sculpture (more than 50 examples), and Quauhtochco served as both a provincial capital and an Aztec fortress, which explains the salient imperial presence there.[8] At both centers, Aztec-style architecture was constructed over preexisting temples, indicating the co-optation of historically important and meaningful loci of local power.

Ohnersorgen (2006:13–14) has identified elements of Aztec-style architecture that suggest the presence of imperial-style buildings, including 86 tenoned cones made of basalt and ceramic that were dispersed throughout Cotaxtla (Figure 7.6). More than 40 percent were associated with large mounds (height ≥ 2.5 m), and almost 25 percent were associated with a single plaza group in the central civic-ceremonial precinct. Only a few tenons were associated with the Grand Platform, however. Tenoned cones were typically placed on the facades of Aztec structures (see Marquina 1964:173, Lam. 52). Sahagún (1950–1982, 11:Drawing 890) further indicates that this type of facade was used in the construction of the noble lords' houses (Figure 7.7). At Cihuatecpan, in the northeastern basin, Evans (1988) found similar tenons associated with both elite and nonelite structures. Tenons also decorated the facade of the Aztec-style pyramid at Quauhtochco.

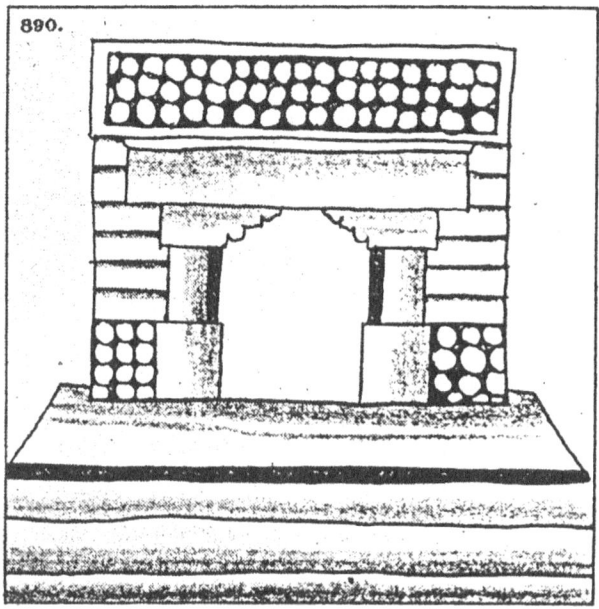

FIGURE 7.7. Drawing of a *tecpilcalli*, or noble lord's house, from Sahagún (1950–1982, 11:Drawing 890). Circular elements in the upper facade and basal platform are tenoned cones. © 2006, Elsevier; reprinted with permission.

Ohnersorgen (2001, 2006:14) suggests that architectural styles at Cotaxtla may have been used to convey political messages and to reinforce imperial political, ethnic, or ideological affiliations. The Aztecs were required to maintain a strong and highly visible political presence, given Cotaxtla's defiance of the imperial regime. The use of tenons on larger structures in the site's civic-ceremonial core suggests a form of public proclamation—a clearly imperial style on what was highly visible architecture associated with civic-ceremonial authority. The tenons on some smaller, outlying structures may signify acceptance of imperial rule by local residents or the presence of foreign residents, that is, Aztec colonists using homeland architectural styles. In either case, the architectural and figurine evidence suggests that material symbols of imperial affiliation permeated Cotaxtla.

Sculpture was another medium of imperial ideology and imagery that served to reinforce the geopolitical changes associated with Aztec conquest and administration. Several Aztec-style sculptures were recovered at Cotaxtla (Medellín 1949), although their original contexts are unknown, including two Aztec-style solar disks (see image in Ohnersorgen 2006:15). The larger disk has elements of the Aztec calendar: a series of 18 points in relief on the front of the stone, corresponding to the 18 months of the indigenous year, and a series of 52 points carved around the border, corresponding to the 52-year cycle (see Ohnersorgen 2006:15–16). Four Chacmool sculptures were also recovered at Cotaxtla. Similar sculptures are known from the Aztec capital of Tenochtitlán, although Chacmools are not solely associated with the Aztec regime (Ohnersorgen 2006:16). Chacmool sculptures are frequently associated with human sacrifice (Miller 1985) and thus would have provided a constant reminder of the consequences of not cooperating with imperial authority. Medellín (1949) also describes six small basalt sculptures found at Cotaxtla that portray possible representations of the Aztec deity Macuilxochitl-Xochipilli. According to Sahagún, Macuilxochitl was "especially the god of those who dwelt in the houses of lords or in the palaces of the chiefs" (1976:35). These representations may

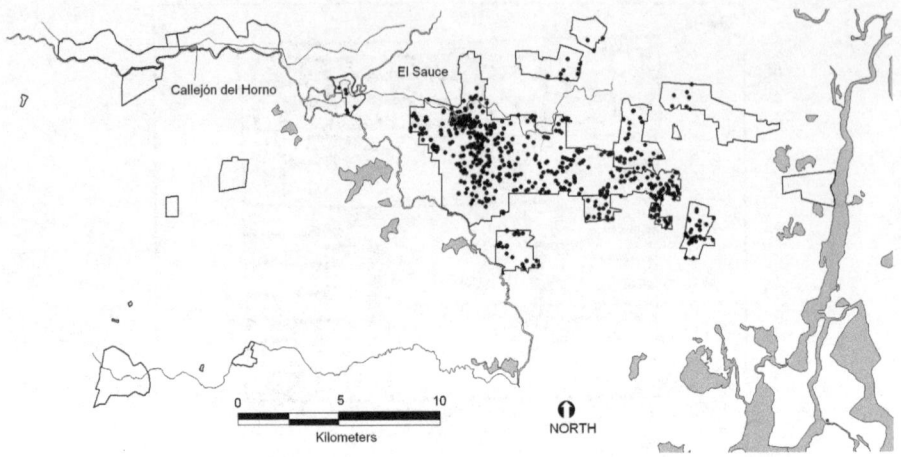

FIGURE 7.8. Middle Postclassic settlement patterns in the Lower Blanco region along the Blanco and Guerengo rivers. Each dot represents a collection area assigned to the Middle Postclassic period through ceramic unmixing (Garraty and Stark 2002:7–10).

have underscored the authority of imperial officials stationed at Cotaxtla (Ohnersorgen 2001).

The Aztec-style sculptures from Cotaxtla are striking in that they highlight themes of imperial authority and dominance. Moreover, calendar dates etched on several of the sculptures may commemorate dates of conquest or dates significant to the history of the empire (see Ohnersorgen 2006:15–16 for details). The celebration of such events at Cotaxtla clearly marked the site as an element within the imperial realm and essentially would have undermined the traditional political and social importance of Cotaxtla, instilling the site with new historical significance in local social memories. The inscribed dates also illustrate the use of the Aztec annalistic system at Cotaxtla, which Boone (1996) suggests was one of the primary media for expressing imperial affiliation.

The Shifting Geopolitical Landscape in the Lower Blanco Region

As stated above, the Lower Blanco region was located about 24 km from Cotaxtla and was likely part of the Cuetlaxtlan province. Changes in the sociopolitical meaning of place in the Lower Blanco region are evidenced through settlement pattern changes, relocation of the local center, and the suppression of pre-imperial (Middle Postclassic) elite traditions.

Imperial Shifts in the Geopolitical Landscape: Settlement Pattern Changes

Settlement pattern changes are one possible line of evidence for inferring external conquest or control in a region (Stark 1990). Although we are unable to definitely date these changes, we suggest that the settlement changes from the Middle to Late Postclassic period resulted from the imposition of Aztec imperial control in the Lower Blanco region. Using a statistical unmixing procedure, Garraty and Stark (2002:7–9) assigned Postclassic collections from the Lower Blanco region to the Middle Postclassic period (611 collections) and the Late Postclassic period (209 collections). Using these unmixed collections, they mapped settlement pattern changes from the pre-imperial Middle to Late Postclassic periods in the Lower Blanco region. The Middle Postclassic settlement is predominantly located in the low-lying delta-distributary zone of the Blanco River (Figure 7.2), which includes the Middle Postclassic center of El Sauce (Figure 7.8). No Middle Postclassic settlement was recorded in upriver survey blocks along the Blanco and Guerengo rivers. In the Late Postclassic period, lower-density settlement continued in the delta-distributary zone, but new settlement sprang up in upriver locations along the Blanco and Guerengo rivers, including the new center of Callejón del Horno (Figure 7.9).

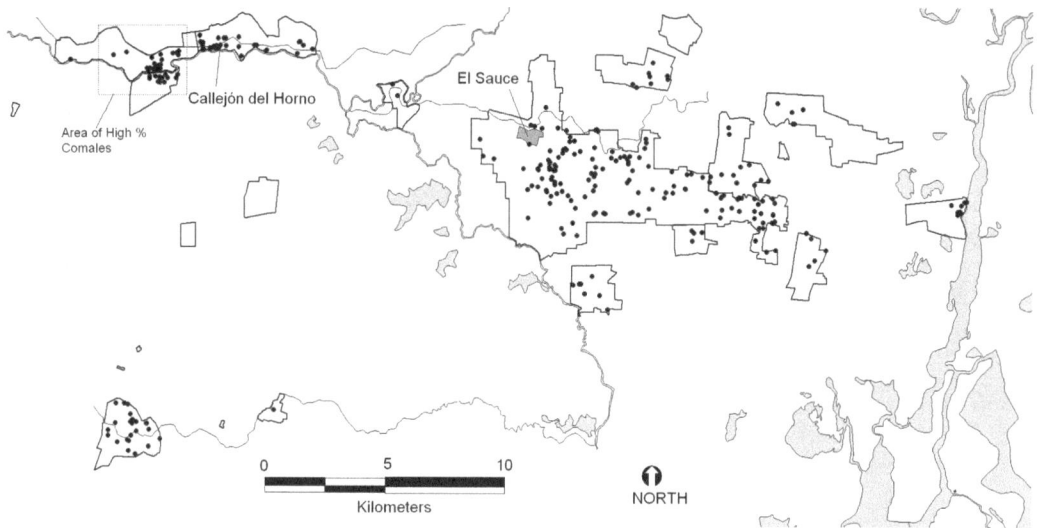

FIGURE 7.9. Late Postclassic settlement patterns in the Lower Blanco region along the Blanco and Guerengo rivers. Each dot represents a collection area assigned to the Late Postclassic period through ceramic unmixing (Garraty and Stark 2002:7–10).

The relocation of the Late Postclassic center to a previously unoccupied area may reflect an imperial strategy to divorce the imperial-affiliated center, Callejón del Horno, from the governing institutions previously centered at El Sauce (Figure 7.8). This relocation would have effectively communicated to the subject population a shift in governing authority with the inception of imperial rule in the areas. The founding of Callejón del Horno might have been part of the imperial conquest and reorganization of Cuetlaxtlan province. The Aztec Empire also might have reorganized previously autonomous polities and founded new centers in other areas of the empire. For example, Garraty (2006) posits an imperial-imposed polity reorganization and center relocation in the Aztec polity of Teotihuacán in the Basin of Mexico. Brumfiel (2000) makes a similar case for imperial subversion of preexisting political institutions and resettlement at Xaltocan, also in the basin.

Imperial officials (or local governing officials affiliated with the empire) in the Lower Blanco region likely chose a location that symbolically communicated the closure of the El Sauce governing regime and that was accessible to Cotaxtla via land transport but was also located near enough to the preexisting populations in the delta-distributary zone to facilitate tribute extraction and shipment. Stark (1999) characterizes the delta-distributary zone as a "capital zone," a subregion in the Lower Blanco area that was continually viewed as a locus of regional power since the Late Preclassic period. If this perception persisted in the Postclassic period, then it may have been especially important for imperial leaders to establish a new center outside the delta-distributary zone to communicate a wholesale shift in the leadership regime. The relocation of the center could also reflect more practical, logistic concerns. The Inca Empire typically constructed provincial centers in previously unoccupied areas that facilitated access to long-distance communications and transport routes (Morris 1972) or to provide better access to previously unused resources (D'Altroy 1994). Perhaps Callejón del Horno was similarly placed along the Blanco River to facilitate communications and riverine transport of tribute and market goods.

The establishment of Callejón del Horno also precipitated substantial resettlement in upstream locations along the Blanco and Guerengo rivers (Figure 7.9). This resettlement probably resulted from both "top-down" processes, such as coercive resettlement (Brumfiel 2000), and "bottom-up" processes of community relocation, for example, to exploit the marketplace opportunities or other

TABLE 7.3. *Comal* Percentages from the Area Just West of Callejón del Horno and Other Zones in the Lower Blanco Region

Zone	% Comales[a]
Settlement Area West of Callejón del Horno	64.18
Callejón del Horno and near Vicinity	34.09
Guerengo Zone	44.74
Delta-Distributary Zone	34.40

Note: See Figure 7.2 for zone designations and the location of the settlement area west of Callejón del Horno.

[a] Calculated as the total comal rim counts per "zone" divided by the total Late Postclassic rim counts.

urban attractions that emerged with the founding of Callejón del Horno. One top-down possibility is that imperial elites, local elites, or both expropriated lands in the delta-distributary zone and repossessed them for agricultural use, which might help explain the lower settlement density in that area. The delta-distributary zone was long perceived as an area of prime agricultural land (Speaker 2001), and landholdings in this area might have been coveted for their productive potential. The *Codex Mendoza* (Berdan and Anawalt 1997) indicates tribute demand for cotton cloth from Cuetlaxtlan, and the delta-distributary zone may have been a major locus of cotton production (Stark et al. 1998). The market demand for cotton in the imperial core and other highland locations likely augmented cotton production in the Gulf lowlands, especially since cotton is not cultivable in most highland locations (Stark et al. 1998). Lowland producers, including those in the Lower Blanco region, thus probably had to increase their output in the Late Postclassic period to satisfy imperial tribute and highland market demands.[9]

Various bottom-up processes also likely promoted settlement relocation near Callejón del Horno. Some communities in the Lower Blanco region probably relocated near the center to exploit a new regional marketplace. Mold fragments for manufacturing Texcoco Molded censers ($n = 5$) and stamped-base Fondo Sellado bowls ($n = 3$) have been recovered at Callejón del Horno (Stark and Garraty 2004). Several collections from Callejón del Horno include diagnostic indicators of obsidian production (Stark 2007). This evidence suggests the possibility that some craft producers, who had previously resided in the delta-distributary zone, chose to relocate to the vicinity of Callejón del Horno to exploit market opportunities. A marketplace at Callejón del Horno presumably would have been linked to others throughout the imperial domain and, if so, would have appealed to commercial craft manufacturers seeking to gain access to a larger consumer population (see Smith 2001). To be sure, one of the key imperial strategies of the empire was to promote commercial exchange and link distant markets to those in the imperial heartland in the Basin of Mexico (Berdan 1988, 1994; Berdan and Smith 1996, 2003; Berdan et al. 2003; Smith 2001).

Also notable is a small, concentrated area with high percentages of *comales* (tortilla griddles) a few kilometers west of Callejón del Horno (Figure 7.9; Table 7.3). This area might have housed a *comal*-production community, perhaps located near the center to gain access to a central marketplace.[10] Curet (1993) located a Middle Postclassic comal-production community roughly 2 km east of El Sauce, indicating a precedent for specialized comal production at a community level. Perhaps this same community relocated near Callejón del Horno to exploit the new marketplace. Another possibility is that this locality represents a deployable tortilla-producing workforce affiliated with the center. Comparable cases of communities with high comal percentages have been found in other Mesoamerican contexts.

Blanton et al. (1999) relate the high percentages of comales in communities surrounding Monte Albán to the production of tortillas as an easily transportable food for a mobile workforce. Brumfiel (1991:239–243) observed higher proportions of comales at Late Postclassic sites in the Basin of Mexico relative to Middle Postclassic sites, which may indicate the development of a more mobile workforce of corvée laborers and soldiers during the period of imperial rule. Fauman-Fichman (2001) also observed higher percentages of comales in the vicinity of Cerro Oztuma than at other areas in the Oztuma-Cutzamala region. The tortilla-producing households in that area might have housed a deployable workforce of tortilla makers servicing government officials, colonists, or imperial troops stationed in the region. The two explanations—a commercial comal-making community and an "attached" community supplying governing officials or soldiers—are not mutually exclusive. Comal producers in the area may have been required to meet a certain quota for governmental demands but also sought to manufacture a surplus for exchange in the marketplace.

Suppression of Preexisting Elite Traditions and Material Expressions

Middle–Late Postclassic shifts in pottery consumption in the Lower Blanco region indicate a suppression or replacement of the pre-imperial elite traditions. In the Middle Postclassic period, several pottery types are strongly connected to the Middle Postclassic center of El Sauce (Table 7.4), including five decorated and one utilitarian type. Of these, only one—Complicated (Cholutecoid) polychromes—continued in the Late Postclassic period. The other elaborate polychromes from the Middle Postclassic period thus fell into disuse. Conversely, the Middle Postclassic types more strongly associated with areas *outside* El Sauce persisted in the Late Postclassic period. In the case of local-style Black-on-Orange and Black-on-Red bowls, Stark and Garraty (2004) found surface evidence for a Middle Postclassic production community located ca. 12 km southeast of El Sauce. If so, this production community may represent a hinterland pottery tradition not affiliated with the center of El Sauce or its resident elites.

Given these results, we argue that, with the imposition of imperial rule at Cuetlaxtlan, Aztec-style pottery replaced the various fine-quality and polychrome pottery types as the class of serving vessels that most effectively symbolized wealth and elite status. The "old ways" of expressing elite status and for garnering popular support shifted. In this sense, the suppression of traditional high-status pottery types may indicate a change in the bases of political power from expressions of common ties with local communities through a medium of local pottery traditions to a "top-down" system based on the allocation of political power by imperial leaders. This interpretation complements above interpretations about the shifts in the locations of the local center at Callejón del

TABLE 7.4. Ceramic Type Percentages from Middle Postclassic Collections by Types Only in Use During the Middle Postclassic Period and Those in Use During Both Middle and Late Postclassic Periods

Locus	Middle Postclassic Period Only						Middle and Late Postclassic Periods				
	White-and-Black-on-Red Polychrome	Frieze Motif	Dull Buff Polychrome	Interior-Banded Decorated	El Sauce Utility Wares	Comal (Griddles)	Complicated Polychrome	Local-Style Black-on-Red	Local-Style Black-on-Orange	Fondo Sellado	Fine-Paste Gray-on-Cream	Total
In and near El Sauce	6.4	2.0	5.3	8.2	3.0	24.2	14.5	31.9	2.1	2.0	0.2	100
Outer Settlements	3.3	1.1	2.7	4.5	1.0	24.8	10.5	39.5	8.8	2.6	1.0	100

Note: The higher of the two percentage values are in boldface. See Garraty and Stark 2002:8 for type codes; Stark 1995 provides detailed type descriptions.

TABLE 7.5. Comparative Data from Three Zones in the Lower Blanco Region, Late Postclassic Period

Zone	Green Obsidian Counts per 100 Clear Gray[a]	% Local-Style Bichrome Bowls[b]	% Complicated Polychromes[c]	% Aztec-Style Pottery[d]
Blanco Zone	73.6	3.8	4.8	4.5
Guerengo Zone	68.8	2.6	0.0	3.9
Delta-Distributary Zone	46.0	9.0	7.1	2.5

Note: Data are combined from all collections assigned to the Late Postclassic period in each zone through ceramic unmixing. The Lower Blanco region is shown in Figure 7.2.

[a] Values are the ratio of piece counts of green obsidian (from Pachuca source, central Mexico) and clear gray obsidian (Pico de Orizaba source, highland Veracruz). All cases with three or more prismatic blade production indicators were eliminated from the analysis, since the inclusion of production loci would bias the count data.

[b] Includes bichrome types BLRD 7a-g and BLOR 53a-c, which were both probably produced in the eastern portions of the delta-distributary zone during the Middle Postclassic (Stark and Garraty 2004). Percentages are rim counts for the combined BLRD and BLOR types divided by the total rim counts for collections assigned to the Late Postclassic period for each of the three zones.

[c] Includes types COMP 7s and 7t, which are Cholutecoid polychromes that were also used during the Middle Postclassic period. Percentages calculated same as above.

[d] Includes Aztec III–style Black-on-Orange pottery (BLOR 57m) and Texcoco Molded censers (TEXM 53a). Percentages calculated same as above.

Horno to divorce imperial from pre-imperial institutions. Not surprisingly, Aztec-style pottery was more prominent in the vicinity of Callejón del Horno than in other areas of the Lower Blanco region (Garraty and Stark 2002). The social negotiations among the imperial and local peoples effected a definitive shift in the geopolitical landscape from local sovereign elite traditions to increased connections with an international, Aztec material idiom.

Tradition and Persistence in the Cuetlaxtlan Hinterland

Although Callejón del Horno emerged as a prominent and salient locus of imperial rule in the Lower Blanco region, a persistence of Middle Postclassic material traditions and networks is evident in the delta-distributary zone—the principal locus of the previous Middle Postclassic settlement and the long-standing "capital zone" of the region (see above). As shown in Table 7.5, some Middle Postclassic pottery types remained prominent in the delta-distributary zone, compared to the later-settled Blanco and Guerengo zones (Garraty and Stark 2002:27). The two bichrome bowl types—local-style Black-on-Orange and Black-on-Red—had been previously associated with the more distant settlements surrounding El Sauce during the Middle Postclassic period (Stark and Garraty 2004). These types persisted in the Late Postclassic period in their traditional place of use in the delta-distributary zone.[11]

The spatial distribution of obsidian complements the pottery distributions in highlighting the continuity of Middle Postclassic interaction networks in the delta-distributary zone (Table 7.5). Clear gray obsidian from the Pico de Orizaba source in highland Veracruz was predominant in the Lower Blanco region during the Middle Postclassic period, and at least one clear gray obsidian workshop has been reported at El Sauce (Heller 2000; Heller and Stark 1998). Green obsidian became more prominent in the Late Postclassic period, however, and was probably exchanged into the area by long-distance commercial traders from central Mexico. To avoid bias in the data and facilitate comparisons of distributions of green and clear gray obsidian, we removed all collections with three or more surface indicators of obsidian production (e.g., various definitive production debris), as identified by Barbara Stark and Lynette Heller (B. Stark, personal communication 2002).[12] Thus, the ratio of green to clear gray obsidian probably accurately reflects differences in obsidian consumption at the household level among the three zones (Figure 7.2). Clear gray obsidian remained prominent throughout the region in the Late Postclassic period. Yet, as is the case with the continuing Middle Postclassic pottery types, the ratio of clear gray to green obsidian is considerably higher in the delta-distributary zone than elsewhere, as shown in Table 7.5.

The upriver settlements along the Blanco and Guerengo rivers appear to have been better integrated into imperial-affiliated economic and political networks, as evidenced by the higher proportions of Aztec-style pottery and green obsidian. Yet pottery and obsidian evidence together suggests the retention of local pottery traditions and interaction networks in the delta-distributary zone. Importantly, Silverstein (2001) found comparable evidence for continuity in local pottery and obsidian-working traditions in areas away from the fortress center of Cerro Oztuma. According to Joyce et al. (2001:368–370), one way that commoners engage in the social negotiation of power—aside from rebellion against, or acceptance of, existing power arrangements—is through *avoidance* of the centers and sources of elite power. Therefore, the retention of local traditions and settlement patterns in both the Lower Blanco and Oztuma-Cutzamala regions might indicate a form of opposition to the imperial intrusion or a strong reluctance to engage in or support imperial-affiliated practices associated with Callejón del Horno (e.g., market production). It may also reflect a lack of concern on the part of the imperial regime about what material culture local peoples used, as long as they produced tribute.

Discussion: Geopolitical Strategies and Imperial Landscapes

Bender (1993:3) argues that landscapes are not static and inert but dynamic and continually reevaluated, reworked, appropriated, and contested. Landscapes are thus continually subject to social negotiation and confrontation among differing geopolitical interests. In the case presented here, the geopolitical landscape was shaped through ongoing processes of social negotiation among the various geopolitical interests, including Aztec imperial rulers, local leaders, and subject populations. In line with Bender's expectations, we suggest possible instances of direct imperial appropriation of the landscape (reinventing place and history at Cotaxtla); reshaping and reworking of the landscape through imperial co-optation of centers and local elites (the adoption of Aztec-style material goods at Callejón del Horno and Cerro Oztuma); and possibly also local opposition to, or avoidance of, imperial-instigated landscape changes (retention of traditional land-use practices and interaction networks in the Lower Blanco region).

A geopolitical landscape perspective, we argue, also provides a helpful vantage point for conceptualizing the whole of the Aztec imperial domain in terms of the extent to which and how provincial populations retained control over the meaning of place and the social definition of landscape features. The geopolitical landscape of the empire was shaped through social negotiation among external imperial forces seeking to cement control over the landscape and local forces aiming to retain sovereignty over the landscape. In this light we can rethink our assumption about the nature of Aztec provincial administration and spatial variation in the extent to which the Aztec imperial presence was manifested in different provinces of the empire.

For example, provincial administration in the Aztec Empire has been widely viewed as largely indirect in nature, especially in the outer provinces (Hassig 1984; Smith and Berdan 1992). This view has been shaped in part by the apparent paucity of Aztec-style material remains in outer provincial areas (Umberger 1996), which suggests that the Aztec imperial regime did not make the material investments in landscape changes commonly associated with more direct forms of administration (D'Altroy 1992; Schreiber 1992; Stark 1990). Aztec-style materials are sparse or absent in the Mixteca Alta (Spores 1984) and in the Valley of Oaxaca (Blanton 1982; Blanton et al. 1999), for instance, but are prevalent in portions of the Gulf lowlands, such as Castillo de Teayo, Quauhtochco, and Cotaxtla. Also perplexing is the lack of Aztec material remains or landscape changes in the eastern Papaloapan Basin, since several known provincial towns were located there (Pool 2006). Umberger (1996:178) attributes the paucity of Aztec materials in the Valley of Oaxaca to distance from the imperial core. Cuetlaxtlan and the Valley of Oaxaca are a comparable distance from Tenochtitlán, however (between ca. 200 and 250 km).

We suggest that factors other than distance from the imperial core should also be factored into the equation. Variability in the degree to which Aztecs left tangible evidence of their presence reflects not only logistical factors but also the social negotiations among imperial elites and local peoples as well as the degree to which imperial and provincial leaders sought to establish a salient, material link to imperial traditions by investing in landscape changes and manipulating the meanings of places. In some cases, it may have been in the best interests of imperial or local rulers to downplay the imperial presence. In other cases, local leaders may have wished to adopt imperial styles and material culture to express affiliation with the empire, possibly to bolster their tribute demands and governing authority. In brief, local sovereignty over the landscape remained intact except where imperial rulers deemed it necessary to support or promote imperial interests or where local leaders or subject peoples opted to express or emphasize their imperial affiliations to promote local interests and agendas.

The imposition of imperial control without alienating local sovereignty may involve subtle, low-cost intrusions by the central state, such as the co-optation of local elites and skimming of local tribute receipts (Berdan and Smith 1996; Smith 1986), with little resulting change in the geopolitical landscape. This strategy can be very effective because, short of coercive labor policies (e.g., corvée), the state can extract tribute and labor from subject populations without reinventing the landscape and drawing attention to the overarching dominance of the central state authority. Certainly, subject populations would have been aware of the state presence, but the controlling state might not attempt to impose its presence or tamper with religious pantheons or other significant dimensions of local identity. Imperial demands may entail relatively subtle or generally acceptable changes in the everyday landscape practices of subject populations, however, such as rescheduling production activities or shifting crop rotations (Thurston 1999).

These shifts in everyday practice might generate complaints or mild opposition, often expressed in private (Joyce et al. 2001; Scott 1990), but intrusions on local sovereignty may be minimal. A subtle presence may have helped curtail local opposition and allowed local leaders to maintain traditional media and methods of expressing governing authority. For example, Smith (1994, 2001)—evaluating the weight of Aztec imperial tribute receipts against local demography in the provinces of Cuauhnahuac and Huaxtepec (in Morelos, central Mexico)—concludes that imperial tribute demands would not have entailed much of a labor burden at the level of individual households (ca. one-half of a cotton manta per household per year). Commoners in these provinces no doubt resented the added tribute burden imposed on them, but the burden was likely not so onerous as to foment serious resistance to imperial control.

Where it was deemed necessary, the imperial presence was more obtrusive and manifested in overt landscape changes, symbols, and material expressions of state power and the presence of Aztec officials or colonists, as is possibly the case at Cotaxtla (Ohnersorgen 2001, 2006; Umberger 1996). In these cases, the imperial regime amplified its presence in subject territories to an extent that fear of imperial retribution and policing agencies became plainly tangible and salient to the subject population. They involved a well-cognized awareness of state power and the implications of nonconformance or opposition to state demands. Such overt tactics are evocative—a way of garnering "hearts and minds," as Brumfiel (2001) puts it—such that state or imperial subjects discursively reevaluate their perceptions of the geopolitical landscape and their place within it. It compels them to acknowledge the shifts in the centers of power (or resistance) and the new meanings afforded to traditional places of power (centers) across the landscape.

More obtrusive tactics include the state-sponsored construction of monuments, human sacrifices of war captives, public humiliations of rebellious individuals, and various forms of state terror tactics or violence (Brumfiel 2000). Generally, however, these latter tactics are more costly than unobtrusive tactics, since they require sufficient capital and labor control to purvey the power and efficacy of the state through a material medium (DeMarrais et al. 1996). Moreover, such overt displays of state power render the state presence conspicuous to subject populations, thus generating active opposition to state control, especially in areas that are difficult for the state to monitor or police (Scott 1990). These forms of controlling landscape thus require extra costs for policing and the enforcement of state decrees.

At Cotaxtla, it appears that obtrusive measures were part of an imperial strategy used to suppress a rebellious population with strong, preexisting ties to an enemy state, Tlaxcalla. Aztec-style remains reflect a strategy designed to create an atmosphere of imperial control through possible colonization and various forms of construction. Tactics used at Cotaxtla included military conquest and threat, the establishment of military garrisons, the installation of imperial administrative personnel, colonization, human sacrifice, imperial-style public art and architecture, and probably state-sponsored public ritual. The overall effect of these measures was to suppress local sovereignty and effect changes in the traditional significance of a powerful sociopolitical center (Ohnersorgen 2001, 2006). In the Lower Blanco region, the establishment of a new center at Callejón del Horno and the abandonment of the former governing center (El Sauce), as well as the abandonment of some of the latter center's pottery types, may suggest that the conquest and reorganization of Cotaxtla extended into its hinterland. The relocation of the local center to an area upstream along the Blanco River could have facilitated communications with and transport to Cotaxtla. It also probably communicated an affiliation with the imperial regime, and the founding of Callejón del Horno in a previously uninhabited area would have detached the local governing regime from its predecessor at El Sauce. Also, given the higher concentrations of Aztec-style pottery types and green obsidian, Callejón del Horno might have been perceived by residents of the Lower Blanco region as a salient locus of imperial practices and material culture (Garraty and Stark 2002).

The degree to which the empire wished to make its presence known, as well as the degree to which local officials negotiated the Aztec presence, produced a mosaic of different and irregular manifestations of imperial presence in the outer provinces (Ohnersorgen 2001, 2006). The geopolitical landscape of the empire was shaped to a large extent by the strategies that imperial and local elites used to communicate the imperial presence. As Duncan argues, "Landscapes are communicative devices that encode and transmit information" (1990:4). As archaeologists continue to examine other Aztec provincial locations in closer detail, we can better "decode" this information and understand the diverse practices and approaches to the negotiation of Aztec imperial rule.

Acknowledgments

This essay benefited from the helpful comments of a number of scholars, including Brenda Bowser, Elizabeth Brumfiel, George Cowgill, Michael Smith, and Barbara Stark. We would like to thank all of them for their insights and suggestions, although we accept responsibility for any errors or omissions. We owe an extra debt of gratitude to Barbara Stark, who generously permitted us access to her extensive, well-maintained database for the Proyecto Arqueológico La Mixtequilla project. The Cotaxtla Archaeological Survey was supported by a National Science Foundation Dissertation Improvement Grant (BNS 97-29317), the Foundation for the Advancement of Mesoamerican Studies, Inc., and Arizona State University. The Proyecto Arqueológico La Mixtequilla was made possible by support from the National Science Foundation (BNS 85-19167, BNS 87-41867, and SBR-9804738), the National Geographic Society, and Arizona State University. Both field projects were conducted with the permission of the Instituto Nacional de Antropología e Historia in Mexico. Figures 7.3, 7.5, and 7.6 are reprinted from Ohnersorgen 2006.

Notes

1. The province of Cuetlaxtlan was governed by the provincial capital town of the same name. To avoid confusion, we refer to the provincial capital town as Cotaxtla (the modern town name); we refer to the remainder of the province as Cuetlaxtlan.
2. Silverstein (2000, 2001) conducted a survey in 1998 in the Oztuma-Cutzamala region of Guerrero, west Mexico. This region includes one known Aztec provincial center, Cerro Oztuma, a military garrison site on the frontier of the enemy Tarascan state (see Figure 7.1).
3. The PALM project involved two stages of survey. The first stage (1986–1989) covered a large

central block that mainly involved the mapping and collection of surface materials in and near a concentration of formal complexes in the delta-distributary zone of the Lower Blanco River (Speaker 2001; Stark 1991). The second stage (1998–2002) was geared toward the identification and mapping of additional formal complexes in the delta-distributary zone and in areas upriver along the Lower Blanco and Guerengo drainages (Figure 7.2). These upriver areas are slightly higher in elevation (20–40 m above sea level) than the delta-distributary zone, with drier soils less amenable to recessional agriculture.

4. Our original intention was to present a table of type percentages for the pottery types listed in Table 7.1. However, this proved overly problematic, since not all of the data are presented in comparable ways, particularly the percentage denominators. For example, in the Lower Blanco region, the percentages represent type counts as a percentage of all sherds from surface collection assigned to the Late Postclassic period through a process of assemblage unmixing (Garraty and Stark 2002). At the same time, the type percentages reported by Olson (2001) from Capilco, Cuexcomate, and Yautepec (in Morelos) derive from percentages of the entire excavated feature units, which may include pottery sherds from earlier and later periods. This latter calculation may underrepresent type percentages relative to the Lower Blanco region. We should also note that the sites and regions chosen for this comparison represent only a sample of the collections from provincial contexts. Smith's (1990, 2003) comparisons of sherd data from provincial contexts are far more comprehensive.

5. It may be significant that, aside from Black-on-Orange serving vessels, Texcoco Molded censer fragments are the only other basin pottery type found in appreciable quantities in south-central Veracruz (Curet et al. 1994; Daneels 1997; Garraty and Stark 2002; Ohnersorgen 2001). Mold fragments for producing Texcoco Molded censers were found both in Cotaxtla and at Callejón del Horno in the Lower Blanco region. These censers may have functioned as ritual paraphernalia and are relatively rare in the Basin of Mexico ceramic assemblages. It is not clear at this point why these *specific* types of censers were adopted and locally reproduced at Cuetlaxtlan; other Aztec censer types have been found in basin assemblages in higher frequencies. Notably, Silverstein (2000, 2001) does not mention the presence of Texcoco Molded censers in the Oztuma-Cutzamala region.

One possibility is that Texcoco Molded censers were used during state- and elite-sponsored rituals and ceremonies and to communicate an affiliation with imperial religion. Indeed, relatively high percentages of Texcoco Molded sherds were recovered from the Grand Platform at Cotaxtla, which might suggest a state association. Charlton et al. (1991:106–107) report a concentrated area of censer production, including Texcoco Molded, at Otumba in the Basin of Mexico. Moreover, they suggest the possibility that censers were produced solely by "religious specialists" for market exchange. Oddly, however, these sherds do not appear to have been strongly associated with state buildings or elite residences in central Mexican contexts. Perhaps local elites in Cuetlaxtlan assigned more symbolic value to these types than did populations in central Mexico and other areas of the empire. Further study is required to better understand this unique pattern.

6. The first Aztec calpixque installed at Cotaxtla was murdered in a rebellion, and Moctezuma I installed a replacement (Alvarado Tezozomoc 1944:122–123, 142–148; Durán 1967, 2:177–183, 197–203). Another rebellion and reconquest during the reign of Axayacatl, and one possibly during the reign of Tizoc, also may have resulted in the murder and subsequent reappointment of imperial officials. At the time of Spanish contact, Cotaxtla housed a calpixque that had been appointed by Moctezuma II (Paso y Troncoso 1905–1906, 5:9).

7. The *Relación Geográfica* of Veracruz notes that the towns of Cotaxtla and Espiche were "populated by people who were disenfranchised and forcibly detained on these frontiers by the Aztec rulers" (Acuña 1985:315; our translation). It is unclear if the *Relación* is referring to people relocated from the highlands; it alternatively may be referring to local groups dispossessed of their lands and resettled into nearby towns, as was the case in Tlalatlauhco, in the western Basin of Mexico (García Payón 1936:196; Torquemada 1969, 1:181; Umberger 1996:155n6). Either way, it is clear that a forced resettlement took place that would have affected local sovereignty and the geopolitical landscape. Alternatively, it is possible that Tlaxcalans introduced Nahuatl in the Middle Postclassic period.

8. It is unclear, however, whether the archaeological site identified by Medellín (1952) as Quauhtochco, located only 18 km west of Cotaxtla, represents the remains of the ethnohistorically documented Aztec provincial capital of Quauhtochco or a possible Aztec garrison in the Cuetlaxtlan province. The debate over the location of the Aztec provincial capital owes to the fact that there are two modern towns in the general area

with similar names derived from Quauhtochco. One candidate is San Antonio Huatusco, between modern Jalapa and Orizaba. This town is located well north of the archaeological remains that Medellín (1952) identifies as Quauhtochco but is much closer to a cluster of other identified towns listed in the Quauhtochco province. However, no known Aztec-period archaeological remains have yet been identified at San Antonio Huatusco. The other candidate is the archaeological site of Quauhtochco, located adjacent to the modern town of Santiago Huatusco, in between Cotaxtla and Orizaba. The site has substantial Aztec-style material remains, including architecture and pottery. Some scholars suggest that archaeological Quauhtochco may have been part of the Cuetlaxtlan province (Umberger 1996:152n2). If so, it may have served as a fortified Aztec garrison associated with Cotaxtla, perhaps forming the western boundary of the province.

9. Unfortunately, we are currently unable to test the possibility of Late Postclassic shifts in cotton production due to an inadequate understanding of the spindle whorl chronology in the Lower Blanco region.

10. More research is required to determine if this locality of collections with high percentages of comales indicates a localized comal-producing community. Garraty has explored this possibility by inspecting surface indicators of pottery production based on comal counts and densities, using the method outlined by Stark and Garraty (2004). The results do not provide clear insights. A few loci in the general area meet the proposed criteria for inferring production localities, but many other loci with high percentages of comal sherds do not meet the proposed density criteria. We are therefore reluctant to interpret those data as indicating a production community. Additional analyses will be needed to further explore this matter.

11. At least one polychrome type that had been well represented at El Sauce, Complicated (Cholutecoid) Polychromes, also shows a continuing association with the delta-distributary zone in the Late Postclassic period. It is unclear why this polychrome type persisted while other types did not; however, Complicated Polychromes were commonly used in the surrounding settlements as well as in El Sauce during the Middle Postclassic period (Table 7.4). Thus, Complicated Polychromes were not solely an elite tradition associated with El Sauce.

12. Stark and Heller have compiled a database of obsidian production indicators, which we used to weed out green and clear gray obsidian production loci. The loci from the Late Postclassic unmixed set of collections with three or more green obsidian production indicators include collection numbers 946, 1392, 6081–6084, 6155, and 6012. For clear gray obsidian, the Late Postclassic collection numbers include 947 and 6234.

8

A Landscape of Gambles and Guts

Commodification of Land on the Arizona Frontier

Michael P. Heilen and J. Jefferson Reid

The sense that resides in me most clearly when I think back on the twelve McMurtrys (all dead now) is of the intensity and depth of their hunger for land: American land, surveyed legal acreage that would relieve them of nomadism (and of the disenfranchisement of peasant Europe) and let everybody know that they were not shiftless people.... To the generation my grandparents belonged to, cut loose by the Civil War, all notions of permanence and respectability were inextricably woven into the dream of land tenure, or acreage that would always be holdable by themselves and their children.
—Larry McMurtry, Walter Benjamin at the Dairy Queen

Southeastern Arizona is one of the most intensively mythologized landscapes of the American West. Stories of gunslingers, raiding Apaches, military forts, and the transcontinental railroad resonate throughout American literature, popular fiction, cinema, and the tourist industry. Stories of the western frontier are part of a nationalistic, American frontier mythology of the Old West, where the interests of lawmen and the lawless, settlers, soldiers, miners, American Indians, and Mexican nationals collide. Rough-and-tumble mining towns like Tombstone, sloganized as "the town too tough to die," highlight the rugged individualism of American frontiersmen, while historical personages that populated them (i.e., the Earp Brothers and "Doc" Holliday) metonymically symbolize the struggle to squeeze prosperity and order out of an unruly yet majestic land.

The territorial history of southeastern Arizona takes place on overlapping series of frontier landscapes, contested borderlands at the edge of a territorially expanding nation. Although places in southeastern Arizona achieve central status in American mythologies of the frontier West, southeastern Arizona was peripheral (on national and international scales) to other major western centers. General histories of the American West often pass superficially over Arizona, hesitating only briefly at major stops. Meinig, for instance, views the Arizona Territory as one of several *secondary* regions of the transcontinental West—"distinctly smaller in population, simpler in economies, without major cities, and more dependent upon external services" (1998:145).

Seeking fortune in the contested, rugged, arid, harsh (yet still promising) landscapes of southeastern Arizona entailed a high degree of risk. Outside the legal hurdles associated with establishing a homestead and obtaining preemptive rights to a parcel of land, attempting to settle frontier Arizona was highly risky. An effort that began with the struggle to carve out a piece of

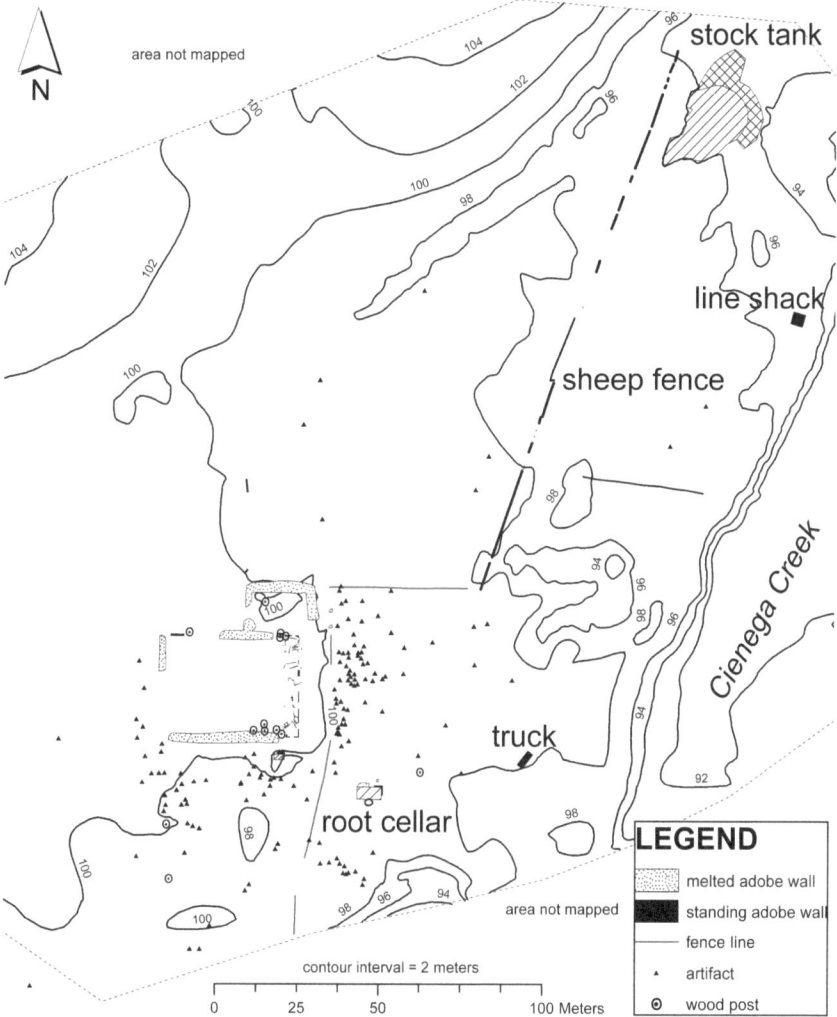

FIGURE 8.1. Map of Sanford Ranch and associated features.

land and make it work could easily end in disaster. On the other hand, the potentially rich resources of Arizona were comparatively untapped. Settlers who had the backing, connections, or gumption to make an attempt at settlement had the opportunity to stake claims on a great many places and convert land and other resources into capital. For the pioneer attempting to settle this rugged landscape, the stakes were high (involving loss of health, wealth, investment, property, or even life), but the potential payoffs were great.

Nestled along the banks of Cienega Creek in southeastern Arizona is Sanford Ranch, an archaeological site consisting of an artifact scatter and a suite of interrelated archaeological features—an adobe compound, a privy, a root cellar, a stock tank, a sheep fence, partially dismantled fence lines, a line shack, and a 1970s pickup truck (Figure 8.1). Significance or meaning can certainly be derived from analysis of the fine-scale distribution of artifacts and features at this archaeological site. Important layers of significance or meaning can also be developed by situating Sanford Ranch as one of many places settled within broad-scale, cultural landscapes. In this essay, we are interested in the broader historical, cultural, and strategic contexts in which Sanford Ranch was selected and transformed into a successful place on a frontier landscape of the American West. Departing from the standard landscape narrative, we conceptualize Sanford Ranch as a complex economic game of land commodification and manipulation. We believe this framework to be more suited to the Sanford Ranch case than complementary approaches framed according to performance characteristics (Schiffer 1995, 2000; Zedeño 2000).

Sanford Ranch was originally homesteaded in 1873 by Don Alonzo Sanford. Don Alonzo selected the location from a finite number of other potential homesteading locations; built domestic and ranching facilities; conducted business with mining towns, commercial centers, and military installations; and continually acquired more landholdings, cattle, horses, and sheep. Nine years after its establishment, he sold his ranch and the better part of his ranching capital for a small fortune. Afterward, Don Alonzo built the largest house in Tucson, became the city's mayor, and in 1886 moved to Washington, D.C., where he and his family circulated in important social circles until his death in 1915 (Reid and Heilen 2005).

Sanford Ranch was at the nexus of multiple intersecting western frontier landscapes. Mining, military, railroad, ranching, homesteading, and commercial frontiers all intersect with the brief history of Sanford Ranch. Though the Homestead Act (1862) had been passed a decade earlier, Sanford Ranch was part of the first small wave of homesteading in southeastern Arizona. It was established in the decade prior to the completion of the transcontinental railroad and was abandoned as an independent ranch shortly after the train's arrival. Sanford Ranch was built and developed during a regional cattle boom and was fortuitously sold before intense drought, falling cattle prices, and overgrazing caused it to bust.

Some historical archaeologists have observed an overabundance of attention paid to examples of "failures." While we can question the validity of treating archaeological test cases as representative of either settlement successes or settlement failures, we can also question what constitutes the "success" of a particular settlement strategy (Adler 1996; Krall 2001). Site duration or site expansion could be interpreted as an indicator of success. Determining the success of any settlement strategy, however, ultimately depends on the intentions or goals of settlers. The goals of settlers are not necessarily consistent with the expectation that settlement duration varies directly with settlement success. Rather, the success of any settlement should depend on how settlers conceptualized places in terms of larger-scale, inclusive social, political, and economic landscapes.

From a capitalist world systems approach, the conversion of resources into capital could be considered an indicator of success. If the accumulation of capital is a primary goal of land-acquisition strategies, then site duration need not have a direct relationship with settlement success. In other words, when land is cognized as a commodity, the goals of some settlers may be to obtain capital gains within the shortest possible time frame.

Sanford Ranch was not a "success" because of its duration of occupation or its transformation into larger, more inclusive entities such as towns or corporations. Although it did increase its landholdings and ranching capital, Sanford Ranch was neither occupied for a long time nor transformed (by its original settlers) into a larger ranching corporation. It was a success because Don Alonzo treated land as a commodity and ultimately transacted a place and its associated capital for liquid capital. Sanford Ranch was a successful outcome in a complex, evolving, spatially explicit, capitalist game—the game of frontier settlement in the American West.

Modeling Settlement in the Frontier American West

The settlement of the frontier American West was a complex, dynamic process involving the interaction of diverse natural and cultural variables at multiple temporal and spatial scales. Competing land disposal systems, historical contingency, changing patterns of resource exploitation, the expansion of national and international market economies, mass migrations of settlers and laborers, emerging transportation and manufacture technologies, spatial and temporal variations in climate, and competing goals and strategies for settlement and land ownership played important roles in shaping frontier settlement in the American West (Meinig 1998). The systemic context of frontier settlement in the American West was a complex mixture of interacting processes that crosscut multiple scales of analysis (see Heilen 2005 for discussion of archaeological and systemic landscapes).

Historians, historical geographers, and historical archaeologists studying the American West are beginning to envision the history and anthropology of the region as taking place on a global stage (Hardesty 1991a, 1991b; Limerick 1987; Limerick et al. 1991; Linklater 2002; Meinig 1998; Purser 1999; Schuyler 1991; Wylie 1993). Theoretical frameworks stress that local and regional frontier processes are intimately related to national and international processes. They also stress that processes of frontier expansion take place within a dense, interconnected web of cultural and natural systems (Hornborg 1998, 2001; Limerick 1987). Only by examining frontier processes at a variety of scales can we interpret the broader significance of individual places on settled landscapes.

The increasing tendency to theoretically model historic frontiers as "the edge of something bigger" parallels attempts to reformulate anthropological questions in terms of more inclusive, broader-scaled analytic constructs. Archaeologists have shifted attention away from the internal structure of individual sites to the relationships of sites as places to larger physical and cultural landscapes. Attempting to reconcile the interpretation of individual places with broad-scale processes, "historical archaeologists struggle to integrate their inexorably physical, bounded sites with global-scale processes that span centuries" (Purser 1999:120).

Theoretical modeling of frontier settlement and exploitation has been attempted from a wide variety of disciplinary perspectives. Recent models have emphasized the economic, political, and technological integration of frontier systems with broad-scale national and international capitalist market systems. In this sense, frontiers are sometimes modeled as internal and external peripheries of cores within broader world systems (Hardesty 1991a; McGuire and Reckner 2002; Nugent 1991; Purser 1999).

Frontier settlement has been modeled as involving the intersection and interaction of multiple, evolving frontier landscapes (Bean 1996). Differing landscape interactions of Anglo-American, Hispanic, and American Indian groups have been used to model multiethnic patterns of land use, resistance, and conflict (Church 2001, 2002; Shackel 2003). Ecological processes of colonization, spread, and competition for niche space have been adapted to fit models of frontier settlement processes (Hudson 1969). Historical geographic models have typologized settlement stages or successions in unfamiliar frontier environments, examined strategic settlement responses to environmental and locational variability, and empirically correlated patterns of land alienation with the application and abuse of federal policies (McIntosh 1976, 1981; Rice 1978; Sauder 1989). Other models, still, have combined both ecological and political economic perspectives to explain the accumulation, control, exploitation, and transformation of interconnected natural and cultural resources at multiple scales of analysis (Greenberg 1998).

A further way to model frontier settlement of the American West is to view it as a complex game (see Dixit and Skeath 1999). The interaction of core systems, such as the public land disposal policy, with local and regional cultural and ecological contexts resulted in the emergence of variable goals and strategies for manipulating core systems. Frontier landscapes are in this sense *strategically cognized landscapes*. The basic mechanisms for game play (i.e., land disposal policies) are specified and articulated by core systems, but the strategic contexts for game play are structured by evolving, peripheral ecological and cultural contexts. Patterns and processes for frontier settlement thus result from the interaction between core system mechanisms and peripheral strategic contexts. Complex patterns of frontier settlement can thus be modeled in terms of the interaction of relatively simple, evolving strategies with evolving rules and procedures for land alienation.

The Commodification of Land

At the heart of frontier settlement of the American West is a single issue: landownership. In both historic documents and later historical analyses, processes linked with alienating and securing unambiguous, legal title to land are seen as fundamental to the expansion of the American nation-state: the conquest, colonization, and control of contested territories; the development of regional and national economic infrastructure; the relief of population pressure in urban centers; and the development of revenue. Land titles were obtained by settlers, corporations, state governments, and speculators for a variety of sometimes-conflicting goals and according to a wide variety of methods. Land built fortunes and lost lives. Land was incorporated in a large, Cartesian grid consisting of standardized, identifiable parcels that left real material traces across landscapes. Land was measured, defined, entered, bought, and sold (Alexander 1977; Gates 1968, 1979; Limerick 1987; Linklater 2002; Meinig 1998; Sheridan 2006). These new meanings and strategic interactions with land were guided by a single, overarching process: the commodification of land.

Commodities and Commodification

Commodities are "things produced for sale on markets" (Schaniel and Neale 1999:96). In analogizing industrial processes to capitalism, Marx considers commodities to have a fairly specific meaning. To Marx, commodities are "(1) produced...(2) in factory-like circumstances...(3) for sale...(4) on a commercial market" (Schaniel and Neale 1999:96; emphasis omitted). Marx's definition of commodity fits certain industrial products well (i.e., lathes, paper clips) but does not include many other things often treated as if they were commodities (i.e., land, labor, and money). Polanyi (1957) refers to land, labor, and money as *fictitious commodities* because they are treated as commodities although they do not fit the classic definition.

Schaniel and Neale (1999) propose that in between commodities and noncommodities a third category exists (somewhat like Polanyi's fictitious commodities): quasi-commodities. Quasi-commodities are things or performances that are "treated as if they were commodities [but] do not behave as proper commodities" (Schaniel and Neale 1999:97). Like commodities, quasi-commodities are produced, but they lack some other characteristic of Marx's definition. Things that are mostly treated like commodities may instead be *quasi-commodities* because they are not sold on a market, produced for profit, or produced in factory-like ways. According to Schaniel and Neale (1999), commodities, quasi-commodities, and noncommodities exist along a pseudo-continuum. Where any particular thing or performance falls on this pseudo-continuum is socially negotiated.

In its simplest form, commodification is the act of treating a thing or performance as if it were a commodity. Commodification is viewed as a process in which nonmarket provisioning systems are replaced by market provisioning systems. Commodification, as it occurs on an economic frontier, incorporates peripheral resources into capitalist market systems by turning those resources into commodities. Land can be treated as a commodity, a quasi-commodity, or a non-commodity depending on social context.

Schaniel and Neale (1999) recognize commodification as a complex, reversible process that allows things and performances to be classified as commodities, noncommodities, or somewhere in between. Whether a thing or performance is treated as a commodity or something else is socially negotiated, contextually variable, and scale dependent. If a state treats land as a commodity in some times and places and as a quasi-commodity in others, determining whether that overall process represents commodification or quasi-commodification is a matter of debate. Although there certainly may have been some contexts in which U.S. public domain land was treated as a noncommodity or quasi-commodity, public land disposal during the homesteading period generally resulted in the *commodification* of land (Krall 2001; Purser 1999).[1]

Land, in a physical sense, was of course not produced under factory-like circumstances. Land existed. Parcels of land were individually surveyed, uniquely identified, and entered according to a common system at a grand scale. Land was for sale on a commercial market. Although title to some land was granted without any payment other than titling fees, the private ownership of land meant that land could be bought and sold on a market.

Territorialization, Globalization, and Commodification

Greenberg (1998) argues that the commodification of nature (as a process) is accomplished through two interconnected processes: territorialization and globalization.[2] In the process of territorialization, "states set the 'rules of the capitalist game' and attempt to control the rights to natural resources" (Greenberg 1998:135). Globalization, as the "dance of commodities as they enter markets," is controlled not simply by "the technologies of power imposed by states" but by strategic decisions made in distant frontiers and markets (Greenberg 1998:136). Commodification, as a process involving both territorialization and globalization, establishes interdependent relationships between states and frontiers.

The commodification of land was intrinsic to the settlement and development of frontier landscapes of the American West.[3] The political and economic power associated with land commodification directly affects how landscapes are cognized. In the frontier American West, landscapes were cognized according to a wide variety of cultural and environmental variables, but in general, variables perceived to influence the exchange value of land as a commodity were most important.

Historical Archaeology of the American West

As a political and geographic area, the American West can be defined in a number of ways. Hardesty (1991a) defines the American West in terms of political boundaries and official survey divisions—as the continental United States west of the ninety-eighth meridian. The American West is environmentally diverse, but in general this vast region is characterized by aridity. As a result, the settlement and exploitation of places and landscapes of the American West necessarily involved the emergence of processes designed to "cope with aridity" (Hardesty 1991a; Whittlesey 2003).

In the past decade, historical archaeologists have conceptualized the West as "a dynamic periphery of an evolving American world system" (Hardesty 1991b:30). Mining and ranching are seen as a "modern capitalistic structure associated with the 19th century expansion of the American nation-state into the American west" (Hardesty 1991b:31). In this sense, mining and ranching in the frontier American West are formulated as "uncertain enterprises" susceptible to boom and bust cycles that are themselves tied to the fluctuating markets of a capitalist world system (Hardesty 1991b:31).

In terms of world systems theory, cores and peripheries are seen as interdependent (Wallerstein 1974). As an "internal periphery…the American West was more culturally, politically, and economically integrated with its core" (McGuire and Reckner 2002:47). The core of the nation-state attempted to "transform periphery production and social relations to conform to or articulate with systems present in the core" (McGuire and Reckner 2002:47).

Along with urbanism and large-scale federal reclamation projects, Hardesty identifies the "technologies of extractive industries such as mining, lumbering, and ranching" (1991a:4) as essential to understanding cultural processes of landscape transformation. The Public Land Survey System was an overarching cultural process that guided and exerted influence over all these processes of landscape transformation and integrated administrative cores with frontier peripheries.

Rather than a vast expanse of empty, "free" land, the American West is increasingly seen as an arena of political, cultural, and economic conflict and conquest (Limerick 1987). Mining communities, ranches, and military outposts are seen as provisioned by distant markets and dependent on the federal government. Heterogeneous natural and cultural landscapes are seen as increasingly homogenized and incorporated into a centralized system of production and control. Urbanized commercial centers are seen as nodes of frontier expansion that connected the frontier population to distant centers of power and commerce (Hardesty 1991b).

Recent critiques of the mythic West have led to exploration of a "counter-classic West." Instead of the classic characters of the western myth, the counter-classic West model is populated by the dispossessed—laborers, tenants, immigrants, American Indians. More broadly, world systems theory and the counter-classic West model conceptualize the American West as "the edge of something bigger" (McGuire and Reckner 2002: 47) that counters mythologies of the American frontier.

Following a series of land policies enacted by Congress, the federal government developed the Public Land Survey System (PLSS). Articulated by a national array of general land offices, the PLSS defined land in order to establish and transfer legal ownership. Ultimately it commodified parcels of public domain land. Articulated across the continent and across a wide array of regional environments with differing political, economic, and cultural histories, implementation of the PLSS was bound to be messy (Cazier 1976).

The PLSS is essentially composed of procedures and processes designed to incorporate peripheral lands and resources into a shared, capitalist, democratic framework. In this sense, the PLSS was a set of rules for game play. The PLSS territorialized frontier resources. However, its interaction with local, peripheral cultural and environmental conditions allowed for variation in implementation and the development of strategies for circumventing or manipulating the system.

To Purser, the West "was a place and time where fundamental material processes worked across grand scales and in often paradoxical fashion" (1999:120). For example, the marginal environments of the West reacted poorly to adverse climate fluctuations, and the predominantly extractive economies of the West were often a victim of wild market fluctuations. The arbitrary partitioning of landscapes by the PLSS was one factor contributing to many of these material processes.

U.S. Public Land Policy

Like classic Turnerian mythologies of the American West, filled with outlaws, lawmen, Indians, gun smoke, and individualistic ideals, a national mythology of frontier homesteading has developed around the disposal of public lands and the settlement of the American West. U.S. public land policy *was* generally structured around idealistic principles (Linklater 2002). Putting land into the hands of actual settlers and discouraging rampant land speculation were recurrent justifications for policy design and adjustment. The model of a 160-acre farming homestead provided free to settlers who improved the land and resided on it was a powerful motivator for the development of congressional legislation during the latter half of the nineteenth century. While Jeffersonian democratic principles may have fueled the enactment of public land disposal policy, the equable disposal of public domain land was also justified by the requirements of nation building. Lands that were "actually settled" and "improved" had the potential to inject resources and capital into the national economy and could act to ensure American economic political and economic control of newly acquired, thinly settled landscapes. Theoretically, higher settlement densities would have also reduced military costs of maintaining public safety and supplied goods, services, and labor to resource-exploitative frontier markets (e.g., Mowry 1857).

The cognitive model of a homestead has an enduring influence on American landscapes and how Americans perceive the connections between citizens and land. The model of a 160-acre homestead was derived from a set of expectations for the agrarian settlement of relatively humid areas of the nation, where essential resources were more evenly distributed. The transfer of the same working model to legislation aimed at settling the American West, where resources essential to successful homesteading were unevenly distributed, led to the development of new sets of strategies to adapt to the evolving rules for patenting land (Krall 2001).

The Origin and Development of the PLSS

The Public Land Survey System originated in the late eighteenth century, closely following the founding of the United States of America. Established initially by the Northwest Ordinance but continually modified through further legislation, the PLSS was largely the brainchild of Thomas Jefferson. The goals of the PLSS were several: (1) to dispose of public lands for settlement, (2) to proliferate democracy, (3) to provide a source of revenue, and (4) to institute a common set of units and measures. As an instrument of a developing democratic state society, the PLSS was designed to promote its principles of governance, facilitate its expansion, and cement political and economic relationships between individual citizens and the federal government (Linklater 2002).

The basic unit of the PLSS was one section of land. Measuring one American mile to a side, each section was individually numbered according to a common numbering system. Thirty-six-square-mile sections constituted a township. By establishing principle meridians and baselines, a vast, arbitrary grid of townships, sections, and quarter-sections could be extended in any direction, allowing for land to be surveyed according to a common system and for each individual unit of land to have a unique name. In this way, the system permitted unambiguous expansion of the survey grid as well as unambiguous identification of any parcel of land (Cazier 1976).

Consequences of the PLSS

Legal ownership of land required that it be surveyed and defined according to the PLSS. Not surprisingly, the demand for land generally outstripped the rate of land survey. Moreover, while the system was intended to democratize landownership, land was initially offered at parcel sizes and prices that were prohibitive to many potential buyers. Over time, Congress passed acts that reduced the minimum parcel size as well as the price per acre. As settlers extended the frontier beyond surveyed areas squatting became commonplace. Settlers eventually realized, however, that landownership was more effective "than a Kentucky long rifle packed full of lead shot and black powder" in protecting rights to land and allowing a landowner to be backed by the "full force of the law" (Linklater 2002:168).

Subdividing and apportioning the landscape into regularly sized quadrangular units had certain consequences. Overlaying naturally and culturally variegated landscapes with a unified Cartesian grid system made the subdivision of natural and cultural resources an arbitrary endeavor, one that did not correspond to the requirements of particular land uses. Thus, the ordering of landscapes as composed of so many places, themselves composed of natural or cultural physiographic features, was replaced by an arbitrary Cartesian system.

Parcel sizes and shapes standardized by public lands policy, a number of scholars have argued, were more reasonable in areas of low relief where resources were more evenly distributed, as on the Plains. As the settlement advanced farther west, however, the "events of western history [became], not a simple process of territorial expansion, but an array of efforts to wrap the concept of property around unwieldy objects" (Limerick 1987:71). The impermanence and mutability of resources such as extractable minerals, grazing lands, and water sources meant that the rights to use these resources were potentially of greater value than the ownership of locations where these performance characteristics might temporarily reside (Limerick 1987).

The choice of homesteads had a lot to do with selecting those units that *happened* to contain desirable performance characteristics, rather than defining operative units according to the characteristics of places. Referring to just this kind of problem in 1851, Samuel D. King, the first surveyor general of California, wrote:

> I am fully convinced, that so far as respects the agricultural lands bordering upon navigable water, and perhaps upon many of the smaller streams, the square system of sectioning should be departed from, and that those lands should be so laid out into lots as to distribute the all-essential advantages, in this country, of water and wood, in such a manner that they might appertain in due proportion to the largest sized tracts in which it may be thought most advisable to subdivide and dispose of those lands, instead of confining the water benefits to only the few forty-acre lots through which the stream may flow [quoted in Uzes 1977:166].

As he was criticizing a survey system that had been deliberately designed to limit variation in the size and shape of land parcels, the surveyor general's concerns fell on deaf ears.

The situation was equally compromising to early homesteaders of southern Arizona. Eventual recognition that 160-acre quarter-sections could not provide adequate acreage for livestock grazing in the parched western lands led to the passing of the Desert Land Act of 1877. While the Desert Land Act raised the maximum allotment to a full section (640 acres), the amount still resulted in ranges that were too small to accommodate the livestock forage capacity of desert grasslands.

In the rangelands of Arizona and other parts of the West, settlers followed multiple strategies for maximizing ownership or control of land. The Desert Land Act of 1877, though designed to improve the chances of ranching homesteaders, "promoted monopolization and speculation and control of land contiguous to Desert Land claims" (Krall 2001:668). A common strategy for controlling rangelands, for instance, was to patent available water sources and establish the de facto right to graze the public lands surrounding them (Ayres 2002; Gates 1968; Krall 2001; Schoenwetter and Hohmann 1997; Sheridan 1995).

Landscapes, Places, and the PLSS

The PLSS imparted to places certain kinds of physical structure. Land parcel boundaries necessarily took the form of regular rectilinear units connected to a giant grid system. The grid system constrained the location of roads, structures, and fences. So long as topography permitted, roads were often placed along section lines, and houses were built near section corners and thus road intersections (Hewes 1996).

The procedures for acquiring the rights to obtain places differed from other land systems, such as the Spanish and later Mexican land-grant systems, which would play a major role in determining landownership after southeastern Arizona became part of the United States. The shapes, orientations, and sizes were more variable for the Spanish system. Parcels were symmetrical, cardinal, and uniform for the U.S. system. The correspondence of land parcels to natural landscape features was more direct in the Spanish system and more arbitrary in the U.S. system (Van Ness 1976; cf. Kish 1962).

The implementation of the PLSS was a monumental effort fraught with difficulties. Given the rapid geographic growth of the United States (the 1790 Census recorded a population of 3,893,874; the 1870 Census recorded a population of 38,155,505) and the demand for land, the PLSS had to be implemented on a grand scale. Fraud was common, as were mistakes. The incidence of fraud and mistakes sometimes required that surveyed areas be resurveyed and section corners be reestablished. The location, extent, and legal bases for preexisting Spanish and Mexican land grants were uncertain and problematic. Previous grants had been measured, described, and allotted according to different land systems. The title to these lands was not always clear.

Competing Land-Tenure Systems

While land policy could be considered representative of a set of cultural ideals, how landscapes are cognized and used results from the interaction of local cultural and natural conditions, cultural ideals, and land-use strategies designed to address both broad-scale cultural ideals and finer-scale local conditions. The many ways landscapes are cognized and used, therefore, are governed by the interaction of culturally motivated goals with local conditions or constraints (Church 2001, 2002; Hardesty 1980).

Spanish Colonial and Hispanic Conceptualizations of Land

Land-use strategies vary according to culturally and historically determined conceptualizations of landscapes. Hispanic conceptualizations of landscapes and resources arose from Spanish colonial political and economic conventions, along with some syncretism of American Indian land-use patterns. Hispanic conceptualizations tended to focus on the *use value* of resources. The spatial allocation of Hispanic land use tended to occur according to more informal, communal, community-negotiated methods of resource partitioning. As a result, Hispanic settlers tended to allocate use rights to the landscape that permitted mixed subsistence activities.

Spanish colonial and Hispanic conceptualizations of landscapes differed markedly from the Anglo-American conceptualizations with which they competed. Spanish land grants were based upon less exacting systems of land disposal that defined land grants on the basis of existing physiographic, environmental, and cultural landscape features. The definition of any particular grant of land was based on a combination of factors: (1) the status of the grantee, (2) the intended use(s) for the land, and (3) the spatial configuration of valued resources. Under the Spanish colonial system, land could be privately owned, but lands surrounding private holdings were often maintained under communal ownership as *ejidos* (Gonzáles 2003; Van Ness 1976). Like the American system of land disposal, Mexican land disposal policies came to favor individually owned haciendas over communally owned ejidos, but community negotiation and sharing of common lands remained important components of Hispanic land use. In the Spanish system, settlers had access to municipal lands, common areas, arable land, and pastureland. Settlers were thus assured access to portions of landscapes that offered the necessary resources for mixed subsistence economies.

Under the Spanish system, land title could be transferred, but this was often done under the agreement of a governor and generally lacked formal instruments of recordation. The usage, conveyance, and legal status of land were thus a community-negotiated process, reliant more on face-to-face agreements than on institutionalized, formal, legal processes. Ultimately, the Spanish land system was based on defining and assigning land according to use value (Van Ness 1976).

Anglo-American Conceptualizations of Land

The Anglo-American land disposal system operated in an entirely different manner. Instead of variable land units with corresponding use values, American land was arbitrarily parceled out in regularly sized and shaped units that had no necessary relationship with the irregular spatial configuration of exploitable resources. These standardized units did, however, contain resources with measurable use values. The major characteristics of the American land system that differentiate it from other competing systems are that land parcels had unique identifiers, were carefully defined and measured, and could be conveyed under a clearly legislated set of nationally recognized rules and procedures (Church 2001, 2002; Linklater 2002; Van Ness 1976).

Instead of defining land according to perceived resource characteristics, settlers *selected* predefined parcels of land according to valued environmental and cultural variables. One could argue that the Anglo-American system permitted more strategically diverse settlement strategies (or at least altered the strategic contexts of land settlement). Rather than being built on a common set of community-negotiated strategies that prefigured a set of potential land-use options, settlers could select parcels for settlement according to different sets of potentially individualized strategies for land use. The most distinguishing feature of the U.S. land disposal system is that it operationalized individual, private landownership and fee simple transfer of title.

Ultimately, the Anglo-American system of land disposal *standardized* land as a *commodity*, allowing for land to be bought and sold in standard, easily transactable units. In this sense, the American land policy favored the *exchange value* of land. Standardization and commodification allowed land to more effectively enter into a capitalist, world systems framework as a transactable unit. This conceptualization and commodification of land opened up a different set of potential strategies for land use and exploitation.

Although cultural ideals may have transferred land title to private individuals for the Jeffersonian purposes of democratized self-sufficiency, to establish pathways for the development of revenue, and to establish direct economic and legal relationships between citizens and their government, it also allowed for the development of land-acquisition strategies based fundamentally on the exchange value of land as a commodity. Furthermore, the commodification of land allowed for landowners to have less of a direct relationship with the land as "actual settlers," who improved the land and extracted its resources, and more of an abstract relationship with land as a commodity. The commodification of land allowed for the possibility of landowners to deal not necessarily in the specific resources landscapes had to offer but in land itself (Krall 2001; Linklater 2002; Sheridan 2006).

Hispanic/Anglo-American Conflict over Land Title

Despite their differences, Spanish land policy in the Southwest did include forms of land speculation. Particularly in California and New Mexico, large grants of land were made under a variety of methods. In the 1830s and 1840s, speculators were able "to secure vast land grants in the name of colonization, Indian defense, or the creation of buffer settlements to hold back Americans" (Lamar 1962:500). Once territories including former Spanish and Mexican land grants came under the jurisdiction of the United States, settling the legal title to earlier land grants became a primary issue.

Lawyers, politicians, and businessmen formed land-speculation rings, attempting to control the transfer of land title. In New Mexico, land attorneys were able to secure some of the territory's first political posts, handle land-grant clients, and amass vast amounts of land and capital. In one famous case, a group of speculators outcompeted other land speculators to obtain the 97,000-acre Maxwell grant for $650,000 ($6.70/acre). As part of the purchase, the speculators established the Maxwell Land Grant and Railroad Company and persuaded the seller to establish a bank (First National of Santa Fe) to handle the new company's securities (Lamar 1962). The speculators then hired a surveyor to generously reinterpret the ambiguously defined grant in order to claim that the tract was two million acres in size. The expanded claim was then sold through a series of buyers for $1,350,000, and $5,000,000 in stock was issued. Though expanded Maxwell grant land claims were questionable, after 10 years of legal battles 1,750,000 acres of land were eventually patented under the grant. Another, the Sangre de Cristo grant, was spuriously inflated from under 100,000 acres to 2,750,000 (Gonzáles 2003; Lamar 1962).

In the case of the Santa Fe ring, relatively small numbers of Anglo-American officials were able to build political and economic power by using "land [as] their first medium of currency" (Lamar 1962: 508). At the same time as vast sums of land were being transferred under the Maxwell grant, less than 10 percent of New Mexican lands had been surveyed, and only 4,475 acres of New Mexican public lands had been sold for cash or entered as homesteads. By the mid-1880s, the new surveyor general of New Mexico, George W. Julian, had "announced that 90 per cent of all land entries in the territory were fraudulent" (Julian 1979; Lamar 1962:512). At the same time, Edmund G. Ross, New Mexico's governor and homesteading advocate, railed against the cattle industry for monopolizing lands that should be reserved exclusively for homesteading. To Lamar (1962), the Spanish pattern of a few *patróns* possessing most of the land and controlling most of the political and economic power persisted in New Mexico. The power simply shifted to a new set of individuals in a position to build economic and political power through the commodification of land.

Historical Analysis of Homesteading Policies and Strategies

Land policy historians have tended to "eulogize" the liberal land policy embodied in the Homestead Act as putting an end to land speculation by putting land in the hands of "actual settlers" who could acquire the land for "free." Gates (1936) concludes to the contrary that the Homestead Act did not reduce land speculation and may have even contributed to its increase. Along with the Homestead Act,

> the existence of the Pre-emption Law and its later variations, the Desert Land Act, the Timber Culture Act, the Timber and Stone Act, the land grants to railroads and states, the cash sale system, the Indian land policy, the acts granting land warrants to ex-soldiers or their heirs, and the Agricultural College Act of 1862, which granted millions of acres of land scrip to Eastern States, tended to make it practically as easy for speculators to engross huge areas of land after 1862 as before [Gates 1936:656].

Within eight years of its passage, almost 130 million acres of land had been granted to private organizations for the construction of railroads, wagon roads, and canals. Over 100 million acres of federal land was offered through the public auction and cash sale system in large and small parcel sizes. As many as 140 million acres of land were granted to states after the passage of the Homestead Act. Indian reservation land also became available for sale after 1862, being initially "sold in large blocks to groups of capitalists and railroads" and later auctioned in smaller parcels at higher rates (Gates 1968:661). At least 100 million acres of Indian reservation land were sold during the homesteading period.

Much of the land granted to transportation companies, state governments, and Indian reservations and offered for sale or auction was higher-quality, more desirable land. Settlers wanting to homestead prime land often had to purchase or lease land from private companies or state governments, rather than obtain land "free" from the federal government (Gates 1936). Settlers were also forced to purchase land at inflated rates. In the settling of the American West, land was the primary currency for developing revenue and expanding capital. The vast majority of public land disposal treated land as a commodity—a commodity that could be traded as currency and used to build revenue, finance infrastructure, and concentrate political and economic power.

The Agricultural College Act of 1862 put 7,672,800 acres of land on the market as land scrip. States sold depreciated land scrip for a fraction of its original value, resulting in some speculators acquiring individually over 50,000 acres of scrip land and groups of speculators acquiring as many as 250,000 acres. In California, where land speculation was rampant, one politically influential speculator, William S. Chapman, was able to acquire title to over one million acres of choice land in California and Nevada through a variety of mechanisms: "cash, scrip, and warrants"; dummy "entrymen"; and vast "swamp" land purchases (Gates 1936:669).

Public Land Disposal and the Tragedy of the Commons

In addressing the global problem of unchecked human population growth, Hardin draws attention to what he refers to as "no technical solution problems" (1968:1243). In Hardin's view, a world of finite resources can only support a finite human population. Thus, human population growth will ultimately have to equal zero in order to avoid outstripping environmental carrying capacities. In Hardin's (1968) view, the population growth problem cannot be solved by technical solutions that increase the efficiency of resource extraction or capitalize on untapped resource pools. Instead, changes in morality, ethics, or policy need to be effected in order to prevent hazardous withdrawals from properties or environments held in common. In effect, populations have to be mutually coerced into protecting the common good, and, to Hardin this coercion would require internal privatization and external regulation. In Hardin's view, failure to externally regulate usage of the commons inevitably leads to a "tragedy of the commons."

Since Hardin's (1968) initial address, as Hardin himself observes, the "tragedy of the commons" has been of interest to practitioners of "ecology, environmentalism, health care, economics, population studies, law, political science, philosophy, ethics, geography, psychology, and sociology" (1998:47). Hardin's (1968, 1998) notion that individual greed leads to short-term gain but ultimately to mutual ruin was taken up by governmental regulatory agencies that perceived traditional common property as effectively unmanaged. What the proponents of Hardin's (1968) thesis failed to recognize, however, was the notion that common property may be effectively controlled by traditional systems of management, in the absence of which the sustainability of resources cannot be supported (Monbiot 1994). Thus, the efforts of governmental agencies to externally regulate traditional common property in order to avoid the tragedy of the commons actually generated another tragedy: the "tragedy of enclosure" (Monbiot 1994).

The Tragedy of Commoditization

As Hornborg (2001) observes, the expansion of market economies is based on unequal distributions of cost. The ability of speculators to use capital to acquire land at a lower energetic cost than those who attempt to acquire "free" land through settlement results in the disproportionate distribution of public lands and subverts the democratic intent of the law. In a different sense, the commodification of land as a resource arbitrarily parcels ecological and cultural resources, depreciating the ability to effectively manage valuable ecological and cultural resources (Polanyi 1957; Sternberg 1993).

Greenberg (1998) argues that the dependency of capitalist economies on the territorialization and commodification of nature (processes fundamental to the public land disposal system) results in a "tragedy of commoditization." In effect, commoditization of natural resources dissipates the inherent order in ecosystems by fragmenting exploitable resources and discharging waste materials that encourage ecosystem entropy. Once alienated, the cultural and ecological resources of public lands are no longer available to common use. Rather, the commodification of land has offered up their private use as capital. At the same time, land as a commodity enters a common market.

U.S. public land policy was designed to put land in the hands of as many citizens as possible, but it had serious unintended consequences. In a sense, it was designed to prevent something like a tragedy of the commons by evening out and partitioning the rights to own and use land. Instead, it allowed land to be commodified, to be converted to capital, and to be accumulated as a commodity in large quantities without regard for management of the cultural and ecological resources it so arbitrarily subdivided.

The Development of Capitalist Land Market Strategies

As discussed above, Hispanic and Anglo-American strategies for settlement and land use differed significantly. Hispanic strategies emphasized community negotiation, shared resource use, and heterogeneous allocation of land use. Anglo-American strategies emphasized individual private ownership, exclusive resource use, and homogeneous allocation of land use. With the passage of the Treaty of Guadalupe Hidalgo (1848) and the Gadsden Purchase (1853), large areas of the American West (including southeastern Arizona) came under the jurisdiction of the United States. Thus, all settlers in these areas were forced to interact with Anglo-American cultural ideals for conceptualizing land as expressed in the Homestead Act of 1862 and related congressionally legislated land policies.

As a result, a variety of new strategies for land use developed. Because American land policy was built on a set of cultural ideals that did not necessarily mesh with local conditions, most strategies were designed to circumvent or manipulate the legal system. Some strategies were based on maintaining the use value of landscapes under a system that promoted a different set of goals. Other strategies were based on capitalizing on the exchange value of land, subverting the idealistic intentions of the system. Divergent strategies that either maintained use value or capitalized on exchange value include the following:

1. Settling a claim, residing for five years, and proving up the claim.
2. Settling claims adjacent to a ranch boss's claim under the agreement of selling to the rancher once the claim had been proved up (Church 2001, citing Friedman 1985).
3. Temporary occupation of land parcels with the intention to sell to large-scale outfits (Allen 1987).
4. Settling sections reserved for education with no intention to legally sell or own parcels (Church 2001).
5. Reciprocal witnessing (or false swearing), often accomplished through real or fictive kinship ties. This strategy took advantage of the limited local knowledge of Government Land Office (GLO) officers and generally entailed traveling to GLO offices in order to witness claims (in order to prevent GLO officers from gaining local knowledge [Allen 1987; Church 2001; Gates 1936; Sauder 1989]).
6. Patenting land containing spatially rare water sources, thereby gaining control of surrounding pasturelands (Church 2001; Schoenwetter and Hohmann 1997; Sheridan 1995).
7. Obtaining title through cash entry rather than demonstrating full-term occupancy and improvements.
8. Antagonizing settlers attempting to homestead land containing valued resources (Allen 1987).
9. Paying "dummy entrymen" to file false claims and transfer title (Gates 1936; Lamar 1962; Sauder 1989).
10. Using family members to file for multiple adjacent claims (McIntosh 1981).
11. Taking advantage of multiple congressional acts in order to obtain title to maximum public land acreage (i.e., filing separate claims under the Pre-Emption Act of 1841, the Homestead Act of 1862, the Timber Culture Act of 1873, and the Desert Land Act of 1877 [Gates 1936; Krall 2001; McIntosh 1981]).
12. Employing banking loan instruments to acquire land from settlers who defaulted on their loans (McIntosh 1981).
13. Voluntarily abandoning a homestead claim, filing for a relinquishment permitting immediate claim by another party, and selling the relinquishment to a land speculator (McIntosh 1981; Panelli 1984).
14. Squatting land in advance of survey in an attempt to gain preemption rights (Linklater 2002).
15. Mortgaging claims to gain capital for improvements (McIntosh 1981).
16. Scheduling relinquishment of a claim upon prior agreement with another party intending to make a claim on the same parcel (McIntosh 1981).
17. Taking advantage of veteran concessions in an 1872 amendment to the Homestead Act allowing for military service to be credited toward occupancy. Land speculators paid widows of veterans to obtain claims and transfer title (McIntosh 1981).
18. Fencing and enclosing large pasturelands by obtaining land patents around the perimeter of a ranch (McIntosh 1981).

Sanford Ranch in Context

The commodification of land as a transactable unit with inherent exchange value transforms the conceptualization and usage of places into a complex, capitalist, spatial game. As legal ownership of land under American land policy of the 1870s and 1880s was contingent upon the survey and legal definition of land parcels, the game board on which the game was played essentially became land parcels within surveyed townships. As discussed above, the potential strategies for the game were numerous, and individual players would likely exploit a number of different strategies depending on the specific context.

While a number of intersecting frontier economies were developing in southeastern Arizona during the 1870s and 1880s (ranching, agriculture, military, railroad, mining), ranching was entering a boom economy for which the control of land was a major component. Ranchers who controlled the best water sources, who had access to the best pasturelands, and who had access to emerging commercial nodes and transportation networks theoretically were in the best position to prosper. Thus ranchers should have sought ownership of land with high ranching-use value.

Sanford Ranch was homesteaded at a time when mass migrations of people were taking place on a global scale. New transportation technologies were connecting distant markets, transporting people and goods across oceans and continents. The United States was expanding its political boundaries and extending its power toward the control, exploitation, and settlement of newly acquired territories and their resources.

The Civil War had ended, and the national economy was entering a depression. The resources of the West needed to be defined, alienated, controlled, and exploited. "Free" land could be settled under the 1862 Homestead Act, but public land could also be bought at auction or entered with cash. Large parcels of choice land were granted to states and railroad companies.

Population across the nation was concentrated in the eastern half of the United States, particularly in the Northeast. The West, in contrast, was thinly settled. The 1870 Census recorded less than 3 percent of the U.S. population in the western frontier. Homesteading was occurring with greatest intensity in the Midwestern states and to a lesser extent in California. Virtually no homesteading occurred in the eastern United States. Arizona was one of the least settled territories of the West when Sanford Ranch was homesteaded.

By the time Sanford Ranch was homesteaded Don Alonzo and Denton Sanford collectively had traveled extensively throughout the far West (Washington and Oregon Territories, Utah, Arizona, Texas, California). Born and raised in an agrarian setting in Holeoye, New York, as young men the two brothers separately headed west, where they became involved in freighting and cattle business. They were thus attracted to the opportunities associated with the supply of mining, military, and other frontiers in the developing far West.

By the time Denton and Don Alonzo settled in Arizona, they had ample opportunity to acquire extensive knowledge of business opportunities available throughout the West. They had knowledge of current transportation systems, ranching technology, and local environments. With this extensive knowledge of local and regional landscapes, they chose to settle an area in which homesteadable land was just becoming available.

In 1873, the southern portion of Arizona had been recently acquired through the Gadsden Purchase. Southeastern Arizona hosted growing mining, ranching, and military frontiers. Publications advertised areas of southeastern Arizona (portions of the Cienega Creek, Sonoita Creek, and San Pedro River valleys) as possessing the finest grasslands in the state. Choice areas of southeastern Arizona had been surveyed, and routes for the transcontinental railroad had been proposed (Hinton 1878). Tucson was the territorial capital, and the political climate was congenial to Anglo-American pioneers (Wagoner 1970).

Apache hostility had kept the area a frontier for centuries. With some prime areas surveyed, legal settlement was now possible but still involved substantial risk. Southeastern Arizona was peppered with Spanish and Mexican land-grant claims. Problems in the settlement of landownership issues in New Mexico and California were legion. In contrast, writers of the time felt that most

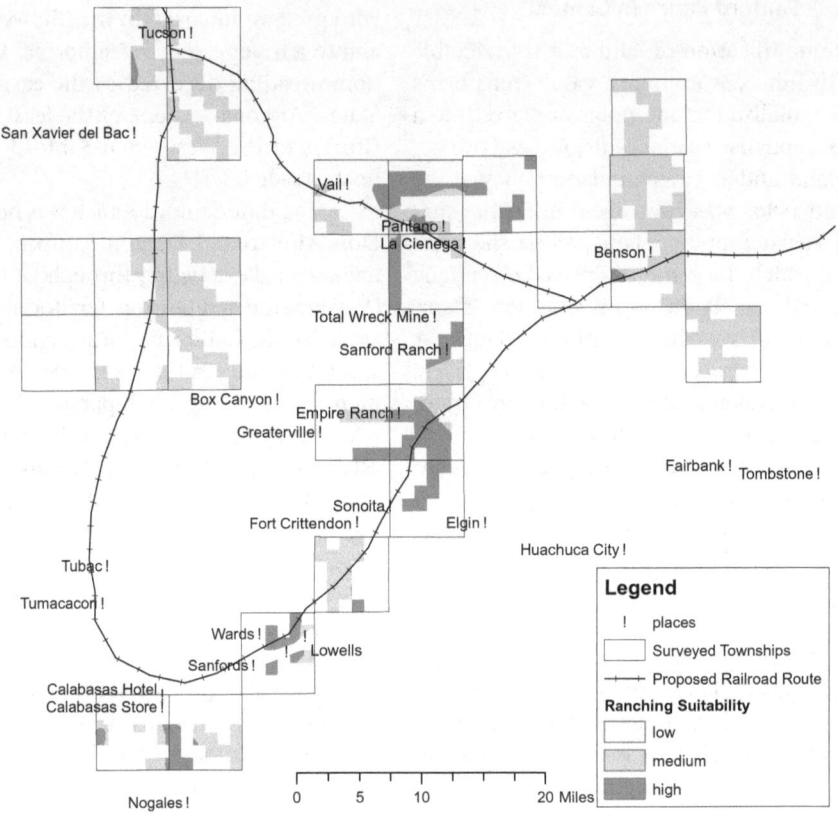

FIGURE 8.2. The cognized landscape of Don Alonzo and Denton Sanford expressed in terms of political and economic variables. The landscape is composed of surveyed and unsurveyed areas, the proposed route of the transcontinental railroad, places, and varying degrees of ranching suitability. Suitable land sections are defined in terms of three ordinal classes—high (high access to water, high livestock forage quality, short distance to proposed railroad route), medium (medium suitability for one variable), or low (medium or low suitability for more than one variable). Both Denton and Don Alonzo appear to have selected homestead parcels that were within small patches of highly suitable ranch land. Through strategic homestead selection, the two were likely gambling on access to railroad, mining, and military frontier markets.

preexisting land grants in the Arizona Territory could not be legally verified (Hinton 1878).

Denton and Don Alonzo settled almost equidistantly from one of the few military forts in the region, within short distances of the proposed railroad route, on high-quality grazing (and in Denton's case, agricultural) land, in locations containing ample water, in an area surrounded by emerging mining districts, at a time when land was just becoming available for settlement. Denton farmed, and Don Alonzo ranched. Clearly, the two strategized where to settle and how to accumulate capital from land (Figure 8.2).

Both brothers continued to acquire land through a variety of strategies rather than invest in upgrading Don Alonzo's primitive ranch house complex (Figure 8.3). They competed with other settlers and businessmen over the control of land and business opportunities and survived Apache scares. Don Alonzo married a woman from Virginia and began raising a family, while Denton remained single. When the railroad eventually came to pass near Denton's Sonoita Creek property, Don Alonzo recycled Johnny Ward's ranch into a grocery store, supplying Chinese American railroad workers (Fontana and Greenleaf 1962).

Within a decade of settling the area, Don Alonzo sold a large proportion of his land and

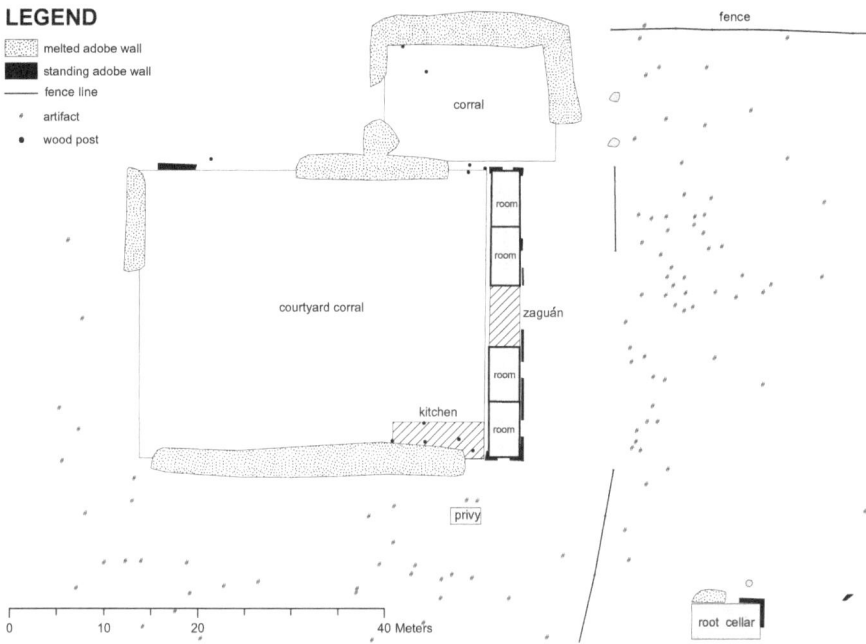

FIGURE 8.3. Reconstruction of structures at Sanford Ranch.

ranching capital, amassing $125,000. He built the largest house in Tucson, became the mayor, and in 1886 moved his family back to the East Coast. Denton's fortunes were different. He eventually lost title to his land once it was officially declared to be within a preexisting Spanish land grant and died a single man in Tucson.

Don Alonzo and Denton Sanford's lives exemplify many of the broad-scale patterns now becoming apparent in the history and anthropology of the American West. Both were relatively young male members of highly mobile populations draining out of the eastern United States and pouring into newly opened lands of the West. They became involved in businesses provisioning emerging local, regional, and national markets. Don Alonzo's fortune, the foundation of his economic and political power, was built upon the commodification of land and his ability to use land as capital.

Discussion

The historical frontier landscapes of southeastern Arizona were defined by processes of conquest and conflict over political borders, resources, landownership, and people. The process of land alienation, as it came to be implemented in different areas of the United States, was rife with conflict over landownership. The game context seemed to generate three general kinds of players: (1) squatters, (2) settlers, and (3) land speculators. Much of the history of land policy legislation and political argument had to do with whether existing systems promoted the disposal of public lands to actual settlers or promoted land monopolization by absentee owners.

Early U.S. land policies set minimum parcel size and pricing structures too high for settlers lacking capital. Moreover, early U.S. land policies did not cap the number of acres that could be purchased outright by any individual party. The result was that small landholdings were rare and land monopoly was common. Instead of owning individual parcels of land, settlers were more often the tenants of absentee landlords.

In order to transfer the ownership of public lands to actual settlers, minimum parcel sizes and price rates were gradually lowered. Still, no policies were enacted to prevent large-scale purchases of federal land. With the passage of the Homestead Act of 1862, Congress made it possible, under certain conditions, to pay nothing but the $14.00 filing fee for a parcel of government land.

After the passage of the Homestead Act, large areas of the western United States were legally opened up for homesteading. Homesteading was not a simple or straightforward process—many variables influenced temporal and spatial homesteading patterns. Along with a series of related acts, the Homestead Act and the process of national frontier expansion led to the alienation of land on a monumental scale and the entry of much of that land into a capitalist market system.

Historic landscapes of southeastern Arizona were cognized by homesteaders like the Sanfords in terms of environmental and cultural variables that were primarily economic and capitalist in nature (Figure 8.2). Homesteaders strategized where to settle in terms of the availability of water, grasslands, agricultural soils, timber, and other ecological resources. They also strategized where to settle in terms of cultural variables: access to existing and future transportation routes, access of mining and military settlements, availability of surveyed land, and the density or locations of pre-existing homesteads. Homesteaders selected areas for settlement to obtain access to ecological and cultural resources in order to exploit those resources for economic gain and to enter emerging local, regional, and national markets.

The success of any particular homesteading strategy depended on its relationship to emerging, capitalist structures. A primary mechanism for succeeding as a homesteader was to capitalize on the commodification of land by using land like currency—as a way to borrow, lend, and accumulate capital. Sanford Ranch, as a homesteaded place in an American frontier landscape, exemplifies processes of commodification. Don Alonzo Sanford began with goals, strategies, and a piece of land; he ended up with wealth, political prominence, and social mobility. Obviously, he played the game well.

Notes

1. The U.S. Public Land Survey System was designed in a similar fashion to the ancient Roman survey system. Cartesian grids of standardized, rectilinear units were defined and surveyed, but concepts such as principle baselines and meridians were not used to connect surveyed areas. A major difference between the two systems is that the Public Land Survey System defines a grid that can be extended across a nation, whereas the Roman system could only be extended over short distances (Kish 1962).
2. Greenberg (1998) uses the term *commoditization* to refer to processes for which the term *commodification* is more often used. Though subtle semantic distinctions between the two terms may exist, we prefer the term *commodification* in order to maintain consistency and avoid confusion.
3. Purser argues that the extractive economies of the frontier American West commodified resources as a general rule—"Even the region's idealized agribusinesses, such as the western cattle industry, could be described quite easily as the mass production and marketing of a basic commodity" (1999:119).

9

Reconstructing an Ndee Sense of Place

John R. Welch

All of us are embedded in places, and scholars are increasingly surrounded by place. Building upon generations of research, advocacy, and creative endeavor that nibbled around the edges, anthropologists, geographers, and historians are now looking more often at the core of places—at the shared meanings of constellations of mineral–plant–animal–human creations and at how these shape and are shaped by environmental, behavioral, cultural, and historical dynamics. Archaeologists are adopting theoretical approaches and methods derived from place-focused scholars and artists (Ashmore 2002, this volume). Historic preservationists, long dedicated to the exacting reconstruction of significant structures and districts, are today showing interest in the nonmaterial dimensions of place (Benton et al. 2001; Stille 2002; Wilson 2002). Anthropologists, geographers, and conservation advocates are recognizing and seeking consideration of the enduring powers of places across time, space, and culture (e.g., Howell 2002; Lane 2002; Sullivan 2000). Planners and tourism professionals are endorsing many of these efforts as bases for promoting the prospects for health and prosperity that typically accompany life in communities willing to conserve and share their authentic places (e.g., McCool and Moisey 2001).

The Ndee (Western Apache) and many other American Indian people have tacitly understood and actively respected the importance of place since time immemorial. It is thus appropriate that the results of Keith Basso's collaborations with the Ndee community of Cibecue, Arizona, are so often credited as inspiring salient elements of the escalating and converging interests in place-based inquiry, planning, and action (e.g., Basso 1996; Feld and Basso 1996). By bridging communication barriers among Ndee and non-Indians through glimpses of the Ndee sense of place, Basso illustrates the connectivity among land, people, culture, and right ways of thinking and acting (Long et al. 2003; Welch and Riley 2001). Cibecue is one of the principal communities making up the White Mountain Apache Tribe of what is now eastern Arizona, and this chapter examines how aspects of an Ndee sense of place have survived to guide the tribe and its members in what is referred to as *reconstructive place making*. Sense of place is considered here in the active terms of engaging geography and culture to create and sustain mutual and meaningful intimacy. The premise is that aspects of the recent history of the White Mountain Apache Tribe may be usefully understood as multifaceted efforts to regain control over important places and to resume place making in accord with both long-standing and contemporary Ndee values, interests, and sensibilities.

Since the rise of tribal sovereignty in the early 1970s, Ndee have engaged in the reconstruction of tangible and intangible aspects of places characterized by both tremendous beauty and resonating meaning. Surviving and growing despite cultural, political, legal, and economic challenges—and employing as a foothold that portion of the core of their ancestral homeland retained as the Fort Apache Indian Reservation—White Mountain Apaches have preserved and continue to actively use aspects of an ancient and distinctive sense of their place. The concept of reconstruction is employed here as a focal point for identifying common ground among archaeological, historical, ecological, and history preservation approaches to place. The discussion proceeds by considering the multiple meanings of reconstruction, reviewing the historical and cultural context for Ndee place making, and examining the guiding principles used and insights gained through Ndee efforts to restore their homeland and reassert control over their history, culture, and destiny. The discussion indicates the need for holism and caution in archaeological efforts to reconstruct places and senses thereof.

Reconstruction Meanings and Methods

Because numerous disciplines and nonacademic pursuits now claim slices of the place pie, it is useful to examine reconstruction from several perspectives. Reconstruction unifies much archaeological discourse and most contributions to this volume, but the term has carried diverse meanings across historical and professional boundaries. In archaeological parlance, *reconstruction* may be defined as the search for increasingly precise understanding of behaviors responsible for material residues. Given the deepening goals of place-focused archaeology, however, little progress in the still incompletely charted terrain scoped out in this volume seems likely if we commit to such rigor.

In historic preservation, reconstruction has been formally codified, through the Secretary of the Interior's Standards and Guidelines, as "depicting, by means of new construction, the form, features, and detailing of a non-surviving site, landscape, building, structure, or object for the purpose of replicating its appearance at a specific period of time and in its historic location" (www.nps.gov/history/local-law/arch_stnds_10.htm). This definition, focused as it is upon the details of architectural treatments, appropriately affirms the important connections among minutia, meanings, and the maintenance of a sense of place. Missing from the definition, though no longer from historic preservation practice, is attention to the overall feeling engendered by buildings and features ordered (or not) within culturally meaningful spaces.

Where used by environmental planners and resource managers, reconstruction most often refers to reassembling the parts and removing the impediments required for healthful and productive ecosystem functions. Here, too, the focus is on the complex relationships among parts of systems and the higher-order processes that may result (Falk et al. 2006).

In historical literature *reconstruction* is most often used in reference to a period in American history, the federal government's post–Civil War policies and practices directed toward restoring the South to the Union. Apparently irrelevant to this discussion at first glance, the historical usage contributes to our understanding of the historical context that created the need for the Ndee place making observable since the 1970s. The Reconstruction period overlapped the era of U.S. subjugation of the Apache, thus highlighting differences in federal policy toward defeated Southerners and defeated American Indian peoples and providing additional background for reconstructive place making by Ndee and other American Indians.

Last, but hardly least, *Webster's* reconstruction is "to rebuild or to form anew...as in the imagination." This definition suggests that archaeologists may need both information and creativity to access domains of culture previously off-limits to analyses of material residues—sense of place could be noted as one such domain. In establishing an archaeologically appropriate framework for pursuing sense of place, Zedeño (Zedeño et al. 1997) suggests describing and understanding places in terms of formal, historical, and relational dimensions. Formal dimensions refer to the physical characteristics and properties of a place: that which can be seen, heard, tasted, or felt. The historical dimension is the sequence of associations among localities, people, and power: what has happened on and with a place through time. The relational dimension is the social and symbolic connections that make places meaningful and useful to groups of people: the linkages among material and conceptual realities. Borrowing from Feld and Basso, it is only through glimpses of "the experiential and expressive ways places are known, imagined, yearned for, held, remembered, voiced, lived, contested, struggled over," and most of all shared, that the road to any place opens (1996:11). Cultural elements must supplement visible features (and may in cases overwhelm them) in efforts to produce and reproduce a sense of place.

Because archaeologists generally rely on data and perspective derived from the observation of material remains, our previous approaches to sense of place too often emphasized formal dimensions and cultural passivity—the inherently ethnocentric reconstruction and interpretation of site settings, architectures, and material cultures as they would have been configured and experienced in times past. Making the inferential leaps from strictly archaeological data to an ancient place's feeling and character—aspects of its relational dimensions—poses serious challenges (see Wylie 1985). As just one example of the problems, archaeologists seldom control sufficient information to enable high-confidence discriminations between alternative behavioral and postbehavioral sources of variation in material remains.

The current interest in place is prompting another surge of archaeological research dedicated to the use of spatial data to make social inferences. Ashmore's review of the diverse approaches being adopted finds particular promise in life histories of place—"examining evidence for human recognition, use, and modification of a particular position, locality, or area over the full time span of its existence" (2002:1178). Clearly essential in cases for which there exist no living representatives of the cultures affiliated with the place, the archaeological emphasis on formal dimensions need not go it alone. Perhaps the most promising means for bridging the gap between formal and relational dimensions involves the use of indigenous peoples' perspectives as guides to place-based sensibilities. The notion that objects and features that share formal attributes are more likely to also share uses and meanings is a pillar of archaeological epistemology. In one example, an archaeologist identifies walls following a steep hillslope's contour. On the basis of observations of American Indian people's use of similar walls as agricultural terraces, an inference is nurtured. Equifinality raises its ugly head with the recognition that similar features may have been used as tactical breastworks, as protection from sheet erosion for a settlement at the base of the hill, and as elements of geoglyphs. The degree of "fit" between an archaeological manifestation and a proposed analogy—environmental/geographic, sociocultural, temporal, and so on—may provide additional criteria for assessing the inferences (Welch 1994).

Given the value of analogical information and reasoning, what information of archaeological use or interest may be gained from the observation or analysis of Ndee reconstructive place making? The answers to this question require an understanding of the cultural foundations for the Ndee–land relationship, the changes to that relationship entailed by the establishment of federal control over the Ndee, and the actions and guiding principles associated with Ndee place making.

Ndee Life as Part of a Sacred Whole

Ndee bonds to land may be discussed in terms of spirituality, history, and exchanges of material support. Land provides points of both departure and convergence for efforts to understand Ndee culture and history. Like all Athabascan speakers, virtually all American Indians (Deloria 1973; Sullivan 2000), and many other land-linked communities, the Ndee are unwilling to think of themselves, their culture, or their history or future without reference to land. This deceptively straightforward truth finds deceptively simple expression in the deceptively small Ndee word *ni'*. In the Apache language *ni'* means both "land" and "mind," as well as "country" and "way of thinking." This is no accident or random convergence. Ndee land is both good to walk and good to think (Welch and Riley 2001). The inseparability of land and thought, of geography and memory, and of place and wisdom has shaped the Ndee and their surroundings (Basso 1996). This unity informs the worldview, social organization, and economic practices of the Ndee and other peoples with spirits embedded in their place and place embedded in their spirits.

Basso's work, especially his *Wisdom Sits in Places* (1996), is the best published source of perspectives on the connections among Ndee places, place names, oral traditions, and systems of memory, morality, and cultural regeneration. Through

FIGURE 9.1. White Mountain Apache Tribe lands.

Basso the Ndee explain the existence of names and meanings for springs, hills, plant constellations, and other landscape features. Places and names are linked to stories and other social memories about the Ndee ancestors who conferred or contributed to the name. Many of these recollections elegantly refer to and reinforce tenets of Ndee morality, and many of these moral tenets exist and recur as core aspects of Ndee culture (see Basso 1996).

To begin to glimpse the connection between place and people one must know something of the Ndee homeland centered on the reservations occupied by the White Mountain and San Carlos Apache tribes, two of the five federally recognized tribes representing the Ndee cultural tradition in Arizona (Figure 9.1). The rugged area north of the Gila River was the exclusive province of the indomitable Apache until 1870. From an Ndee perspective the 1.7 million acres under the immediate control of the White Mountain Apache start at the top, the summits of Arizona's White Mountains—the source for water, life, history, and culture (Figure 9.2). From these peaks above 3,354 m the land descends through high-elevation *cienegas* and about 400,000 acres of commercial forest, with precious surface water cascading along about 600 km of perennial streams. (Prior to the Rodeo-Chediski wildfire of 2002 there were over 600,000 acres of commercial timberlands on the Fort Apache Indian Reservation.) Most of the tribe's briskly expanding population of about 14,000 tribal members live in the piñon-juniper woodland belt, from about 1,980 m to 1,220 m above sea level. Below these woodlands the country breaks up even more into buttes and canyons, before yielding to true desert at the reservation's southwestern border at about 760 m. A personal visit may not allow an outsider to grasp an Ndee sense of the place, but few leave without an appreciation of the pride Apaches rightfully take in their land, one of their enduring birthrights and sources of distinctive identity.

How the Land Was Lost

Ndee connections to their land remain vital in spite of a century of historical forces and government policies that systematically sought to dismantle Ndee senses of place. The establishment of Fort Apache by the U.S. Army marked the beginning of a century-long interruption in Ndee dominion over their homeland. Seeking a site for a military post to keep the formidable White Mountain Apaches out of hostilities escalating to the south and west, in 1869 Major John Green led the Army's first scouting expedition onto the southern flanks of the White Mountains. The cavalry's mission was to locate an army post and prevent White Mountain bands from providing corn and supplies to hostile bands. But Green had received dubious intelligence, and the reportedly nomadic barbarians greeted him as an ambassador and assisted in situating Fort Apache in exchange for cavalry protection from non-Indian incursions into their homeland (Davisson 1976, 1978). Green wrote,

> It seems this one corner of Arizona were almost a garden spot, the beauty of its scenery, the fertility of its soil and facilities for irrigation are not surpassed.... This post would be of greatest advantage for the following reasons: It would compel the White Mountain Indians to live on their reservation or be driven from their beautiful country which they almost worship. (1896)

Green's words proved prophetic. Capitalizing on Ndee affection for their land and the fractiousness of Ndee bands and subtribes, the Army seized strategic ground and political control. But the frontier's predatory character ruled the era, and the government promptly broke the promise to protect the integrity of the 14 million-acre Ndee homeland. With initial reservation establishment in 1871 the government "restored to the public domain" millions of acres of the Ndee territory, conveying vast tracts of Ndee land to non-Indians at little or no cost (see, e.g., U. S. Grant Executive Orders dated November 9, 1871; August 5, 1873; July 21, 1874; and April 27, 1876). This denied Ndee

FIGURE 9.2. Louie Zospah, White Mountain Apache Tribe Wildlife and Outdoor Recreation Ranger. Photograph by John R. Welch; courtesy of the White Mountain Apache Tribe Heritage Program.

use and enjoyment of 10 million acres, including virtually all of the land possessing noteworthy commercial or industrial value by nineteenth-century standards (Welch 1997).

By the later 1870s—as the availability of open land beyond reservation boundaries dwindled and as resource pressures on Ndee lands increased—the qualitative land losses were almost as traumatic (Buskirk 1986). The tribe's federal trustees often took the lead in opening the land reserved for the exclusive use and benefit of the White Mountain Apache people—the reservation itself—to non-Indian cattlemen, shepherds, loggers, farmers, miners, missionaries, hunters, fishermen, and museum collectors. Non-Ndee approached the land as a commodity instead of a birthright and mandate for stewardship: overgrazing the rangelands, high grading the forests, overhunting the game herds, looting and desecrating the cultural sites, extracting minerals, degrading the stream channels, building roads and ditches without attention to erosion or other risks, creating toxic waste and other pollutants and liabilities, and so on. Among the innumerable instances of shortsighted resource management was a ca. 1960 experiment to increase runoff from the Cibecue watershed through the removal of "thirsty" cottonwood trees from stream courses by poisoning and girdling. The result, perhaps needless to say, was disastrous erosion and reductions in the diversity and resilience of one of Arizona's most beautiful and productive mid-elevation riparian areas (Long et al. 2003).

From the Ndee perspective the greedy and foolhardy destruction of a part of creation was likened to witchcraft (Basso 1970). More generally, the rapacious character of non-Indian land use was viewed as disrespectful. Because the new arrivals came from places not known to Ndee and moved often, depleting and sometimes destroying the land, the Ndee viewed the newcomers as apparently placeless, likely senseless, and certainly dangerous. Ndee lifeways quickly changed dramatically, and opportunities for farming, hunting, and plant gathering declined along with resource conditions across the tribe's aboriginal and trust lands. Various courts have recognized the massive erosion of Ndee tangible assets through their trustees' neglect and mismanagement, but not enough has been said about the violence done and losses to the people's distinctive, geography-linked identity and senses of places.

As has occurred across the globe, the separation of indigenous people from place brought a spiral of ecological disaster (Nabhan 1997; Naveh 1998). Aspects of the relationship between the Ndee and their homeland unraveled quickly and irrevocably. The ensuing century of despair on Apache reservations resulted directly from the federal effort to eliminate Ndee identity by severing ties between the people and their "geocultural" birthright. The late Raymond Kane, a director of the tribe's Heritage Program and a member of the Cultural Advisory Board, said that his grandfather described the loss of land as an unanesthetized amputation.

As federal policy shifted, new challenges to the Ndee–land bonds emerged. In 1922, when the Army concluded, at last, that the Apache wars were over, Fort Apache was transferred to the Interior Department for use as a Bureau of Indian Affairs (BIA) boarding school. In this incarnation, Fort Apache served as a center for the acculturation of American Indian youth. Mandatory Christian prayer, an English-only regimen, periodic submersion in vats of sheep dip, a psychological warfare of ethnic cleansing, and the sorts of corporal punishments that would be prosecuted today were part of the curriculum at the early Theodore Roosevelt School (Welch 2004, 2008; see also Adams 1995). Young Ndee minds and bodies were aggressively separated from their geographic and social birthright in the name of education and progress. Removing children from their families and lands broke links in a great chain that had provided for the Ndee since time immemorial.

Anthropology and archaeology also played roles in interrupting Ndee connections to their lands. The Field Museum, Gila Pueblo, and University of Arizona projects that harvested data and objects from Ndee lands violated Ndee behavioral and ethical principles by desecrating sacred places, removing ceremonial objects, and using cultural resources to augment personal and professional status (Welch 2000, 2007; Welch and Ferguson 2005, 2007). Increasingly liberated from the fear of BIA retribution, and empowered by the Native American Graves Protection and Repatriation Act and other favorable changes in federal authorities, many Ndee express bitterness toward archaeology, anthropology, and other pursuits that have collected materials and information without giving back (Welch 2000).

The final threats to land, people, and their connections are clear and present. One is at least as likely to find Apache youth in a mall or in front of a TV as with their parents or grandparents out on the land, coming to know their country, their mind, their place. As is true across much of Indian Country, the White Mountain Apache Tribe is facing daunting challenges associated with rapidly increasing population densities on and around reservation lands, the incursions of non-Indian communities, the limitations of extractive industries and federal fiduciary responsibilities, and global warming–related environmental degradation (Welch 2002).

Forward-Looking Reconstruction

In the wake of the Confederacy's defeat, the federal government reached out, "with malice toward none, with charity for all...to bind up the nation's wounds, to care for him who shall have borne the battle and for his widow and his orphan, to do all which may achieve and cherish a just and lasting peace among ourselves and with all nations" (Lincoln 1865). Lincoln's evocative words became the basis for a sustained federal commitment to reestablish the decimated links between North and South. No such commitment to mitigating the impact of subjugation in Indian Country was forthcoming, and none is on the horizon. To Ndee and other American Indian people, conquest efforts have persisted except as repulsed by tribal government and community countermeasures. The conflict continues.

Using the land as both a weapon and a call to arms, the White Mountain Apache Tribe has been engaged in regaining control of its place for much of the last four decades. Neither the Army nor the BIA was successful in eliminating Ndee senses of place, and their famous spirit of resilience and defiance was bent but never broken. This spirit, coupled with useful policies, practices, and technologies borrowed from non-Ndee, is facilitating progress toward the regeneration of Ndee–land linkages. The guiding light is the recognition that the Ndee homeland—as it has nurtured countless Apache generations and been shaped both physically and conceptually through actions, reflections, and oral traditions—holds keys to restoring much of the harmony and health of the White Mountain Apache community. The tribe's general strategy is to take care of the land so that the land, once again, can take better care of the people.

Place names have proved indispensable tools and points of orientation for reconstructive place making. Building on the efforts of Grenville Goodwin and Keith Basso, the White Mountain, San Carlos, and Payson Tonto Apache tribes and the Yavapai-Apache Nation have joined forces in the Western Apache Place Names Project. With financial assistance from the National Park Service Historic Preservation Fund Grants to Indian Tribes program, project teams have collected names and other oral traditions linked to more than 1,500 places scattered across the Ndee homeland, both within and beyond reservation, state, and national boundaries. There is no surer initial indicator of Ndee cultural and historical significance than an Ndee place name, and these records are serving as the foundations for educational and management programs, including consultations with the government agencies that now manage portions of the Ndee homeland.

In conjunction with the ongoing "re-placement" of an American Indian geographic framework, the White Mountain Apache Tribe is reasserting virtually total management control over its reservation lands. For example, as a result of successful assertions of tribal rights and prerogatives, the tribe, not its government trustees, now sets policies and program parameters for mineral extraction; livestock grazing; and how much, where, and how timber is to be harvested. Through enforcement of the tribe's water-quality standards and best management practices, cattle have been removed from degraded ranges (Long et al. 2003). Riparian areas are being allowed to recover and repair themselves, while Apache high school, college, and graduate students learn the Apache names of the plants and the places (Long 2002). Ndee foresters employed by the BIA and the tribe act as liaisons between the cultural and professional perspectives on timber harvesting, fire management, pest control, and post-wildfire rehabilitation. Exclosures keep elk out and allow for aspen and then spruce and fir trees to regenerate in areas affected by catastrophic pest infestations, blowdown events, and fires. Younger and older students collaborate during annual watershed-restoration summer camps. Active and ongoing consultations among students, elders, and Tribal Council members concern how place- and species names and other Ndee traditions provide clues to land history, capacity, functions, and stewardship (Long 2002; see also Maines and Bridger 1992).

The tribe has concluded an agreement with the U.S. Fish and Wildlife Service that ensures tribal control over research and management of threatened and endangered species. The programs include an extensive effort to restore the high-elevation riparian habitat of the Apache trout, Arizona's state fish. Additionally, since 1997 the tribe has closed all 40 of the small dump sites on its land and opened a single, state-of-the-art landfill. Draft tribal ordinances covering natural

FIGURE 9.3. Perry Tsadiasi (cultural adviser, Zuni Pueblo), Levi Dehose (cultural adviser, White Mountain Apache Tribe), Harold Polingyumptewa (cultural adviser, Hopi Tribe), and Karl Hoerig (museum director, White Mountain Apache Tribe). Photograph by John R. Welch; courtesy of the White Mountain Apache Tribe Heritage Program.

and cultural resource protection are under consideration. With grant assistance from the Environmental Protection Agency, a heritage tourism program targeting the development of a cadre of Apache tribal guides was launched in summer 1999 (Aleshire 2002). Destinations include some of the outstanding cultural, geological, and birding sites that the reservation is well known for by refugees from the Tucson and Phoenix summers. Visitors now have the option to visit ecological, historical, and cultural sites in the company of an Apache interpreter trained to offer information from both Ndee and scholarly perspectives and to highlight the differences between the two.

Repatriation initiatives—entailing the reunion of specific places with the human remains, funerary objects, and sacred objects that were inappropriately removed from Ndee contexts—are proceeding as one sensitive and significant component of reconstructive place making (Welch and Ferguson 2005, 2007). Because Zuni Pueblo and Hopi Tribe ancestors also occupied the Ndee homeland, and because the federal government divided the Ndee Nation into different tribes, intertribal cooperation is crucial in many aspects of reconstruction. Long-term partnerships exist between the White Mountain Apache Tribe and Zuni Pueblo, the Yavapai-Apache Nation, and the Hopi, Tonto Apache, and San Carlos Apache tribes. In place and thriving since the early 1990s, these collaborations have made it possible to identify an impressive range of reconstruction concepts and tactics while minimizing prospects for intertribal conflicts and other procedural delays. As an alternative to cultural affiliation discussions focused exclusively on objects and archaeological traditions, the tribe is working to establish *patria*, land, as the focus for processes of cultural affiliation assessment, consultation, and the disposition aspects of repatriation. By reuniting tribal elders with places, objects, and knowledge important in regional history, elders and cultural advisers are comparing and experiencing Pueblo and Apache senses of the same places (Welch and Ferguson 2007). Figure 9.3 shows some of the participants on one of the many trips taken to reestablish and document diverse cultural connections to significant places as the basis for follow-up stewardship initiatives. The investigation of oral traditions—sometimes distinctive, sometimes similar, invariably reverent—raises provocative questions concerning the geographic and cultural sources of senses of place. The consensus goal of the repatriation efforts is to respectfully restore the places diminished by the removal of ancestors and objects. According to the Ndee, Hopi, and Zuni cultural advisers, the achievement of this objective will not only sustain tribal authority over these places but assist in reconciling and repairing the relationships among Indians and non-Indians.

Archaeologists have also contributed to the reconstruction of Ndee places through the University of Arizona's Summer Field School in Archaeology and Heritage Resource Management (Mills et al. 2008). With funding from the National Science Foundation's Research Experiences for Undergraduates Sites Program, this unique field school was designed to achieve a fully integrated combination of research and Ndee community objectives. The field school provided students with excellent field training while simultaneously benefiting the cultural heritage stewardship and place-focused reconstruction goals espoused by the tribe. Students assisted in the stabilization and interpretation of the fourteenth-century site of Kinishba Ruins National Historic Landmark (Welch 2007) and conducted site survey, mapping, damage assessment, and post-looting site repair in the archaeologically dense zone of the Forestdale Valley. The tribe retains discretion over the publication or other release of all information derived from and pertaining to tribal lands, and Ndee elders are featured as lecturers and fieldwork consultants. No other field school has integrated cultural heritage stewardship and academic archaeology at every stage of the teaching and research program (Mills et al. 2008). Time and the level of respect accorded the Forestdale heritage by both Ndee and non-Ndee will judge whether the project was worthwhile.

The tribe's Fort Apache and Theodore Roosevelt School Historic Park initiative represents another unique and important effort to reconstruct a place in accord with Ndee sensibilities (Welch and Riley 2001). Seeking to reverse the place's function as an instrument for the implementation of generally short-sighted federal Indian policy, the tribe is converting the former Army post and current BIA-funded boarding school from a symbol and tool of political subjugation and cultural oppression into a beacon of hope and a means for enhancing and expanding the most important elements of sovereignty—that is, self-governance, self-determination, self-representation, and self-knowledge coupled with peer recognition. In addition to restoring Fort Apache's physical appearance to the period, ca. 1935, when the facility retained the character of both an Army post and the Theodore Roosevelt School, the tribe is employing Ndee stewardship principles as well as historical traditions as guides to operational and planning policy and practice. The goals are to use Fort Apache and the Theodore Roosevelt School as a context to interpret Ndee heritage and regional history to outsiders, to perpetuate Ndee language and culture, and to serve dynamic community needs through tourism- and community-focused economic development.

The Fort Apache historical district's worldwide name recognition and the tribe's 1993 Master Plan have helped the tribe to develop partnerships with the World Monuments Fund, the National Park Service, Arizona State Parks, the U.S. Postal Service, the Fort Apache Heritage Foundation nonprofit corporation, and the BIA. Ten of the fort's 26 historic buildings have been partially or completely restored and given revitalized roles (Figure 9.4). The tribe has opened within the Historic District the Nohwiké Bagowa (House of Our Footprints), the Apache Cultural Center and Museum. As an official *Save America's Treasures* project recognized by the White House Millennium Council, Fort Apache is becoming a forum for celebrating Ndee survival and sharing Apache perspectives on their culture and history (Welch et al. 2000).

With the most imminent threats to individual historic structures addressed, the tribe has initiated interpretive and site-development projects intended to return Fort Apache to active duty—this time in support of, instead of against, White Mountain Apache sovereignty and Ndee communities. The representation to the public of Fort Apache as a place with multiple distinctive histories is the central theme being explored in the interpretive planning and plan-implementation processes being supported by the National Endowment for the Humanities (Mahaney and Welch 2002). The processes are providing Ndee and non-Ndee access to previously unavailable White Mountain Apache perspectives on their culture, ancient traditions, contacts with non-Indians, and contemporary status and interests. The interpretive effort also encourages Ndee and non-Ndee to confront ambiguous and occasionally hostile sentiments relating to events, individuals, and groups and to think about links among

FIGURE 9.4. View to the west along Officer's Row at Fort Apache. Photograph courtesy of the White Mountain Apache Tribe Heritage Program.

TABLE 9.1. Ndee Principles for Reconstructive Place Making

Long-Standing Ndee Values and Interests	Contemporary Ndee Values and Interests
• Behavior and attitude should reflect respect for all spiritual, animal, vegetal, and mineral elements as parts of a seamless, sacred whole • Knowledge is power; power is available only to those with respect, strength, patience, and stewardship ethics • Pursuit of profit or self-aggrandizement entailing the disturbance of places or objects associated with the deceased or the use of Ndee cultural knowledge is harmful, as well as dangerous to one's self, family, and community • Clear thinking is pursued and maintained through balancing what is taken with what is given	• Enhance and expand sovereignty through internal nation building and external recognition of Ndee rights and duties in the control and protection of places, objects, traditions, and other resources vital to community, culture, and language survival • Self-governance—through improved local capacity and authorities, as well as external partnerships • Self-determination—through planning for the protection and sustainable use of vital resources and for economic and educational opportunities aligned with cultural values • Self-representation—through accurate and balanced first-person portrayals of community-derived cultural values, histories, visions, and goals • Tribe or tribal members must harvest the majority of benefits from any activity involving Ndee lands or resources • Sustainable job creation is better than either nonsustainable resource extraction or other short-term revenue streams; the quality of visitor experiences is more important than quantity

places, memories, emotions, and imagined historical and future frontiers.

Through a unique integration of physical restoration and social reconciliation the White Mountain Apache Tribe is reconnecting to Fort Apache as a significant, though briefly foreign, place within an Apache landscape. At no other place has an American Indian tribe adopted the frontier military outpost that was established to control them, reasserted control over that place, and put it to use to promote their interests and reconstruct and revalidate their sense of place.

Toward an Ndee Model for Place Management

What planting willows, repatriating cultural items, growing rare fish, closing dumps, restoring and reinterpreting historic sites, and participating in the rehabilitation of lands scorched by wildfire have in common is the reconnection of people and land and the reconstruction of Ndee senses of places. Although the inseparability of people and place may be old news, it is worth emphasizing how this concept is being applied by the White Mountain Apache in service to a unique combination of long-standing and emergent values and interests (Table 9.1). The critical importance of place is at last receiving well-deserved attention from resource managers, linguists, historic preservationists, educators, tribal advocates, and archaeologists. Be this as it may, the concept that cultural traditions are intertwined and interdependent with lands is so foreign to most thinking and acting in the industrial world that it has yet to receive attention from those concerned with the understanding and governance of communities, lands, and the world heritage.

As a complement to physical and biological treatments intended to return landscapes and specific places to their ideal conditions, as determined by Ndee perspectives, the diverse projects and programs reviewed here are united by the deceptively straightforward principle of reestablishing Ndee stewardship (Long 2002). As distinct from more mechanistic or rigorously scientific non-Indian approaches to place-focused caretaking, Ndee stewardship is built on the premise that physical, mental, social, and ecosystem health are all interwoven. The mind-set or sense that individuals or groups bring to a place or project may be at least as important as the scientific information or technical skills or specifications motivating the effort. Goals for Ndee cultural and environmental heritage stewardship are less focused on the protection or survival of specific objects, places, or traditions than on the perpetuation of the most meaningful and productive contexts for the continuing evolution of Ndee communities and their spiritual, linguistic, cultural, and geographic well-being (see Naveh 1998).

Wisdom Sits in Reconstruction: Some Implications for Archaeology and Heritage Stewardship

Many indigenous nations are today expanding and reasserting use of their homelands by moving beyond natural resource extraction and tourism and turning back to the land as a source of pride, inspiration, and strength. The ongoing experience of White Mountain Apache reconstruction can and should inform archaeologically driven reconstruction. Most relevant in this discussion are the many instances in which the tribe and the Ndee are asserting their distinctive perspectives and ways of doing business. Such assertions afford glimpses into Apache culture, including Ndee senses of place, while also offering possible guidance for efforts involving the reconstruction of places and the senses embedded therein and evoked thereby.

Perhaps the most valuable lesson comes from the Ndee emphasis on wholes instead of parts, connections instead of differences. Ndee increasingly question the imposition of analytic and management concepts and vocabulary, especially site vs. nonsite, prehistory vs. history, nature vs. culture, and politically imposed land jurisdictions. Such intrusive distinctions can impede understanding of land and people and history; they generally detract from collaborations between place-based and professional communities. Why, given the existence of widely shared best management practices, are state and federal lands managed so differently? Why is a landscape a cultural resource, while the rocks and trees and streams are considered natural? What management or scientific benefits derive from drawing rigid boundaries—based on distributions of stone cairns and tools—around shrine localities occupying the same landform instead of identifying the landform itself as a sacred site (Welch 1997)? In the absence of additional information, why refer to such shrines as "prehistoric" or assume that the site's primary value or highest and best use is scientific or economic rather than spiritual or community oriented?

Another question deserving attention is why and how Ndee-place linkages survived in the face of the momentous changes that the last 150 years have brought to Ndee material and social conditions of existence. Among the provocative insights gained from the Ndee reconstruction initiatives is the possibility that one or more essential characteristics of a particular place—as described in an Ndee place name or narrative—will remain intact and available for reemergence despite poor management or other factors "masking" the place's natural appearance and functions. From this perspective places have intrinsic qualities—formal and possibly relational properties that may be identified and put to work in the oral traditions and social processes of the people who know the places the best. Alternatively, reconstruction may result, at least in part, through the reunion of place and people and through the elimination of alienating influences (see Anderson and Nabhan 1991). Applied communally, this principle helps to explain how the Ndee sense of place has endured, only awaiting a lack of interference to reassert itself.

Research into the life histories of place, as advocated by Ashmore (2002), should assist in assessing the intriguing possibility of inherent place characteristics. Using this approach to inform stewardship policy and practice opens doors to the benefits of management regimes and strategies that facilitate the unencumbered assertion and reassertion of the intrinsic characteristics of resources, communities, and ecosystems. This means spending passive time—sometimes a lot of it—observing people and places and allowing their authentic interactions to recommend or define their ways of being and trajectories of change. This is hard on those who, like most archaeologists, want to obtain "hard" data and solve problems without delay.

In the rush to constructively expand archaeology to embrace place we must bear in mind that senses of place may be elusive even to those who have a detailed target in mind. As with the Emperor's Nightingale, so with a sense of place: even the most painstaking reconstruction of the formal attributes may not foster or sustain emotional and symbolic associations on individual or group levels. Three-dimensional rigor may not, except in special circumstances, be sufficient to shed light on the historical, social, moral, and spiritual connections experienced and employed by the original *sensers* of a place. The White Mountain Apache Tribe has been working for more than four decades to reconstruct senses of places, but few Ndee would argue that broad-scale success is at hand. Archaeological efforts will obviously require diligence, not to mention imagination and attention to living communities with cultural and emotional links to the places under study. Archaeologists would do well to listen carefully to the representatives of descendant communities. We may also find inferential insight and assistance through comparisons of places based on relational dimensions rather than formal dimensions.

A final recommendation for archaeologists interested in place stems from the prospective value of developing mutually beneficial relationships with people who know and care about places being subjected to archaeological research. The apparent decline in the volume and diversity of meanings and values that link American Indian peoples to their places deserves serious consideration and concerted response. Landscapes and communities, along with the values and individual localities from which we derive our distinctive and sustaining identities, are the ultimate cultural resources. As the veritable wellsprings of sites, objects, knowledge, and meanings, communities deserve at least the same careful, conservation-oriented attention as archaeological sites, endangered species, or other elements of the physical world (see Netting 1993; Western et al. 1994). Archaeologists have now been digesting and incorporating the conservation ethic as a disciplinary principle for about three decades (Lipe 1974), and there are both moral and instrumental benefits to be realized from offering to extend this ethic, without paternalism or intrusion, to the people whose lives and cultures and senses of place may be affected by our work (see Watkins 2000). One criterion for assessing proposals for archaeological research and cultural resource management should be the degree to which the proposed activities will strengthen place-based communities and enhance their ties to lands and other resources. If such benefits are absent or recondite, the proposal should be rethought and revised in consultation with community representatives. This simple principle might do much to facilitate dialogue and limit the need for juridical attention to cultural and intellectual property rights and the ongoing friction between archaeologists and descendant communities.

The notion of making people and communities priorities in archaeology strikes many as counterproductive, but discussions of archaeological reconstructions of senses of place should make it clear that archaeologists need living communities. People are required to provide insight and assign values to our findings. Extending the logic of this requirement to its far reaches, communities, especially indigenous communities, are to archaeology and historic preservation what rain forests are to biomedical research and conservation biology. Archaeology of the sort we are learning about from landscape-level analyses cannot be done without reference to long-standing place-focused ways of dwelling and sensing. Similarly, participation in community-driven reconstruction projects can offer archaeologists superb opportunities to learn about the generation, expression, and perpetuation of senses of place. When and where mutually beneficial partnerships between indigenous and professional communities can be forged, the daunting challenges of reconstructing senses of places and managing resources for our great-grandchildren's great-grandchildren become dazzling landscapes of faces and names, hopes and dreams, places and connections.

A Once and Future Place

Once sovereigns over and intimately dependent upon a region larger than the State of West Virginia, Ndee today reside on and maintain intimate links to only a small fraction of their great-grandparents' landscapes. More than a century of federal policies have systematically alienated Ndee from their land and the material and cultural vitality they once derived from it, but Apache elders, cultural specialists, and other sources have safeguarded vast knowledge of oral traditions associated with landscape features, functions, and values. Ongoing intertribal efforts to document place-based oral traditions and give them new uses in this challenging postcolonial period are finding success in conserving fragile and beautiful places, objects, knowledge, and the links among them that create and maintain senses of places.

The processes employed have well-established, though still-unfolding uses in ecological restoration, cultural education, the protection of sacred sites, and the reconstruction of Ndee authority over their land, history, and future.

Acknowledgments

I am well beyond grateful for guidance received from the Ndee: Glenn Cromwell, the late Nashley Tessay, Ronnie Lupe, Eva Watt, Ramon Riley, and other Apache wisdom keepers too numerous to name.

I hope Grenville Goodwin and Keith Basso will be long recognized for laying the scholarly foundations for the reconstruction under way across the Ndee homeland and beyond.

10

Lost Cities, Prairie Castles

Stephen H. Lekson

Mesa Verde and Bent's Old Fort, both in Colorado, are iconic places in our national heritage. Mesa Verde, the great thirteenth-century Pueblo center, is the most famous American Indian site. Bent's Old Fort is less well known. It was a post in the fur-trapper era, built in 1833, and a key place in America's rise to empire. Two other Colorado places provide interesting contrasts and comparisons. Manitou Cliff Dwellings is a re-creation and relocation of Mesa Verde ruins, a creation of the very early twentieth century. The Fort restaurant is a meticulous reconstruction of Bent's Old Fort and opened for business in 1963. Each year, Mesa Verde averages about 625,000 visitors; Bent's Old Fort receives a little over 40,000. About 100,000 tourists enjoy Manitou Cliff Dwellings each year. Comparable figures are harder to calculate for The Fort restaurant, but we know that over 50,000 bison entrées (the house specialty) are served each year. Double that, at least, for the number of satisfied customers, including trout eaters.

These are public places, places of interpretation. Contemporary archeology, we are told, should be interpretive. But what does archaeological "interpretation" mean?[1] American archaeology seems ever ready to let other fields do its theoretical thinking. Curiously, American archaeology has been uncurious about other fields' thinking on interpretation. There are whole disciplines of interpretation (Beck and Cable 1997; Tilden 1957), indeed career paths and professional organizations for interpreters (most often in natural sciences but also strongly in history). For archaeologist Ian Hodder (1999:66), interpretation is any statement that goes beyond simple description. For interpreter Tilden (1957), interpretation is *telling a story*. In both cases, interpretation should be accurate (i.e., true to the data) and should convey information. For Hodder, this requires ascending the hermeneutic spiral. For Tilden, this requires telling a story—a harder task, perhaps.

On a sliding scale of reality, Mesa Verde is *real*; Manitou is *relocated*; Bent's Old Fort is *reconstructed*; and The Fort restaurant is *really tasty*. All four places are interesting, and all four tell us useful things about interpretive archaeology, because all four are interpretations of archaeological places. How do we tell stories, and how do we interpret archaeological places?

Lost Cities: Mesa Verde and Manitou Cliff Dwellings

The small New Zealand town of Wanaka marked the year 2000 with a line of 2,000 tiles, each about 30 cm square, along a lakeside walk. Each tile, of course, represents a year. Important events were glazed onto appropriate tiles: for example, Cook's arrival in 1769, Wilding's Wimbledon victory in 1910. Many years lacked noteworthy happenings, and their tiles are blank. One thousand one hundred fifty tiles into the Millennium Walk the text states, "Cliff homes built at Mesa Verde." Mesa Verde is honored even in the Antipodes.

Mesa Verde is unquestionably the best-known archaeological site in the United States and among

FIGURE 10.1. Square Tower House, Mesa Verde.

the most famous in the world (Figure 10.1).[2] It was one of the first archaeological preserves created by the government in 1906 (largely as the result of the lobbying of the Colorado Cliff Dwellings Association), and it is one of the largest such areas, at 210 km². Mesa Verde was listed as a World Heritage Site in 1978, the first American Indian place in the United States so honored. Thousands of sites have been located, and, after recent fires cleared trees, plants, and duff, hundreds more are being found. The key sites span eight centuries, from AD 500 to 1300, but Mesa Verde's fame rests with the cliff dwellings of AD 1150 to 1300. Cliff or alcove-sheltered sites include Cliff Palace, Spruce Tree House, and Long House. A dozen large cliff dwellings and scores of smaller alcove-sheltered ruins are spectacular in their settings, astonishing in their preservation. Abandoned seven centuries ago, they look like *people just left*. Archaeologists call those vanished people "Anasazi" or, more accurately, "ancestral Pueblo" (for that is who they were).

The history of Mesa Verde, as a place and a park, has been well told by Duane Smith (2002). The history of Mesa Verde in the American imagination has yet to be written. Mesa Verde's "lost cities" were America's answer to the spectacular archaeological discoveries of the Old World at the end of the nineteenth and beginning of the twentieth centuries. They had Troy and Tut. We had Mesa Verde. Mesa Verde featured prominently at national expositions and in print media, and by the early twentieth century, it was a well-known but seldom visited place.

Its discovery was a romance, with hard-bitten cowboys sighting Cliff Palace through a driving winter snowstorm. Willa Cather turned the real Richard Wetherill of 1888 into a fictional Tom Outland. Outland recounts the "discovery":

> Far up above me, a thousand feet or so, set in a great cavern in the face of the cliff, I saw a little city of stone, asleep.... Such silence and stillness and repose—immortal repose. That village sat looking down into the canyon with the calmness of eternity. The falling snowflakes, sprinkling the piñons, gave it a special kind of solemnity. I can't describe it. It was more like a sculpture than anything else. I knew at once I had come upon the city of some extinct civilization, hidden away in this inaccessible mesa for centuries [Cather 1973:201–202].

Lost cities in the wilderness! Themes of mystery and antiquity run through all interpretations of

FIGURE 10.2. Manitou Cliff Dwellings.

Mesa Verde: "The mystery of the Anasazi: Why did they leave? Where did they go?" This bromide became a slogan for the local Chamber of Commerce and, despite their drama, these questions still underwrite much archaeological research in the region.

In 1906, 52,000 acres of southwestern Colorado (including large parts of the Ute Reservation) were declared Mesa Verde National Park. After an unsteady start, the National Park Service (NPS) cleared away the rubble and repaired crumbling walls, graded trails and installed ladders. John D. Rockefeller chipped in to build facilities. With a few important exceptions (discussed below), nothing further was needed to present these magnificent ruins to the public. But Mesa Verde's remote location discouraged that public from actually visiting the ruins. Mesa Verde was 400 straight-line kilometers from Denver. A half-dozen mountain ranges made those straight-line kilometers many more on the ground. Days of difficult travel, by wagon, coach, and mining trains separated Denver from Mesa Verde. And, in 1900, Easterners considered Denver a distant cow town. It was hard to reach the park, and very few people were able to do so or cared to try.

Colorado Springs, 100 km to the south of Denver, rivaled and perhaps even surpassed the Mile High City as a cosmopolitan center in early-twentieth-century Colorado. Local promoters wanted Colorado Springs to become a destination for eastern travelers, with resorts (like the magnificent Broadmoor) and rail connections to St. Louis, Chicago, and all points east. A few years before Mesa Verde was declared a national park, a Texas entrepreneur named Harold Ashenhurst and a Colorado Springs businessman named W. S. Crosby proposed building a replica cliff dwelling near Manitou, just outside Colorado Springs. "Why visit Mesa Verde when you can see it all here for a dollar?" they asked (quoted in Smith 1987:125). Ashenhurst procured wagonloads of building stone from ruins in McElmo Canyon (near Mesa Verde) and freighted rocks and artifacts over the passes back to Colorado Springs. The local newspaper headlined: "CLIFF DWELLINGS TO BE PUT CLOSE TO MANITOU. Colorado Springs capitalists plan novel scenic feature for edification of summer throngs of tourists, will spend $50,000. It is the idea of the promoters to have ruins, real ruins here in Manitou" (*Colorado Springs Gazette*, May 1, 1906). Manitou Cliff Dwellings (Figure 10.2) was on the streetcar line from Colorado Springs.

A rift in the Colorado Cliff Dwellings Association (the organization responsible for the creation of Mesa Verde National Park) provided the project legitimacy. The association's estranged founder became a stockholder and director of Crosby and Ashenhurst's company. It was even rumored that Edgar Hewett, director of the Museum of New Mexico, attended the opening of Manitou Cliff Dwellings on June 2, 1907, one year after Mesa Verde had been declared a park.

To build Manitou Cliff Dwellings, Crosby and Ashenhurst enlarged a small alcove in Phantom Canyon, blasting it to a suitably large site. The ruin built there was a hybrid, in large part recreations of real McElmo Canyon sites, relocated to Manitou, and in smaller part replicas of elements of Cliff Palace, Square Tower House, and other sites. The building stones came from sites off the mesa, sandstones similar to those used in the cliff dwellings of Mesa Verde. A large museum, modeled on the Pueblo of Taos, was built to display a collection of Mesa Verde artifacts. Crosby and Ashenhurst hired Indians from Tesuque and San Juan pueblos to work at Manitou and later developed a long-term relationship with the Tafoya family from Santa Clara Pueblo. Members of the Tafoya family acted as guides and danced at specified hours; some relocated to Colorado Springs. Manitou Cliff Dwelling was an immediate success and continues to be a major tourist attraction. Many visitors believed it to be an authentic ruin, and the management did (and does) little to discourage that impression. And, indeed, much of Manitou *is* real but relocated.

NPS officials at Mesa Verde were incensed. They decried Manitou as a fraud; and so it was, if presented as authentic and in situ. The idea (if not the motive) behind Manitou Cliff Dwellings, however, was perhaps not so far removed from other "building museums" of the time. The museum village of Skansen, opened in 1881 in Sweden, was one of the first such institutions; today there are thousands of "open-air" museums throughout Europe. Old Sturbridge Village and Greenfield Village were American counterparts, both begun in the 1920s and still in operation today.

Building museums removed folk or vernacular buildings from farms and pioneer settlements and reconstructed them in settings more convenient to population centers. Museums, after all, were all about logistical concentration: bringing objects from distant places into cities, allowing more people to see them and, hopefully, learn from them. After several trips to Manitou Cliff Dwellings, I am of the opinion that people do indeed learn from these reconstructed ruins. It would be interesting to evaluate what they learn, compared to the messages visitors receive at Mesa Verde. I suspect the "take-home messages" are not that different. One difference is clear, however: Manitou, built stoutly with cement, allows visitors to clamber over, around, and through the "ruins" with a freedom unthinkable in the fragile originals at Mesa Verde. At Mesa Verde, you can look but not touch; at Manitou, almost anything goes, limited only by the owner's understandable concerns for injury liability.

Manitou is relocated: out of context, out of place. So is a triptych in an art museum. A barn at Greenfield Village is also displaced, but unlike much of Manitou, the barn and (one hopes) the triptych are *authentic*. Manitou is in part authentic ruins relocated to a resort town and in part an imaginary site built of authentic materials. In the latter case, Crosby, Ashenhurst, and company could do more than reassemble; they could reconstruct and present rooms and chambers as if they were new and not ruins.

Reconstruction is a perennial and troublesome issue. Is it wrong to reconstruct? The National Park Service has almost always avoided reconstruction. *Stabilization* is the term for NPS preferred treatment of its buildings: minimal (but often significant) repair to maintain the structure as much as possible as it exists, in the present, rather than restoration to its original condition and appearance. Today, it is fair to say that NPS eschews reconstructions and is even embarrassed by existing reconstructions within the parks. For there are reconstructions in parks (national and local) to rival Manitou. And there is a curious dichotomy as to what can or cannot be reconstructed: rooms are generally not reconstructed, whereas kivas—the subterranean chambers so characteristic of Mesa Verde ruins—are sometimes restored, rebuilt, and maintained for visitor experiences.

Above-ground "pueblo" rooms were reconstructed at only a few southwestern ruins: Puye

FIGURE 10.3. Kiva, Spruce Tree House, Mesa Verde.

near Santa Fe, Kinishba near Fort Apache, Besh-ba-gowa near Globe, and Tuzigoot in the Verde Valley, among others. Several of these, and perhaps most, were reconstructed during the 1920s and 1930s, when reconstruction probably seemed preferable to excavation by large numbers of untrained Civilian Conservation Corps workers. Kinishba, on the Fort Apache Indian Reservation in Arizona, was perhaps the most extensively reconstructed ruin; it was rebuilt in the 1920s, and it has since fallen back into ruin (Welch 2007). A similar history marks Besh-ba-gowa, a ruin near Globe, Arizona, which was excavated, rebuilt, and then (like Kinishba) fell back into ruin, only to be rebuilt again.

The NPS itself very seldom reconstructs (only Tuzigoot, of the ruins named above, is an NPS unit; the rest are local, state, or tribal parks). The kivas at Spruce Tree House are a significant departure from that policy at Mesa Verde; two of them were reroofed for visitors to enter—an extremely popular experience (Figure 10.3). A few other park units have reconstructed kivas, including Aztec Ruins and Pecos Pueblo, and some state or local parks also feature reconstructed kivas (e.g., Kuaua at Coronado State Park, near Albuquerque). In ruin, kivas are usually greatly reduced: amorphous depressions with an occasional roof beam projecting from the rubble. Kivas at Spruce Tree House (and elsewhere) have been almost entirely reconstructed, based on a few more or less intact kivas in other cliff-sheltered sites. The propriety of these reconstructions is still a matter of hot debate within the NPS. Are they too "Disney"? Are they too much like Manitou?

Soul-searching is compounded today by heightened sensitivities toward American Indians: kivas, after all, are kivas. According to the Mesa Verde pamphlet:

> Anasazi kivas were underground chambers which may be compared to churches of later times. Based upon modern Pueblo practice, the Anasazi may have used them to conduct healing rites or to pray for rain, luck in hunting, or good crops. Kivas also served as gathering places, and weaving was sometimes done there [NPS 1994].

As the NPS brochure notes, kivas at modern pueblos are particularly sacred and restricted spaces. The idea of half a million visitors each year climbing in and out of the Spruce Tree House kivas, if they are indeed ritual structures, probably does not sit well with Pueblo people.

Kivas at Mesa Verde, however, present an archaeological conundrum: while Pueblo people, NPS interpretive brochures, and coffee-table books present Mesa Verde kivas as ancient versions of modern ceremonial structures, the archaeology of Mesa Verde kivas suggests that they were probably the last, most elaborate version of pit houses. The argument is too long to review here (see Lekson 1988), but the number of kivas at each settlement suggests that we might question the equivalence of ancient and modern kivas. At Rio Grande pueblos, from the fourteenth century until today, there are only a few kivas at each town (sometimes as few as one or two). At large Mesa Verde sites, such as Yellow Jacket Pueblo, there are hundreds of kivas (in fact, one "kiva" for every household). Whatever ancient kivas were, they were not the same thing we see today in the plazas at San Juan Pueblo. What, then, could they be? Pueblo people had been living in pit houses for at least seven centuries prior to Spruce Tree House and Cliff Palace. At Mesa Verde, we see one "kiva" for each household. The kivas of Spruce Tree House were probably the last pit houses and not the first kivas. But the experience of entering a reconstructed kiva is important for many, perhaps most, visitors. It adds immeasurably to the sense of place. Most cliff dwellings are experienced at a distance, from viewpoints on valley rims opposite the sites. A few can be entered, on restricted paths. Stay on the trail! Don't touch the walls!

In a few rooms, visitors can stick their heads through doors to glance up, awkwardly, at intact roofs. In reconstructed kivas, people can actually enter the structure. With the interpretive spin on kivas as ritual structures, it is a spiritual moment. Or it would be, if one did not climb the entry ladder in a long line of fellow pilgrims, nose-to-bottom.

Cliff dwellings are an icon of ancient America, but that is in large part an accident of preservation: cliff dwellings are famously well preserved by their placement in deep alcoves and overhangs. Most Mesa Verde sites were not so happily placed. Yellow Jacket Pueblo, seven or eight times bigger than Cliff Palace, sits today in the bean fields northwest of Cortez, Colorado, its 100 acres of tumbled masonry mounds representing the largest (by far!) Mesa Verde town/city ever constructed. It is not a national park because it does not *look like* a national park.[3]

Prairie Castles: Bent's Old Fort and The Fort Restaurant

After solving the world's economic problems, the boys knocked off for drinks and dinner: Bill Clinton, Boris Yeltsin, Jacques Chirac, Tony Blair, Helmut Kohl, Romano Prodi, Ryutaro Hashimoto, and Jean Chrétien. Limos took them from Denver hotels, through the shadows of the foothills, to a wooden gate in a tall adobe wall (Figure 10.4). An American flag flapped above the gate, in the dusk. To seasoned diplomatic eyes, the flag seemed strange: too few stars? Beyond the gate was a dark courtyard. Light from a bonfire flickered on the barrel of a big brass cannon.

Seated at tables in a long adobe hall, below a ceiling of dark vigas and *latillas*, they examined the bill of fare. Their waiter was a rough-looking fellow, dressed like a mountain man (Figure 10.5); he may have tempted them with buffalo tongue or bison "oysters" or marrow bones—"Julia Child's favorite," according to the mountain man—but they chose instead to open their meal with fried squash blossoms, filled with wild mushrooms and rattlesnake. Their entrées were buffalo in whiskey sauce, mesquite-grilled quail with prickly pear, and Clear Creek trout; washed down with Hailstorms, mint juleps, and (perhaps) sweet Santa Fe cocktails. The Italian prime minister demanded that the cannon be fired; its boom alarmed the Secret Service. When calm returned, fiddlers scraped old-time tunes.

The Summit of the Eight met in Denver in 1997. They dined at Bent's Old Fort in 1846. Or, rather, they dined at a re-creation of Bent's Old Fort, a restaurant called The Fort, a few kilometers and a century and a half away from Denver. We will first visit the original Bent's Old Fort before returning to its modern counterpart, The Fort restaurant.

The real Bent's Old Fort (Figure 10.6) was 385 km southeast of Denver (which did not exist when Bent's Fort was in operation). It was a vital outpost of the American empire from 1833 to 1849. Bent's Old Fort on the Arkansas River was built at a time and a place critical in American history, so it is remembered when scores of similar but smaller edifices are forgotten. The architecture of

FIGURE 10.4. The Fort.

Bent's Old Fort matched its historic importance: instead of the typical fur-trader's ragtag timber stockade, Bent's Old Fort was an adobe castle, reputedly the largest building between St. Louis and San Francisco. (Bent's Fort would fit easily into the plaza at the Pueblo of Taos.)

Bent's Old Fort owed as much to the architecture of presidios as it did to the military architecture taught at West Point. It was built for the Bents by 100 men from Taos, who had their own ideas about how forts should look. Its thick adobe walls with tall round *torreons* at the corners marked an island of civility in the vast, empty Plains. Travelers who survived the Santa Fe Trail to its bend at the Arkansas River could hardly believe their eyes (Figure 10.7). In a modern fictional account (owing much to old travel diaries), a guide describes Bent's Fort to a discouraged traveler:

> "You'll be wonderstruck, ma'am," laughs he. "You haven't seen a building worth the name since we left Westport, have you? Well, tomorrow, after a thousand miles of desolation, you'll see a veritable castle on the prairie, with towers and ramparts—oh, and shops too! It's a fact, and all as busy as Stephen's Green. This time tomorrow you'll be watching the captain here playing skittle pool in the billiard room, with a wee man in a white coat skipping in with

FIGURE 10.5. The Fort wait staff.

FIGURE 10.6. Bent's Old Fort, main gate.

refreshment, and you'll sleep on a down mattress after a hot bath and the best dinner west of St. Louis, so you will" [Fraser 1982:115].

Bent's Old Fort was officially named Fort William, after William Bent, its last proprietor and (possible) demolisher. William was one of three traders who built the structure in 1833 and from it administered a vast commercial empire. William and his brother Charles partnered with Ceran St. Vrain (all from St. Louis, Missouri) to found the Bent & St. Vrain Company, dealing first in beaver pelts and later in buffalo hides. They operated at the very edge of old (New) Mexico: the Arkansas was the boundary between the United States and Mexico. Life was good on the frontier: trade between St. Louis and Santa Fe was even more lucrative than the fur business, and much of it passed through Bent's Old Fort. The trappers built Fort William (Bent's Old Fort) at a spot suggested by Yellow Hand, a Cheyenne leader, as a place where his people gathered yearly for trading.

The Old Fort was used and occupied from 1833 to 1849. It was a prominent place when the United States invaded Mexico, and it played a key role in bringing Texas and California into the Union.

St. Vrain had become a Mexican citizen, to facilitate trade in Santa Fe; the Bents themselves had strong connections among New Mexicans (and the Arapaho and Cheyenne people of the Plains). When the United States began to move against Mexico, the army marching to New Mexico mustered at Bent's Fort. Before that army moved, the Bents and St. Vrain negotiated with the Mexican officials in Santa Fe, and the invasion was almost bloodless. (A short-lived revolt in Taos, two years later, cost Charles Bent his life.) The Bent & St. Vrain Company dissolved and abandoned Bent's Old Fort shortly after the end of the Mexican War. In August 1849, William Bent loaded 20 wagons with stock and tack and left the "Prairie Castle." Shortly thereafter, the fort collapsed in fire; rumor had it that William Bent blew it up (he went on to build another, Bent's New Fort).

Six decades after Bent left his fort, the local chapter of the Daughters of the American Revolution declared Bent's Old Fort the most important historic site in Colorado and determined that it should be rebuilt. Bent's Old Fort was touted as one of the first, and certainly the most impressive, early American structures in the state, as Colorado's "number one historic shrine" and "most important site in Colorado." The Daughters of

FIGURE 10.7. Bent's Old Fort, billiard room and laundry.

the American Revolution lobbied hard for preservation and reconstruction, but, by the 1920s, the ruins were sadly reduced. After the standing portions of the fort were briefly reused as a stage stop, farmers and ranchers of the Arkansas Valley helped themselves to roof beams and adobe bricks. The fort was reduced to wall stubs. A legendary flood in 1921 ("the Great Pueblo Flood") covered the surviving remnants deep in sand and clay. By the time the site was transferred to the NPS, in 1960, little of the original fort was visible.

Hard lobbying by the Colorado congressional delegation and the Colorado Historical Society eventually overcame the National Park Service's reluctance to reconstruct sites. In 1965, a "blue-ribbon" committee appointed by the NPS split down the middle on the question: two for and two against reconstruction. Nothing happened until the approach of the national bicentennial and the Colorado state centennial tipped the scale.

Once approved, the project moved forward rapidly. National Park Service archaeologist "Smokey" Moore outlined what was left of the foundations in 1964. Travelers' descriptions, including excellent drawings and sketch maps, provided information on wall heights, second stories, and so forth. Like the Bent & St. Vrain Company, the NPS contractor brought builders from Taos—who knows?—perhaps a few great-great-great-grandsons of the original artisans. The work was completed by 1976, in time for the centennial and bicentennial. An NPS video concluded: "After years of research and planning, a year of labor, the task of building is finished. Every detail, every aspect was carefully researched and executed, to ensure that many generations of the future will come here and feel the vestiges of our past" (Fouschee n.d.). Those details include radiant subfloor heat and flush toilets, new from Bent's day, but otherwise the re-creation is remarkable—and remarkably successful.[4]

Bent's Old Fort is, today, a fur-trade Williamsburg: a careful re-creation of a fur station, peopled by a staff in period costumes and personae. The visitor experience is quiet but intense. The site is rural; the nearest town is La Junta, with a population of less than 7,500. The fort itself is a rectangle only 45 m on a side. The NPS wisely took 325 ha of surrounding bottomland to preserve a semblance of remoteness. Absent school groups, there are seldom many people in the fort, increasing its atmosphere of isolation: Bent's Old Fort feels *out there, isolated, remote*. Annual "rendezvous" events bring large numbers of mountain man reenactors camping outside the fort and doing mountain man things. Despite the Bents' close ties to American Indian groups, few Plains Indians participate. The few Arapahos and Cheyennes who make the trip from Oklahoma stay in motels, not tepees.

A decade before the NPS opened its reconstruction of Bent's Old Fort, The Fort restaurant had opened for business in the outskirts of Denver. This wonderful re-creation of Bent's Old Fort realized the dream of the late Samuel P. Arnold, a Yale graduate and avid avocational historian. Arnold moved from northern New Mexico to Denver in 1951 and determined to build his family a Santa Fe–style home outside the city. He chanced upon old drawings of Bent's Fort and, working with Santa Fe architect Bill Lumpkins, designed his fort. Like Bent before and the NPS after, Arnold hired 25 Taos workmen to make adobes, hew beams, and raise walls. Expenses mounted; a restaurant was added to the home plans to secure a business loan. The restaurant opened in 1963. Arnold became an authority on frontier cooking, hosting a PBS series on western cuisine called *Frying Pans West*.

Today, The Fort is considered one of the premier dining experiences in the Denver area and indeed the West. The Summit of the Eight are only a few of the famous patrons who have dined on bison, elk, trout, and other frontier fare in the remarkable setting of Sam Arnold's re-creation. In 1999, a parallel nonprofit was created to expand Arnold's goals of education and interpretation at The Fort. The Tesoro Foundation's mission is "from art to cuisine to historical re-enactments and music…to create community based events and educational outreach programs" centering on the history and cultures of Colorado and the Southwest. The Fort has evolved from a family home, to a successful restaurant, to an educational nonprofit.

A Summary: Towns and Castles

Mesa Verde and Manitou, Bent's Old Fort and The Fort: each of these places offers different insights on interpretation of the past in place. Mesa Verde is real, Manitou is relocated, Bent's Old Fort is reconstructed, and The Fort is a gastronomic fantasy.

Mesa Verde, the lost city of the Anasazi, was our first cultural national park and a World Heritage Site, the most famous archaeological site in the United States. With over half a million visitors a year, Mesa Verde is by far the largest draw of these four places. On my sliding scale of reality, Mesa Verde is *most* real. But Mesa Verde, too, is a production. It is, at least, heavily edited: we booted out the Utes, blazed roads and trails, stabilized the walls, cleaned up the ancient trash, built museums and infrastructure, all to let our people see their ancient cities. Mesa Verde is very much a place in the present (Fine 1988). Rows of tour buses, lines of people snaking down trails and up ladders, shuttle trains to and from the parking lots: in high season, it is a zoo. But if you are there off season, or get an opportunity to visit a remote ruin, it is still a magical place. Recall the Tom Outland story: "Far up above me, a thousand feet or so, set in a great cavern in the face of the cliff, I saw a little city of stone, asleep." Sometimes the magic works.[5]

Manitou Cliff Dwellings is Mesa Verde relocated, transposed, and dislodged. It is part reconstruction, part replica. And Manitou itself is a piece of history: it celebrated its centennial in 2007. In a country that officially recognizes 50 years as the threshold for "historic," Manitou is old. It can be seen as a monument to the early days of historic preservation and the turbulent era of private reclamation in the late nineteenth and early twentieth century just before the West was fully federalized.

Today 100,000 people visit Manitou every year, one-sixth of the Mesa Verde total. In the early days, Mesa Verde griped that Manitou was cutting into its business, siphoning off visitors. These days, Mesa Verde worries, justly, about too many visitors. Maybe it should rethink its relationship with Manitou. Build a few more Manitous: ring the park with fake cliff dwellings at Grand Junction, at Gallup, at Flagstaff, and head off the hordes. Many visitors, I am reasonably certain, do not realize that Manitou is a replica; they think it is the real thing. That is probably fine with the Colorado Springs Chamber of Commerce, and I am not sure that we should mind, either. Consider Bent's Old Fort.

Bent's Old Fort, another NPS unit, is a complete reconstruction. The only original bits are a flagstone floor in the kitchen and some short spans of wall. Bent's Old Fort is a cautious, careful, brilliant attempt at false authenticity. Was it a brilliant mistake? No, it works, but perhaps it works too well. According to the NPS staff, many (most?) of the 40,000 annual visitors think they have seen the real thing, not unlike at Manitou.

The reconstruction of Bent's Old Fort was a project conceived in an era that glorified Manifest Destiny, but after decades of delay, it opened at a time when our ideas about western history were under revision. Douglas Comer's postmodern take on Bent's Old Fort, *Ritual Ground* (1996), expands a dissertation based on excavations he conducted at the National Historic Site in 1976, during the final stages of reconstruction. Comer offers some real insights into how Bent's Old Fort worked within the greater world system of its times, and in the worlds of the Arapaho and Cheyenne, and in the thin line between Manifest Destiny and Old Mexico. Comer reinterprets Bent's Old Fort as the Edge of Empire, in not an altogether positive light. We are revising our history of places like Bent's Fort in the western wilderness, and one wonders if it would be rebuilt today. Would we want to rebuild it? Perhaps not. And, certainly, current NPS interpretive policies and philosophies would not countenance reconstruction.[6]

The Fort restaurant is a delightful reconstruction and a complete fabrication! The Fort averages 50,000 bison dinners a year: more people eat buffalo at The Fort than visit Bent's Old Fort National Historic Site. (Since bison is featured in only one-third of the entrées, we can extrapolate the real number of visitors to The Fort to at least double that number.) It began as a country home but turned into a historically "themed" restaurant, and now with the Tesoro Foundation, it is changing again into an educational and cultural nonprofit.

But The Fort *always was* a cultural institution. That was Sam'l Arnold's vision (as he signed himself, in character). Yes, The Fort is "fake." But The Fort is, by every measure, an interpretive success. Do you want to experience the entrepreneurial enthusiasm that propelled the fur-trade frontier, the spirit of William Bent at its best? Have a mint julep with the proprietor or the mountain man staff. Then start your meal with quail eggs wrapped in buffalo sausage or the "Historian's Platter" of mixed appetizers. For the entrée: Uncle Dick's Buffalo Sirloin with the Dixon Red Chile Sauce or the Elk Chop St. Vrain. And for dessert: Chocolate Chile Bourbon Cake. You will learn a lot and heal your spirit.

Conclusions: Places in Our Past

All four of these places are archaeological: Mesa Verde and Bent's Old Fort are archaeological sites; Manitou Cliff Dwellings and The Fort are recreations of archaeological sites. As public places, they are archaeological interpretations (whether or not we agree with their content). I focus here on three criteria with which to examine and perhaps evaluate these archaeological interpretations: authenticity, context, and history.

Places should be authentic, that is, genuine. Mesa Verde is certainly the most authentic of the four sites: real ruins in situ. That is Mesa Verde's indisputable attraction and the reason why people drive for days through deserts and mountains to visit the national park. But it is important to remember that Mesa Verde's ruins have been edited, fixed, and (to some extent) sanitized. It is not what it was in the late thirteenth century, when its people moved away, but few archaeological sites are "Pompeii" (indeed, Pompeii itself is not really a "Pompeii"). More importantly, Mesa Verde is far removed from what it was in 1888, when cowboys first saw Cliff Palace through the snow. Cowboys (and "archaeologists") looted the ruins, removing trainloads of pots and baskets they had found sitting in the rooms and kivas. The Bureau of American Ethnology sent out scientists to complete that process and to begin "stabilization" of the ruins. Stabilization—minimal (if often significant) repair rather than restoration—is the National Park Service's preferred treatment of ruins. Particularly in the early days of stabilization, the appearances of many buildings changed markedly, as falling walls were righted, cracks were filled, and corners were squared.[7] The landscape itself changed, too, with suppression of fires altering the natural succession of plant communities.

Increasing interest and mounting numbers of visitors made paving roads, building stairs, and creating interpretive trails through the ruins necessary. Cliff Palace today is grouted, routed, railed, and *cleaned*. Undeveloped cliff dwellings in the backcountry are notable for their messiness: sherds, corncobs, burned wood, and yucca fiber all attest to a living history for these places. Indeed, these debris are part of the charm of backcountry ruins. A few visitors see these materials at Mug House and other Wetherill Mesa sites, but most visitors stay on Chapin Mesa to see Cliff Palace and Spruce Tree House, squeaky clean. The messiness of Cliff Palace's archaeology is gone. Many sites are off limits, viewed only from distant viewpoints. They are stops on the trail, photo ops, Stations of the Camera. The sites become, in Tom Outland's words, "like a sculpture": compositions with planes, masses, textures. Wonderful sculpture, to be sure; there is no counting the number of photo essays, calendars, and coffee-table books featuring Mesa Verde's ruins. They are authentic *ruins* but no longer authentic *places*.

More so Manitou. As a building museum, some of its structures are authentic but out of context. Manitou is heavily edited: a *Reader's Digest* Mesa Verde. In its favor, having reassembled its ruins with cement, Manitou allows actual contact with the buildings, an intimacy literally illegal at Mesa Verde. You can crawl all over Manitou, *just like they did* in ancient times. Contact and use, possible at Manitou, add experiential dimensions largely missing from Mesa Verde (the conspicuous exception being the crowded, claustrophobic kiva experience at Spruce Tree House). Manitou is not genuine, but Manitou (and other reconstructions) serves a purpose as a hands-on replica of the real thing. Crow Canyon Archaeological Center, a superb archaeological institution of experiential learning, recently built an accurate (but of course not authentic) replica of a Mesa Verde pueblo, for just this reason: much can be learned by contact and use.

If we seek a sense of place, we must serve senses other than sight, and Manitou adds touch. Ambient environments are important, too. Mesa Verde is in situ, and its flora and fauna are (of course) more authentic than Manitou's; but gas and diesel engines are the ambient environment of both. At least this is the case in front-country Mesa Verde: on Wetherill Mesa, visitors can escape the busloads of German tourists and the parking lot confrontations of the Chapin Mesa center.

Authenticity assumes accuracy, but archaeological places can be accurate without being authentic. Consider Bent's Old Fort and The Fort. Both, in fact, are fake. The Fort began as a family home and then added the facilities of a major restaurant. It looks like the original Bent's Fort, from some angles; but then the visitor rounds a corner to the service entrance and sees refrigeration units, loading docks, and garbage cans. It would be easy to dismiss The Fort as parody, like roadside attraction "forts" and frontier facades at souvenir shops; but there was honesty and integrity in The Fort's creation, which elevates it far above Fort Courage and Frontier Town. Indeed, Samuel Arnold was a consultant in the furnishing and programming for Bent's Old Fort National Historic Site. The NPS version of Bent's Old Fort is almost entirely reconstructed (and NPS staff repeatedly emphasize this to visitors). It is built on the original foundations, so it is in place. Its authenticity is, of course, greater than The Fort's. The restaurant was built in the red rock foothills of the Rocky Mountains, quite unlike the flat floodplain of the Arkansas River, where Bent's Old Fort was and is. Bent's Old Fort remains a reconstruction, however, with all the negative and positive aspects of replicas.

All four sites provide context, to greater or lesser degrees. By "context," I mean a sense of the site's place within its larger world. No man is an island, and neither are human places. Even islands are not islands: the context of Polynesian islands must include settlement by humans from other, far distant places. How do places—the small areas occupied and observed by archaeologists and visitors—provide their own context, a sense of their larger worlds?

When the NPS purchased land around Bent's Old Fort, that excess acreage ensured a sense of isolation appropriate to the Prairie Castle's place in the early nineteenth century. One does not get that sense at Fort Vasquez (in the highway median, with trucks roaring by) or, for that matter, at The Fort. Originally rural, The Fort is now firmly surrounded by suburbs of Denver. At all three, museum displays and interpreters also serve up context, but Bent's Old Fort best presents context through landscape, a sense of place. The apparent isolation underscores Bent's Fort's role in a larger world system, an isolated node in a global economy that brought beaver felt to Europe and bison leather to New York.

This is not to say that Bent's Old Fort stood alone on the Plains. This was the homeland of the Arapaho and Cheyenne peoples. Their presence, then, is honored in absence, today. And other fur-trade entrepôts were built along rivers to the north. Bent's Old Fort, moreover, was historically and strategically important as the last developed stop on the Santa Fe Trail, before it went into New Mexico. Santa Fe was far closer than St. Louis to Bent's Fort. The Hispanic context is reflected in the adobe fabric of the building and its presidio-like form. But Bent's Fort was an isolated outpost; that was its whole purpose.

Manitou Cliff Dwellings offers up context through interpretative programs and American Indian performance. With the cliff dwellings removed from their original locations to a streetcar stop of Colorado Springs, the building museum cannot pretend to present context in place. The Manitou museum tries, without great success, to re-place the buildings in their original historical and spatial contexts through exhibits, maps, and text; but it accomplishes mainly the display of objects, artifacts, and humans (not seen at the national park!). The museum is, despite good intentions, simply another attraction, something else included in the price of admission. Manitou Cliff Dwellings, from its opening, has done far better by engaging American Indians to provide context for the buildings. Pueblo people on the payroll ensure that (living) human faces are associated with the cliff dwellings and resolve to some extent a larger context that resolves "the Mystery of the Anasazi: Where did they go?": to San Juan, to Tesuque, to Santa Clara, and to the other modern pueblos, from whence come the Indians who interact with Manitou tourists. Visitors learn that the people who built the cliff dwellings are, in fact, still here. This is, perhaps, the best we can hope for at Manitou, and it is not a small thing.

Surprisingly, Mesa Verde National Park provides less context for the cliff dwellings than we might wish. The large and professional staff of interpreters and educators do a superb job presenting the archaeology of the park and include American Indians in programming. Mesa Verde answers "Where did they go?" and visitors who leave still asking that question must willfully choose romance or ignorance. But the task of interpretation is almost impossible if we extend *context* to include the much larger historical dynamics in which the ancient buildings and peoples of Mesa Verde were embedded. Manitou sidesteps this responsibility by removing the ruins to another world; Mesa Verde, because it is in situ, cannot.

Park interpretation suggests containment and local sufficiency. A long, plodding history-in-place is suggested by several sites, earlier than the cliff dwellings, excavated and preserved as exhibits. The park brochure sums up this view (I omit ellipses in the interest of clarity): "About 1400 years ago a group of Indians chose Mesa Verde for their home. For over 700 years their descendents lived and flourished here. Then in the late 1200s, within the span of one or two generations, they abandoned their homes and moved away" (NPS 1994).

The only interesting thing that happened at Mesa Verde, it seems, was: they left. But many archaeologists believe that the history of those seven centuries leading up to the abandonment is far more dynamic and (importantly) far larger in scope than suggested by Mesa Verde, both as a place and as a park (e.g., Lekson 1999; Lipe et al. 1999). I intend no criticism of Mesa Verde National Park with this statement: as I hope I will explain, it is nearly impossible for Mesa Verde to contextualize its world, because its world was very, very large.

Mesa Verde represents an odd sampling of its local region. The national park was created because of the extraordinary preservation of the cliff dwellings, but cliff dwellings were a relative rarity in the thirteenth-century Mesa Verde world. Far more numerous (and presumably important) were scores of large towns (nearly urban in size) in the plains west of Mesa Verde (such as Yellow Jacket, described briefly above [see Rohn 1982, among the first of many studies addressing this shift of emphasis]). And it appears that the Mesa Verde region was abandoned and resettled at least once and perhaps twice prior to the final thirteenth-century abandonment (Lipe et al. 1999)—a fact that provides critical context for the central drama of Mesa Verde, the Mystery of the Anasazi. Moreover, at no time was Mesa Verde *a center*; that is, during those seven centuries, bigger, more central things were happening elsewhere in the Anasazi world, things that were reflected at but never directed from Mesa Verde. I will return to this idea in my final paragraphs.

Thus, Mesa Verde is a difficult place from which to present the larger Anasazi world. This chapter is not the place to review Anasazi prehistory, but suffice it to say that it was dynamic, large scale, and enormously interesting (Lekson 1999; Lipe et al. 1999). I am not sure visitors to Mesa Verde (or most other southwestern archaeological parks) learn that the ancient southwestern peoples had histories as complex and dramatic as any other peoples' histories. To appreciate Mesa Verde's place in its world requires knowledge of, and visits to, places like Chaco Canyon, Yellow Jacket, and hundreds of other sites scattered over thousands of square miles. There is, of course, no way to present, directly, large-scale contexts at the smaller, human scales of parks and places. Larger scales require visual aids: maps, diagrams, charts, museum displays, interpretation.

But perhaps the place can present its larger context. I offer one example. At Mesa Verde, there is one possible aspect of its larger context that can, in fact, be seen. During the eleventh century, Mesa Verde was part of a much larger political network centered on Chaco Canyon. An outpost of Chaco was built at Far View House, aptly named as it commands a spectacular panorama. That "far view" was a design criterion: Far View House was a node on a complex, wide-ranging line-of-sight communication system (using fire, smoke, and mirrors) through which Chaco administered its vast, but largely empty, domain. You (and they) can see distant Chaco from Far View House, and Chaco can see you. Or, at least, that is one story (Lekson 1999); right or wrong, it is indeed *a story* and an interpretation of Mesa Verde's history that re-places Mesa Verde in its larger context.

My final criterion for exploring archaeological places is history. A mountain stands eternal, but human places have histories. Do these places have histories? Yes and no: yes, for the two versions of Bent's Fort, and no, for the two versions of cliff dwellings. Bent's Old Fort and The Fort have history galore: names, dates, events. The events of Bent's Old Fort were tumultuous, dramatic, and even important in the national heritage. We know from diaries and reports the names and characters of people who spent time there; reenactors at both places adopt their names and adapt their personalities. The fort was an act of will: it was built, used, and destroyed by people we know. The sense of history is palpable: things happened.

Less so at Manitou and Mesa Verde. Manitou largely abrogates history to the Mystery—Where did they go? Why did they leave?—and answers those questions by importing Indians to dance and tell stories. Mesa Verde does much the same. Consider this quote (again with ellipses omitted) from the official park brochure:

> Despite decades of excavation, analysis, classification, and comparison our knowledge is still sketchy. We will never know the whole story of their existence, for they left no written records and much that was important in their lives has perished. Archeology has yielded some information, but without written documents, there is no way to be sure about their social, political, or religious ideas. We probably will never know a great deal more about these people. We must rely for insight on comparisons with the modern Pueblo people of New Mexico and Arizona [NPS 1994].

As an archaeologist, I find these statements appalling. You should, too. We have learned much and can learn more about what the past was like through archaeology.[8] If we cannot, we should hang up our trowels and unplug our PCs.

What we can know extends, I think, to history. Historicity has returned to southwestern archaeology with an attitude, through postprocessual relocation of archaeology in the humanities, and with a vengeance, through the *Native American Graves Protection and Repatriation Act* (NAGPRA). Many of my colleagues insist that archaeology cannot write narrative history; but I think that NAGPRA and interpretive archaeology demand that we do precisely that. As a closing example, I focus historically on Mesa Verde and Bent's Old Fort (and assume extension to their counterparts, Manitou Cliff Dwellings and The Fort).

Bent's Old Fort has history, and perhaps the

most compelling theme of that history is edge of empire. Bent's Fort was on the edge—the cutting edge, to be sure—of Manifest Destiny, the American Empire. Bent's Old Fort was on the distant fringe of civilization, as that term was understood in New York, Charleston, and London. Bent's Fort lasted less than a lifetime; it waxed and waned, and the frontier shifted. That history is so much a part of the American heritage that there is no need to recount it further here, but it is important to point to revisionist histories, like Doug Comer's (1996), that place Bent's Old Fort clearly at the end of the capitalist world system, evanescent and exploitive.

Mesa Verde, in contrast, is presented today as a deeply permanent place: centuries of in-place, internal development. There is a trope of timelessness that suffuses most writing about Anasazi and Pueblo "history," as evidenced by our appeal to modern Pueblos to illuminate ancient history. This interpretive tactic assumes that *nothing changed*. But Pueblo traditional histories are all about change: migrations, wars, lessons learned, places and people lost. These oral histories explain how Pueblos came to be as they are today, and it was a long and bumpy road. Pueblo stories are far less teleological than our interpretive equation of modern Pueblos with ancient times: in the Pueblo stories, people made choices. Some of those choices led to the modern condition, and others did not.

The final abandonment of Mesa Verde would seem to challenge timelessness: at least once, something did indeed happen. And if one historical thing happened, once, why not more? There is a past, a history, to Anasazi and Pueblo places like Mesa Verde.

Mesa Verde itself can be seen as a frontier, like and unlike Bent's Fort. Bent's Fort was an outpost of a capitalist world system (its products went to the East Coast and thence to Europe). Mesa Verde was the product of a very different economic and political structure but still continental in scale—as big as the world could be, absent deep-ocean ships. Mesa Verde's world encompassed Mexico, or vice versa. I assert, but do not demonstrate here, that Mesa Verde was the distant fringe of civilization, as that term (or its local linguistic equivalent) was understood in Tula, El Tajín, or Culiacán. Beyond Mesa Verde, to the north, there were no sizable farming towns, no "budding urban centers." It was the frontier. Bent's Old Fort represented an extractive, expansive economy and the edge of empire. Chaco and Mesa Verde were not quite like that; they were agricultural at their base. And the cities of central Mexico were probably more modest in their territorial goals than was Washington, D.C. But both Bent's Old Fort and Mesa Verde were at the very edge of civilization, as that was understood by the people who considered themselves civilized at their respective times.

We need revisionist archaeologies of these ancient places, just as we have revisionist histories of Bent's Old Fort. We need to rethink our givens, like "kivas." We can do this with an archaeology that recognizes (and honors) the dynamic nature of American Indian traditional histories. Pueblo people recall very well that their past was different from their present. They have *history*: heroes and villains, rises and falls, grand narratives—all the things we expect to see in history books. But the NPS and most archaeologists say we cannot tell that history, that we cannot know it. I strongly disagree. We can know its broad outlines and often its telling details. Let these places have history: they have earned it.

Acknowledgments

I greatly appreciate the invitation of Brenda Bowser and María Nieves Zedeño to participate in this interesting volume; I hope my chapter is not too many standard deviations from what they meant when they asked me to contribute. I very sincerely thank the staffs of Mesa Verde National Park, Manitou Cliff Dwellings, Bent's Old Fort National Historic Site, and The Fort restaurant for sharing their knowledge and enthusiasm and for answering my many questions: I am sure they all have been burned by smarmy journalists, and in this age of anthropology-as-journalism I would not blame them for doubting my motives. Everyone I talked to was invariably polite and open, so one compliment fits all: they do not get paid enough! I spent 10 years working for the National Park Service, and I stand in awe of the amazing work of its staff, meeting ever-increasing demands with ever-diminishing budgets. Every archaeologist (regardless of academic specialty) owes a lot to the rangers and interpreters of Mesa Verde and Bent's Old Fort! They are the front line of public archaeology: take a seasonal to lunch. The staff at Manitou work equally hard to give the customer value for dollar, and I appreciate their good humor and patience with my queries. And, last but not least, I thank Holly Arnold Kinney of the Tesoro Foundation and The Fort for taking time out of her busy schedule to meet with me, and I thank the late Sam'l Arnold for reviving a great American cuisine! I believe the proper expression is: waugh?

Notes

1. One reviewer of this chapter asked: "Is archaeology interpretive by nature? Should it be? Please explain." Archaeology, in my opinion, *is* interpretation, *must be* interpretation. Getting things out of the ground is a craft—an exercise of considerable skill, complexity, and sophistication but essentially a suite of techniques shared with forensic sciences and paleontology and various quasi-archaeologies. Archaeology is the *interpretation* of the objects and information recovered from excavation, survey, and collection. Everything archaeologists write, beyond the measurements of a posthole or a bead, is interpretive (and some argue that measurements are interpretations—a pox on them, I say). *How we interpret* separates the archaeology of this book from doctrinal archaeology, treasure hunting, or "forbidden archaeology" of the fringe. During the last four decades (i.e., my career), the fundamental argument in archaeology has been *how we interpret*. In the 1970s and 1980s, Lewis Binford (and other archaeologists trained as or with natural history scientists) proposed that interpretations should use the tactics and strategies of science. *Middle-range theory* was precisely that: scientifically developed interpretive tools. But science is very hard to do: middle-range theory required the accumulation of great masses of carefully sifted data (mostly, and intentionally, unrelated to the case at hand) and years of analysis. In the end, that process produced tomes like *Constructing Frames of Reference*—Binford's (2001) impossible masterpiece. Rough going: the interpretations had to be interpreted! And even then, *Constructing Frames of Reference* left many wondering, So what? Easier by far—and more immediately engaging—are the tropes and styles of the humanities. In the late 1980s, 1990s, and 2000s, humanistic approaches were advocated by Ian Hodder (and other archaeologists trained as or with historians). It is easier to do humanistic interpretation: some soul-searching, a spark of imagination, a few appeals to philosophical authority, a basic facility with language, and there you are. This is not to denigrate the *scholarship* of humanistic archaeology; *method*, not scholarship, is the issue here. Most importantly, humanistic approaches have immediate interest. An essay, if well constructed, has a point or thesis that the reader immediately perceives; we need not suffer the delayed gratifications of science. It comes to this: it is more fun to read Hodder than Binford. This chapter is clearly in the humanities camp, but I have not given up on science. Science will give us sounder interpretations, if we have the discipline to follow it out. Science is hard work.

2. The literature on Mesa Verde is enormous. An excellent summary of Mesa Verde region archaeology was assembled by Lipe, Varien, and Wilshusen (1999) and Noble (2006). Jack Smith (1987) provides a good history of archaeology at the park, and Duane Smith (2002) wrote the standard history of the park itself. The standard history of Bent's Fort was written by David Lavender (1954). An accessible history and the best account of Bent's Fort archaeology appears in a collection of papers published first in a journal and then republished by the State Historical Society of Colorado (1979).

   I occasionally use the term *site* to refer to Mesa Verde, a national park that preserves thousands of individual sites. Mesa Verde is a landscape: the allusion of wilderness is a major part of the interpretive experience. I use *site* for Mesa Verde in the encompassing sense of landscape, just as we refer to Tikal or Zimbabwe or Chaco Canyon as "sites."

3. About two-thirds of the site is protected by the Archaeological Conservancy, and someday Yellow Jacket may be incorporated into one of the several NPS units in southwestern Colorado. Yellow Jacket was, for the Southwest, a huge site (Kuckelman 2003; Lange et al. 1988). Many of the very largest Mesa Verde sites were recently preserved by the creation of Canyons of the Ancients National Monument.

4. There are other reconstructed fur-trapper forts, perhaps less successful than Bent's Old Fort: Fort Vasquez was an 1835 fur-trading fort, built by founders Louis Vasquez and Andrew Sublette. The traders employed many of their mountain man friends, including Baptiste Charbonneau and Jim Beckwourth, at their adobe outpost on the South Platte River. A reconstruction, less faithful to the original than Bent's, today it is

on the median of four-lane Highway 85, 35 mi north of Denver. It is, literally, a wide spot in the road and shares its space with a truck inspection station.

5. Sometimes, the magic works, for us. It is, perhaps, less successful for the descendants of its builders. Simon Ortiz, from the Pueblo of Acoma, wrote a poem titled "A Designated National Park." Here are two lines from that poem:

> This morning
> I have to buy a permit to get back home.

There is still work to be done with and for the people who built Mesa Verde. As I write this, the National Park Service is locked in a contentious *Native American Graves Protection and Repatriation Act* dispute with many of the pueblos.

6. Sand Creek, to the northeast of Bent's Old Fort, was a "battle" widely recognized even at the time as an indefensible massacre. On November 29, 1864, Col. Chivington led the 3rd Regiment of Colorado Volunteers from Denver to a peaceful Cheyenne village at Sand Creek. The soldiers massacred and mutilated 200 people. Four of William Bent's children were present: three (George, Julia, and Charles) living in the camp and a fourth (Robert) acting under duress (threat of death) as a guide for Chivington.

    Almost all our national parks and monuments (and state parks, for that matter) that deal with Indian history (*not* archaeology) in the West are forts or battlefields. For "Indian history," as we interpret it through places, we could as easily say "Indian Wars." It is my impression that Indian people would not want their most important places—places really significant in their history, such as Devils Tower—singled out for national park status, but maybe Sand Creek will offer some balance for the account. The National Park Service is developing plans to interpret the Sand Creek site. Geographically and administratively, Sand Creek is linked to Bent's Old Fort. Bent's Fort was not the actual beginning of Manifest Destiny in the West, but it stood near that beginning in both time and space. Sand Creek was not the end of the Indian Wars, but it stands as an eloquent example of their waning decades. Bent's Old Fort and Sand Creek, in tandem, may send a powerful new message. Perhaps there is a healing there; it is not for me to say.

7. Christopher Woodward, in his short, intriguing book *In Ruins*, suggests that ruins should be allowed to decay: "No ruin can be suggestive to the visitor's imagination…unless its dialogue with the forces of nature is visibly alive and dynamic" (2001:73). In other words, things should fall apart. But we will not have it so. For decades, hardworking NPS stabilization crews have battled erosion and gravity. The idea of preservation outruns its technology. Today, stabilization is giving way to reburial. Sites in Chaco Canyon and at Aztec Ruins are being reburied as a preservation strategy. For many Pueblo people, our attempts at stabilization wrongly arrest cycles of life and death: buildings, like all things, were created to live for a while in this world and then pass on to another, perhaps coming back as new buildings.

8. Mesa Verde no longer welcomes archaeology. At the recent public centennial celebration of the park's creation, it was very clear that new research was not wanted. Archaeology will be only ancillary, and a very distant second, to ruins preservation. Archaeology can indeed answer questions, but park policies give us a self-fulfilling prophecy: "We probably will never know a great deal more about these people" (NPS 1994). In part, those policies reflect American Indian peoples' understandable doubts about archaeology. If there is a polarity between archaeology and American Indian histories in NPS interpretation (and there is), the pendulum has swung far to the latter. Interpretation should and must be informed by the insights and guidance of American Indian peoples; but archaeology remains a useful tool for understanding the past. We could indeed learn a great deal more about these people, with archaeology.

References Cited

Ackerly, N. W., J. B. Howard, and R. H. McGuire
1987   *La Ciudad Canals: A Study of Hohokam Irrigation Systems at the Community Level.* Anthropological Field Studies No. 17. Arizona State University, Tempe.

Acuña, R. (editor)
1985   *Relaciones geográficas del siglo XVI: Tlaxcala*, Vol. 5. Universidad Nacional Autónoma de México, Instituto de Investigaciones Antropológicas, Mexico City.

Adams, D. W.
1995   *Education for Extinction: American Indians and the Boarding School Experience, 1875–1928.* University Press of Kansas, Lawrence.

Adams, E. C.
1986   Hopi Use, Occupancy, and Possession of the Indian Reservation Defined by the Act of June 14, 1934: An Archaeological Perspective. Manuscript on file, Laboratory of Anthropology, Museum of New Mexico, Santa Fe.

Adler, M. A.
1996   Land Tenure, Archaeology, and the Ancestral Pueblo Landscape. *Journal of Anthropological Archaeology* 15:337–371.

Agnew, J. A.
1987   *Place and Politics: The Geographical Mediation of State and Society.* Allen and Unwin, Boston.

Agurcia Fasquelle, R., and B. W. Fash
2005   The Evolution of Structure 10L-16, Heart of the Copán Acropolis. In *Copán: The History of an Ancient Maya Kingdom*, edited by E. W. Andrews and W. L. Fash, pp. 201–237. School of American Research Press, Santa Fe.

Alcock, S. E., T. N. D'Altroy, K. D. Morrison, and C. M. Sinopoli (editors)
2001   *Empires: Perspectives from Archaeology and History.* Cambridge University Press, Cambridge.

Aleshire, P.
2002   Cibecue Canyon: A Guided Tour Through a Spiritual Center of Serenity in Apache Country. *Arizona Highways* 78(5):18–23.

Alexander, T. G.
1977   *A Clash of Interests: Interior Department and Mountain West 1863–96.* Brigham Young University Press, Provo.

Allen, B.
1987   *Homesteading the High Desert.* University of Utah Press, Salt Lake City.

Alvarado Tezozomoc, H.
1944   *Crónica mexicana.* Editorial Leyenda, S. A., Mexico City.
1975   *Crónica mexicana.* Edited by M. Orozco y Berra. Porrúa, Mexico City.

Anderson, K., and G. P. Nabhan
1991   Gardeners in Eden. *Wilderness* 55(194):27–30.

Anschuetz, K. F.
1996   Of Pueblos, Fields, and Shrines: Steps Beyond Archaeological Landscapes in the Northern Rio Grande. Paper presented at the 61st Annual Meeting of the Society for American Archaeology, New Orleans.

Anschuetz, K. F., and C. L. Scheick
1998   Unveiling Archaeological Tierra Incognita: Evaluating Time, Place-Making, and Tradition Through a Cultural Landscape Paradigm. Paper presented at the symposium "Beyond Settlement Systems: Archaeology and Cultural Landscapes," 63rd Annual Meeting of the Society for American Archaeology, Seattle.

Anschuetz, K. F., R. H. Wilshusen, and C. L. Scheick
2001   An Archaeology of Landscapes: Perspectives

and Directions. *Journal of Archaeological Research* 9:157–211.

Ashmore, W.
1980a The Classic Maya Settlement at Quiriguá. *Expedition* 23(1):20–27.
1980b Discovering Early Classic Quiriguá. *Expedition* 23(1):35–44.
1981 Precolumbian Occupation at Quiriguá, Guatemala: Settlement Patterns in a Classic Maya Center. Unpublished Ph.D. dissertation, Department of Anthropology, University of Pennsylvania.
1984 Quiriguá Archaeology and History Revisited. *Journal of Field Archaeology* 11:365–386.
1987 Cobble Crossroads: Gualjoquito Architecture and External Elite Ties. In *Interaction on the Southeast Mesoamerican Periphery*, edited by E. J. Robinson, pp. 28–48. BAR International Series 327. British Archaeological Reports, Oxford.
1989 Construction and Cosmology: Politics and Ideology in Lowland Maya Settlement Patterns. In *Word and Image in Maya Culture: Explorations in Language, Writing, and Representation*, edited by W. F. Hanks and D. S. Rice, pp. 272–286. University of Utah Press, Salt Lake City.
1991 Site Planning and Concepts of Directionality Among the Ancient Maya. *Latin American Antiquity* 2:199–226.
2002 "Decisions and Dispositions": Socializing Spatial Archaeology. *American Anthropologist* 104:1172–1183.
2004a Classic Maya Landscapes and Settlement. In *Mesoamerican Archaeology: A Sourcebook*, edited by J. A. Hendon and R. A. Joyce, pp. 169–191. Blackwell, Oxford.
2004b Social Archaeologies of Landscape. In *A Companion to Social Archaeology*, edited by L. Meskell and R. W. Preucel, pp. 255–271. Blackwell, Oxford.
2007a Building Social History at Pueblo Bonito: Footnotes to a Biography of Place. In *Chaco Architecture: Ancient Buildings and Landscapes of Chaco Canyon*, edited by S. H. Lekson, pp. 179–198. University of Utah Press, Salt Lake City.
2007b Settlement Archaeology at Quiriguá, Guatemala: Aspects of a Precolumbian Landscape, Quiriguá Reports, IV. Museum Monograph 126. University of Pennsylvania Museum, Philadelphia.

Ashmore, W., and A. B. Knapp (editors)
1999 *Archaeologies of Landscape: Contemporary Perspectives*. Blackwell, Oxford.

Ashmore, W., and J. A. Sabloff
2002 Spatial Orders in Maya Civic Plans. *Latin American Antiquity* 13:201–215.
2003 Interpreting Ancient Maya Civic Plans: Reply to Smith. *Latin American Antiquity* 14:229–236.

Ashmore, W., E. M. Schortman, and R. J. Sharer
1983 The Quiriguá Project: 1979 Season. In *Quiriguá Reports, II*, edited by R. J. Sharer, E. M. Schortman, and P. A. Urban, pp. 55–78. Paper No. 8, University Museum Monograph 49. University of Pennsylvania, Philadelphia.

Aveni, A. F.
1980 *Skywatchers of Ancient Mexico*. University of Texas Press, Austin.

Ayres, J. E.
2002 Agua Caliente: The Life of a Southern Arizona Ranch. *Journal of Arizona History* 43(4):309–342.

Balkansky, A. K.
2002 *The Sola Valley and the Monte Albán State: A Study of Zapotec Imperial Expansion*. Memoirs of the Museum of Anthropology No. 36. University of Michigan, Ann Arbor.

Bamforth, D.
1988 *Ecology and Human Organization on the Great Plains*. Plenum Press, New York.

Banyacya, T.
1966 Pottery Chips. MS Collection #245 (Louis A. Hieb, ed., *The Hopi Traditionalist Movement, a Documentary History, 1948–1971*), Special Collections, Cline Library, Northern Arizona University, Flagstaff.

Barber, S. B., and A. A. Joyce
2006 When Is a House a Palace? Elite Residences in the Valley of Oaxaca. In *Palaces and Power in the Americas*, edited by J. J. Christie and P. J. Sarro, pp. 211–255. University of Texas Press, Austin.

Barrett, J. C.
1999 The Mythical Landscapes of the British Iron Age. In *Archaeologies of Landscape: Contemporary Perspectives*, edited by W. Ashmore and A. B. Knapp, pp. 253–265. Blackwell, Oxford.

Bartolomé, M., and A. Barabas
1982 *Tierra de la Palabra: Historia y etnografía de los Chatinos de Oaxaca*. Colección Científica 108. Instituto Nacional de Antropología e Historia, Mexico City.

Basso, K. H.
1970 *The Cibecue Apache*. Holt, Rinehart, and Winston, New York.
1990 "Wise Words" of the Western Apache: Metaphor and Semantic Theory. In *Western Apache*

Language and Culture, by K. H. Basso, pp. 53–79. University of Arizona Press, Tucson.

1996 *Wisdom Sits in Places: Landscape and Language Among the Western Apache.* University of New Mexico Press, Albuquerque.

Bean, K. M.

1996 Settlement Stages and Frontier Systems: The Historic American Settlement of New Mexico's Black Hill Range. Unpublished Ph.D. dissertation, State University of New York, Buffalo.

Beck, L., and T. Cable

1997 *Interpretation for the 21st Century: Fifteen Guiding Principles for Interpreting Nature and Culture.* Sagamore, Champaign.

Becker, M. J.

1988 Caches as Burials, Burials as Caches: The Meaning of Ritual Deposits Among the Classic Period Lowland Maya. In *Recent Studies in Pre-Columbian Archaeology*, edited by N. J. Saunders and O. de Montmollin, pp. 117–142. BAR International Series 421. British Archaeological Reports, Oxford.

Bell, E. E., R. J. Sharer, L. P. Traxler, D. W. Sedat, C. W. Carrelli, and L. A. Grant

2004 Tombs and Burials in the Early Classic Acropolis at Copán. In *Understanding Early Classic Copán*, edited by E. E. Bell, M. A. Canuto, and R. J. Sharer, pp. 131–157. University of Pennsylvania Museum, Philadelphia.

Bender, B.

1993 Introduction: Landscape—Meaning and Action. In *Landscape: Politics and Perspectives*, edited by B. Bender, pp. 1–17. Berg, Oxford.

1998 *Stonehenge: Making Space.* Berg, Oxford.

1999 Introductory Comments. *Antiquity* 73: 632–634.

Bender, B. (editor)

1993 *Landscape: Politics and Perspectives.* Berg, Oxford.

Benítez, F.

1993 Tumba 7 de Monte Albán. *Arqueología Mexicana* 1(3):28–34.

Benton, J. C., J. Goodwyn, and R. C. Gamble

2001 *A Sense of Place: Montgomery's Architectural Heritage.* River City, Montgomery, Alabama.

Benyo, J. C.

1979 The Pottery Censers of Quiriguá, Izabal, Guatemala. Unpublished Master's thesis, State University of New York, Albany.

Berdan, F. F.

1988 Principles of Regional and Long-Distance Trade in the Aztec Empire. In *Smoke and Mist: Mesoamerican Studies in Memory of Thelma D. Sullivan*, Vol. 2, edited by J. K. Josserand and K. Dakin, pp. 639–655. BAR International Series 402(ii). British Archaeological Reports, Oxford.

1994 Economic Alternatives Under Imperial Rule: The Eastern Aztec Empire. In *Economies and Polities in the Aztec Realm*, edited by M. G. Hodge and M. E. Smith, pp. 291–312. University of Texas Press, Austin.

Berdan, F. F., and P. R. Anawalt

1997 *The Essential Codex Mendoza.* University of California Press, Berkeley.

Berdan, F. F., and P. R. Anawalt (editors)

1992 *The Codex Mendoza*, 4 vols. University of California Press, Berkeley.

Berdan, F. F., R. E. Blanton, E. H. Boone, M. G. Hodge, M. E. Smith, and E. Umberger

1996 *Aztec Imperial Strategies.* Dumbarton Oaks Research Library and Collection, Washington, D.C.

Berdan, F. F., M. A. Masson, J. Gasco, and M. E. Smith

2003 An International Economy. In *The Postclassic Mesoamerican World*, edited by M. E. Smith and F. F. Berdan, pp. 96–108. University of Utah Press, Salt Lake City.

Berdan, F. F., and M. E. Smith

1996 Imperial Strategies and Core–Periphery Relations. In *Aztec Imperial Strategies*, by F. F. Berdan, R. E. Blanton, E. H. Boone, M. G. Hodge, M. E. Smith, and E. Umberger, pp. 209–217. Dumbarton Oaks Research Library and Collection, Washington, D.C.

2003 The Aztec Empire. In *The Postclassic Mesoamerican World*, edited by M. E. Smith and F. F. Berdan, pp. 67–72. University of Utah Press, Salt Lake City.

Berlo, J. C.

1992 Icons and Ideologies at Teotihuacan: The Great Goddess Reconsidered. In *Art, Ideology, and the City of Teotihuacan*, edited by J. C. Berlo, pp. 129–168. Dumbarton Oaks, Washington, D.C.

Bernardini, W.

2005a *Hopi Oral Tradition and the Archaeology of Identity.* University of Arizona Press, Tucson.

2005b *The Tutuveni Petroglyph Site.* Report on file at the Hopi Cultural Preservation Office, Kykotsmovi, Arizona.

Binford, L.

1962 Archaeology as Anthropology. *American Antiquity* 28:217–225.

1982 The Archaeology of Place. *Journal of Anthropological Archaeology* 1:5–31.

2001 *Constructing Frames of Reference.* University of California Press, Berkeley.

Blake, E.
1999 Coming to Terms with Local Approaches to Sardinia's Nuraghi. In *Archaeology and Folklore*, edited by A. Gazin-Schwartz and C. Holtorf, pp. 230–239. Routledge, London.
2003 The Familiar Honeycomb: Byzantine Era Reuse of Sicily's Prehistoric Rock-Cut Tombs. In *Archaeologies of Memory*, edited by R. M. Van Dyke and S. E. Alcock, pp. 203–220. Blackwell, Oxford.
2004 Space, Spatiality, and Archaeology. In *A Companion to Social Archaeology*, edited by L. Meskell and R. W. Preucel, pp. 230–254. Blackwell, Oxford.

Blanton, R. E.
1978 *Monte Albán: Settlement Patterns at the Ancient Zapotec Capital*. Academic Press, New York.
1982 *Monte Albán's Hinterland*. Memoirs of the Museum of Anthropology No. 15. University of Michigan, Ann Arbor.
1983 The Urban Decline of Monte Albán. In *The Cloud People: Divergent Evolution of the Zapotec and Mixtec Civilizations*, edited by K. V. Flannery and J. Marcus, p. 186. Academic Press, New York.
1996 The Basin of Mexico Market System and the Growth of Empire. In *Aztec Imperial Strategies*, by F. F. Berdan, R. E. Blanton, E. H. Boone, M. G. Hodge, M. E. Smith, and E. Umberger, pp. 47–84. Dumbarton Oaks Research Library and Collection, Washington, D.C.

Blanton, R. E., G. M. Feinman, S. A. Kowalewski, and L. M. Nicholas
1999 *Ancient Oaxaca: The Monte Albán State*. Cambridge University Press, Cambridge.

Blitz, J. H.
1993 Big Pots for Big Shots: Feasting and Storage in a Mississippian Community. *American Antiquity* 58:80–96.

Blouet, B. W.
2001 *Geopolitics and Globalization in the Twentieth Century*. Reaktion, London.

Boone, E. H.
1996 Manuscript Painting in Service of Imperial Ideology. In *Aztec Imperial Strategies*, by F. F. Berdan, R. E. Blanton, E. H. Boone, M. G. Hodge, M. E. Smith, and E. Umberger, pp. 181–207. Dumbarton Oaks Research Library and Collection, Washington, D.C.

Borhegyi, S. F. de
1969 The Pre-Columbian Ballgame: A Pan-Mesoamerican Tradition. *Proceedings of the 38th International Congress of Americanists* 1:498–515. Stuttgart.

Bostwick, T. W.
1992 Platform Mound Ceremonialism in Southern Arizona: Possible Symbolic Meanings of Hohokam and Salado Platform Mounds. In *Proceedings of the Second Salado Conference: Globe, AZ 1992*, edited by R. C. Lange and S. Germick, pp. 78–85. Occasional Paper 1992. Arizona Archaeological Society, Phoenix.
2002 *Landscape of the Spirits: Hohokam Rock Art at South Mountain Park*. University of Arizona Press, Tucson.

Bourdieu, P.
1977 *Outline of a Theory of Practice*. Translated by R. Nice. Cambridge University Press, Cambridge.

Bowser, B. J.
2002 *The Perceptive Potter: An Ethnoarchaeological Study of Pottery, Ethnicity, and Political Action in Amazonia*. Ph.D. dissertation, Department of Anthropology, University of California, Santa Barbara. University Microfilms, Ann Arbor.
2004 Prologue: Toward an Archaeology of Place. *Journal of Archaeological Method and Theory* 11(1):1–3.

Bowser, B. J., and J. Q. Patton
2004 Domestic Spaces as Public Places: An Ethnoarchaeological Case Study of Houses, Gender, and Politics in the Ecuadorian Amazon. *Journal of Archaeological Method and Theory* 11(2):157–181.

Bradley, R. J.
1987 Time Regained: The Creation of Continuity. *Journal of the British Archaeological Association* 140:1–17.
1993 *Altering the Earth: The Origins of Monuments in Britain and Continental Europe*. Society of Antiquaries of Scotland, Edinburgh.
1998 *The Significance of Monuments*. Routledge, London.
2000 *The Archaeology of Natural Places*. Routledge, London.
2003 The Translation of Time. In *Archaeologies of Memory*, edited by R. M. Van Dyke and S. E. Alcock, pp. 221–227. Blackwell, Oxford.

Bradomin, J. M.
1955 *Toponimia de Oaxaca: Crítica etimológica*. Manuscript on file at the Welte Institute, Oaxaca.

Brady, J. E., and W. Ashmore
1999 Mountains, Caves, Water: Ideational Land-

scapes of the Ancient Maya. In *Archaeologies of Landscape: Contemporary Perspectives*, edited by W. Ashmore and A. B. Knapp, pp. 124–145. Blackwell, Oxford.

Braswell, G. E.
2003   Obsidian Exchange Spheres. In *The Postclassic Mesoamerican World*, edited by M. E. Smith and F. F. Berdan, pp. 131–158. University of Utah Press, Salt Lake City.

Braudel, F.
1980   *On History*. Weidenfeld and Nicolson, London.

Breternitz, C. D.
1991   Preface. In *The Operation and Evolution of an Irrigation System: The East Papago Canal Study*, by J. B. Howard and G. Huckleberry, p. v. Soil Systems, Phoenix.

Broda, J.
1991   The Sacred Landscape of Aztec Calendar Festivals: Myth, Nature, and Society. In *To Change Place: Aztec Ceremonial Landscapes*, edited by D. Carrasco, pp. 74–120. University Press of Colorado, Niwot.

Brown, L. A.
2004   Dangerous Places and Wild Spaces: Creating Meaning with Materials and Space at Contemporary Maya Shrines on El Duende Mountain. *Journal of Archaeological Method and Theory* 11(1):31–58.

Brumfiel, E. M.
1991   Tribute and Commerce in Imperial Cities: The Case of Xaltocan, Mexico. In *Early State Dynamics*, edited by H. Claessen and P. van de Velde, pp. 223–251. Transaction, New Brunswick, New Jersey.
1992   Distinguished Lecture in Archaeology: Breaking and Entering the Ecosystem—Gender, Class, and Faction Steal the Show. *American Anthropologist* 94:551–567.
1994   Ethnic Groups and Political Development in Ancient Mexico. In *Factional Competition and Political Development in the New World*, edited by E. M. Brumfiel and J. W. Fox, pp. 89–102. Cambridge University Press, Cambridge.
1998   Huitzilopochtli's Conquest: Aztec Ideology in the Archaeological Record. *Cambridge Archaeological Journal* 81:3–13.
2000   The Imperial Subversion of Aztec Xaltocan. In *Precious Greenstone, Precious Quetzal Feather: Mesoamerican Studies in Honor of Doris Heyden*, edited by E. Quiñones Keber, pp. 169–181. Labyrinthos, Culver City.
2001   Aztec Hearts and Minds: Religion and the State in the Aztec Empire. In *Empires: Perspectives from Archaeology and History*, edited by S. E. Alcock, T. N. D'Altroy, K. D. Morrison, and C. M. Sinopoli, pp. 283–310. Cambridge University Press, Cambridge.

Brumfiel, E. M., and J. W. Fox (editors)
1994   *Factional Competition and Political Development in the New World*. Cambridge University Press, Cambridge.

Buikstra, J. E., and D. K. Charles
1999   Centering the Ancestors: Cemeteries, Mounds, and Sacred Landscapes of the Ancient North American Midcontinent. In *Archaeologies of Landscape: Contemporary Perspectives*, edited by W. Ashmore and A. B. Knapp, pp. 201–228. Blackwell, Oxford.

Bureau of Indian Affairs
1955   *Hopi Hearings, July 15–30, 1955*. Bureau of Indian Affairs Phoenix Area Office, Hopi Agency, Phoenix.

Burland, C., and W. Forman
1975   *Feathered Serpent and Smoking Mirror*. Orbis, London.

Buskirk, W.
1986   *The Western Apache: Living with the Land Before 1950*. University of Oklahoma Press, Norman.

Byland, B. E., and J. M. D. Pohl
1994   *In the Realm of 8 Deer*. University of Oklahoma Press, Norman.

Carmichael, D., J. Hubert, B. Reeves, and A. Schanche (editors)
1994   *Sacred Sites, Sacred Places*. Routledge, New York.

Carnap, R.
1955   *Philosophy and Logical Syntax*. MIT Press, Cambridge, Massachusetts.

Carrasco, P.
1996   *Estructura Político-Territorial del Imperio Tenochca: La Triple Alianza de Tenochtitlan Tetzcoco, y Tlacopan*. El Colegio de México, Fideicomiso Historia de las Américas, Fondo de Cultura Económica, Mexico City.
1999   *The Tenochca Empire of Ancient Mexico: The Triple Alliance of Tenochtitlan, Tetzcoco, and Tlacopán*. University of Oklahoma Press, Norman.

Carrelli, C. W.
2004   Measures of Power: The Energetics of Royal Construction at Early Classic Copán. In *Understanding Early Classic Copán*, edited by E. E. Bell, M. A. Canuto, and R. J. Sharer, pp. 113–127. University of Pennsylvania Museum, Philadelphia.

Carroll, A. K., M. N. Zedeño, and R. Stoffle
2004 Landscapes of the Ghost Dance: A Cartography of Numic Ritual. *Journal of Archaeological Method and Theory* 11(2):127–156.

Carroll, K. J.
2007 Place, Performance, and Social Memory in the 1890s Ghost Dance. Unpublished Ph.D. dissertation, Department of Anthropology, University of Arizona, Tucson.

Caso, A.
1932 Monte Albán, Richest Archaeological Find in America. *National Geographic Magazine* 62(4):487–512.
1938 *Exploraciones en Oaxaca. Quinta y Sexta Temporadas 1936–37*. Instituto Panamericano de Geografía e Historia No. 34. Mexico City.
1939 Resumen del Informe de las Temporadas en Oaxaca, durante la 7a y la 8a Temporadas (1937–38 y 1938–39). *27 Congreso Internacional de Americanistas* 2:159–187. Mexico City.
1947 Calendario y escritura de las antiguas culturas de Monte Albán. *Obras Completas de Miguel Othón de Mendizábal* 1:116–143.
1982 *El Tesoro de Monte Albán*. Memorias del Instituto Nacional de Antropología e Historia III. Mexico City.

Caso, A., I. Bernal, and J. R. Acosta
1967 *La cerámica de Monte Albán*. Memorias del Instituto Nacional de Antropología e Historia No. 13. Mexico City.

Castellanos, A.
1989 *Monte Albán, Danni Dipaa: Cerro Fortificado*. Lásser Plus, Oaxaca.

Cather, W.
1973 *The Professor's House*. Reprinted. Vintage Books, New York. Originally published 1925, Knopf, New York.

Cazier, L.
1976 *Surveys and Surveyors of the Public Domain: 1785–1975*. U.S. Department of the Interior, Bureau of Land Management, U.S. Government Printing Office, Washington, D.C.

Charles, D. K., J. Van Nest, and J. E. Buikstra
2004 From the Earth: Minerals and Meaning in the Hopewellian World. In *Soils, Stones and Symbols: Cultural Perceptions of the Mineral World*, edited by N. Boivin and M. A. Owoc, pp. 43–70. University College London Press, London.

Charlton, T. H., D. L. Nichols, and C. O. Charlton
1991 Aztec Craft Production and Specialization: Archaeological Evidence from the City-State of Otumba, Mexico. *World Archaeology* 23:98–114.

Chippindale, C.
1986 Stoned Henge: Events and Issues at the Winter Solstice, 1985. *World Archaeology* 18:38–58.

Chippindale, C., P. Devereux, P. Fowler, R. Jones, and T. Sebastian
1990 *Who Owns Stonehenge?* B. T. Batsford, London.

Church, M. C.
2001 Homesteads on the Purgatoire: Frontiers of Culture Contact in 19th Century Colorado. Unpublished Ph.D. dissertation, Department of American Civilization, University of Pennsylvania, Philadelphia.
2002 The Grant and the Grid: Homestead Landscapes in the Late Nineteenth-Century Borderlands of Southern Colorado. *Journal of Social Archaeology* 2(2):220–244.

Clarke, D. L. (editor)
1972 *Models in Archaeology*. Methuen, London.

Cleere, H.
1995 Cultural Landscapes as World Heritage. *Conservation and Management of Archaeological Sites* 1:63–68.

Clemmer, R. O.
1993 Hopi. In *An Investigation of AIRFA Concerns Relating to the Fruitland Coal Gas Development Area*, edited by D. M. Brugge, pp. 77–89. Office of Contract Archaeology, University of New Mexico, Albuquerque.

Coe, M. D.
1956 The Funerary Temple Among the Classic Maya. *Southwestern Journal of Anthropology* 12:387–394.

Coggins, C. C.
1980 The Shape of Time: Some Political Implications of a Four-Part Figure. *American Antiquity* 45:727–739.

Cohen, S. B.
2003 *Geopolitics of the World System*. Rowman and Littlefield, Lanham, Maryland.

Cohodas, M.
1975 The Symbolism and Ritual Function of the Middle Classic Ballgame in Mesoamerica. *American Indian Quarterly* 2:99–130.
1991 Ballgame Imagery of the Maya Lowlands: History and Iconography. In *The Mesoamerican Ballgame*, edited by V. L. Scarborough and D. R. Wilcox, pp. 251–288. University of Arizona Press, Tucson.

Colton, M. R. F., and H. S. Colton
1931 Petroglyphs, the Record of a Great Adventure. *American Anthropologist* 33(1):32–37.

Comer, D. C.
1996 *Ritual Ground: Bent's Old Fort, World Forma-*

tion, and the Annexation of the Southwest. University of California Press, Berkeley.

Connerton, P.
1989   *How Societies Remember*. Cambridge University Press, Cambridge.

Cosgrove, D. E., and S. Daniels (editors)
1988   *The Iconography of Landscape: Essays on the Symbolic Representation, Design and Use of Past Environments*. Cambridge University Press, Cambridge.

Crumley, C. L.
1994   Historical Ecology: A Multidimensional Ecological Orientation. In *Historical Ecology: Cultural Knowledge and Changing Landscapes*, edited by C. L. Crumley, pp. 1–16. School of American Research Press, Santa Fe.

Crumley, C. L., and W. H. Marquardt
1990   Landscapes: A Unifying Concept in Regional Analysis. In *Interpreting Space: GIS and Archaeology*, edited by K. M. S. Allen, S. W. Green, and E. B. W. Zubrow, pp. 73–79. Taylor and Francis, London.

Cruz, W.
1946   *Oaxaca Recóndita: Razas, Idiomas, Costumbres, Leyendas, y Tradiciones del Estado de Oaxaca, México*. W. Cruz, Mexico City.

Curet, L. A.
1993   Regional Studies and Ceramic Production Areas: An Example from La Mixtequilla, Veracruz, Mexico. *Journal of Field Archaeology* 20:427–440.

Curet, L. A., B. L. Stark, and S. Vásquez Z.
1994   Postclassic Changes in Veracruz, Mexico. *Ancient Mesoamerica* 5:13–32.

D'Altroy, T. N.
1992   *Provincial Power in the Inka Empire*. Smithsonian Institution Press, Washington, D.C.
1994   Public and Private Economy in the Inka Empire. In *The Economic Anthropology of the State*, edited by E. M. Brumfiel, pp. 171–222. Society for Economic Anthropology Monograph No. 11. University Press of America, Lanham, Maryland.
2002   *The Incas. The Peoples of the Americas*. Blackwell, Oxford.

Daneels, A.
1997   Settlement History in the Lower Cotaxtla Basin. In *Olmec to Aztec: Settlement Patterns in the Ancient Gulf Lowlands*, edited by B. L. Stark and P. J. Arnold, pp. 206–252. University of Arizona Press, Tucson.

Daniels, S., and D. E. Cosgrove
1988   Introduction: Iconography and Landscape. In *The Iconography of Landscape: Essays on the Symbolic Representation, Design and Use of Past Environments*, edited by D. E. Cosgrove and S. Daniels, pp. 1–10. Cambridge University Press, Cambridge.

Dart, A.
1989   *Prehistoric Irrigation in Arizona: A Context for Canals and Related Cultural Resources*. Technical Report 89-1. Center for Desert Archaeology, Tucson.

David, B., and H. Lourandos
1999   Landscapes as Mind: Land Use, Cultural Space, and Change in North Queensland. *Quaternary International* 59:107–123.

Davisson, L.
1976   Fifty Years at Fort Apache. *Journal of Arizona History* 17:301–320.
1978   Arizona's White River: A Working Watercourse. *Journal of Arizona History* 19:55–72.

Dean, J. S.
1991   Thoughts on Hohokam Chronology. In *Exploring the Hohokam: Prehistoric Desert Peoples of the American Southwest*, edited by G. J. Gumerman, pp. 61–149. Amerind Foundation, Dragoon, Arizona; and University of New Mexico Press, Albuquerque.

de Certeau, M.
1984   *The Practice of Everyday Life*. University of California Press, Berkeley.

de Coppet, D.
1985   Land Owns People. In *Contexts and Levels: Anthropological Essays in Hierarchy*, edited by R. Barnes, D. de Coppet, and R. Park, pp. 78–90. Occasional Papers No. 4. Journal of the Anthropological Society of Oxford, Oxford.

de la Cruz, V.
2004   Cambios religiosos en Monte Albán a fines del período Clásico. In *Estructuras políticas en el Oaxaca antiguo*, edited by N. M. Robles García, pp. 159–173. Instituto Nacional de Antropología e Historia, Mexico City.

Deloria, V., Jr.
1973   *God Is Red*. Grosset and Dunlap, New York.

DeMarrais, E., L. J. Castillo, and T. Earle
1996   Ideology, Materialization, and Power Strategies. *Current Anthropology* 17:15–31.

Dimmitt, M. A.
2000   Biomes and Communities of the Sonoran Desert Region. In *A Natural History of the Sonoran Desert*, edited by S. J. Phillips and P. W. Comus, pp. 3–18. Arizona–Sonora Desert Museum, Tucson.

Di Peso, C. C.
1956   *The Upper Pima of San Cayetano del Tumacacori: An Archaeological Reconstruction of the*

Ootam of the Pimería Alta. Publication No. 7. Amerind Foundation, Dragoon, Arizona.

Dixit, A., and S. Skeath
1999 *Games of Strategy*. W. W. Norton, New York.

Doelle, W. H., and H. D. Wallace
1991 The Changing Role of the Tucson Basin in the Hohokam Regional System. In *Exploring the Hohokam: Prehistoric Desert Peoples of the American Southwest*, edited by G. J. Gumerman, pp. 279–345. Amerind Foundation, Dragoon, Arizona; and University of New Mexico Press, Albuquerque.

Downum, C. E., and T. W. Bostwick
2003 The Platform Mound. In *Centuries of Decline During the Hohokam Classic Period at Pueblo Grande*, edited by D. R. Abbott, pp. 166–200. University of Arizona Press, Tucson.

Doyel, D. E.
1980 Hohokam Social Organization and the Sedentary to Classic Transition. In *Current Issues in Hohokam Prehistory*, edited by D. Doyel and F. Plog, pp. 23–40. Anthropological Research Papers No. 23. Arizona State University, Tempe.
1991 Hohokam Cultural Evolution in the Phoenix Basin. In *Exploring the Hohokam: Prehistoric Desert Peoples of the American Southwest*, edited by G. J. Gumerman, pp. 231–278. Amerind Foundation, Dragoon, Arizona; and University of New Mexico Press, Albuquerque.
1992 On Models and Methods: Comments on the History of Archaeological Research in the Southern Southwest. In *Proceedings of the Second Salado Conference: Globe, AZ, 1992*, edited by R. C. Lange and S. Germick, pp. 345–351. Occasional Paper 1992. Arizona Archaeological Society, Phoenix.

Duncan, J. S.
1990 *The City as Text: The Politics of Landscape Interpretation in the Kandyan Kingdom*. Cambridge University Press, Cambridge.

Durán, F. D.
1967 *Historia de las Indias de Nueva España e islas de la Tierra Firme*, 2 vols. Edited by A. M. Garibay K. Editorial Porrúa, Mexico City.

Ebert, J.
1992 *Distributional Archaeology*. University of New Mexico Press, Albuquerque.

Eggan, F.
1994 The Hopi Indians, with Special Reference to Their Cosmology or World View. In *Kachinas in the Pueblo World*, edited by P. Schaafsma, pp. 7–16. University of New Mexico Press, Albuquerque.

Eiseman, F. B., Jr.
1959 The Hopi Salt Trail. *Plateau* 32(2):25–32.
1961 Discovery of the Hopi Salt Cave. *Spout*, November: 2–7.

Elson, M. D.
1986 *Archaeological Investigations at the Tanque Verde Wash Site, a Middle Rincon Hamlet in the Eastern Tucson Basin*. Anthropological Paper No. 7. Institute for American Research, Tucson.

Entrikin, J. N.
1991 *The Betweenness of Place: Toward a Geography of Modernity*. Johns Hopkins University Press, Baltimore.

Evans, S. T. (editor)
1988 *Excavations at Cihuatecpan: An Aztec Village in the Teotihuacan Valley*. Vanderbilt University Publications in Anthropology No. 36. Vanderbilt University Press, Nashville.

Ezzo, J. A., and J. H. Altschul (compilers)
1993 *Glyphs and Quarries of the Lower Colorado River*. Technical Series 44. Statistical Research, Tucson.

Fairley, H. C.
2003 *Changing River: Time, Culture, and the Transformation of Landscape in the Grand Canyon*. Technical Series No. 79. Statistical Research, Tucson.

Falk, D. A., M. A. Palmer, and J. B. Zedler (editors)
2006 *Foundations of Restoration Ecology*. Island Press, Washington, DC.

Fash, W. L.
2001 *Scribes, Warriors, and Kings: The City of Copán and the Ancient Maya*. Rev. ed. Thames and Hudson, New York.
2005 Toward a Social History of the Copán Valley. In *Copán: The History of an Ancient Maya Kingdom*, edited by E. W. Andrews and W. L. Fash, pp. 73–101. School of American Research Press, Santa Fe.

Fash, W. L., and D. S. Stuart
1991 Dynastic History and Cultural Evolution at Copán, Honduras. In *Classic Maya Political History: Hieroglyphic and Archaeological Evidence*, edited by T. P. Culbert, pp. 147–179. Cambridge University Press, Cambridge.

Fauman-Fichman, R.
2001 An Aztec Case Study to Highlight Problems in Development of Material Evidence of Indirectly Controlled Empires. Paper presented at the 66th Annual Meeting of the Society for American Archaeology, New Orleans.

Feld, S., and K. H. Basso (editors)
1996 *Senses of Place*. School of American Research Press, Santa Fe.

Ferg, A., and J. I. Mead
1993   *Red Cave: A Prehistoric Cave Shrine in Southeastern Arizona.* Arizona Archaeologist No. 26. Arizona Archaeological Society, Phoenix.

Ferguson, T. J.
1996   *Historic Zuni Architecture and Society: An Archaeological Application of Space Syntax.* Anthropological Papers of the University of Arizona No. 60. University of Arizona, Tucson.
1998   *Öngtupka niqw Pisisvayu (Salt, Salt Canyon, and the Colorado River), the Hopi People and the Grand Canyon.* Final ethnohistoric report for the Hopi Glen Canyon Environmental Studies. Hopi Cultural Preservation Office, Kykotsmovi, Arizona.

Ferguson, T. J., K. E. Dongoske, L. Jenkins, M. Yeatts, and E. Polingyouma
1993   Working Together, the Roles of Archeology and Ethnohistory in Hopi Cultural Preservation. *CRM: The Journal of Heritage Stewardship* 16 (special issue): 27–37.

Ferguson, T. J., K. E. Dongoske, and L. J. Kuwanwisiwma
2001   Hopi Perspectives on Southwestern Mortuary Studies. In *Ancient Burial Practices in the American Southwest*, edited by D. R. Mitchell and J. L. Brunson-Hadley, pp. 9–26. University of New Mexico Press, Albuquerque.

Ferguson, T. J., and M. Loma'omvaya
1999   *Hoopoq'yaqam niqw Wukoskyyavi (Those Who Went to the Northeast and Tonto Basin), Hopi–Salado Cultural Affiliation Study.* Hopi Cultural Preservation Office, the Hopi Tribe, Kykotsmovi, Arizona.
2000   *Nuvatukya'ovi, Palatsmo niqw Wupatki*: Hopi History, Culture, and Landscape. Manuscript on file, Desert Archaeology, Tucson.

Fewkes, J. W.
1897   Tusayan Totemic Signatures. *American Anthropologist* 10:1–11.
1900   Property-Right and Eagles Among the Hopi. *American Anthropologist* 2:690–707.
1906   Hopi Shrines near the East Mesa, Arizona. *American Anthropologist* 8:346–375.
1910   Shrines. In *Handbook of the American Indians North of Mexico*, Pt. 2, edited by F. W. Hodge, pp. 558–559. U.S. Government Printing Office, Washington, D.C.

Fine, K.
1988   The Politics of "Interpretation" at Mesa Verde National Park. *Anthropological Quarterly* 61(4):177–186.

Fish, S. K.
1995   Mixed Agricultural Technologies in Southern Arizona and Their Implications. In *Soil, Water, Biology, and Belief in Prehistoric and Traditional Southwestern Agriculture*, edited by H. W. Toll, pp. 101–116. Special Publication No. 2. New Mexico Archaeological Council, Albuquerque.

Fish, S. K., and G. P. Nabhan
1991   Desert as Context: The Hohokam Environment. In *Exploring the Hohokam: Prehistoric Desert Peoples of the American Southwest*, edited by G. J. Gumerman, pp. 29–60. Amerind Foundation, Dragoon, Arizona; University of New Mexico Press, Albuquerque.

Fisher, C. T., and T. L. Thurston
1999   Dynamic Landscapes and Socio-Political Process: The Topography of Anthropogenic Environments in Global Perspective. *Antiquity* 73:630–631.

Flannery, K. V., and J. Marcus
1983a The Rosario Phase and the Origins of Monte Albán. In *The Cloud People: Divergent Evolution of the Zapotec and Mixtec Civilizations*, edited by K. V. Flannery and J. Marcus, pp. 74–77. Academic Press, New York.
1983b The Origins of the State in Oaxaca: Editors Introduction. In *The Cloud People: Divergent Evolution of the Zapotec and Mixtec Civilizations*, edited by K. V. Flannery and J. Marcus, pp. 79–83. Academic Press, New York.

Fleming, A.
2006   Post-Processual Landscape Archaeology: A Critique. *Cambridge Archaeological Journal* 16(3):267–280.

Flores, D. L.
1998   Environmentalism and Multiculturalism. In *Reopening the American West*, edited by H. K. Rothman, pp. 24–37. University of Arizona Press, Tucson.

Fontana, B. L., and J. C. Greenleaf
1962   Johnny Ward's Ranch. *Kiva* 28(1–2):1–115.

Foster, G.
1954   Petrographic Art in Glen Canyon. *Plateau* 27(1):6–18.

Foucault, M.
1977   *Discipline and Punish: The Birth of the Prison.* Vintage, New York.
1986   Of Other Spaces. *Diacritics* 16:22–27.

Fouschee, Richard E. (writer/director)
n.d.   *They Came to Build: The Reconstruction of Bent's Old Fort.* Eugene-Clair Productions, Denver. VHS, National Park Service, distributed by INTERPark, Cortez, Colorado.

Fowler, D. D.
1987 Uses of the Past in the Service of the State. *American Antiquity* 52(2):229–248.

Fox, G. L., and J. S. Dean
1996 Dating the Upper Ruin. In *Archaeological Investigations at the Upper Ruin, Tonto National Monument*, Pt. 1, edited by G. L. Fox, pp. 181–189. Western Archeological and Conservation Center Publications in Anthropology 70. Tucson.

Fox, J. G.
1994 Putting the Heart Back in the Court: Ballcourts and Ritual Action in Mesoamerica. Ph.D. dissertation, Harvard University. University Microfilms, Ann Arbor.
1996 Playing with Power: Ballcourts and Political Ritual in Southern Mesoamerica. *Current Anthropology* 37:483–509.

Fraser, G. M.
1982 *Flashman and the Redskins*. Plume/Penguin, New York.

Frazer, S.
1998 The Public Forum and the Space Between: The Materiality of Social Strategy in the Irish Neolithic. *Proceedings of the Prehistory Society* 64:203–224.

Freidel, D. A.
1979 Culture Areas and Interaction Spheres. *American Antiquity* 44:36–54.

Freidel, D. A., L. Schele, and J. Parker
1993 *Maya Cosmos: Three Thousand Years on the Shaman's Path*. William Morrow, New York.

Friedman, P. D.
1985 Final Report of History and Oral History Studies of the Fort Carson Piñon Canyon Maneuver Area, Las Animas County, Colorado. Report submitted by Powers Elevation, Archaeology Division, to the National Park Service Rocky Mountain Regional Office, Denver, for the Department of the Army, Fort Carson, Colorado.

Frigout, A.
1979 Hopi Ceremonial Organization. In *Southwest*, edited by A. Ortiz, pp. 564–576. *Handbook of North American Indians*, Vol. 9, William C. Sturtevant, general editor. Smithsonian Institution, Washington, D.C.

Fritz, J. M.
1978 Paleopsychology Today: Ideational Systems and Human Adaptation in Prehistory. In *Social Archeology: Beyond Subsistence and Dating*, edited by C. L. Redman, M. J. Berman, F. V. Curtin, W. T. Langhorne Jr., N. M. Versaggi, and J. C. Wanser, pp. 37–59. Academic Press, New York.

Fung, C.
1995a Domestic Labor, Gender and Power on the Mesoamerican Frontier. In *Debating Complexity: Proceedings of the 26th Annual Chac Mool Conference*, edited by D. Meyer, P. Dawson, and D. Hanna, pp. 65–75. Archaeology Association, University of Calgary, Calgary.
1995b *Domestic Labor, Gender and Social Power: Household Archaeology in Terminal Classic Yoro, Honduras*. Ph.D. dissertation, Harvard University. University Microfilms, Ann Arbor.

Gailey, C. W., and T. C. Patterson
1987 Power Relations and State Formation. In *Power Relations and State Formation*, edited by C. W. Gailey, pp. 1–26. Sheffield, Salem, Wisconsin.

Gallivan, M. D.
2006 Powhatan's Werowocomoco: Constructing Place, Polity, and Personhood in the Chesapeake, C.E. 1200–C.E. 1609. *American Anthropologist* 109(1):85–100.

Gámez Goytia, G.
2002 El eje sagrado en Monte Albán: Elemento central de la arquitectura religiosa zapoteca. In *La Religión de los Binnigula'sa'*, edited by V. de la Cruz and M. Winter, pp. 197–217. Fondo Editorial, Instituto Estatal de Educación Pública de Oaxaca (IEEPO), Oaxaca.

García Icazbalceta, J. (editor)
1943 *Relaciones históricas estadísticas*. 2 vols. MS from the Collection of Federico Gómez de Orozco.

García Márquez, A.
1998 Los Aztecas en el sur-centro de Veracruz. Unpublished Master's thesis, Universidad Autónoma de México, Mexico City.

García Moll, R., D. W. Patterson Brown, and M. Winter
1986 *Monumentos escultóricos de Monte Albán*. Verlag C. H. Beck, Munich.

García Payón, J.
1936 *La zona arqueológica de Tecaxic-Calixtlahuaca y los Matlatzincas*, Pt. I. Secretaría de Educación Publica, Mexico City.

Garraty, C. P.
2006 Aztec Teotihuacan: Political Processes at an Aztec City-State in the Basin of México, AD 1200–1650. *Latin American Antiquity* 17(4):363–387.

Garraty, C. P., and B. L. Stark
2002 Imperial and Social Relations in Postclassic South-Central Veracruz, México. *Latin American Antiquity* 13:3–33.

Gasser, R. E., and S. J. Kwiatkowski
1991   Food for Thought: Recognizing Patterns in Hohokam Subsistence. In *Exploring the Hohokam: Prehistoric Desert Peoples of the American Southwest*, edited by G. J. Gumerman, pp. 417–460. Amerind Foundation, Dragoon, Arizona; and University of New Mexico Press, Albuquerque.

Gates, P. W.
1936   The Homestead Law in an Incongruous Land System. *American Historical Review* 41(4):652–681.
1968   *History of Public Land Law Development*. Public Land Law Review Commission, Washington, D.C.
1979   *The Fruits of Land Speculation*. Arno Press, New York.

Geertz, Armin
1994   *The Invention of Prophecy, Continuity and Meaning in Hopi Indian Religion*. University of California Press, Berkeley.

Gerstle, A. I.
1988   Maya–Lenca Ethnic Relations in Late Classic Period Copán, Honduras. Unpublished Ph.D. dissertation, Department of Anthropology, University of California, Santa Barbara.

Giddens, A.
1979   *Central Problems in Social Theory*. University of California Press, Berkeley.
1984   *The Constitution of Society: Outline of the Theory of Structuration*. Polity Press, Cambridge.

Gillespie, S. D.
1991   Ballgames and Boundaries. In *The Mesoamerican Ballgame*, edited by V. L. Scarborough and D. R. Wilcox, pp. 317–345. University of Arizona Press, Tucson.
1993   Power, Pathways, and Appropriation in Mesoamerican Art. In *Imagery and Creativity: Ethnoaesthetics and Art Worlds in the Americas*, edited by D. Whitten and N. Whitten Jr., pp. 67–107. University of Arizona Press, Tucson.

Gladwin, H. S., E. W. Haury, E. B. Sayles, and N. Gladwin
1937   *Excavations at Snaketown I: Material Culture*. Medallion Papers No. 25. Gila Pueblo, Globe, Arizona.

Goldstein, P.
1993   Tiwanaku Temples and State Expansion: A Tiwanaku Sunken-Court Temple in Moquegua, Peru. *Latin American Antiquity* 4:22–47.

Golledge, R.
2003   Human Wayfinding and Cognitive Maps. In *Colonization of Unfamiliar Landscapes*, edited by M. Rockman and J. Steele, pp. 25–43. Routledge, London.

Gonzáles, P. B.
2003   Struggle for Survival: The Hispanic Land Grants of New Mexico, 1848–2001. *Agricultural History* 77(2):293–324.

Gorenstein, S.
1973   *Tepexi el Viejo: A Postclassic Fortified Site in the Mixteca–Puebla Region of México*. American Philosophical Society, Philadelphia.

Gossen, G. H.
1986   Mesoamerican Ideas as a Foundation for Regional Synthesis. In *Symbol and Meaning Beyond the Closed Community: Essays in Mesoamerican Ideas*, edited by G. H. Gossen, pp. 1–8. Studies on Culture and Society, Vol. 1. Institute for Mesoamerican Studies, State University of New York, Albany.

Gould, R. A.
1980   *Living Archaeology*. Cambridge University Press, Cambridge.

Green, J.
1896   Letter to the Acting Assistant Adjutant General, Department of California, U.S. Army. Copy on file, White Mountain Apache Tribe Heritage Program Archives, Fort Apache, Arizona.

Greenberg, J. B.
1998   The Tragedy of Commodification: The Political Ecology of the Colorado River Delta's Distruction. *Research in Economic Anthropology* 19:133–149.

Greider, T., and L. Garkovich
1994   Landscapes: The Social Construction of Nature and the Environment. *Rural Sociology* 59:1–24.

Griffith, J. S.
1992   *Beliefs and Holy Places: A Spiritual Geography of the Pimería Alta*. University of Arizona Press, Tucson.

Grove, D. C.
1999   Public Monuments and Sacred Mountains: Observations on Three Formative Period Sacred Landscapes. In *Social Patterns in Pre-Classic Mesoamerica*, edited by D. C. Grove and R. A. Joyce, pp. 255–299. Dumbarton Oaks, Washington, D.C.

Grove, D. C., and S. D. Gillespie
1992   Ideology and Evolution at the Pre-State Level: Formative Period Mesoamerica. In *Ideology and Pre-Columbian Civilizations*, edited by A. A. Demarest and G. W. Conrad, pp. 15–36. School of American Research Press, Santa Fe.

Gumerman, G. J. (editor)
1991 *Exploring the Hohokam: Prehistoric Desert Peoples of the American Southwest*. Amerind Foundation New World Studies Series 1, Anne I. Woosley, series editor. Amerind Foundation, Dragoon, Arizona; and University of New Mexico Press, Albuquerque.

Gumerman, G. J., and E. W. Haury
1979 Prehistory: Hohokam. In *Southwest*, edited by A. Ortiz, pp. 75–90. *Handbook of North American Indians*, Vol. 9, William C. Sturtevant, general editor. Smithsonian Institution, Washington, D.C.

Gussow, A.
1995 Beauty in the Landscape: An Ecological Viewpoint. In *Landscape in America*, edited by G. F. Thompson, pp. 223–231. University of Texas Press, Austin.

Hamann, B.
2002 The Social Life of Pre-Sunrise Things. *Current Anthropology* 43(3):351–382.
2003a Reply to M. E. Smith, "What Did Mesoamerican Commoners Think About 'Pre-Sunrise Things'?" *Current Anthropology* 44(2):272–274.
2003b High Culture, Mesoamerican Civilization, and the Classic Oaxacan Tradition. Paper presented at the 68th Annual Meeting of the Society for American Archaeology, Milwaukee, Wisconsin.

Hardesty, D. L.
1980 Historic Sites Archaeology on the Western Frontier: Theoretical Perspectives and Research Problems. *North American Archaeologist* 2(1):67–81.
1991a Historical Archaeology in the American West. *Historical Archaeology* 25(3):3–5.
1991b Toward an Historical Archaeology of the Intermountain West. *Historical Archaeology* 25(3):29–35.

Hardin, G.
1968 The Tragedy of the Commons. *Science* 162: 1243–1248.
1998 Extensions of "The Tragedy of the Commons." *Science* 280:47–48.

Hassig, R.
1984 The Aztec Empire: A Reappraisal. In *Five Centuries of Law and Politics in Central Mexico*, edited by R. Spores and R. Hassig, pp. 15–24. Publications in Anthropology No. 30. Vanderbilt University, Nashville.
1985 *Trade, Tribute and Transportation: The Sixteenth-Century Political Economy of the Valley of Mexico*. University of Oklahoma Press, Norman.

Haury, E. W.
1932 *Roosevelt 9:6, a Hohokam Site of the Colonial Period*. Medallion Papers No. 11. Gila Pueblo, Globe, Arizona.
1945 *The Excavations of Los Muertos and Neighboring Ruins in the Salt River Valley, Southern Arizona*. Papers of the Peabody Museum of American Archaeology and Ethnology Vol. 24, No. 1. Harvard University, Cambridge, Massachusetts.
1950 *The Stratigraphy and Archaeology of Ventana Cave*. University of Arizona Press, Tucson; and University of New Mexico Press, Albuquerque.
1965 Pottery Types at Snaketown. In *Excavations at Snaketown: Material Culture*, by H. S. Gladwin, E. W. Haury, E. B. Sayles, and N. Gladwin, pp. 169–229. Reprinted. University of Arizona Press, Tucson. Originally published 1937, Medallion Papers No. 25, Gila Pueblo, Globe, Arizona.
1976 *The Hohokam: Desert Farmers and Craftsmen: Excavations at Snaketown, 1964–1965*. University of Arizona Press, Tucson.

Hawley, F. G.
1965 Chemical Investigation of the Incrustation on Pottery Vessels and Palettes from Snaketown. In *Excavations at Snaketown: Material Culture*, by H. S. Gladwin, E. W. Haury, E. B. Sayles, and N. Gladwin, Appendix 4, pp. 282–289. Reprinted. University of Arizona Press, Tucson. Originally published 1937, Medallion Papers No. 25, Gila Pueblo, Globe, Arizona.

Head, L.
1993 Unearthing Prehistoric Cultural Landscapes: A View from Australia. *Transactions of the Institute of British Geographers*, n.s., 18: 481–499.

Hegmon, M., S. G. Ortman, and J. L. Mobley-Tanaka
2000 Women, Men, and the Organization of Space. In *Women and Men in the Prehispanic Southwest: Labor, Power, and Prestige*, edited by P. L. Crown, pp. 43–90. School of American Research Press, Santa Fe.

Heilen, M. P.
2005 An Archaeological Theory of Landscapes. Unpublished Ph.D. dissertation, Department of Anthropology, University of Arizona, Tucson.

Heller, L.
2000 Postclassic Obsidian Workshop Debris from El Sauce, Veracruz, Mexico. *Mexicon* 22:139–146.

Heller, L., and B. L. Stark
1998 Classic and Postclassic Obsidian Tool Production and Consumption: A Regional Per-

spective from the Mixtequilla, Veracruz. *Mexicon* 20:119–128.

Henderson, T. K. (editor)
1987   *Structure and Organization at La Ciudad.* Anthropological Field Studies No. 18. Arizona State University, Tempe.

Hendon, J. A.
2002   Social Relations and Collective Identities: Household and Community in Ancient Mesoamerica. In *The Dynamics of Power*, edited by M. O'Donovan, pp. 273–300. Center for Archaeological Investigations, Occasional Paper 30. Southern Illinois University, Carbondale.
2007   Memory, Materiality, and Practice: House Societies in Southeastern Mesoamerica. In *The Durable House: House Society Models in Archaeology*, edited by R. A. Beck, pp. 292–316. Center for Archaeological Investigations, Occasional Paper 35. Southern Illinois University, Carbondale.

Hendon, J. A., and J. L. Lopiparo
2004   Investigaciones recientes en Cerro Palenque, Cortés, Honduras. In *Memoria VII Seminario de Antropología de Honduras, "Dr. George Hasemann,"* edited by C. J. Fajardo, pp. 187–195. Instituto Hondureño de Antropología e Historia, Tegucigalpa.

Hermequaftewa, A.
1953   *The Hopi Way of Life Is the Way of Peace.* Hopi Friendship Association, Santa Fe.

Herrera, A. de
1952   *Historia General de los Hechos de los Castellanos en las Islas y Tierrafirme del Mar Océano.* Década cuarta, libro séptimo. Tipografía y Archivos de la Real Academia de Historia, Madrid.

Herrera Muzgo Torres, A.
2002   Ritos postclásicos en Monte Albán. In *La Religión de los Binnigula'sa'*, edited by V. de la Cruz and M. Winter, pp. 343–370. Fondo Editorial, Instituto Estatal de Educación Pública de Oaxaca (IEEPO), Oaxaca.

Hewes, L.
1996   Making a Pioneer Landscape in the Oklahoma Territory. *Geographical Review* 86(4):588–603.

Heyden, D.
1975   La supervivencia del uso mágico de las figurillas y miniatures arqueológicas. In *XII Mesa Redonda, Sociedad Mexicana de Antropología: Historia, Religión, y Escuelas*, edited by J. Litvak King and N. Castillo Tejero, pp. 341–349. Sociedad Mexicana de Antropología, Mexico City.

Hicks, F.
1992   Subject States and Tribute Provinces: The Aztec Empire in the Northern Valley of Mexico. *Ancient Mesoamerica* 3:1–10.
1994   Alliance and Intervention in Aztec Imperial Expansion. In *Factional Competition and Political Development in the New World*, edited by E. M. Brumfiel and John W. Fox, pp. 111–116. Cambridge University Press, Cambridge.

Hill, W. D., and J. E. Clark
2001   Sports, Gambling, and Government: America's First Social Compact? *American Anthropologist* 103:331–345.

Hillier, B., and J. Hanson
1984   *The Social Logic of Space.* Cambridge University Press, Cambridge.

Hinton, R. J.
1878   *The Handbook to Arizona: Its Resources, History, Towns, Mines, Ruins and Scenery.* Arizona Silhouettes, Tucson.

Hirsch, E.
1995   Landscape: Between Place and Space. In *The Anthropology of Landscape: Perspectives on Place and Space*, edited by E. Hirsch and M. O'Hanlon, pp. 1–30. Clarendon Press, Oxford.

Hirsch, E., and M. O'Hanlon (editors)
1995   *The Anthropology of Landscape: Perspectives on Place and Space.* Clarendon Press, Oxford.

Hodder, I.
1999   *The Archaeological Process: An Introduction.* Blackwell, Malden, Massachusetts.
2002   Comment on "The Social Life of Pre-Sunrise Things" by Byron Hamaan. *Current Anthropology* 43(3):373–374.

Hodder, I., and C. Orton
1976   *Spatial Analysis in Archaeology.* Cambridge University Press, Cambridge.

Hopi Dictionary Project
1998   *Hopi Dictionary, Hopíikwa LaváyTutuveni, a Hopi–English Dictionary of the Third Mesa Dialect.* University of Arizona Press, Tucson.

Hopi Tribe
n.d.   *Hopi: The Story of Our People.* Office of Public Relations, Hopi Tribe, Kykotsmovi, Arizona.

Hornborg, A.
1998   Ecosystems and World Systems: Accumulation as an Ecological Process. *Journal of World-Systems Research* 4:169–177.
2001   *The Power of the Machine: Global Inequalities of Economy, Technology, and Enivroment.* AltaMira Press, Walnut Creek, California.

Howard, A. V.
1993   Marine Shell Artifacts and Production Processes at Shelltown and the Hind Site. In

Shelltown and the Hind Site: A Study of Two Hohokam Craftsman Communities in Southwestern Arizona, Vol. 1, edited by W. S. Marmaduke and R. J. Martynec, pp. 321–448. Northland Research, Flagstaff.

Howard, J. B.
1985 Courtyard Groups and Domestic Cycling: A Hypothetical Model of Growth. In *Proceedings of the 1983 Hohokam Symposium*, edited by A. E. Dittert Jr. and D. E. Dove, pp. 311–326. Occasional Paper No. 2. Arizona Archaeological Society, Phoenix.

Howell, B. J.
2002 *Culture, Environment, and Conservation in the Appalachian South*. University of Illinois Press, Urbana.

Hudson, J. C.
1969 A Location Theory for Rural Settlement. *Annals of the Association of American Geographers* 59:365–381.

Hunt, E.
1977 *The Transformation of the Hummingbird*. Cornell University Press, Ithaca, New York.

Huntington, F. W.
1986 *Archaeological Investigations at the West Branch Site: Early and Middle Rincon Occupation in the Southern Tucson Basin*. Anthropological Paper No. 5. Institute for American Research, Tucson.

Hutson, S. R.
2002 Built Space and Bad Subjects: Domination and Resistance at Monte Albán, Oaxaca, Mexico. *Journal of Social Archaeology* 2:53–80.

Inglis, F.
1977 Nation and Community: Landscape and Its Morality. *Sociological Review* 25:489–514.

Ingold, T.
1986 *The Appropriation of Nature*. Manchester University Press, Manchester.
1993 The Temporality of the Landscape. *World Archaeology* 25(2):152–174.

Jackson, J. B.
1984 *Discovering the Vernacular Landscape*. Yale University Press, New Haven.
1995 In Search of the Proto-Landscape. In *Landscape in America*, edited by G. F. Thompson, pp. 43–50. University of Texas Press, Austin.

Jansen, M.
1998 Monte Albán y Zaachila en los códices mixtecos. In *The Shadow of Monte Albán: Politics and Historiography in Postclassic Oaxaca, Mexico*, edited by M. Jansen, P. Krofges, and M. R. Oudijk, pp. 67–122. Research School for Asian, African, and Amerindian Studies, Leiden University, Leiden.
2004 La transición del Clásico al Posclásico, una interpretación a partir de los códices mixtecos. In *Estructuras políticas en el Oaxaca antiguo*, edited by N. M. Robles García, pp. 121–146. Instituto Nacional de Antropología e Historia, Mexico City.

Jenkins, L., T. J. Ferguson, and K. E. Dongoske
1994 A Reexamination of the Concept of *Hopitutskwa*. Paper presented at the Annual Meeting of the American Society for Ethnohistory, Tempe.

Johnston, R. J., D. Gregory, and D. M. Smith (editors)
1994 *The Dictionary of Human Geography*. 3rd ed. Blackwell, Oxford.

Jones, A.
1998 Where Eagles Dare: Landscape, Animals and the Neolithic of Orkney. *Journal of Material Culture* 3(3):301–324.

Jones, C.
2007 Archaeological Investigations in the Site Core, Quiriguá, Guatemala. In *Settlement Archaeology at Quiriguá. Quiriguá Reports, V*. University of Pennsylvania, Philadelphia.

Jones, C., W. Ashmore, and R. J. Sharer
1983 The Quiriguá Project: 1977 Season. In *Quiriguá Reports, II*, edited by R. J. Sharer, E. M. Schortman, and P. A. Urban, pp. 1–38. Paper No. 6, University Museum Monograph 49. University of Pennsylvania, Philadelphia.

Jones, C., and R. J. Sharer
1980 Archaeological Investigations in the Site Core of Quiriguá. *Expedition* 23(1):11–19.

Joyce, A. A.
2000 The Founding of Monte Albán: Sacred Propositions and Social Practices. In *Agency in Archaeology*, edited by M.-A. Dobres and J. Robb, pp. 71–91. Routledge, London.
2004 Sacred Space and Social Relations in the Valley of Oaxaca. In *Mesoamerican Archaeology*, edited by J. A. Hendon and R. A. Joyce, pp. 192–216. Blackwell, Oxford.

Joyce, A. A., L. A. Bustamante, and M. N. Levine
2001 Commoner Power: A Case Study from the Classic Period Collapse on the Oaxaca Coast. *Journal of Archaeological Method and Theory* 8(4):343–385.

Joyce, A. A., and M. Winter
1996 Ideology, Power, and Urban Society in Prehispanic Oaxaca. *Current Anthropology* 37:33–86.

Joyce, R. A.
1991 *Cerro Palenque: Power and Identity on the*

Maya Periphery. University of Texas Press, Austin.

2003 Concrete Memories: Fragments of the Past in the Classic Maya Present (500–1000 AD). In *Archaeologies of Memory*, edited by R. M. Van Dyke and S. E. Alcock, pp. 104–125. Blackwell, Oxford.

2004 Unintended Consequences? Monumentality as a Novel Experience in Formative Mesoamerica. *Journal of Archaeological Method and Theory* 11(1):5–29.

Joyce, R. A., and J. A. Hendon

2000 Heterarchy, History, and Material Reality: "Communities" in Late Classic Honduras. In *The Archaeology of Communities: A New World Perspective*, edited by M. A. Canuto and J. Yaeger, pp. 143–159. Routledge, New York.

Julian, G. W.

1979 Our Land Policy: Its Evils and Their Remedy (reprinted from Speech of Hon. George W. Julian, of Indiana, in the House of Representatives, March 6, 1868). In *The Fruits of Land Speculation*, edited by P. W. Gates. Arno Press, New York.

Keller, A. H.

2006 Roads to the Center: A Study of the Design, Use, and Abandonment of the Roads of Xunantunich, Belize. Unpublished Ph.D. dissertation, Department of Anthropology, University of Pennsylvania.

Kelley, J. C.

1966 Mesoamerica and the Southwestern United States. In *Archaeological Frontiers and External Connections*, edited by G. F. Ekholm and G. R. Willey, pp. 95–111. *Handbook of Middle American Indians*, Vol. 4, R. Wauchope, general editor. University of Texas Press, Austin.

King, T. F.

2003 *Places That Count: Traditional Cultural Properties in Cultural Resource Management*. AltaMira, Walnut Creek, California.

Kish, G.

1962 *Centuratio*: The Roman Rectangular Land Survey. *Surveying and Mapping* 22:233–244.

Knapp, A. B., and W. Ashmore

1999 Archaeological Landscapes: Constructed, Conceptualized, Ideational. In *Archaeologies of Landscape: Contemporary Perspectives*, edited by W. Ashmore and A. B. Knapp, pp. 1–30. Blackwell, Oxford.

Kowalewski, S., G. Feinman, L. Finsten, R. Blanton, and L. M. Nicholas

1989 *Monte Albán's Hinterland, Pt. II: Prehispanic Settlement Patterns in Tlacolula, Etla, and Ocotlán, the Valley of Oaxaca, Mexico*. Memoirs No. 23. Museum of Anthropology, University of Michigan, Ann Arbor.

Krall, L.

2001 US Land Policy and the Commodification of Arid Land (1862–1920). *Journal of Economic Issues* 35(3):657–674.

Küchler, S.

1993 Landscape as Memory: The Mapping of Process and Its Representation in a Melanesian Society. In *Landscape: Politics and Perspectives*, edited by B. Bender, pp. 85–106. Berg, Oxford.

Kuckelman, K. A. (editor)

2003 The Archaeology of Yellow Jacket Pueblo (Site 5MT5): Excavations at a Large Community Center in Southwestern Colorado. Electronic document, http://www.crowcanyon.org/yellowjacket, accessed July 10, 2006.

Kuus, M.

2002 Sovereignty for Security? The Discourse on Sovereignty in Estonia. *Political Geography* 21:393–412.

Kuwanwisiwma, L.

2002 *Hopit Navotiat*, Hopi Knowledge of History: Hopi Presence on Black Mesa. In *Prehistoric Culture Change on the Colorado Plateau: Ten Thousand Years on Black Mesa*, edited by S. Powell and F. E. Smiley, pp. 161–163. University of Arizona Press, Tucson.

Lakoff, G., and M. Johnson

1980 *Metaphors We Live By*. University of Chicago Press, Chicago.

Lamar, H. R.

1962 Land Policy in the Spanish Southwest, 1846–1891: A Study in Contrasts. *Journal of Economic History* 22(4):498–515.

Lane, B. C.

2002 *Landscapes of the Sacred: Geography and Narrative in American Spirituality*. Johns Hopkins University Press, Baltimore.

Lange, F., N. Mahaney, J. B. Wheat, M. L. Chenault, and J. Cater

1988 *Yellow Jacket: A Four Corners Anasazi Ceremonial Center*. Bison Books, Boulder.

Lansing, J. S.

1991 *Priests and Programmers: Technologies of Power in the Engineered Landscape of Bali*. Princeton University Press, Princeton.

Lavender, D.

1954 *Bent's Fort*. University of Nebraska Press, Lincoln.

LeCount, L. J.

2001 Like Water for Chocolate: Feasting and

Political Ritual Among the Late Classic Maya of Xunantunich, Belize. *American Anthropologist* 103:935–953.

Lekson, S. H.
1988 The Idea of the Kiva in Anasazi Archaeology. *Kiva* 53(3):213–234.
1999 *Chaco Meridian: Centers of Political Power in the Ancient Southwest*. AltaMira, Walnut Creek, California.

Leone, M. P.
1984 Interpreting Ideology in Historical Archaeology. In *Ideology, Power, and Prehistory*, edited by D. Miller and C. Tilley, pp. 25–35. Cambridge University Press, Cambridge.

Levinson, S. C.
1996 Language and Space. *Annual Review of Anthropology* 25:353–382.

Levy, R. I.
1990 *Mesocosm: Hinduism and the Organization of a Traditional Newar City in Nepal*. University of California Press, Berkeley.

Limerick, P. N.
1987 *The Legacy of Conquest: The Unbroken Past of the American West*. W. W. Norton and Co., New York.

Limerick, P. N., C. A. Milner II, and C. E. Rankin (editors)
1991 *Trails: Toward a New Western History*. University Press of Kansas, Lawrence.

Lincoln, Λ.
1865 Second Inaugural Address, March 4, Washington, D.C. http://www.bartleby.com/124/pres32.html

Lind, M.
1994 Monte Albán en el valle de Oaxca durante la fase Xoo. In *Monte Albán: Estudios Recientes*, edited by M. Winter, pp. 99–111. Contribución No. 2. del Proyecto Especial Monte Albán 1992–1994. Oaxaca.

Linklater, A.
2002 *Measuring America: How the United States Was Shaped by the Greatest Land Sale in History*. Plume-Penguin Group, New York.

Lipe, W. D.
1974 A Conservation Model for American Archaeology. *Kiva* 39:213–245.

Lipe, W. D., and M. Hegmon (editors)
1989 *The Architecture of Social Integration*. Crow Canyon Archaeological Center, Cortez, Colorado.

Lipe, W. D., M. D. Varien, and R. H. Wilshusen
1999 *Colorado Prehistory: A Context for the Southern Colorado River Basin*. Colorado Council of Professional Archaeologists, Denver.

Loma'omvaya, M., and T. J. Ferguson
1999 *Hisatqatsit Aw Maamatslalwa*—Comprehending Our Past Lifeways: Thoughts About a Hopi Archaeology. Paper presented at the 1999 Chac Mool Conference, University of Calgary, Calgary.

Loma'omvaya, M., T. J. Ferguson, and M. Yeatts
2001 *Öngtuvqava Sakwtala, Hopi Ethnobotany in the Grand Canyon*. Hopi Cultural Preservation Office, Kykotsmovi, Arizona.

Lomayaktewa, S., M. Lansa, N. Nayatewa, C. Kewanyama, J. Pongayesvla, T. Banyacya, and D. Monogya
1971 Statement of Hopi Religious Leaders. Exhibit A to *Starlie Lomayaktewa v. Rogers C. B. Morton and Peabody Coal Company*, "Complaint for Declaratory Relief and to Set Aside Agency Action," filed May 14, 1971. MS Collection #245 (Louis A. Hieb, ed., *The Hopi Traditionalist Movement, a Documentary History, 1948–1971*), Special Collections, Cline Library, Northern Arizona University, Flagstaff.

Long, J. W.
2002 Evaluating Recovery of Riparian Wetlands on the White Mountain Apache Reservation. Unpublished Ph.D. dissertation, Northern Arizona University, Flagstaff.

Long, J. W., A. Tecle, and B. Burnette
2003 Cultural Foundations for Ecological Restoration on the White Mountain Apache Reservation. *Conservation Ecology* 8(1):4. Electronic document, http://www.consecol.org/vol8/iss1/art4, accessed 2006.

Looper, M. G.
1995 The Sculpture Programs of Butz'-Tiliw, an Eighth-Century Maya King of Quiriguá, Guatemala. Unpublished Ph.D. dissertation, Department of Art History, University of Texas, Austin.
1999 New Perspectives on the Late Classic Political History of Quiriguá, Guatemala. *Ancient Mesoamerica* 9:263–280.
2001 Dance Performances at Quiriguá. In *Landscape and Power in Ancient Mesoamerica*, edited by R. Koontz, K. Reese-Taylor, and A. Headrick, pp. 113–135. Westview Press, Boulder.
2003 *Lightning Warrior*. University of Texas Press, Austin.

Lopiparo, J.
2003 *Household Ceramic Production and the Crafting of Society in the Terminal Classic Ulúa Valley, Honduras*. Ph.D. dissertation, Department of Anthropology, University of

California, Berkeley. University Microfilms, Ann Arbor.

2004 La evidencia arqueológica de la producción doméstica de las cerámicas en el valle del río Ulúa. In *Memoria VII Seminario de Antropología de Honduras, "Dr. George Hasemann,"* edited by C. J. Fajardo, pp. 151–160. Instituto Hondureño de Antropología e Historia, Tegucigalpa.

2006 Crafting Children: Materiality, Social Memory, and the (Re)Production of Terminal Classic House Societies in the Ulúa Valley, Honduras. In *The Social Experience of Childhood in Ancient Mesoamerica*, edited by T. Ardren and S. Hutson, pp. 133–168. University Press of Colorado, Boulder.

2007 House Societies and Heterarchy in the Terminal Classic Ulúa Valley, Honduras. In *The Durable House: House Society Models in Archaeology*, edited by R. A. Beck, pp. 73–96. Center for Archaeological Investigations, Occasional Paper 35. Southern Illinois University, Carbondale.

Lopiparo, J., R. A. Joyce, and J. A. Hendon

2005 Terminal Classic Pottery Production in the Ulúa Valley, Honduras. In *Geographies of Power: Understanding the Nature of Terminal Classic Pottery in the Maya Lowlands*, edited by S. L. López Varela and A. E. Foias, pp. 107–119. BAR International Series 1447. British Archaeological Reports, Oxford.

Love, M.

1999 Ideology, Material Culture, and Daily Practice in Pre-Classic Mesoamerica: A Pacific Coast Perspective. In *Social Patterns in Pre-Classic Mesoamerica*, edited by D. C. Grove and R. A. Joyce, pp. 127–154. Dumbarton Oaks, Washington, D.C.

Low, S. M.

2000 *On the Plaza: The Politics of Public Space and Culture*. University of Texas Press, Austin.

Low, S. M., and D. Lawrence-Zúñiga

2003 Locating Culture. In *The Anthropology of Space and Place: Locating Culture*, edited by S. M. Low and D. Lawrence-Zúñiga, pp. 1–47. Blackwell, Oxford.

Mack, A.

2004 One Landscape, Many Experiences: Differing Perspectives of the Temple Districts of Vijayanagara. *Journal of Archaeological Method and Theory* 11(1):59–81.

Mahaney, N., and J. R. Welch

2002 The Legacy of Fort Apache: Interpretive Challenges at a Community Historic Site. *Journal of the Southwest* 44(1):35–47.

Maines, D. R., and J. C. Bridger

1992 Narratives, Community, and Land Use Decisions. *Social Science Journal* 29(4): 363–380.

Malotki, E., and M. Lomatuway'ma

1987 *Maasaw: Profile of a Hopi God*. University of Nebraska Press, Lincoln.

Marcus, J.

1983 Aztec Military Campaigns Against the Zapotec: The Documentary Evidence. In *The Cloud People: Divergent Evolution of the Zapotec and Mixtec Civilizations*, edited by K. V. Flannery and J. Marcus, pp. 314–318. Academic Press, New York.

Marcus, J., and K. Flannery

1996 *Zapotec Civilization*. Thames and Hudson, London.

Markens, R.

2004 *Ceramic Chronology in the Valley of Oaxaca, Mexico, During the Classic and Postclassic Periods and the Organization of Ceramic Production*. Ph.D. dissertation, Department of Anthropology, Brandeis University. University Microfilms, Ann Arbor.

Markman, R. H., and P. T. Markman

1992 *The Flayed God: The Mythology of Mesoamerica: Sacred Texts and Images from Pre-Columbian Mexico and Central America*. Harper San Francisco, New York.

Marmaduke, W. S., and R. J. Martynec (editors)

1993 *Shelltown and the Hind Site: A Study of Two Hohokam Craftsman Communities in Southwestern Arizona*, Vol. 1. Northland Research, Flagstaff.

Marquina, I.

1964 *Arquitectura prehispánica*. Instituto Nacional de Antropología e Historia, Secretária de Educación Pública, Mexico City.

Martin, S., and N. Grube

2000 *Chronicle of the Maya Kings and Queens: Deciphering the Dynasties of the Ancient Maya*. Thames and Hudson, London.

Martínez López, C.

1998 Contextos mortuorios en unidades habitacionales de Monte Albán, Oaxaca, de la época II temprana a la época V. Unpublished Licenciatura thesis, Escuela Nacional de Antropología e Historia, Mexico City.

2002 La residencia de la tumba 7 y su templo: Elementos arquitectónico-religiosos en Monte Albán. In *La Religión de los Binnigula'sa'*, edited by V. de la Cruz and M. Winter, pp. 219–272. Fondo Editorial, Instituto Estatal de Educación Pública de Oaxaca (IEEPO), Oaxaca.

Martínez López, C., and R. Markens
2004 Análisis de la función político-económica del conjunto Plataforma Norte lado poniente de la Plaza Principal de Monte Albán. In *Estructuras políticas en el Oaxaca antiguo*, edited by N. M. Robles García, pp. 75–99. Instituto Nacional de Antropología e Historia, Mexico City.

Martínez López, C., M. Winter, and P. A. Juárez
2002 Las tumbas exploradas durante el Proyecto Especial Monte Albán 1992–94. Informe final, vol. 7. Instituto Nacional de Antropología e Historia, Mexico City.

Masayesva, V.
1994 The Problem of American Indian Religious Freedom: A Hopi Perspective. *American Indian Religions* 1:93–96.

Matthews, C. N.
2002 Power in Place: Site, Region, and Landscape in Historical Archaeology. In *The Dynamics of Power*, edited by O'Donovan, M., pp. 324–340. Center for Archaeological Investigations, Occasional Paper No. 30. Southern Illinois University, Carbondale.

Maudslay, A. P.
1889– *Biologia Centrali-Americana: Archaeology*,
1902 Vol. 5 [2]. Porter, London.

McAnany, P. A.
1995 *Living with the Ancestors: Kinship and Kingship in Ancient Maya Society*. University of Texas Press, Austin.

McCafferty, S. D., and G. G. McCafferty
1994 Engendering Tomb 7 at Monte Albán: Respinning an Old Yarn. *Current Anthropology* 35(2):143–166.

McClelland, L. F.
1991 Imagery, Ideals, and Social Values: The Interpretation and Documentation of Cultural Landscapes. *Public Historian* 13(2):107–124.

McClelland, L. F., J. T. Keller, G. P. Keller, and R. Z. Melnick
n.d. *Guidelines for Evaluating and Documenting Rural Historic Landscapes*. National Register Bulletin 30. U.S. Department of the Interior, National Park Service, Interagency Resources Division, Washington, D.C.

McCool, S. F., and R. N. Moisey
2001 *Tourism, Recreation and Sustainability: Linking Culture and the Environment*. Wallingford Press, New York.

McCreery, P., and E. Malotki
1994 *Tapamveni, the Rock Art Galleries of the Petrified Forest and Beyond*. Petrified Forest Museum Association, Petrified Forest, Arizona.

McGuire, R. H., and P. Reckner
2002 The Unromantic West: Labor, Capital, Struggle. *Historical Archaeology* 36(3):44–58.

McIntosh, C. B.
1976 Patterns from Land Alienation Maps. *Annals of the Association of American Geographers* 66(4):570–582.
1981 One Man's Sequential Land Alienation on the Great Plains. *Geographical Review* 71(4): 427–455.

Medellín Zenil, A.
1949 Informe de la primera exploración en Cotaxtla, Cueva Pintada, y Mictlancuauhtla. Manuscript, Archivo Técnico, Instituto Nacional de Antropología e Historia, Mexico City.
1952 *Exploraciones en Quauhtochco, Temporada I*. Gobierno del Estado de Veracruz, Jalapa.

Meighan, C. W.
1999 The Mexican West Coast and the Hohokam Region. In *The Casas Grandes World*, edited by C. F. Schaafsma and C. L. Riley, pp. 206–212. University of Utah Press, Salt Lake City.

Meinig, D. W.
1998 *The Shaping of America: A Geographical Perspective on 500 Years of History, Vol. 3: Transcontinental America, 1850–1915*. Yale University Press, New Haven.

Meskell, L.
2002 Negative Heritage and Past Mastering in Archaeology. *Anthropological Quarterly* 75(3): 557–574.
2003 Memory's Materiality: Ancestral Presence, Commemorative Practice and Disjunctive Locales. In *Archaeologies of Memory*, edited by R. M. Van Dyke and S. E. Alcock, pp. 34–55. Blackwell, Oxford.

Michaelis, H.
1981 Willowsprings: A Hopi Petroglyph Site. *Journal of New World Archaeology* 4:1–23.

Middleton, W. D., G. M. Feinman, and G. Molina Villegas
1998 Tomb Use and Reuse in Oaxaca, Mexico. *Ancient Mesoamerica* 9(2):297–308.

Miller, A. G.
1995 *The Painted Tombs of Oaxaca, Mexico*. Cambridge University Press, Cambridge.

Miller, M. E.
1985 A Re-Examination of the Mesoamerican Chacmool. *Art Bulletin* 67(1):7–17.
1988 The Meaning and Function of the Maya Acropolis, Copán. In *The Southeast Classic Maya Zone*, edited by E. H. Boone and

G. R. Willey, pp. 149–194. Dumbarton Oaks, Washington, D.C.

Miller, M. E., and K. Taube
1993   *An Illustrated Dictionary of the Gods and Symbols of Ancient Mexico and the Maya*. Thames and Hudson, New York.

Miller, R. N.
n.d.   Figurines and Ethnicity in the Late Postclassic Aztec Empire (AD 1350–1521). Manuscript on file, Department of Anthropology, Arizona State University, Tempe.

Millian, A. C.
1981   The Iconography of Aztec Ceramic Figurines. Unpublished Master's thesis, Columbia University, New York.

Millon, R.
1981   Teotihuacan: City, State, and Civilization. In *Archaeology*, edited by J. Sabloff, pp. 198–243. Supplement to the *Handbook of Middle American Indians*, Vol. 1, Victoria Bricker, general editor. University of Texas Press, Austin.

Mills, B. J., M. Altaha, T. J. Ferguson, and J. R. Welch
2008   Field Schools Without Trowels: Teaching Archaeological Ethics and Heritage Preservation in a Collaborative Context. In *Collaborating at the Trowel's Edge*, edited by S. W. Silliman, pp. 25–49. Amerind Foundation, Dragoon, Arizona.

Miranda Flores, F. A.
1998   *Proyecto Quauhtochco*. Informe Técnico Final, 1a Temporada. Manuscript, Archivo Técnico, Instituto Nacional de Antropología e Historia, Mexico City.

Moholy-Nagy, H.
1978   Social and Ceremonial Uses of Mollusks at Tikal, Guatemala. Paper presented at the 43rd Annual Meeting of the Society for American Archaeology, Tucson.

Monaghan, J.
1990   Sacrifice, Death, and the Origins of Agriculture in the Codex Vienna. *American Antiquity* 55:559–569.
1994   Sacrifice and Power in Mixtec Kingdoms. Paper presented at the 59th Annual Meeting of the Society for American Archaeology, Anaheim.
1995   *The Covenants with Earth and Rain*. University of Oklahoma Press, Norman.

Monbiot, G.
1994   The Tragedy of Enclosure. *Scientific American*, January: 159.

Moore, J. D.
1992   Pattern and Meaning in Prehistoric Peruvian Architecture: The Architecture of Social Control in the Chimu State. *Latin American Antiquity* 3:95–113.

Morley, S. G.
1935   *Guide Book to the Ruins of Quiriguá*. Supplementary Publication 16. Carnegie Institution of Washington, Washington, D.C.

Morphy, H.
1995   Landscape and the Reproduction of the Ancestral Past. In *The Anthropology of Landscape: Perspectives on Place and Space*, edited by E. Hirsch and M. O'Hanlon, pp. 184–209. Clarendon Press, Oxford.

Morris, B.
2004   What We Talk About When We Talk About "Walking in the City." *Cultural Studies* 18: 675–697.

Morris, C.
1972   State Settlement at Tawantisuyu: A Strategy of Compulsory Urbanism. In *Contemporary Archaeology*, edited by M. Leone, pp. 393–401. Southern Illinois University Press, Carbondale.
1995   Symbols to Power: Styles and Media in the Inka State. In *Style, Society, and Person: Archaeological and Ethnological Perspectives*, edited by C. Carr and J. E. Neitzel, pp. 419–433. Plenum Press, New York.

Mowry, S.
1857   *Memoir of the Proposed Territory of Arizona*. Henry Polkinhorn, Washington, D.C.

Mrozowski, S. A., and M. C. Beaudry
1990   Archaeology and the Landscape of Corporate Ideology. In *Earth Patterns: Essays in Landscape Archaeology*, edited by W. M. Kelso and R. Most, pp. 189–208. University Press of Virginia, Charlottesville.

Myers, F.
1991   *Pintupi Country, Pintupi Self*. University of California Press, Berkeley.

Nabhan, G. P.
1997   *Cultures of Habitat*. Counterpoint, Washington, D.C.

National Park Service
1994   *Mesa Verde National Park, Colorado*. U.S. Government Printing Office, Washington, D.C.

Naveh, Z.
1998   Ecological and Cultural Landscape Restoration and the Cultural Evolution: Toward a Post-Industrial Symbiosis Between Human Society and Nature. *Restoration Ecology* 6: 135–143.

Neitzel, J. E. (editor)
2003   *Pueblo Bonito: Center of the Chacoan World*.

Smithsonian Institution Press, Washington, D.C.

Nelson, M.
2000   Abandonment: Conceptualization, Representation, and Social Change. In *Social Theory in Archaeology*, edited by M. B. Schiffer, pp. 52–62. University of Utah Press, Salt Lake City.

Netting, R. McC.
1993   *Smallholders, Stakeholders*. University of Arizona Press, Tucson.

Nials, F., D. A. Gregory, and D. A. Graybill
1989   Salt River Streamflow and Hohokam Irrigation Systems. In *Environment and Subsistence*, edited by C. Heathington and D. Gregory, pp. 59–78. *The 1982–1984 Excavations at Las Colinas*, Vol. 5. Archaeological Series 162. Arizona State Museum, University of Arizona, Tucson.

Nielsen, A. E.
1995   Architectural Performance and the Reproduction of Social Power. In *Expanding Archaeology*, edited by J. M. Skibo, W. H. Walker, and A. E. Nielsen, pp. 47–66. University of Utah Press, Salt Lake City.

Noble, D. (editor)
2006   *The Mesa Verde World*. School of American Research Press, Santa Fe.

Norton, W.
1989   *Explorations in the Understanding of Landscape*. Greenwood Press, New York.

Nugent, W.
1991   Frontiers and Empires in the Late Nineteenth Century. In *Trails: Toward a New Western History*, edited by P. N. Limerick, C. A. Milner II, and C. E. Rankin, pp. 161–181. University Press of Kansas, Lawrence.

Ohnersorgen, M. A.
2001   Social and Economic Organization in the Postclassic Gulf Lowlands: A View from Cotaxtla, Veracruz, Mexico. Unpublished Ph.D. dissertation, Arizona State University, Tempe.
2006   Aztec Provincial Administration at Cuetlaxtlan, Veracruz. *Journal of Anthropological Archaeology* 25:1–32.

Olson, J. M.
2001   Unequal Consumption: A Study of Domestic Wealth Differentials in Three Late Postclassic Mexican Communities. Unpublished Ph.D. dissertation, University at Albany, State University of New York, Albany.

Orozco, R., and R. Bronson
1991   *Proyecto Arqueológico Izabal, Fase II*. Unpublished report on file at the Centro de Investigaciones Regionales de Mesoamérica, Antigua, Guatemala.

Orr, H. S.
1997   *Power Games in the Late Formative Valley of Oaxaca: The Ballplayer Sculptures at Dainzú*. Ph.D. dissertation, Department of Art and Art History, University of Texas. University Microfilms, Ann Arbor.
2001   Processsion Rituals and Shrine Sites: The Politics of Sacred Space in the Late Formative Valley of Oaxaca. In *Landscape and Power in Ancient Mesoamerica*, edited by R. Koontz, K. Reese-Taylor, and A. Headrick, pp. 55–79. Westview Press, Boulder.

Ortman, S. G.
2000   Conceptual Metaphor in the Archaeological Record: Methods and an Example from the American Southwest. *American Antiquity* 65: 613–645.

Ortman, S. G., and B. A. Bradley
2002   Sand Canyon Pueblo: The Container in the Center. In *Seeking the Center Place: Archaeology and Ancient Communities in the Mesa Verde Region*, edited by M. D. Varien and R. H. Wilshusen, pp. 41–78. University of Utah Press, Salt Lake City.

O'Tuathail, G.
1996   *Critical Geopolitics: The Politics of Writing Global Space*. University of Minnesota Press, Minneapolis.

Oudijk, M. R.
2002   The Zapotec City-State. In *A Comparative Study of Six City-State Cultures*, edited by M. H. Hansen, pp. 73–90. Royal Academy of Sciences and Letters, Copenhagen.

Owens, B. McC.
2002   Monumentality, Identity, and the State: Local Practice, World Heritage, and Heterotopia at Swayambhu, Nepal. *Anthropological Quarterly* 75:269–316.

Page, J.
1982   Inside the Sacred Hopi Homeland. *National Geographic* 162(5):606–629.

Panelli, M. D.
1984   *An Ethnoarchaeological Study of Homesteading in Central Nevada*. University of Nevada, Reno.

Parker, G.
1998   *Geopolitics: Past, Present, and Future*. Pinter, London.

Parker Pearson, M., J. Pollard, C. Richards, J. Thomas, C. Tilley, K. Welham, and U. Albarella
2006   Materializing Stonehenge: The Stonehenge Riverside Project and New Discoveries. *Journal of Material Culture* 11:227–261.

Parker Pearson, M., and Ramilisonina
1998   Stonehenge for the Ancestors: The Stones Pass on the Message. *Antiquity* 72:308–326.

Parker Pearson, M. P., and C. Richards (editors)
1994   *Architecture and Order: Approaches to Social Space*. Routledge, New York.

Parsons, E. C.
1936   *Mitla: Town of the Souls*. University of Chicago Press, Chicago.

Parsons, M. H.
1972   Aztec Figurines from the Teotihuacan Valley, Mexico. In *Miscellaneous Studies in Mexican Prehistory*, edited by M. W. Spence, J. R. Parsons, and M. H. Parsons, pp. 81–117. Anthropological Papers No. 45. Museum of Anthropology, University of Michigan, Ann Arbor.

Paso y Troncoso, F. del (editor)
1905–   *Papeles de Nueva España. Segunda serie,*
 1906   *geografía y estadística*, 7 vols. Tipográfico Sucesores de Rivandeneyra, Mexico City.

Pasztory, E.
1997   *Teotihuacan: An Experiment in Living*. University of Oklahoma Press, Norman.

Patterson, T. C.
1987   Tribes, Chiefdoms, and Kingdoms in the Inca Empire. In *Power Relations and State Formation*, edited by C. W. Gailey, pp. 117–127. Sheffield, Salem, Wisconsin.
1991   *The Inca Empire: The Formation and Disintegration of a Pre-Capitalist State*. Berg, New York.

Pauketat, T. R.
1998   Refiguring the Archaeology of Greater Cahokia. *Journal of Archaeological Research* 6(1):45–89.
2000   The Tragedy of the Commoners. In *Agency in Archaeology*, edited by M.-A. Dobres and J. Robb, pp. 113–129. Routledge, London.

Pauketat, T. R., and S. M. Alt
2003   Mounds, Memory, and Contested Mississippian History. In *Archaeologies of Memory*, edited by R. M. Van Dyke and S. E. Alcock, pp. 151–179. Blackwell, Oxford.

Pauls, E. P.
2006   The Place of Space: Architecture, Landscape, and Social Life. In *Historical Archaeology*, edited by M. Hall and S. W. Silliman, pp. 65–83. Blackwell, Oxford.

Percy, W.
1958   Metaphor as Mistake. *Sewanee Review* 66:79–99.

Pohl, J. M. D.
1999   The Lintel Paintings of Mitla and the Function of the Mitla Palaces. In *Mesoamerican Architecture as a Cultural Symbol*, edited by J. K. Kowalski, pp. 176–197. Oxford University Press, New York.
2002   Los dinteles pintados de Mitla. *Arqueología Mexicana* 10(55):64–67.
2003a   Creation Stories, Hero Cults, and Alliance Building: Confederacies of Central and Southern Mexico. In *The Postclassic Mesoamerican World*, edited by M. E. Smith and F. F. Berdan, pp. 61–66. University of Utah Press, Salt Lake City.
2003b   Royal Marriage and Confederacy Building Among the Eastern Nahuas, Mixtecs, and Zapotecs. In *The Postclassic Mesoamerican World*, edited by M. E. Smith and F. F.Berdan, pp. 243–248. University of Utah Press, Salt Lake City.
2005   The Arroyo Group Lintel Painting at Mitla, Oaxaca. In *Painted Books and Indigenous Knowledge in Mesoamerica: Manuscript Studies in Honor of Mary Elizabeth Smith*, edited by E. H. Boone, pp. 109–127. Middle American Research Institute Publication 69. Tulane University Press, New Orleans.

Pohl, J. M. D., J. Monaghan, and L. Stiver
1997   Religion, Economy, and Factionalism in Mixtec Boundary Zones. In *Códices y Documentos sobre México: Segundo Simposio, Vol. 1*, edited by S. Rueda Smithers, C. Vega Sosa, and R. Martínez Baracas, pp. 205–232. Instituto Nacional de Antropología e Historia y Consejo Nacional para la Cultura y las Artes, Mexico City.

Pohl, M.
1983   Maya Ritual Faunas: Vertebrate Remains from Burials, Caches, Caves, and Cenotes in the Maya Lowlands. In *Civilization in the Ancient Americas: Essays in Honor of Gordon R. Willey*, edited by R. M. Leventhal and A. L. Kolata, pp. 55–103. University of New Mexico Press, Albuquerque; and Peabody Museum of Archaeology and Ethnology, Harvard University, Cambridge, Massachusetts.

Polanyi, K.
1957   *The Great Transformation*. Beacon Press, Boston.

Pool, C. A.
1992   Strangers in a Strange Land: Ethnicity and Ideology at an Enclave Community in Middle Classic Mesoamerica. In *Ancient Images, Ancient Thought: The Archaeology of Ideology*, edited by A. S. Goldsmith, pp. 41–55. University of Calgary, Calgary.
2006   Current Research on the Gulf Coast of

Mexico. *Journal of Archaeological Research* 14:189–241.

Pred, A.
1984 Place as Historically Contingent Process: Structuration and the Time-Geography of Becoming Places. *Annals of the Association of American Geographers* 74:279–297.

Preucel, R. W.
1996 Cooking Status: Hohokam Ideology, Power, and Social Reproduction. In *Interpreting Southwestern Diversity: Underlying Principles and Overarching Patterns*, edited by P. R. Fish and J. J. Reid, pp. 125–131. Anthropological Research Papers No. 48. Arizona State University, Tempe.

Purser, M.
1999 *Ex Occidente Lux?* An Archaeology of Later Capitalism in the Nineteenth-Century West. In *Historical Archaeologies of Capitalism*, edited by M. P. Leone and P. B. Potter Jr., pp. 115–141. Kluwer Academic/Plenum, New York.

Quirarte, J.
1977 The Ballcourt in Mesoamerica: Its Architectural Development. In *Pre-Columbian Art History*, edited by A. Cordy-Collins and J. Stern, pp. 191–212. Peek, Palo Alto.

Rafferty, K.
1982 Hohokam Micaceous Schist Mining and Ceramic Craft Specialization: An Example from Gila Butte, Arizona. *Anthropology* 6:199–222.

Ramos Gomez, J. H.
2006 Temple 16: Yax Pasaj and the Revival of Antiquity at Late Classic Copán. Unpublished Ph.D. dissertation, Department of Anthropology, University of California, Riverside.

Rapoport, A.
1989 On the Attributes of "Tradition." In *Dwellings, Settlements and Tradition: Cross-Cultural Perspectives*, edited by J.-P. Bourdier and N. Alsayyad, pp. 77–105. International Association for the Study of Traditional Environments, University Press of America, Lanham, Maryland.
1990 *The Meaning of the Built Environment: A Nonverbal Communication Approach*. University of Arizona Press, Tucson.

Rathje, W. L., and M. B. Schiffer
1982 *Archaeology*. Harcourt Brace Jovanovich, New York.

Redfield, R., and A. Villa Rojas
1962 *Chan Kom: A Maya Village*. University of Chicago Press, Chicago.

Reese-Taylor, K., and R. Koontz
2001 The Cultural Poetics of Power and Space in Ancient Mesoamerica. In *Landscape and Power in Ancient Mesoamerica*, edited by R. Koontz, K. Reese-Taylor, and A. Headrick, pp. 1–27. Westview Press, Boulder.

Reid, J. J., and M. P. Heilen
2005 *Collection of Cultural Resource Information at Sanford Ranch*. Submitted to the Bureau of Land Management, Tucson Area Field Office, Tucson.

Reid, J. J., and S. Whittlesey
1997 *The Archaeology of Ancient Arizona*. University of Arizona Press, Tucson.

Rice, J. G.
1978 The Effect of Land Alienation on Settlement. *Annals of the Association of American Geographers* 68(1):61–72.

Rice, P. M.
1999 Rethinking Classic Lowland Maya Pottery Censers. *Ancient Mesoamerica* 10:25–50.

Richards, C. C.
1996 Monuments as Landscape: Creating the Centre of the World in Late Neolithic Orkney. *World Archaeology* 28:190–208.

Ringle, W. M.
1999 Pre-Classic Cityscapes: Ritual Politics Among the Early Lowland Maya. In *Social Patterns in Pre-Classic Mesoamerica*, edited by D. C. Grove and R. A. Joyce, pp. 183–223. Dumbarton Oaks, Washington, D.C.

Robin, C.
2002 Outside of Houses: The Practices of Everyday Life at Chan Nòohol, Belize. *Journal of Social Archaeology* 2:245–268.

Robinson, E. J. (editor)
1987 *Interaction on the Southeast Mesoamerican Periphery: Prehistoric and Historic Honduras and El Salvador*. BAR International Series 327. British Archaeological Reports, Oxford.

Robles García, N. M.
2001a Breve historia de las discusiones sobre Monte Albán. In *Procesos de cambio y conceptualización del tiempo: Memoria de la primera mesa redonda de Monte Albán*, edited by N. M. Robles García, pp. 13–21. Instituto Nacional de Antropología e Historia, Mexico City.

Robles García, N. M. (editor)
2001b *Procesos de cambio y conceptualización del tiempo: Memoria de la primera mesa redonda de Monte Albán*. Instituto Nacional de Antropología e Historia, Mexico City.

Rodman, M.
1992 Empowering Place: Multilocality and

Multivocality. *American Anthropologist* 94:640–656.

Rohn, A. H.
1982 Budding Urban Settlements in the Northern San Juan. In *Proceedings of the First Anasazi Symposium*, edited by J. E. Smith, pp. 175–180. Mesa Verde Museum Association, Mesa Verde National Park, Mesa Verde, Colorado.

Rossignol, J., and L. Wandsnider (editors)
1992 *Space, Time, and Archaeological Landscapes*. Plenum Press, New York.

Russell, F.
1908 *The Pima Indians*. 26th Annual Report of the Bureau of American Ethnology, 1904–1905. Smithsonian Institution, Washington, D.C.

Rykwert, J.
1988 *The Idea of a Town: The Anthropology of Urban Form in Rome, Italy and the Ancient World*. Massachussetts Institute of Technology Press, Cambridge.

Sahagún, F. B. de
1950– *Florentine Codex: General History of the Things of New Spain*, 13 vols. Edited and translated by Arthur J. O. Anderson and Charles E. Dibble. University of Utah, Salt Lake City; and School of American Research, Santa Fe.
1953 The Sun, Moon, and Stars, and the Binding of the Years. In *Florentine Codex: General History of the Things of New Spain*, Book 7. Translated by A. J. O. Anderson and C. E. Dibble. University of Utah, Salt Lake City; and School of American Research, Santa Fe.
1976 *A History of Ancient Mexico, 1547–1577: The Religion and Ceremonies of the Aztec Indians*. Rio Grande Press, Glorieta, New Mexico.

Sahlins, M.
1996 The Sadness of Sweetness: The Native Anthropology of Western Cosmology. *Current Anthropology* 37(3):395–428.

Sanders, W. T., J. R. Parsons, and R. S. Santley
1979 *The Basin of Mexico: Ecological Processes in the Evolution of a Civilization*. Academic Press, New York.

Santley, R. S., C. M. Yarborough, and B. A. Hall
1987 Enclaves, Ethnicity, and the Archaeological Record at Matacapan. In *Ethnicity and Culture*, edited by R. Auger, M. F. Glass, S. MacEachern, and P. H. McCartney, pp. 85–100. Archaeological Association of the University of Calgary, Calgary.

Sauder, R. A.
1989 Patenting an Arid Frontier: Use and Abuse of the Public Land Laws in Owens Valley, California. *Annals of the Association of American Geographers* 79(4):544–569.

Sauer, C. O.
1925 The Morphology of Landscapes. *University of California Publications in Geography* 2(2):19–54.

Scarborough, V. L.
1991 Courting in the Southern Maya Lowlands: A Study in Pre-Hispanic Ballgame Architecture. In *The Mesoamerican Ballgame*, edited by V. L. Scarborough and D. R. Wilcox, pp. 129–144. University of Arizona Press, Tucson.

Schaafsma, P.
1999 Tlalocs, Kachinas, Sacred Bundles, and Related Symbolism in the Southwest and Mesoamerica. In *The Casas Grandes World*, edited by C. F. Schaafsma and C. L. Riley, pp. 164–192. University of Utah Press, Salt Lake City.

Schama, S.
1995 *Landscape and Memory*. Vintage Books, New York.

Schaniel, W. C., and W. C. Neale
1999 Quasi Commodities in the First and Third Worlds. *Journal of Economic Issues* 33:95–115.

Schele, L.
1990a Early Quiriguá and the Kings of Copán. *Copán Notes* 75. Austin and Tegucigalpa.
1990b Speculations from an Epigrapher on Things Archaeological. *Copán Notes* 80. Austin and Tegucigalpa.

Schele, L., and D. A. Freidel
1990 *A Forest of Kings: The Untold Story of the Ancient Maya*. William Morrow, New York.

Schele, L., and J. Guernsey Kappelman
2001 What the Heck's Coatépec? The Formative Roots of an Enduring Mythology. In *Landscape and Power in Ancient Mesoamerica*, edited by R. Koontz, K. Reese-Taylor, and A. Headrick, pp. 29–53. Westview Press, Boulder.

Schele, L., and M. E. Miller
1986 *The Blood of Kings: Dynasty and Ritual in Maya Art*. Kimball Art Museum, Fort Worth.

Schiffer, M. B.
1982 Hohokam Chronology: An Essay on History and Method. In *Hohokam and Patayan: Prehistory of Southwestern Arizona*, edited by R. H. McGuire and M. B. Schiffer, pp. 299–344. Academic Press, New York.
1995 Social Theory and History in Behavioral Archaeology. In *Expanding Archaeology*, edited by J. M. Skibo, W. H. Walker, and A. E. Nielsen, pp. 22–35. University of Utah Press, Salt Lake City.
2000 Indigenous Theories, Scientific Theories and Product Histories. In *Matter, Materiality*

and Modern Culture, edited by P. G. Brown, pp. 72–96. Routledge, London.

Schiffer, M. B., and A. R. Miller
1999 *The Material Life of Human Beings: Artifacts, Behavior, and Communication*. Routledge, London.

Schill, K.
1993 Hopis Honor Vast Land. *Arizona Daily Sun* 48(56):1, 13.

Schlanger, S.
1992 Recognizing Persistent Places in Anasazi Settlement Systems. In *Space, Time, and Archaeological Landscapes*, edited by J. Rossignol and L. Wandsnider, pp. 91–112. Plenum Press, New York.

Schoenwetter, J., and J. W. Hohmann
1997 Land Use Reconstruction at the Founding Settlement of Las Vegas, Nevada. *Historical Archaeology* 31(4):41–58.

Schortman, E. M.
1986 Interaction Between the Maya and Non-Maya Along the Late Classic Southeast Maya Periphery: The View from the Lower Motagua Valley, Guatemala. In *The Southeast Maya Periphery*, edited by P. A. Urban and E. M. Schortman, pp. 114–137. University of Texas Press, Austin.
1989 Interregional Interaction in Prehistory: The Need for a New Perspective. *American Antiquity* 54:52–65.
1993 Archaeological Investigations in the Lower Motagua Valley, Izabal, Guatemala. *Quiriguá Reports, III*. University Museum Monograph 80. University of Pennsylvania, Philadelphia.

Schortman, E. M., and S. Nakamura
1991 A Crisis of Identity: Late Classic Competition and Interaction on the Southeast Maya Periphery. *Latin American Antiquity* 2:311–336.

Schreiber, K. M.
1992 *Wari Imperialism in Middle Horizon Peru*. Museum of Anthropology Papers No. 87. University of Michigan, Ann Arbor.

Schroeder, S.
2004 Power and Place: Agency, Ecology, and History in the American Bottom, Illinois. *Antiquity* 78:812–827.

Schuyler, R. L.
1991 Historical Archaeology in the American West: The View from Philadelphia. *Historical Archaeology* 25(3):7–17.

Schwartz, D. W.
1989 *On the Edge of Splendor, Exploring Grand Canyon's Human Past*. School of American Research Press, Santa Fe.

Scott, J. C.
1990 *Domination and the Arts of Resistance: Hidden Transcripts*. Yale University Press, New Haven.

Scott, J. F.
1978a *The Danzantes of Monte Albán, Pt. I: Text*. Studies in Pre-Columbian Art and Archaeology No. 19. Dumbarton Oaks, Washington, D.C.
1978b *The Danzantes of Monte Albán, Pt. II: Catalogue*. Studies in Pre-Columbian Art and Archaeology No. 19. Dumbarton Oaks, Washington, D.C.

Seaman, P. D.
1985 *Hopi Dictionary*. Northern Arizona University Anthropological Paper No. 2. Department of Anthropology, Northern Arizona University, Flagstaff.

Secakuku, F.
1993 The Hopi View of Wilderness. *Federal Archaeology Report* 6(3):9.

Séjourné, L.
1976 *Burning Water: Thought and Religion in Ancient Mexico*. Random House, New York.

Shackel, P. A.
2003 Archaeology, Memory, and Landscapes of Conflict. *Historical Archaeology* 37(3):3–13.

Sharer, R. J.
1978 Archaeology and History at Quiriguá, Guatemala. *Journal of Field Archaeology* 5:51–70.
1988 Quiriguá as a Classic Maya Center. In *The Southeast Classic Maya Zone*, edited by E. H. Boone and G. R. Willey, pp. 31–65. Dumbarton Oaks, Washington, D.C.
1990 *Quiriguá: A Classic Maya Center and Its Sculptures*. Centers of Civilization Series. Carolina Academic Press, Durham.
2002 Early Classic Dynastic Origins in the Southeastern Maya Lowlands. In *Incidents of Archaeology in Central America and Yucatan: Essays in Honor of Edwin M. Shook*, edited by M. W. Love, M. Popenoe de Hatch, and H. L. Escobedo, pp. 459–476. University Press of America, Lanham, Maryland.

Sharer, R. J., and W. R. Coe
1979 The Quiriguá Project: Origins, Objectives and Research in 1973 and 1974. In *Quiriguá Reports, I*, edited by R. J. Sharer and W. Ashmore, pp. 1–11. Paper No. 1, Monograph 37. University of Pennsylvania Museum, Philadelphia.

Sharer, R. J., J. C. Miller, and L. P. Traxler
1992 Evolution of Classic Period Architecture in the Eastern Acropolis, Copán: A Progress Report. *Ancient Mesoamerica* 3:145–159.

Sharer, R. J., D. W. Sedat, L. P. Traxler, J. C. Miller, and E. E. Bell
2005   Early Classic Royal Power in Copán: The Origins and Development of the Acropolis (ca. AD 250–600). In *Copán: The History of an Ancient Maya Kingdom*, edited by E. W. Andrews and W. L. Fash, pp. 139–199. School of American Research Press, Santa Fe.

Sharer, R. J., L. P. Traxler, D. W. Sedat, E. E. Bell, M. A. Canuto, and C. Powell
1999   Early Classic Architecture Beneath the Copán Acropolis: A Research Update. *Ancient Mesoamerica* 10:3–23.

Sheridan, T. E.
1995   *Arizona: A History*. University of Arizona Press, Tucson.
2006   *Landscapes of Fraud: Mission Tumacácori, the Baca Float, and the Betrayal of the O'Odham*. University of Arizona Press, Tucson.

Silverstein, J.
2000   A Study of the Late Postclassic Aztec–Tarascan Frontier in Northern Guerrero, México: The Oztuma-Cutzamala Project. Unpublished Ph.D. dissertation, Department of Anthropology, Pennsylvania State University, University Park.
2001   Aztec Imperialism at Oztuma, Guerrero: Aztec–Chontal Relations During the Late Postclassic and Early Colonial Periods. *Ancient Mesoamerica* 12:31–48.

Simmons, L. W. (editor)
1942   *Sun Chief: The Autobiography of a Hopi Indian*. Yale University Press, New Haven.

Sinopoli, C. M.
2003   Echos of Empire: Vijayanagara and Historical Memory, Vijayanagara as Historical Memory. In *Archaeologies of Memory*, edited by R. M. Van Dyke and S. E. Alcock, pp. 17–33. Blackwell, Oxford.

Skoglund, T., B. L. Stark, H. Neff, and M. D. Glascock
2006   Compositional and Stylistic Analysis of Aztec-Era Ceramics: Provincial Strategies at the Edge of Empire, South-Central Veracruz, Mexico. *Latin American Antiquity* 17:541–559.

Smith, A.
1996   Imperial Archipelago: The Making of the Urartian Landscapes in Southern Transcaucasia. Unpublished Ph.D. dissertation, Department of Anthropology, University of Arizona, Tucson.

Smith, A. L.
1961   Types of Ballcourts in the Highlands of Guatemala. In *Essays in Pre-Columbian Art and Archaeology*, edited by S. K. Lothrop, pp. 100–125. Harvard University Press, Cambridge, Massachusetts.

Smith, D. A.
2002   *Mesa Verde National Park: Shadows of the Centuries*. University Press of Colorado, Boulder.

Smith, J. E.
1987   *Mesas, Cliffs and Canyons: The University of Colorado Survey of Mesa Verde National Park 1971–1977*. Mesa Verde Research Series 3. Mesa Verde Museum Association, Mesa Verde, Colorado.

Smith, Mary E.
1973   *Picture Writing from Ancient Southern Mexico: Mixtec Place Signs and Maps*. University of Oklahoma Press, Norman.

Smith, Michael E.
1986   The Role of Social Stratification in the Aztec Empire: A View from the Provinces. *American Anthropologist* 88:70–91.
1987   The Expansion of the Aztec Empire: A Case Study in the Correlation of Diachronic Archaeological and Ethnohistoric Data. *American Antiquity* 52:37–54.
1990   Long-Distance Trade Under the Aztec Empire: The Archaeological Evidence. *Ancient Mesoamerica* 1:153–169.
1992   *Archaeological Research in Aztec-Period Rural Sites in Morelos, Mexico, Vol. 1: Excavations and Architecture*. Memoirs in Latin American Archaeology No. 4. Department of Anthropology, University of Pittsburgh, Pittsburgh.
1994   Social Complexity in the Aztec Countryside. In *Archaeological Views from the Countryside: Village Communities in Early Complex Societies*, edited by G. Schwartz and S. Falconer, pp. 143–159. Smithsonian Institution Press, Washington, D.C.
2001   The Aztec Empire and the Mesoamerican World System. In *Empires: Perspectives from Archaeology and History*, edited by S. E. Alcock, T. N. D'Altroy, K. D. Morrison, and C. M. Sinopoli, pp. 128–154. Cambridge University Press, Cambridge.
2003   *Comercio postclásico en la cerámica decorada: Malinalco, Toluca, Guerrero y Morelos*. Departamento de Arqueología, Instituto Nacional de Antropología e Historia, Mexico City.

Smith, M. E., and F. F. Berdan
1992   Archaeology of the Aztec Empire. *World Archaeology* 23:353–367.
2003   Postclassic Mesoamerica. In *The Postclassic Mesoamerican World*, edited by M. E. Smith and F. F. Berdan, pp. 3–13. University of Utah Press, Salt Lake City.

Solís Olgún, F. R.
1986 La estructura piramidal de Castillo de Teayo: Un edificio en proceso constructivo o un peculiar estilo arquitectónico. In *Cuadernos de Arquitectura Mesoamericana* 8:73–79. División de Estudios de Posgrado, Facultad de Arquitectura, Universidad Nacional Autónoma de México, Mexico City.

Speaker, J. S.
2001 Settlement and Agricultural Land Use in Ancient Mixtequilla, Veracruz, Mexico. Unpublished Ph.D. dissertation, Department of Anthropology, Tulane University, New Orleans.

Spencer, C. S., and E. M. Redmond
2001 Multilevel Selection and Political Evolution in the Valley of Oaxaca, 500–100 BC. *Journal of Anthropological Archaeology* 20:195–229.

Spores, R.
1984 *The Mixtecs in Ancient and Colonial Times*. University of Oklahoma Press, Norman.

Stark, B. L.
1974 Geography and Economic Specialization in the Lower Papaloapan, Veracruz, Mexico. *Ethnohistory* 21:199–221.
1990 The Gulf Coast and the Central Highlands of Mexico: Alternative Methods for Interaction. *Research in Economic Anthropology* 12:243–285.
1991 *Settlement Archaeology of Cerro de las Mesas*. Institute of Archaeology, University of California, Los Angeles.
1995 Introducción a la alfarería del posclásico en La Mixtequilla, sur-centro de Veracruz. *Arqueología* 13–14:17–36.
1999 Formal Architectural Complexes in South-Central Veracruz, Mexico: A Capital Zone? *Journal of Field Archaeology* 26:197–225.
2007 Diachronic Change in Crafts and Centers in South-Central Veracruz, Mexico. In *Craft Production in Complex Societies: Multicraft and Producer Perspectives*, edited by Izumi Shimada, pp. 227–261. University of Utah Press, Salt Lake City.

Stark, B. L., and C. P. Garraty
2004 Evaluation of Systematic Surface Evidence for Pottery Production in Veracruz. *Latin American Antiquity* 15:123–143.

Stark, B. L., L. Heller, and M. A. Ohnersorgen
1998 People with Cloth: Mesoamerican Economic Change from the Perspective of Cotton in South-Central Veracruz. *Latin American Antiquity* 9:1–30.

Stark, M. T., J. M. Vint, and J. M. Heidke
1995 Compositional Variability in Utilitarian Ceramics at a Colonial Period Site. In *Ceramic Chronology, Technology, and Economics*, edited by J. M. Heidke and M. T. Stark, pp. 273–295. Roosevelt Community Development Study, Vol. 2. Anthropological Papers No. 14. Center for Desert Archaeology, Tucson.

State Historical Society of Colorado
1979 *Bent's Old Fort*. State Historical Society of Colorado, Denver.

Stephen, A. M.
1929 Hopi Tales. *Journal of American Folklore* 42:1–72.

Sternberg, E.
1993 Justifying Public Intervention Without Market Externalities: Karl Polanyi's Theory of Planning in Capitalism. *Public Administration Review* 53(2):100–109.

Steward, J. H.
1955 *Theory of Culture Change: The Methodology of Multilinear Evolution*. University of Illinois Press, Urbana.

Steward, J. H., and F. M. Seltzer
1938 Function and Configuration in Archaeology. *American Antiquity* 4(1):4–10.

Stewart, A. M., D. Keith, and J. Scottie
2004 Caribou Crossings and Cultural Meanings: Placing Traditional Knowledge and Archaeology in Context in an Inuit Landscape. *Journal of Archaeological Method and Theory* 11:183–211.

Stille, A.
2002 *The Future of the Past*. Farrar, Strauss, and Giroux, New York.

Stoddart, S. (editor)
2000 *Landscapes from Antiquity*. Antiquity Papers 1. Antiquity Publications, Cambridge.

Stoffle, R. W., D. B. Halmo, and D. E. Austin
1997 Cultural Landscapes and Traditional Culture Properties: A Southern Paiute View of the Grand Canyon and Colorado River. *American Indian Quarterly* 21(2):229–249.

Stoffle, R. W., and M. N. Zedeño
2001a American Indian Worldviews I: The Concept of "Power" and Its Connection to People, Places, and Resources. In *American Indians and the Nevada Test Site*, edited by R. W. Stoffle, M. N. Zedeño, and D. B. Halmo, pp. 58–76. U.S. Government Printing Office, Washington, D.C.
2001b American Indian Worldviews II: Power and Cultural Landscapes. In *American Indians and the Nevada Test Site*, edited by R. W. Stoffle, M. N. Zedeño, and D. B. Halmo, pp. 139–152. U.S. Government Printing Office, Washington, D.C.

Stoffle, R. W., M. N. Zedeño, J. K. Eyrich, and P. Barabe
2000   *The Wellington Canyon Ethnographic Study at Pintwater Range, Nevada*. Bureau of Applied Research in Anthropology, University of Arizona, Tucson.

Stone, A. J.
1983   The Zoomorphs of Quiriguá. Unpublished Ph.D. dissertation, Department of Art History, University of Texas, Austin.

Stromsvik, G.
1941   *Substela Caches and Stela Foundations at Copán and Quiriguá*. Publication 528, Contribution 37. Carnegie Institution of Washington, Washington, D.C.

Stuart, D.
1984   Blood Symbolism in Maya Iconography. *Res* 7/8:6–20.
1998   "The Fire Enters His House": Architecture and Ritual in Classic Maya Texts. In *Function and Meaning in Classic Maya Architecture*, edited by S. D. Houston, pp. 373–425. Dumbarton Oaks, Washington, D.C.

Sugiyama, S.
1993   Worldview Materialized in Teotihuacan, Mexico. *Latin American Antiquity* 4(2):103–129.

Sullivan, L. E. (editor)
2000   *Native Religions and Cultures of North America: Anthropology of the Sacred*. Continuum Press, New York.

Swanton, J. R.
1952   *The Indian Tribes of North America*. Smithsonian Institution Bureau of American Ethnology Bulletin 145. U.S. Government Printing Office, Washington, D.C.

Talahaftewa (and Others)
1949   Letter to the President of the United States, March 28, 1949. MS Collection #245 (Louis A. Hieb, ed., *The Hopi Traditionalist Movement, a Documentary History, 1948–1971*), Special Collections, Cline Library, Northern Arizona University, Flagstaff.

Taube, K. A.
1998   The Jade Hearth: Centrality, Rulership, and the Classic Maya Temple. In *Function and Meaning in Classic Maya Architecture*, edited by S. D. Houston, pp. 427–478. Dumbarton Oaks, Washington, D.C.
2000   The Turquoise Hearth: Fire, Self-Sacrifice, and the Central Mexican Cult of War. In *Mesoamerica's Classic Heritage: From Teotihuacan to the Aztecs*, edited by D. Carrasco, L. Jones, and S. Sessions, pp. 269–340. University Press of Colorado, Boulder.
2004   Structure 10L-16 and Its Early Classic Antecedents: Fire and the Evocation and Resurrection of K'inich Yax K'uk' Mo'. In *Understanding Early Classic Copán*, edited by E. E. Bell, M. A. Canuto, and R. J. Sharer, pp. 265–295. University of Pennsylvania Museum, Philadelphia.

Thomas, D. H.
1973   An Empirical Test of Steward's Model of Great Basin Subsistence. *American Antiquity* 38:155–176.
1974   An Archaeological Perspective on Shoshonean Bands. *American Anthropologist* 76:11–23.
1981   Complexity Among Great Basin Shoshoneans: The World's Least Affluent Hunter-Gatherers? In *Affluent Foragers: Pacific Coast East and West*, edited by S. Koyama and D. H. Thomas, pp. 19–52. Senri Ethnological Studies No. 9. National Museum of Ethnology, Osaka.

Thomas, J.
1993   The Politics of Vision and the Archaeologies of Landscape. In *Landscape: Politics and Perspectives*, edited by B. Bender, pp. 49–84. Berg, Oxford.
2001   Archaeologies of Place and Landscape. In *Archaeological Theory Today*, edited by I. Hodder, pp. 165–186. Polity Press, Malden, Massachusetts.

Thompson, G. F.
1995   A Message to the Reader. In *Landscape in America*, edited by G. F. Thompson, pp. xi–xiv. University of Texas Press, Austin.

Thurston, T. L.
1999   The Knowable, the Doable, and the "Becoming" of Rural Landscapes in Denmark's Iron Age. *Antiquity* 73:661–671.

Tilden, F.
1957   *Interpreting Our Heritage; Principles and Practices for Visitor Services in Parks, Museums, and Historic Places*. University of North Carolina Press, Chapel Hill.

Tilley, C.
1993   Art, Architecture, Landscape [Neolithic Sweden]. In *Landscape: Politics and Perspectives*, edited by B. Bender, pp. 49–84. Berg, Oxford.
1994   *A Phenomenology of Landscape: Places, Paths and Monuments*. Berg, Oxford.
1999   *Metaphor and Material Culture*. Blackwell, Oxford.
2004   Mind and Body in Landscape Research. *Cambridge Archaeological Journal* 14(1):77–80.

Tilley, C., and W. Bennett
2001   An Archaeology of Supernatural Places: The

Case of West Penwith. *Journal of the Royal Anthropological Institute* 7(2):335–362.

Torquemada, F. J. de
1943 *Monarquía indiana*, 3 vols. Editorial Salvador Chávez Hayhoe, Mexico City.
1969 *Monarquía indiana*, 3 vols. Porrúa, Mexico City.

Townsend, R. F.
1992a The Renewal of Nature at the Temple of Tlaloc. In *The Ancient Americas: Art from Sacred Landscapes*, edited by R. F. Townsend, pp. 171–186. Art Institute of Chicago, Chicago.
1992b *The Aztecs*. Thames and Hudson, London.

Tozzer, A. M. (translator)
1941 *Landa's Relación de las Cosas de Yucatán: A Translation*. Papers of the Peabody Museum of American Archaeology and Ethnology 18. Harvard University, Cambridge, Massachusetts.

Traxler, L. P.
2001 The Royal Court of Early Classic Copán. In *Royal Courts of the Ancient Maya, Vol. 2: Data and Case Studies*, edited by T. Inomata and S. D. Houston, pp. 44–73. Westview Press, Boulder.
2004 Redesigning Copán: Early Architecture of the Polity Center. In *Understanding Early Classic Copán*, edited by E. E. Bell, M. A. Canuto, and R. J. Sharer, pp. 51–64. University of Pennsylvania Museum, Philadelphia.

Tress, B., and G. Tress
2001 Capitalizing on Multiplicity: A Transdisciplinary Systems Approach to Landscape Research. *Landscape and Urban Planning* 57(3–4):143–157.

Tuan, Y.
1977 *Space and Place: The Perspective of Experience*. University of Minnesota Press, Minneapolis.

Turner, C. G.
1963 *Petroglyphs of the Glen Canyon Region, Styles, Chronology, Distribution, and Relationships from Basketmaker to Navajo*. Museum of Northern Arizona Bulletin 38. Glen Canyon Series No. 4. Museum of Northern Arizona, Flagstaff.

Umberger, E.
1996 Aztec Presence and Material Remains in the Outer Provinces. In *Aztec Imperial Strategies*, by F. F. Berdan, R. E. Blanton, E. H. Boone, M. G. Hodge, M. E. Smith, and E. Umberger, pp. 151–179. Dumbarton Oaks Research Library and Collection, Washington, D.C.

Umberger, E., and C. Klein
1993 Aztec Art and Imperial Expansion. In *Latin American Horizons*, edited by D. S. Rice, pp. 295–336. Dumbarton Oaks, Washington, D.C.

Urban, P. A., and E. M. Schortman
1988 The Southeast Zone Viewed from the East: Lower Motagua–Naco Valleys. In *The Southeast Classic Maya Zone*, edited by E. H. Boone and G. R. Willey, pp. 223–267. Dumbarton Oaks, Washington, D.C.

Urban, P. A., and E. M. Schortman (editors)
1986 *The Southeast Maya Periphery*. University of Texas Press, Austin.

Urcid, J., and M. Winter
2003 Nuevas variantes glíficas zapotecas. *Mexicon* 25:123–128.

Urcid, J., M. Winter, and R. Matadamas
1994 Nuevos monumentos grabados en Monte Albán, Oaxaca. In *Escritura zapoteca prehispánica*, edited by M. Winter, pp. 2–52. Contribución No. 4. del Proyecto Especial Monte Albán 1992–1994. Oaxaca.

Urcid Serrano, J.
1992 *Zapotec Hieroglyphic Writing*. Ph.D. dissertation, Department of Anthropology, Yale University. University Microfilms, Ann Arbor.
1994a Mound J at Monte Albán and Zapotec Political Geography During Period II (200 BC–AD 200). Paper presented at the 59th Annual Meeting of the Society for American Archaeology, Anaheim.
1994b Un sistema de nomenclatura para los monolitos grabados y los materiales con inscripciones de Monte Albán. In *Escritura zapoteca prehispánica*, edited by M. Winter, pp. 53–79. Contribución No. 4. del Proyecto Especial Monte Albán 1992–1994. Oaxaca.
2001 *Zapotec Hieroglyphic Writing*. Dumbarton Oaks Studies in Pre-Columbian Art and Archaeology 34. Washington, D.C.
2005 *Zapotec Writing: Knowledge, Power, and Memory in Ancient Oaxaca*. Foundation for the Advancement of Mesoamerican Studies, Inc., Crystal River, Florida. Available at http://www.famsi.org/zapotecwriting/.
2008 The Writing Surface as a Cultural Code: A Comparative Perspective of Scribal Traditions from Southwestern Mesoamerica. Paper presented at the Scripts and Notational Systems in Pre-Columbian America Symposium, Dumbarton Oaks, Washington, D.C.

Uzes, F. D.
1977 *Chaining the Land: A History of Surveying in California*. Landmark Enterprises, Sacramento.

Vanderpot, R., S. D. Shelley, and S. Benaron
1994 Riser Site AZ U:8:225/1580. In *Prehistoric*

Rural Settlements in the Tonto Basin, edited by R. Ciolek-Torrello, S. D. Shelley, and S. Benaron, pp. 292–337. Roosevelt Rural Sites Study, Vol. 2, Pt. 1. Technical Series 28. Statistical Research, Tucson.

van Dommelen, P.
1999 Exploring Everyday Places and Cosmologies. In *Archaeologies of Landscape: Contemporary Perspectives*, edited by W. Ashmore and A. B. Knapp, pp. 277–285. Blackwell, Oxford.

Van Dyke, R. M.
2003 Memory and the Construction of Chacoan Society. In *Archaeologies of Memory*, edited by R. M. Van Dyke and S. E. Alcock, pp. 180–200. Blackwell, Oxford.

Van Dyke, R. M., and S. E. Alcock (editors)
2003 *Archaeologies of Memory*. Blackwell, Oxford.

Van Ness, J. R.
1976 Spanish American vs. Anglo American Land Tenure and the Study of Economic Change in New Mexico. *Social Science Journal* 13(3):45–50.

van Zantwijk, R.
1981 The Great Temple at Tenochtitlan: Models of Aztec Cosmovision. In *Mesoamerican Sites and World-Views*, edited by E. P. Benson, pp. 71–84. Dumbarton Oaks Research Library and Collections, Washington, D.C.

Vogt, E. Z.
1969 *Zinacantan*. Harvard University Press, Cambridge, Massachusetts.
1976 *Tortillas for the Gods: A Symbolic Analysis of Zinacantan Ritual*. Harvard University Press, Cambridge, Massachusetts.
1981 Some Aspects of the Sacred Geography of Highland Chiapas. In *Mesoamerican Sites and World-Views*, edited by E. P. Benson, pp. 119–142. Dumbarton Oaks Research Library and Collections, Washington, D.C.

Wagoner, J. J.
1970 *Arizona Territory 1863–1912: A Political History*. University of Arizona Press, Tucson.

Walker, D. E.
1991 Protection of American Indian Sacred Geography. In *Handbook of American Indian Religious Freedom*, edited by C. Vecsey, pp. 100–115. Crossroad, New York.

Walker, W. H.
1995 Ceremonial Trash? In *Expanding Archaeology*, edited by J. Skibo, W. H. Walker, and A. Nielsen, pp. 67–79. University of Utah Press, Salt Lake City.

Wallace, H. D.
1995 *Archaeological Investigations at Los Morteros, a Prehistoric Settlement in the Northern Tucson Basin*. Anthropological Papers No. 17. Center for Desert Archaeology, Tucson.

Wallace, H. D., J. M. Heidke, and W. H. Doelle
1995 Hohokam Origins. *Kiva* 60(4):575–618.

Wallace, H. D., and J. P. Holmlund
1986 *Petroglyphs of the Picacho Mountains, South Central Arizona*. Anthropological Papers No. 6. Institute for American Research, Tucson.

Wallerstein, I.
1974 *The Modern World System I: Capitalist Agriculture and the Origins of the European World-Economy in the Sixteenth Century*. Academic Press, New York.

Walsh-Anduze, M. E.
1993 The Sourcing of Hohokam Red-on-Buff Ceramics Using Inductively Coupled Plasma Spectroscopy: "Schist Happens." Unpublished Master's thesis, Department of Anthropology, Northern Arizona University, Flagstaff.

Waring, A. J., Jr.
1968 The Southern Cult and Muskhogean Ceremonial. In *The Waring Papers: The Collected Works of Antonio J. Waring, Jr.*, edited by S. Williams, pp. 9–29. Papers of the Peabody Museum of Archaeology and Ethnology Vol. 58. Harvard University, Cambridge, Massachusetts.

Waring, A. J., Jr., and P. Holder
1968 A Prehistoric Ceremonial Complex in the Southeastern United States. In *The Waring Papers: The Collected Works of Antonio J. Waring, Jr.*, edited by S. Williams, pp. 30–69. Papers of the Peabody Museum of Archaeology and Ethnology Vol. 58. Harvard University, Cambridge, Massachusetts.

Watkins, J.
2000 *Indigenous Archaeology*. AltaMira Press, Walnut Creek, California.

Weaver, M. P.
1981 *The Aztecs, Maya, and Their Predecessors: Archaeology of Mesoamerica*. 2nd ed. Studies in Archaeology, Academic Press, New York.

Webster, D.
1999 The Archaeology of Copán, Honduras. *Journal of World Prehistory* 7(11):1–53.

Wedel, W.
1941 *Environment and Native Subsistence Economies in the Central Great Plains*. Smithsonian Miscellaneous Collections 101(3). Smithsonian Institution, Washington, D.C.
1953 Some Aspects of Human Ecology in the Central Great Plains. *American Anthropologist* 55(4):499–514.

1977   The Education of a Plains Archeologist. *Plains Anthropologist* 22(75):1–11.

Weed, C. S., and A. E. Ward
1970   The Henderson Site: Colonial Hohokam in North Central Arizona. *Kiva* 36:1–12.

Welch, J. R.
1994   Ethnographic Models for Tonto Basin Land Use. In *Changing Land Use in the Tonto Basin*, edited by R. S. Ciolek-Torrello and J. R. Welch, pp. 79–120. The Roosevelt Rural Sites Study, Vol. 3: Technical Series 28. SRI Press, Statistical Research, Tucson.
1997   White Eyes' Lies and the Battle for *Dzil Nchaa Si An*. *American Indian Quarterly* 27(1):75–109.
2000   The White Mountain Apache Tribe Heritage Program: Origins, Operations, and Challenges. In *Working Together: Native Americans and Archaeologists*, edited by K. E. Dongoske, M. Aldenderfer, and K. Doehner, pp. 67–83. Society for American Archaeology, Washington, D.C.
2002   The Rodeo-Chediski Fire and Cultural Resources. *Arizona Archaeological Council Newsletter* 26(3):1–3.
2004   *National Historic Landmark Nomination for Fort Apache and Theodore Roosevelt School*. Submitted to the National Parks Advisory Board, Washington, D.C.
2007   A Monument to Native American Civilization: Byron Cummings' Still-Unfolding Vision for Kinishba Ruins. *Journal of the Southwest* 49:1–94.
2008   *Fort Apache and Theodore Roosevelt School National Historic Landmark Nomination*. Under consideration by the National Historic Landmarks Subcommittee of the Secretary of the Interior's Advisory Board on National Parks and Monuments. Washington, D.C.

Welch, J. R., and T. J. Ferguson
2005   *Cultural Affiliation Assessment of White Mountain Apache Tribal Lands (Fort Apache Indian Reservation)*. Historic Preservation Office, Heritage Program, White Mountain Apache Tribe, Fort Apache, Arizona.
2007   Putting Patria into Repatriation: Cultural Affiliations of White Mountain Apache Tribe Lands. *Journal of Social Archaeology* 7:171–198.
2008   Putting *Patria* Back into Repatriation: Cultural Affiliation Assessment of White Mountain Apache Tribal Lands. *Journal of Social Archaeology* 7:171–198.

Welch, J. R., N. Mahaney, and R. Riley
2000   The Reconquest of Fort Apache: The White Mountain Apache Tribe Reclaims Its History and Culture. *Cultural Resource Management* 23(9):16–19.

Welch, J. R., and R. Riley
2001   Reclaiming Land and Spirit in the Western Apache Homeland. *American Indian Quarterly* 25(1):5–12.

Wellman, K. D., and A. Dart
1996   Feature Descriptions. In *Archaeological Data Recovery Project at the Cook Avenue Locus of the West Branch Site, AZ AA:16:3 (ASM)*, edited by A. Dart and D. L. Swartz, pp. 21–52. Technical Report No. 96-9. Center for Desert Archaeology, Tucson.

Western, D. R., M. Wright, and S. C. Strum (editors)
1994   *Natural Connections: Perspectives in Community-Based Conservation*. Island Press, Washington, D.C.

Whalen, M. E.
1988   Small Community Organization During the Late Formative Period in Oaxaca, Mexico. *Journal of Field Archaeology* 15:291–306.

Wheatley, P.
1971   *The Pivot of the Four Quarters: A Preliminary Inquiry into the Origins and Character of the Ancient Chinese City*. Aldine, Chicago.

Whiteley, P. M.
1989   *Hopitutskwa*: An Historical and Cultural Interpretation of the Hopi Traditional Land Claim. Manuscript on file, Hopi Cultural Preservation Office, Kykotsmovi, Arizona.

Whitridge, P.
2004   Landscapes, Houses, Bodies, Things: "Place" and the Archaeology of Inuit Imaginaries. *Journal of Archaeological Method and Theory* 11(2):213–250.

Whittaker, G.
1980   *The Hieroglyphics of Monte Albán*. Ph.D. dissertation, Department of Anthropology, Yale University. University Microfilms, Ann Arbor.

Whittlesey, S. M.
1998a   Archaeological Landscapes: A Methodological and Theoretical Discussion. In *Vanishing River: Landscapes and Lives of the Lower Verde Valley: The Lower Verde Archaeological Project. Overview, Synthesis, and Conclusions*, edited by S. M. Whittlesey, R. Ciolek-Torrello, and J. H. Altschul, pp. 17–28. SRI Press, Tucson.
1998b   Rethinking the Core–Periphery Model of the Pre-Classic Period Hohokam. In *Vanishing River: Landscapes and Lives of the Lower Verde Valley: The Lower Verde Archaeological Project. Overview, Synthesis, and Conclu-

sions, edited by S. M. Whittlesey, R. Ciolek-Torrello, and J. H. Altschul, pp. 597–628. SRI Press, Tucson.

2003 *Rivers of Rock: Stories from a Stone-Dry Land: Central Arizona Project Archaeology*. SRI Press, Tucson.

Whittlesey, S. M. (editor)
2004 *Pots, Potters, and Models: Archaeological Investigations at the West Branch Site*. Technical Series 80. SRI Press, Tucson.

Whittlesey, S. M., R. Ciolek-Torrello, and J. H. Altschul (editors)
1998 *Vanishing River: Landscapes and Lives of the Lower Verde Valley: The Lower Verde Archaeological Project. Overview, Synthesis, and Conclusions*. SRI Press, Tucson.

Widdison, J. G. (editor)
1991 *The Anasazi, Why Did They Leave? Where Did They Go?* Southwest Natural and Cultural Heritage Association, New Mexico University, Albuquerque.

Wilcox, D. R.
1979 The Hohokam Regional System. In *An Archaeological Test of Sites in the Gila Butte–Santan Region, South-Central Arizona*, edited by G. Rice, D. Wilcox, K. Rafferty, and J. Schoenwetter, pp. 77–116. Technical Papers No. 3. Anthropological Research Papers No. 18. Arizona State University, Tempe.

1991 The Mesoamerican Ballgame in the American Southwest. In *The Mesoamerican Ballgame*, edited by V. L. Scarborough and D. R. Wilcox, pp. 101–125. University of Arizona Press, Tucson.

Wilcox, D. R., T. R. McGuire, and C. Sternberg
1981 *Snaketown Revisited: A Partial Cultural Resource Survey, Analysis of Site Structure, and an Ethnohistoric Study of the Proposed Hohokam–Pima National Monument*. Archaeological Series No. 155. Arizona State Museum, University of Arizona, Tucson.

Wilcox, D. R., and L. O. Shenk
1977 *The Architecture of the Casa Grande and Its Interpretation*. Archaeological Series No. 115. Arizona State Museum, University of Arizona, Tucson.

Wilcox, D. R., and C. Sternberg
1983 *Hohokam Ballcourts and Their Interpretation*. Archaeological Series No. 160. Arizona State Museum, University of Arizona, Tucson.

Willey, G. R.
1973 Mesoamerican Art and Iconography and the Integrity of the Mesoamerican Ideological System. In *The Iconography of Middle American Sculpture*, by I. Bernal, M. D. Coe, G. Kubler, G. R. Willey, J. E. Thompson, pp. 153–161. Metropolitan Museum of Art, New York.

Wilson, G. L.
1928 Hidatsa Eagle Trapping. *Anthropological Papers of the American Museum of Natural History* 30(4):99–245.

Wilson, R. (editor)
2002 *A Certain Somewhere: Writers on the Places They Remember*. Random House, New York.

Wingard, J. D.
1996 Interactions Between Demographic Processes and Soil Resources in the Copán Valley, Honduras. In *The Managed Mosaic: Ancient Maya Agriculture and Resource Use*, edited by S. L. Fedick, pp. 207–235. University of Utah Press, Salt Lake City.

Winter, M.
1974 Residential Patterns at Monte Albán, Oaxaca, Mexico. *Science* 186(4168):981–987.

1989 *Oaxaca: The Archaeological Record*. Minutiae Mexicana, Mexico City.

1995 Introducción. In *Entierros humanos de Monte Albán*, edited by M. Winter, pp. 2–9. Contribución No. 7 del Proyecto Especial Monte Albán 1992–1994. Centro Instituto Nacional de Antropología e Historia, Oaxaca.

2001 Palacios, templos y 1300 años de vida urbana en Monte Albán. In *Reconstruyendo la ciudad maya: El Urbanismo en las sociedades antiguas*, edited by A. Ciudad Ruiz, M. J. I. Ponce de Léon, and M. del Carmen Martínez Martínez, pp. 253–301. Sociedad Española de Estudios Mayas, Madrid.

2003 Monte Albán and Late Classic Site Abandonment in Highland Oaxaca. In *The Archaeology of Settlement Abandonment in Middle America*, edited by T. Inomata and R. W. Webb, pp. 103–119. University of Utah Press, Salt Lake City.

Woodward, C.
2001 *In Ruins: A Journey Through History, Literature and Art*. Vintage Books, New York.

Wylie, A.
1985 The Reaction Against Analogy. In *Advances in Archaeological Method and Theory*, Vol. 8, edited by M. B. Schiffer, pp. 63–112. Academic Press, Orlando.

1993 Invented Lands/Discovered Pasts: The Westward Expansion of Myth and History. *Historical Archaeology* 27(4):1–19.

Yaeger, J.
2000 The Social Construction of Communities in the Classic Maya Countryside: Strategies of Affiliation in Western Belize. In *The

Archaeology of Communities: A New World Perspective, edited by M. A. Canuto and J. Yaeger, pp. 123–142. Routledge, New York.

Yaeger, J., and M. A. Canuto
2000   Introducing an Archaeology of Communities. In *The Archaeology of Communities: A New World Perspective*, edited by M. A. Canuto and J. Yaeger, pp. 1–15. Routledge, New York.

Yamin, R., and K. B. Metheny (editors)
1996   *Landscape Archaeology: Reading and Interpreting the American Historical Landscape*. University of Tennessee Press, Knoxville.

Yava, A.
1978   *Big Falling Snow*. Edited by H. Courlander. Crown, New York.

Yorke, S. S.
2006   More Things of Heaven and Earth: Reading Ancient Landscapes of the Americas. Unpublished Ph.D. dissertation, Department of Anthropology, Rutgers, State University of New Jersey, New Brunswick.

Zedeño, M. N.
1997   Landscapes, Land Use, and the History of Territory Formation: An Example from the Puebloan Southwest. *Journal of Archaeological Method and Theory* 4:67–103.

2000   On What People Make of Places: A Behavioral Cartography. In *Social Theory in Archaeology*, edited by M. B. Schiffer, pp. 97–111. University of Utah Press, Salt Lake City.

Zedeño, M. N., D. Austin, and R. Stoffle
1997   Landmark and Landscape: A Contextual Approach to the Management of American Indian Resources. *Culture and Agriculture* 19(3):123–129.

Zedeño, M. N., K. L. Hollenback, and C. Grinnell
2009   From Path to Myth: Journeys and the Naturalization of Nation Along the Missouri River. In *The Anthropology of Paths, Trails, and Roads*, edited by James E. Snead, Clark L. Erickson, and J. Andrew Darling. University of Pennsylvania Press, Philadelphia.

Zedeño, M. N., and N. Laluk
2008   When Is a Site Culturally Viable? Landscape Evolution and Ojibwa Heritage Building on the St. Croix National Scenic Riverway, Minnesota and Wisconsin. *Heritage Management* 1(1):71–98.

Zedeño, M. N., R. Stoffle, G. Dewey-Hefley, and D. Shaul
1999   *Storied Rocks: American Indian Inventory and Interpretation of Rock Art on the Nevada Test Site*. Desert Research Institute Technical Reports No. 93. University of Nevada, Las Vegas.

Contributors

Wendy Ashmore is a professor of anthropology at the University of California, Riverside.

Brenda J. Bowser is an assistant professor of anthropology at California State University, Fullerton.

T. J. Ferguson owns Anthropological Research, LLC, in Tucson, where he is also a professor of practice in anthropology at the University of Arizona.

Christopher P. Garraty is an adjunct faculty member in the School of Human Evolution and Social Change, Arizona State University, Tempe.

Michael P. Heilen is a research director and principal investigator at Statistical Research Incorporated in Tucson.

Julia A. Hendon is an associate professor of anthropology at Gettysburg College.

Arthur A. Joyce is an associate professor of anthropology at the University of Colorado, Boulder.

Rosemary A. Joyce is a professor of anthropology and chair of the Department of Anthropology at the University of California, Berkeley.

Leigh J. Kuwanwisiwma is the director of the Hopi Cultural Preservation Office and a member of the Greasewood Clan at Paaqavi Village on Third Mesa, Arizona.

Stephen H. Lekson is a curator and professor of anthropology at the University of Colorado, Boulder.

Jeanne Lopiparo is an assistant professor of anthropology at Rhodes College, Memphis.

Michael A. Ohnersorgen is an assistant professor of anthropology at the University of Missouri, St. Louis.

J. Jefferson Reid is a professor of anthropology and University Distinguished Professor at the University of Arizona, Tucson.

John R. Welch is an associate professor and Canada Research Chair in Indigenous Heritage Stewardship at Simon Fraser University, British Columbia.

Stephanie M. Whittlesey is a senior principal investigator at SWCA Environmental Consultants, Flagstaff.

María Nieves Zedeño is an associate research anthropologist at the Bureau of Applied Research in Anthropology and an associate professor of anthropology at the University of Arizona, Tucson.

Index

abandonment: of Mesa Verde, 175–76; and persistent places, 12. *See also* settlement patterns

Acosta, Jorge, 48

acropolis, and architecture of Classic Maya sites, 19, 22, 27, 29

agency, and archaeology of place, 5–6

Agnew, J. A., 1

Agricultural College Act of 1862, 142–43

agriculture: and cultural landscape of Hohokam, 77, 78, 87; and cultural landscape of Hopi, 94, 97–98. *See also* food preparation and production

Akimel O'odham (Pima), 79

Alcock, S. E., 107

ancestral villages, and cultural landscape of Hopi, 95–97, 105

Ang Kuktota, and cultural landscape of Hopi, 92–95

Anschuetz, K. F., 76

anthropology, and landscape as metaphor, 74

Apache: and Anglo-American settlement on Arizona frontier, 145; and reconstruction of sense of place, 149–62

Arapaho (Colorado), 175

archaeology: and authenticity in preservation or reconstruction of sites, 173–75; and concept of meaningful places, 13; and development of frameworks for place, 4–13; and field schools in Arizona, 157; interpretation of public places in contemporary, 163, 178n1, 179n8; and reconstructive place making by indigenous nations, 160–61; and revisionist histories, 177; role of in definition of Hopi cultural landscapes, 90–106; and spatial analyses, 53. *See also* architecture; art; burials; historical archaeology; mounds; obsidian; pottery; shell artifacts

architecture: of Bent's Old Fort, 169; ceremonial at Snaketown (Hohokam), 81; and material culture in outer provinces of Aztec empire, 119–22; meaning and spatial organization at Quiriguá, 19–22. *See also* acropolis; ballcourts; pit structures; plazas

Arizona: landscape and commodification of land during frontier period, 132–48; Ndee (Western Apache) and reconstruction of sense of place, 149–62. *See also* Hohokam

Arnold, Samuel P., 172, 173, 174

art: and cultural landscape of Hohokam, 78; and imperial ideology in outer provinces of Aztec empire, 119–22; and portraits of Zapotec nobles, 39–40. *See also* petroglyphs; sculpture

Ashenhurst, Harold, 165–66

Ashmore, Wendy, 2–3, 5, 9, 53, 55, 56, 58, 74, 88, 151, 160

authenticity, and reconstruction or preservation of archaeological sites, 173–75

authority, communal identity and sacred at Monte Albán, 34–39

Aztec: and creation myths, 47, 83, 85; and invasion of Valley of Oaxaca, 45; imperial landscape and geopolitics of control of empire, 107–29

Aztec Ruins (New Mexico), 167

ballcourts: and Classic Maya sites in Honduras, 56–57, 63–70, 71; and Hohokam sites, 77, 78, 81, 86

Barrett, John C., 34, 50

Basso, Keith H., 1, 2, 12, 76, 149, 151–52, 155

Becker, M. J., 86

Bender, B., 107, 127

Bent, Charles, 170

Bent & St. Vrain Company, 170

Bent's Old Fort (Colorado), 163, 168–73, 174–75, 176–77, 179n6

Berdan, F. F., 110, 114

Bernal, Ignacio, 48

Besh-ba-gowa (Arizona), 167

Binford, Lewis, 1, 4, 7, 178n1

biographies, of place: and Classic Maya site of

215

Index

Quiriguá, 15–31; and frameworks for archaeological research, 9; and main plaza of Monte Albán, 32–51
Blanton, R. E., 40, 124
Boone, E. H., 110, 111, 122
Bostwick, T. W., 85
Bowser, Brenda J., 5
Bradley, B. A., 76–77
Bradley, R. J., 31, 34, 50
Brown, Linda A., 29
Brumfiel, E. M., 108, 123, 124, 128
built environment, and concept of place, 5
Bureau of American Ethnology, 173
Bureau of Indian Affairs (BIA), 91, 154, 155
burials: and cultural landscape of Hohokam, 78, 86, 89; and cultural landscape of Hopi, 97; and main plaza of Monte Albán, 45
burnt offerings, and rituals at Quiriguá, 28–30

caches, and termination rituals at Quiriguá, 27–28
Cahokia (Illinois/Missouri), 15
Calakmul (Yucatan), 26
California: and Hispanic/Anglo-American conflicts over land titles, 141; homesteading policies and land tenure in, 142–43
Callejón del Horno (Mexico), and geopolitics of Aztec empire, 109, 113, 117, 122–24, 126, 127, 129
capitalism, and commodification of land in American West, 143–44
Carrasco, P., 113, 118
Caso, Alfonso, 48
Castellanos, A., 46
Castillo de Teayo (Veracruz, Mexico), 120
Cather, Willa, 164
caves: and cultural landscape of Hohokam, 88; as metaphors at Classic Maya sites, 85
Cerro Oztuma (Veracruz, Mexico), 117, 120, 127, 129n2
Cerro Palenque (Honduras), 54–71
Chaco Canyon (New Mexico), 15, 176, 177
Chapman, William S., 142–43
Charlton, T. H., 130n5
Charnay, Désireé, 48
Cheyenne (Colorado), 175
chronology, of Hohokam, 79
Cibecue (Arizona), 149
city planning models, 19
civic gatherings, at Quiriguá, 30
Civilian Conservation Corps, 167
clan glyphs (Hopi), 100–101, 104
Cleere, H., 88
cliff dwellings: frequency of in thirteenth century, 175; preservation of in American West, 168. *See also* Manitou Cliff Dwellings; Mesa Verde National Park
Cocijo (Zapotec god), 37, 38

Codex Mendoza (Berdan and Anawalt 1997), 124
Coggins, Clemency, 19
cognitive dimension, of cultural landscapes, 75, 80–85
Cohen, S. B., 109
colonialism: and geopolitical landscape of Cotaxtla, 118–22; and Hispanic conceptualizations of land, 140–43; and main plaza of Monte Albán, 47–48, 50
Colorado, and interpretation of archaeological and historic places, 163–77
Colorado Cliff Dwellings Association, 164, 166
Colorado Historical Society, 171
Colorado Springs (Colorado), 165
comales (tortilla griddles), 124–25, 131n10
Comer, Douglas C., 173, 177
commodification, of land on frontier of American West, 132–48
community: perceptions of landscapes and formation of, 118; place and continuity of at Quiriguá, 25–30, 50–51
Copán (Guatemala): and ballcourt, 64; comparison of with Cerro Palenque, 54–60; Quiriguá and biographies of place, 18–19, 22, 24, 26–27, 30
Cosgrove, D. E., 2
cosmology: and ballcourts in Mesoamerica, 64; and construction projects of Maya elites, 55–56; and cultural landscape of Hohokam, 80, 81; dualities in Mesoamerican, 81; and main plaza of Monte Albán, 33, 46
Cotaxtla (provincial capital of Cuetlaxtlan), and geopolitics of Aztec empire, 108, 112, 113, 114, 117, 118–22, 128, 130n6-7. *See also* Cuetlaxtlan
Cotaxtla Archaeological Survey, 112
creation myths: and main plaza of Monte Albán, 42–47, 50, 51; symbolism in Mesoamerican, 37. *See also* oral traditions
Crosby, W. S., 165–66
Crow Canyon Archaeological Center (Colorado), 174
Crumley, C. L., 75
Cuetlaxtlan (Veracruz, Mexico), and geopolitics of Aztec empire, 108, 111–13, 114, 122–27. *See also* Cotaxtla
cultural landscape: definition of, 73, 74; meaning and metaphor in Hohokam, 73–89; role of archaeological sites in definition of Hopi, 90–106

Daughters of the American Revolution, 170–71
David, B., 5
de Certeau, Michel, 71
defensive structures, and ceremonial spaces at Monte Albán, 35, 45. *See also* warfare
desert(s), and cultural landscape of Hohokam, 77
Desert Archaeology, Inc., 102–4
Desert Land Act of 1877, 139
Double Butte Cave (Arizona), 88
Duncan, J. S., 107, 129

Dupaiz, Guillaume, 48
Durán, Diego, 119

economics. *See* agriculture; capitalism; commodification; globalization; land tenure; Tragedy of the Commons
Eggan, F., 95–96
elites: and control of Aztec empire, 110–11, 116–18, 125–26; and control of ceremonial space in Mesoamerica, 34; cosmology and construction projects of Maya, 55–56; and emergence of empires, 108; and main plaza of Monte Albán, 38, 39–42, 45–47
El Palenque (Oaxaca Valley), 39, 49
El Sauce (Mexico), 108–9, 123, 125, 129, 131n11
emplacement, and orientation of Classic Maya settlements, 60, 63
Entrikin, J. Nicholas, 54
Environmental Protection Agency, 156
ethnicity, and imperial colonialism in Veracruz (Mexico), 118–22
Evans, S. T., 120
exchange value, and commodification of land, 141

Far View House (Chaco Canyon), 176
Fauman-Fichman, R., 124
Ferguson, T. J., 3, 10, 13
fictitious commodities, 136
fire rituals, and Classic Maya, 28–30
Flores, D. L., 73
food preparation and production: and cultural landscape of Hopi, 98–99; and feasting at Quiriguá, 30; and place networks, 10. *See also* agriculture
formal dimension, of cultural landscape, 75, 85–86
Fort Apache Heritage Foundation, 157
Fort Apache Indian Reservation (Arizona), 150, 153, 154, 167
Fort Apache and Theodore Roosevelt School Historic Park, 157, 158
Fort restaurant (Colorado), 163, 168, 172, 173
Fort Vasquez (Colorado), 174, 178–79n4
Foster, G., 101
Foucault, Michel, 5, 60
Fouschee, Richard E., 171
Fox, John G., 67
Frazer, S., 83
frontier, and commodification of land in Arizona, 132–48
Fung, Christopher, 69
fur trade, and Bent's Old Fort, 170, 171, 175

Gadsden Purchase (1853), 144, 145
Gallivan, M. D., 9
Gamio, Manuel, 48
García Márquez, A., 113
Garkovich, L., 74

Garraty, Christopher P., 3–4, 6, 9, 11–12, 113, 122, 123, 131n10
Gates, P. W., 142
Giddens, A., 5
Gila Butte (Arizona), 83–85, 87, 88, 89
Gila Pueblo Archaeological Foundation, 78–79
Gillespie, Susan D., 64
Gladwin, Harold S., 78
Glen Canyon (Arizona), and Hopi petroglyphs, 101
globalization: and commodification of land in American West, 137; and life history of main plaza at Monte Albán, 49, 51
Golledge, R., 10–11
Goodwin, Grenville, 155
Grand Canyon, and cultural landscape of Hopi, 95–102
Green, Major John, 153
Greenberg, J. B., 136–37, 143, 148n2
Greenfield Village (Michigan), 166
Greider, T., 74
Grube, N., 24
Guadalupe Hidalgo, Treaty of (1848), 144
Gussow, A., 75

Hamana, Walter, 96
Hamann, B., 47, 50–51
Hardesty, D. L., 137
Hardin, G., 143
Haury, Emil W., 79, 83, 88
Heilen, Michael P., 4, 6, 9, 11, 12
Heller, Lynette, 126, 131n12
Hendon, Julia A., 3, 64
heritage, and meaningful places, 13. *See also* historic preservation
Hermequaftewa, Andrew, 91
Hewett, Edgar, 166
Hicks, F., 110
Hidatsa (North Dakota), 6, 7
Hisatsinom (Hopi ancestral villages), 96, 97
historical archaeology, and American West, 137–38
historical dimension, of cultural landscape, 75, 87
historic preservation: National Park Service grants for, 155; and reconstruction of sites, 150
history: and historicity of southwestern archaeology, 176–77; national parks and interpretation of Indian, 179n6, 179n8; phenomenology of Hopi, 105; and revisionism in archaeology, 177. *See also* historical archaeology; historical dimension; historic preservation; oral traditions
Hodder, Ian, 51, 163, 178n1
Hohokam (Arizona), meaning and metaphor in cultural landscape of, 73–89
Holmes, William Henry, 48
Homehongva, Charlie, 91, 92
Homestead Act (1862), 134, 142, 144, 145, 147

Index

homesteading, in American West, 138–40, 142–44, 145, 148
Homvi'ikya (Hopi pilgrimage routes), 92, 93
Honawa, Jerry, 97
Honduras, and landscape of Classic Maya sites in northwest, 53–71
Hopi: and concept of meaningful place, 6–7; and Ndee homeland, 156; role of archaeological sites in definition of cultural landscape, 90–106
Hopi Cultural Preservation Office, 102–4
Hopi Cultural Resources Advisory Task Team, 94–95
Hopitutskwa (Hopi land), 90–92, 93
Hornborg, A., 143
Huitzilopochtli (Aztec god), 83

iconography: and cultural landscape of Hohokam, 86, 88; and main plaza of Monte Albán, 37; of Mesoamerican ceremonial centers, 35–36. *See also* cosmology; symbolism
identity: Monte Albán and communal, 34–39; prehispanic past and Mexican national, 48, 50
ideological dimension, of cultural landscape, 76, 87–88
ideology, art and architecture in outer provinces of Aztec empire and imperial, 119–22. *See also* cosmology; iconography
image censers, and Classic Maya, 28–29
Inca Empire, and resettlement policy, 110
indigenismo, and Mexican national identity, 48
Ingold, T., 53, 66, 67, 70, 71
itaakuku (Hopi "footprints"), 90

Jackson, John B., 2, 74
Jade Sky (king of Quiriguá), 22, 24
Jefferson, Thomas, 138
Jenkins, Leigh, 101
Joyce, Arthur A., 3, 5, 41
Joyce, Rosemary A., 3, 5, 8, 9–10, 13, 64, 127
Julian, George W., 142

K'ak' Tiliw' (king of Quiriguá), 16, 18, 19, 22, 23, 24–25, 26, 29, 30
Kane, Raymond, 154
Kappelman, J. Guernsey, 83, 85
kiikiqo (ancestral settlements of Hopi), 95
King, Samuel D., 139
Kinishba Ruins National Historic Landmark (Arizona), 157, 167
kivas, and Mesa Verde National Park, 167–68
Knapp, A. B., 74, 88
Koontz, R., 76
Krall, L., 139
Kuwanwisiwma, Leigh, 3, 10, 13

Lamar, H. R., 141, 142
landscape: and commodification of land on Arizona frontier, 132–48; definition of, 76, 107; development of concept, 2; dimensions of contemporary approaches to, 7; and geopolitics of Aztec empire, 107–29; identity and experience at Classic Maya sites in Honduras, 53–71; memory and metaphor in modifications of, 8; and Mesa Verde National Park, 178n2; multiple meanings of, 74. *See also* cultural landscape; place
land tenure, and U.S. public land policy, 138–42
language: cultural concepts in Tewa, 76–77; outer provinces of Aztec empire and Nahuatl, 119
Lavender, David, 178n2
Lekson, Stephen H., 4, 5, 13
Leone, M. P., 73
Levy, Robert I., 63
Limerick, P. N., 139
Lincoln, A., 155
Linklater, A., 139
Lipe, W. D., 178
logic, and concept of place, 10–11
Lomakema, Milland, 97
Looper, Matthew G., 18, 24
Lopiparo, Jeanne, 3, 60, 63
Los Naranjos (Honduras), 64
Lourandos, H., 5
Lumpkins, Bill, 172

Màasaw (Hopi god), 90
Manifest Destiny, and Bent's Old Fort, 173, 177, 179n6
Manitou Cliff Dwellings (Colorado), 163–68, 172, 173, 174, 175, 176
Marquardt, W. H., 75
Martin, S., 24
Masayesva, Vernon, 99
Mastutskwa (Hopi "land"), 90–91
materiality, and archaeology of place, 5–6
Maya: and caves as metaphors, 85; and landscape of Classic period sites in northwest Honduras, 53–71; and multiplicity of cultural landscape, 88–89; Quiriguá and biographies of place, 15–31. *See also* Cerro Palenque; Copán; Mesoamerica
Maxwell Land Grant and Railroad Company, 141
McAnany, P. A., 86
McCafferty, S. D. and G. G., 45
McGuire, R. H., 137
meaning, of place: and archaeology of meaningful places, 13; continuity of at Monte Albán, 50–51; and definition of "meaningful" places, 13; memory and materialization of, 15–16; place networks and layering of, 10; simultaneous existence of alternative forms of, 15; and spatial organization of Quiriguá, 19–22
Medellín Zenil, A., 121, 130–31n8
Meinig, D. W., 132
memory: ceremonial centers and social, 33–34; and

concept of place, 8; main plaza of Monte Albán and social, 43–44; and materialization of meaning, 15–16
Mesa Verde National Park (Colorado), 163–68, 172, 173–77, 179n8
Mesoamerica: cosmology and ballcourts in, 64; and creation stories, 37; dualities in cosmology of, 81; Hohokam and "Mesoamerican worldview," 80; and iconography of ceremonial centers, 35–36; mountains in religious beliefs of, 80; and power of ceremonial precincts, 33. *See also* Aztec; Maya; Mexico
metaphor: and concept of place, 8; and mountains in cultural landscape of Hohokam, 79–89; role of in cultural-landscapes studies, 76–77
Mexican War (1849), 170
Mexico: and land disposal policies, 140; prehispanic past and national identity of, 48, 50. *See also* Aztec; Maya; Mesoamerica; Oaxaca Valley; Tenochtitlán; Teotihuacán
migration traditions: and concept of place, 8; Snake Mountain as metaphor in Aztec, 85. *See also* oral traditions
Mitla (Oaxaca Valley), 46, 47
Mixtec (Mexico), 46, 47, 48, 52n5
Monte Albán (Oaxaca Valley), and main plaza as life history of place, 32–51
monuments, and Hohokam iconography, 86. *See also* acropolis; plazas
Moore, "Smokey," 171
Morley, S. G., 22
mounds, and cultural landscape of Hohokam, 85–86, 88, 89
mountains, and cultural landscape of Hohokam, 79–89
Muhlenpfordt, Eduard, 48
museums, and "open-air" concept, 166
mythology: of American West, 132; about lost cities, 164–65. *See also* creation myths

Nahuatl language, 119
Nankoweap (Grand Canyon), 97, 98, 104
National Endowment for the Humanities, 157
National Geographic Magazine, 48
National Interagency Wilderness Conference (1993), 94
National Park Service: and Bent's Old Fort, 171, 174, 175; and Fort Apache historic district, 157; and Historic Preservation Fund Grants, 155; and interpretation of Indian history, 179n6, 179n8; and Mesa Verde National Park, 165, 166, 167; and Native American Graves Protection and Repatriation Act, 179n5
National Science Foundation, 79, 157
Native Graves Protection and Repatriation Act (NAGPRA), 154, 176, 179n5
navoti (Hopi history), 105

Ndee (Western Apache), and reconstruction of sense of place, 149–62
Neale, W. C., 136
networks, and archaeological concepts of place, 9–10
New Age spiritualism, and Monte Albán site, 49
New Archaeology, 2
New Mexico, and Hispanic/Anglo-American conflicts over land titles, 141–42. *See also* Chaco Canyon; Pueblos
New Zealand, and Mesa Verde Pueblo, 163

Oaxaca Valley (Mexico): Aztec invasion of, 45; and history of Monte Albán, 34, 39, 52n5
obsidian: and bloodletting rituals at Quiriguá, 28; and influence of Aztec empire in outer provinces, 117, 118, 126–27, 129, 131n12
Ohnersorgen, Michael, 3–4, 9, 11–12, 120, 121
Old Sturbridge Village (Massachusetts), 166
Olson, J. M., 130n4
Öngtupqa (Grand Canyon), 95–102
oral traditions: and change in Pueblo traditional histories, 177; and cultural landscape of Hopi, 95; and reconstructive place making by Ndee, 156, 162. *See also* creation myths; migration traditions; origin myths
origin myths, and concepts of place and landscape, 8. *See also* creation myths
Orr, H. S., 47
Ortiz, Simon, 179n5
Ortman, S. G., 76–77, 80
Owens, Bruce McC., 63

PACO 14 and 15 (Honduras), 70
Parsons, Elsie Clews, 47
Pasiwvi (Hopi place name), *103*, 104
Payson Tonto Apache Tribe, 155. *See also* Tonto Apache
Pecos Pueblo (New Mexico), 168
persistent places, 12–13
petroglyphs and pictographs: and cultural landscape of Hohokam, 88; and cultural landscape of Hopi, 100–102, 104
phenomenology, of Hopi history, 105
pilgrimages, and cultural landscape of Hopi, 91–92, 93, 99–100
Pima (Arizona), 79
pit structures: and Hohokam, 77–78, 81; and kivas at Mesa Verde National Park, 168
place: approaches to in current volume, 2–4; archaeological sites and definition of Hopi cultural landscapes, 90–106; Classic Maya site of Quiriguá and biographies of, 15–31; and commodification of land on Arizona frontier, 132–48; definition of, 1, 5, 6–7; development of concept, 2; and development of frameworks for archaeological research, 4–13;

and geopolitics of Aztec empire, 107–29; and interpretation of historic and archaeological sites in Colorado, 163–77; and landscape of Classic Maya sites in northwest Honduras, 53–71; main plaza of Monte Albán as life history of, 32–51; meaning and metaphor in Hohokam cultural landscape, 73–89; Ndee (Western Apache) and reconstruction of sense of, 149–62. *See also* biographies; landscape; meaning

place names, and reconstructive place making, 155

plazas: and Great Plaza at Quiriguá, 19, 22, 23–24; and life history of place at Monte Albán, 32–51, 52n2; and Snaketown (Hohokam), 81, 82

Pohl, J. M. D., 45, 46

Polingyumptewa, Simon, 97

politics: and archaeological concept of place, 6, 11–12; imperial landscape and control of Aztec empire, 107–29; and main plaza at Monte Albán, 34–42; and U.S. public land policy, 138–40, 143, 144, 147–48. *See also* elites; sovereignty

portrait stelae, at Quiriguá, 22–25

postmodernism, and perspectives on cultural landscape, 76

pottery: and Aztec influence in outer provinces of empire, 113–16, 125, 127, 129, 130n4–5, 131n11; and Hohokam artwork, 78, 87

power: of ceremonial precincts in Mesoamerica, 33; and portraits of Zapotec nobles, 39–40

Pred, A., 2, 67, 71

Preucel, R. W., 80

Proyecto Arqueológico La Mixtequilla (PALM), 112–13, 129–30n3

Public Land Survey System (PLSS), 137–40, 148n1

Pueblos, change in traditional histories of, 177. *See also* Mesa Verde National Park; Yellow Jacket Pueblo; Zuni Pueblo

Purser, M., 135, 138, 148n3

Puye (New Mexico), 166–67

quasi-commodities, 136

Quauhtochco (Veracruz, Mexico), 120, 130–31n8

Quiriguá (Guatemala), and biographies of place, 15–31

Rapoport, A., 75, 76

Reckner, P., 137

reconstruction: definitions of, 150–51; and Manitou Cliff Dwellings, 166; and Ndee (Western Apache) sense of place, 155–59

Red Cave (Arizona), 88

Redmond, E. M., 39

redundancy, and Hohokam cultural landscape, 81, 87

Reese-Taylor, K., 76

Reid, J. Jefferson, 4, 6, 9, 11, 12

relational dimension, of cultural landscape, 75–76, 86–87

religion: concept of Hopitutskwa in Hopi, 90–92; and main plaza at Monte Albán, 34–42; mountains in Mesoamerican beliefs, 80. *See also* cosmology; kivas; pilgrimages; rituals; sacrifice and sacrificial practices; shrines

replication, in Hohokam cultural landscape, 81, 87

Rice, Prudence M., 28–29

Richards, C. C., 81, 83

rituals: and Aztec-style figurines in Cotaxtla households, 119; and burnt offerings at Quiriguá, 28–30; and cultural landscape of Hohokam, 78, 88; and Hopi shrines, 91–92; and main plaza of Monte Albán, 37, 38, 43–44; of renewal and termination at Quiriguá, 27–28, 29; symbolism and use of ballcourts at Classic period Maya sites, 70. *See also* religion

roasting pits, and cultural landscape of Hopi, 98–99

rock art. *See* petroglyphs

Rockefeller, John D., 165

Rodman, Margaret, 53, 70

Ross, Edmund G., 142

sacred geography, and main plaza of Monte Albán, 39, 42, 48–49

sacrifice and sacrificial practices, and main plaza of Monte Albán, 37, 38, 39. *See also* religion; rituals

Sahagún, F. B. de, 120, 121

Sahlins, M., 50

St. Vrain, Ceran, 170

San Carlos Apache Tribe. *See* Ndee

Sand Creek Massacre (1864), 179n6

Sanford, Denton, 145, 146, 147

Sanford, Don Alonzo, 134, 145, 146–47

Sanford Ranch (Arizona), and historical archaeology, 133–34, 145–47, 148

San José Mogote (Oaxaca Valley), 34–35

San Juan Pueblo (New Mexico), 168

Santa Fe Trail, and Bent's Old Fort, 175

Sauer, Carl O., 1–2, 74

Schaniel, W. C., 136

Scheick, C. L., 76

Schele, Linda, 18, 83, 85

Schill, K., 95

Schlanger, S., 12

Schortman, Edward M., 18, 26

Schwartz, D. W., 95

sculpture: and Aztec-style art in outer provinces of empire, 119, 121–22; and portrait stelae at Quiriguá, 22–25. *See also* art

Secakuku, Ferrell, 94, 95, 97, 101–2

Sekaquaptewa, Abbott, 97, 100

Seler, Eduard, 48

settlement patterns: and concept of landscape, 53; and control of outer provinces in Aztec empire, 119, 122–25, 130n7; frontier American West and model-

ing of, 134–35; and resettlement policy of Inca Empire, 110. *See also* abandonment
Sharer, R. J., 22
shell artifacts, and Hohokam artwork, 78
shrines: and cultural landscape of Hohokam, 88; and cultural landscape of Hopi, 91–92, 99–100. *See also* religion
Silverstein, J., 116–17, 127, 129n2, 130n5
site, and definition of place, 7
Skoglund, T., 113, 114
Sky Xul (king of Quiriguá), 22
Smith, Duane A., 164, 178n2
Smith, J. E., 178n2
Smith, Michael E., 110, 114, 130n4
Snake Mountain, as metaphor in Aztec migration epic, 85
Snaketown (Arizona), 77–79, 81, 82
social organization. *See* community; elites; memory; settlement patterns
Sonoran Desert (Arizona), 77
sovereignty: definition of, 108; and geopolitics of Aztec empire, 109–11, 128, 129. *See also* politics
Spain. *See* colonialism
spatial organization: of Classic Maya sites, 55, 60–63; and cultural landscape of Hohokam, 81; and meaning at Quiriguá, 19–22; and symbolism at Monte Albán, 35–36
Spencer, C. S., 39
Spruce Tree House (Mesa Verde), 167
stabilization, and National Park Service management of archaeological sites, 166, 173
Stark, Barbara L., 112, 113, 122, 123, 126, 131n10, 131n12
Stephen, A. M., 90
Stone, Andrea J., 18
Stonehenge (England), 15
symbolism: of Hopi rattles, 105–6; and main plaza of Monte Albán, 37, 38, 41, 42, 50–51; and spatial organization of Monte Albán, 35–36. *See also* cosmology; iconography
"systems of settings," and place networks, 10

taskscapes, 67
Taube, Karl A., 28, 29
Taylor, Dalton, 94–95, 102
temple-patio-altar (TPA) complexes, and Monte Albán, 40–41, 42, 43–44, 52n4
Tenochtitlán (Mexico), 34, 85, 121
Teotihuacán (Mexico), 34, 41, 110, 123
termination rituals, at Quiriguá, 27–28, 29
territorialization, and commodification of land on Arizona frontier, 136–37
Tesoro Foundation, 172, 173
Tewa language, 76–77
Thurston, T. L., 107
Tikal (Classic Maya), 19

Tilden, F., 163
Tilley, C., 76
time, and Hopi archaeological sites, 104–5
Tlaloc (Mesoamerican god), 80, 81
Tlaloque (spirits of mountains and weather phenomena), 80
Tlaxcalla (Veracruz, Mexico), 114, 129
Tonto Apache, 156. *See also* Payson Tonto Apache Tribe
Tonto Cliff Dwellings (Arizona), 104
tourism, and Monte Albán site, 49, 51
Townsend, R. F., 80
Tragedy of the Commons, and public land policy, 143
trail markers, and cultural landscape of Hopi, 100
Travesía (Honduras), 60, 62, 63, 64
Traxler, L. P., 26
Tuan, Yi-Fu, 2, 75, 80
Turner, C. G., 101
Tutskwa (Hopi "land"), 90, 91
Tuzigoot (Arizona), 167

Umberger, E., 119, 120, 127
U.N. Educational Scientific and Cultural Organization. *See* World Heritage List
U.S. Fish and Wildlife Service, 155
U.S. Postal Service, 157
University of Arizona, 154, 157
University of Pennsylvania Museum, 17
use value, and Hispanic conceptualizations of land, 140

van Dommelen, P., 75, 88
Varien, M. D., 178n2
Vogt, Evon Z., 19

Wanaka (New Zealand), 163
warfare, and main plaza of Monte Albán, 38
Wedel, Waldo, 1–2
Welch, John R., 4, 6, 11, 12, 13
West (American): and historical archaeology, 137–38; and modeling of settlement on frontier, 134–35; and mythology of frontier, 132. *See also* Arizona; California; Colorado; New Mexico
Western Apache Place Names Project, 155
Wetherill, Richard, 164
White Mountain Apache Tribe. *See* Ndee
Whittaker, G., 46–47
Whittlesey, Stephanie M., 3, 7, 8, 13
wiimi (Hopi history), 105
Wilcox, D. R., 77, 79, 81, 87
Wilshusen, R. H., 178n2
Woodward, Christopher, 179n7
World Heritage Sites, 49, 164, 172
World Monuments Fund, 157
world systems theory, 137

Wukoskyavi (Tonto Basin), 104–5
Wupatki National Monument (Arizona), 102
wuuya (Hopi totemic symbols), 100–101

Xunantunich (Belize), 15

Yavapai-Apache nation, 155, 156
Yellow Jacket Pueblo (Colorado), 168, 176, 178n3

Zapotec. *See* Monte Albán
Zedeño, M. Nieves, 89, 150–51
Zospah, Louie, *153*
Zuni Pueblo (New Mexico), 156